COLLEGE ACCOUNTING 22e

Chapters 1-9

James A. Heintz, DBA, CPA
Professor of Accounting
School of Business
University of Kansas
Lawrence, Kansas

Robert W. Parry, Jr., Ph.D.
Professor of Accounting
Kelley School of Business
Indiana University
Bloomington, Indiana

CENGAGE
Learning·

Australia • Brazil • Japan • Korea • Mexico • Singapore • Spain • United Kingdom • United States

College Accounting, 22nd edition, Chapters 1-9

James A. Heintz and Robert W. Parry

Vice President, General Manager: Balraj Kalsi,
  Vice President, General Manager, Math &
  Quantitative Business

Product Director: Mike Schenk

Product Manager: Jason Guyler

Associate Content Developer: Jennifer Reed

Product Assistant: Trisha Makley

Associate Marketing Manager: Charisse Darin

Sr. Content Project Manager: Tim Bailey

Sr. Digital Production Project Manager: Sally Neiman

Content Digitization Project Manager: Thomas Burns

Manufacturing Planner: Doug Wilke

Production Service: Cenveo Publisher Services

Sr. Art Director: Linda May

Internal Designer: Joe Devine/Red Hangar Design

Cover Designer: Jen2 Design

Cover Image: Shutterstock.com/Nomadic Media Lab

Intellectual Property
  Analyst: Brittani Morgan
  Project Manager: Betsy Hathaway

DEDICATION

We are grateful to our wives, Celia Heintz and Jane Parry, and our children, Andrea Heintz Tangari, John Heintz, Jessica Parry, and Mitch Parry, for their love, support, and assistance during the preparation of the 22nd edition. We especially want to thank Anita Bhushan and Mitch Parry for granting permission to use Professor Parry's grandson's name, Rohan Macsen Parry, throughout the first six chapters.

For product information and technology assistance, contact us at
Cengage Learning Customer & Sales Support, 1-800-354-9706

For permission to use material from this text or product,
submit all requests online at **www.cengage.com/permissions**
Further permissions questions can be emailed to
permissionrequest@cengage.com

Library of Congress Control Number: 2015950603

ISBN: 978-1-305-66618-4

Cengage Learning
20 Channel Center Street
Boston, MA 02210
USA

Cengage Learning is a leading provider of customized learning solutions with employees residing in nearly 40 different countries and sales in more than 125 countries around the world. Find your local representative at **www.cengage.com.**

Cengage Learning products are represented in Canada by Nelson Education, Ltd.

To learn more about Cengage Learning Solutions, visit **www.cengage.com**

Purchase any of our products at your local college store or at our preferred online store **www.cengagebrain.com**

Printed in Canada
Print Number: 01   Print Year: 2015

James A. Heintz

James A. Heintz was Professor of Accounting and Information Systems for 15 years, including 13 years as the Director, in the School of Business at the University of Kansas. He is now Professor Emeritus at Kansas and teaches for the University of Iowa in a study abroad program in Northern Italy. Prior to joining the University of Kansas, he was Accounting Department Head at the University of Connecticut for eight years, and Assistant, Associate and Full Professor at Indiana University for 20 years. His doctorate is from Washington University in St. Louis, and he is a CPA. He was Price Waterhouse Faculty Fellow at Indiana, Arthur Andersen Faculty Fellow at Connecticut, and Deloitte & Touche Faculty Fellow at Kansas. Professor Heintz has won numerous school and university teaching awards, including five teaching awards from Doctoral Student Associations. He has served in various capacities on 27 doctoral dissertation committees. Professor Heintz has published numerous articles in accounting and business journals, such as *The Accounting Review; Auditing: A Journal of Practice and Theory; Accounting Horizons; Accounting and Business Research; Journal of Business Finance and Accounting;* and *International Journal of Accounting Education and Research.* He served on the editorial board of *Auditing: A Journal of Practice and Theory* for seven years and was president of the Accounting Programs Leadership Group of the AAA. He also has participated in external reviews of accounting programs at 12 major universities.

Robert W. Parry

Robert W. Parry is Professor Emeritus of Accounting at Indiana University's Kelley School of Business in Bloomington, Indiana. An accomplished teacher, Professor Parry has taught accounting at virtually all levels. While earning his MBA, he taught accounting at Bishop Klonowski High School in Scranton, Pennsylvania. While earning his Ph.D., he taught introductory financial and managerial accounting at Northampton County Community College and Lehigh University. At Indiana, he taught in the Undergraduate, MBA, MBA in Accounting, Master of Science in Accounting, the online Kelley Direct MBA Program, and Ph.D. Programs. In addition, he has taught accounting in the Consortium of Universities for International Studies in Asolo, Italy. During his 35 years at Indiana University, he won or was nominated for a total of 27 teaching excellence awards, including recognition twice by *Business Week* as one of the country's Outstanding MBA Faculty. In addition, he was awarded the Indiana University Distinguished Service Award for his efforts in planning and deploying a new, integrated MBA Core Program. He also received the Kelley School of Business Innovative Teaching Award for his role in designing and implementing the curriculum for the Master of Science in Accounting Program.

Parry has conducted research in the areas of public finance, governmental accounting, and accounting education. His work has been published in many journals, including *Public Finance Quarterly, Public Budgeting and Financial Management, Financial Analysts Journal, Accounting Horizons, Management Accounting, Research in Accounting Regulation, Research in Governmental and Non-Profit Accounting, Issues in Accounting Education,* and *Journal of Accounting Education.* Professor Parry was a lead author on the *Service Efforts and Accomplishments* research report published by the Governmental Accounting Standards Board. He also served on many committees of the American Accounting Association, including President of the Government and Nonprofit Accounting Section.

Rob and his wife, Jane, enjoy golf, ballroom dancing, hiking, kayaking, travel, and working in the yard. They have two children, Mitchell and Jessica, and four grandchildren, Anya Catrin Parry, Rohan Macsen Parry, Damon Robert Williams, and Mitchell David Williams.

Where *Accounting Education* and the *Real World* Meet

As the leading choice in college accounting, Heintz & Parry's *College Accounting, 22e* combines a proven, step-by-step approach and excellent examples with a tightly integrated online homework tool that makes accounting understandable to every student, regardless of their accounting background or business experience. The Heintz & Parry program, well-known for its quality, consistency, and technology, focuses on the practical skills students need to transition from the classroom to the workplace. With even more practice opportunities and independent study resources than ever before, the 22nd edition delivers the tools students need to succeed.

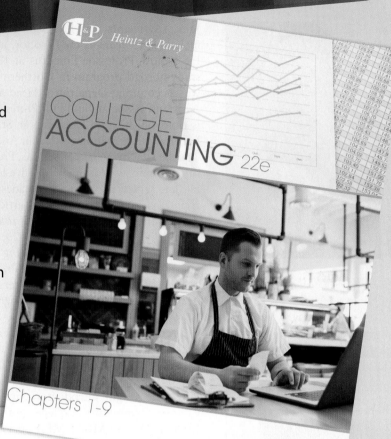

As the authors of *College Accounting 22e*, we are excited about this new edition and the enhancements made to the CengageNOWv2 online homework system. We believe that a truly integrated textbook and online homework system that serves as an extension of the classroom will help students be more successful in the college accounting course and better prepared for the real world.

In this edition, we have inserted a "Show Me How" icon next to many of the end-of-chapter exercises and problems. If you are having difficulty with an assignment, this icon indicates that additional help is available on CengageNOWv2. There, you can click on the icon. A voice-over, power-point video presentation will pop up with an explanation of how to solve a similar exercise. We think these videos are similar to a quick visit to our offices. Hope you find them helpful.

Chapters 1-9: 9781305666184

Throughout the revision process, we spent much of our time participating in the CengageNOWv2 development. We viewed it as essential to clearly connect CengageNOWv2 with the *College Accounting 22e* text by ensuring consistent terminology use, meaningful feedback for the students, and examples consistent with those in the textbook.

We hope this preface will serve as a guide to help you gain the most knowledge from this text and its supporting materials.

Sincerely,

Jim Heintz and Rob Parry

Where *Accounting Education* and Digital Learning Meet

College Accounting 22e combined with CengageNOWv2 elevates student thinking with unique content that addresses each phase of the learning process. The text combined with the digital content in **CengageNOWv2** offers students clearly defined tools to optimize their learning experience. Included are many proven resources including algorithmic activities, test bank, course management tools, reporting and assessment options, and much more.

Recent CengageNOWv2 Enhancements

- Refreshed Design: This refreshed look will help you and your students focus easily and quickly on what is important, while maintaining the same functionality that CengageNOW users know and love.

- Better Date Management: When modifying assignment due dates for a whole course, the system will now automatically adjust due dates based on a new start date, making it easier to reuse a course from one term to the next and adjust for snow days.

- Streamlined Assignment Creation Process: A simplified and streamlined Assignment Creation process allows instructors to quickly set up and manage assignments from a single page!

- New Report Options: New reporting options allow you to get better reports on your students' progress.

NEW! Blank Sheet of Paper Experience A less-leading Blank Sheet of Paper Experience discourages overreliance on the system.

- The use of drop down menus and Smart Entry (type-ahead) has been eliminated.

- Students must refer to the Chart of Accounts and decide for themselves which account is impacted.

- The number of accounts in each transaction is not given away.

- Whether the account should be debited or credited is not given away.

- Transactions may be entered in any order (as long as the entries are correct).

- Check My Work feedback only reports on what students have actually attempted, which prevents students from "guessing" their way through the assignment.

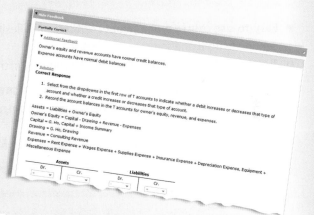

NEW! Mastery Problems now available in Blank Sheet of Paper offer students a real-world opportunity to test their expertise in each chapter's content. Check My Work feedback provides truly helpful guidance to assist in the completion of a question before the student submits the assignment for grading. This feature can be turned on or off by the instructor.

Where *Accounting Education* and Digital Learning Meet

- **Animated Activities** are assignable animated scenarios that provide an overview of the chapter concepts. Each activity uses a realistic company example to illustrate how the concepts relate to the everyday activities of a business. These activities include multiple-choice questions that gauge student understanding of the overarching chapter concepts. **Show Me How Videos** provide students with an opportunity to revisit what you've covered in class.

- **Blueprint Problems**, specifically designed for the text, are assignable teaching problems that require students to think through the problem solving process. These longer problems tie concepts together, giving students a more complete picture of the most fundamental accounting concepts.

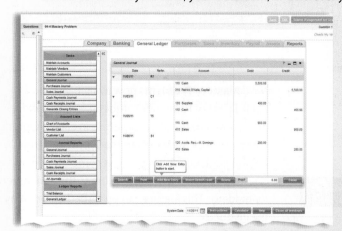

- **Easy-to-use course management options** offer flexibility and continuity from one semester to the next.
- The most **robust** and **flexible assignment options** in the industry.

- NEW! **Cengage Learning Testing Powered by Cognero** is a flexible, online system that allows you to:
  - author, edit, and manage test bank content from multiple Cengage Learning solutions
  - create multiple test versions in an instant
  - deliver tests from your LMS, your classroom, or wherever you want

- Each problem is tagged by topic, learning objectives, level of difficulty, Bloom's Taxonomy, AICPA, ACBSP, and general business program standards allowing you to **analyze student work from the gradebook and generate reports on learning outcomes**.

- **Cengage Learning General Ledger Software (CLGL) is now included in CengageNOWv2.** CLGL provides introductory exposure to general ledger software through the completion of select end-of-chapter assignments. Activities can be assigned as homework or tests and are automatically graded.

Where Accounting Education, the Classroom, and the Workplace Meet

Real-World Examples, bringing accounting concepts to life.

College Accounting, 22e maintains its dedication to its proven step-by-step style, clear explanations, excellent examples, and a relevant approach. Practical learning aids and fine-tuned pedagogy highlight and build upon key content to reinforce the accounting principles.

■ **Chapter openers** feature small companies from throughout the United States, setting the stage for why each chapter's content is relevant and important in the business world.

Chapter 2

LEARNING OBJECTIVES

Careful study of this chapter should enable you to:

LO1 Define the accounting elements.

LO2 Construct the accounting equation.

LO3 Analyze business transactions.

LO4 Show the effects of business transactions on the accounting equation.

LO5 Prepare and describe the purposes of a simple income statement, statement of owner's equity, and balance sheet.

LO6 Define the three basic phases of the accounting process.

Analyzing Transactions: The Accounting Equation

At Rob's Bike Courier Service in Fort Collins, Colorado, Rob believes "less is more." His small company doesn't "have a fleet of vehicles, just some pretty cool bicycles." His mission is providing successful bike delivery service, perfect for both traditional business delivery services and residential errands. Since January of 2005, Rob's Bike Courier Service has been the alternative to gas-powered vehicle delivery. Thus, besides great rates and friendly, reliable service, Rob offers earth-friendly service.

Currently, he delivers wholesale bagels from a mid-town baker to several downtown coffee shops. He does the same for another pastry chef. Rob also picks up recycling materials, offers bike towing services, and will go to a customer's home to fix flat bike tires and make repairs.

Though his company is small, Rob still needs an accounting system to maintain records of his business transactions and to prepare financial statements. Currently, he uses Quickbooks®, an accounting program used by many small companies. In Chapters 2 through 6, we learn how to account for a service business like Rob's by using an example of a similar company, Rohr's Lamp...

Your Perspective   SALES ASSOCIATE

As a Sales Associate at a department store such as Macy's, you assist customers in finding products that meet their needs, make sales and accept returns, stock clothing racks and shelves, mark prices, prepare displays and take inventory.

Did you know that when you are recording inventory, you are actually assisting with the calculation of gross profit and net income for Macy's? As you are learning in this chapter, determining the dollar amounts assigned to cost of goods sold and ending inventory is used to prepare financial statements. Your help with tracking inventory at Macy's assists external and internal users of financial statements to make key decisions regarding finances.

■ **Your Perspective** showcases everyday student jobs, such as a stockperson, cashier, or bank teller to illustrate how accounting relates to tasks that students encounter on a daily basis.

A Broader View

All Kinds of Businesses Need Accounting Systems

Even small businesses like those that provide guided horseback tours of the Rocky Mountains need good accounting systems. Proper records must be maintained for the cost of the horses, feed, food served, tour guides' salaries, and office expenses. Without this information, the company would not know how much to charge and whether a profit is made on these trips.

■ **A Broader View** feature provides captivating examples of actual business events or situations that relate to each chapter's accounting topics. Students more easily retain topics when they understand the connection to the business world.

ETHICS CASE

Electronics, Inc., is a high-volume, wholesale merchandising company. Most of its inventory turns over four or five times a year. The company has had 50 units of a particular brand of computers on hand for over a year. These computers have not sold and probably will not sell unless they are discounted 60 to 70%. The accountant is carrying them on the books at cost and intends to recognize the loss when they are sold. This way, she can avoid a significant write-down in inventory on the current year's financial statements.

1. Is the accountant correct in her treatment of the inventory? Why or why not?

2. If the computers cost $1,000 each and their market value is 40% of their cost, journalize the entry necessary for the write-down.

3. In a short paragraph, explain what is meant by conservatism and how it ties in with the lower-of-cost-or-market method of accounting for inventory.

4. In groups of three or four, make a list of reasons why inventories of electronic equipment might have to be written down.

■ **Ethics Cases** provide future business leaders with a clear understanding of the important ethical implications in modern accounting procedures and decisions. These cases highlight work-related ethical dilemmas and invite further analysis by the student independently or through classroom discussions.

Where *Accounting Education*, the *Classroom*, and the *Workplace* Meet

Superior Pedagogy, designed to keep students on track and truly help them succeed.

- **Learning Objectives** connect the chapter coverage from beginning to end.

  Problems in CengageNOWv2 are linked to the eBook, by Learning Objective, to guide students as they complete their homework.

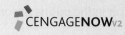

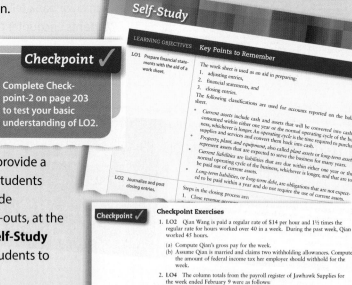

- **Excellent Examples, Clear Illustrations,** and **Step-by-Step Instructions** guide students visually through the steps of learning accounting. Heintz & Parry are well known for thorough, relevant, and visually simple examples.

- **Color-Coding System** helps students understand how accounts are classified and assists them with following the key transactions presented, clarifying the impact of transactions on the accounting equation.

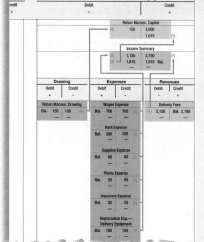

- **Self-Study featuring Checkpoint Exercises** offers the best in ongoing, self-review. These end-of-chapter summaries provide a strong framework for study and consistent progress as students recap chapter content, emphasize key points, and provide demonstration problems and solutions. Checkpoint call-outs, at the end of each learning objective, direct students to the **Self-Study Test Questions and Checkpoint Exercises**, allowing students to check their understanding of each learning objective.

- **The Adaptive Study Plan within CengageNOWv2** allows students to focus their study on the areas they are weakest. First, students take a **quiz** to assess where they are now. An **Adaptive Study Plan** will be crafted based on their results. After working through the study plan resources, students can take a **another quiz** to see how they have improved.

CENGAGE**NOW**v2

Where *Accounting Education,* the *Classroom,* and the *Workplace* Meet

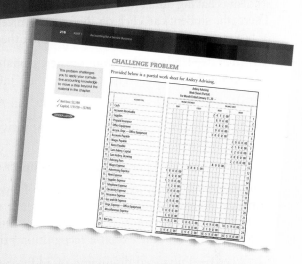

Real-World Preparation, giving students the experience to apply accounting knowledge and prepare them for real-world success.

■ **End-of-Chapter** material provides students the opportunity to apply chapter content to current business situations, strengthening decision-making skills and reinforcing the ability to follow proper procedures as they progress through the course. **Mastery and Challenge Problems** give students the opportunity to apply their cumulative accounting knowledge and move a step beyond the material in the chapter, sharpening their problem solving and critical thinking skills.

MANAGING YOUR WRITING

☑ Check List
☐ Managing
☐ Planning
☐ Drafting
☐ Break
☐ Revising
☐ Managing

You are a public accountant with many small business clients. During a recent visit to a client's business, the bookkeeper approached you with a problem. The columns of the trial balance were not equal. You helped the bookkeeper find and correct the error, but believe you should go one step further. Write a memo to all of your clients that explains the purpose of the double-entry framework, the importance of maintaining the equality of the accounting equation, the errors that might cause an inequality, and suggestions for finding the errors.

■ **Managing Your Writing** teaches students how to be efficient and effective writers. Writing assignments at the end of each chapter are accompanied by a **Checklist of tips** presented in Chapter 1, serving as a reminder to students to seek the additional help as they complete their assignment.

• Selected problems that can be solved using CLGL are designated by an icon in the textbook and are listed in the assignment preparation grid in the Instructor's Manual.

CLGL

■ **Comprehensive Problems are available to be solved using Cengage Learning General Ledger Software, or QuickBooks®,** as well as using the manual method. These are only available to select problems identified by the icons.

■ **Excel templates** are provided for selected exercises and problems, designated by an Excel icon. To help students stay on track, certain cells are coded to display a red asterisk when an incorrect answer is entered.

■ **Comprehensive Problems** tie content together, giving students a chance to apply accounting procedures, which helps them understand the processes they studied in a series of chapters (1-6, 7-15, and 16-19). As students complete the End-of-Chapter Material and Comprehensive Problems, **Hints and "Check My Work" feedback** (available in CengageNOWv2) remind students of the things they need to consider when thinking through the problem. This creates an online instructional tool to help students reach deeper understanding.

CENGAGENOWv2

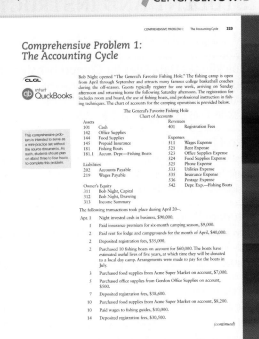

CHAPTER-BY-CHAPTER ENHANCEMENTS

The authors have inserted a "Show Me How" icon next to many of the end-of-chapter exercises and problems. If the student is having difficulty with an assignment, this icon indicates that additional help is available on CengageNOWv2. There, the student can click on the icon. A voice-over, PowerPoint video presentation will pop up with an explanation of how to solve a similar exercise. We think these videos are similar to a quick office visit.

Chapter 1—Updated Jets.com opener; Updated statistics on job opportunities for Figures 1-6 and 1-7; Updated accounting position descriptions and salary information.

Chapter 2—Updated "A Broader View" on AT&T.

Chapter 3—Updated information on AppRiver opener; Enhanced discussion of debits and credits; Enhanced learning key and added margin note.

Chapter 4—Added paragraph on the impact of computerized accounting systems on correcting entries.

Chapter 5—Updated chapter opener on Floyd's 99 Barbershop; Added discussion of the expense recognition principle. Enhanced discussion of the revenue recognition principle and the role of matching; Enhanced discussion of prepaid insurance; New work sheet illustrations in Figures 5-16, 5-17, and 5-18; New end of chapter review question on the expense recognition principle.

Chapter 6—Enhanced discussion of additional investments and the interpretation of the owner's capital account balances.

Chapter 7—Added new illustration of bank reconciliation form from bank statement; Added new illustrations for voucher and voucher check (in APX); Updated "A Broader View" with new fraud information.

Chapter 8—Updated text and end-of-chapter materials for new FIT withholding tables and Social Security maximum; Added description of new Medicare tax on earnings greater than $200,000.

Chapter 9—Updated text for EFTPS tax deposit rules; Provided new Forms 941 and 940; Added Self-Employment Contributions Act (SECA) coverage.

STUDENT AND INSTRUCTOR RESOURCES

Student Supplements and Resources

QuickBooks Data Files for Comprehensive Problems CD-ROM

These data sets allow you to complete the requirements of the Comprehensive Problems using QuickBooks software. (The software is not included on this CD-ROM.) Students can purchase the CD-ROM through www.cengagebrain.com.
(ISBN-10: 1-305-66990-8/ISBN-13: 978-1-305-66990-1)

Excel Templates

These templates are provided for selected end-of-chapter exercises and problems, designated by an icon in the text. They are designed to help you set up and work the assignment. To help you stay on track, certain cells are coded to display a red asterisk when an incorrect answer is entered. Your instructor may ask you to use the template for homework assignments. All templates can be downloaded for free from the student website located at www.cengagebrain.com.

Student Website

Now, mastering accounting concepts is easier than ever with the rich array of learning resources at the Heintz & Parry student website found at www.cengagebrain.com. Designed specifically to help you learn the most from your course and earn the grade you want, this website's interactive study center features chapter-by-chapter PowerPoint® student slides, online quizzes, flashcards, outlines, key terms, and a final exam, as well as links to accounting resources and more.

Study Guide and Working Papers

The study guide and working papers for the text assignments are provided together in one resource for your convenience. Written by the text authors to ensure accuracy and consistent quality, this resource provides chapter outlines linked to learning objectives and a set of "C" assignments that include review questions, exercises, and problems to enhance your learning experience. Students can purchase the study guide and working papers at www.cengagebrain.com.
Chapters 1–9: (ISBN-10: 1-305-66767-0/ISBN-13: 978-1-305-66767-9)

Trey's Fast Cleaning Service Practice Set

This practice set features a sole proprietorship service business simulation. It reviews the accounting cycle and accounting for cash. The practice set can be solved manually with Cengage Learning General Ledger software. The student CD includes the relevant data files (appropriate for use after Chapter 7). Students can purchase this practice set through www.cengagebrain.com.

Using QuickBooks Accountant for Accounting

This book teaches fundamental accounting concepts and principles while developing students' proficiency with the market-leading accounting software, QuickBooks Accountant by Intuit. This well-organized and concise text teaches the technology and application of accounting skills by illustrating how accounting information is created and used.
2015 edition: (ISBN-10: 1-305-08477-2/ISBN-13: 978-1-305-08477-3)

Using Excel and Access for Accounting

This textbook teaches students how businesses use spreadsheets and databases in accounting. It explains how to use these tools in solving real accounting problems and is written in a step-by-step format, with plenty of screenshots making it easy to follow. This textbook presents a tour of Microsoft Excel, along with an explanation of how that software is used in business. Next, a "Basics" chapter provides students with an immediate opportunity to begin using Excel with a real accounting problem and concept. The same process follows for chapters that teach Microsoft Access.
2013 edition: (ISBN-10: 1-285-18347-9/ISBN-13: 978-1-285-18347-3)

Instructor Supplements

CengageNOWv2

CengageNOWv2 is a powerful course management and online homework resource that provides control and customization to optimize the student learning experience. Included are many proven resources including algorithmic activities, test bank, course management tools, reporting and assessment options, and much more.

Instructor Resource Guide

The Instructor Resource Guide is available in print-on-demand and electronic format and contains a correlation grid with changes from the 21st edition to the 22nd edition, enhanced chapter outlines with teaching tips, suggested in-class exercises, figure references, and homework suggestions.
Chapter 1-15: (ISBN-10: 1-305-66771-9/ISBN-13: 978-1-305-66771-6)

Solutions Manual

The Solutions Manual is available in print and electronic format and contains carefully verified solutions for all text assignments, including Review Questions, all Exercises and Problem sets, Challenge and Mastery problems, Comprehensive Problems 1–3, as well as suggested answers to the Ethics Cases and the Managing Your Writing exercises.
Chapters 1–15: (ISBN-10: 1-305-66773-5/ISBN-13: 978-1-305-66773-0)

Test Bank

The Test Bank has been revised and verified and tagging standards have been added including level of difficulty, learning objectives, Bloom's Taxonomy, AICPA, ACBSP, and general business program standards (BUSPROG) to allow greater guidance in developing assessments and evaluating student progress.
Chapters 1–15: (ISBN-10: 1-305-66775-1/ISBN-13: 978-1-305-66775-4)

Cognero information Testing Software

Cengage Learning Testing powered by Cognero is a flexible, online system that allows you to author, edit, and manage test bank content from multiple Cengage Learning solutions, create multiple test versions in an instant, and deliver tests from your LMS, your classroom, or wherever you want.
(ISBN-10: 1-305-66777-8/ISBN-13: 978-1-305-66777-8)

Study Guide Solutions

Solutions to all Study Guide set "C" assignments are located here and are available on the Instructor Website.

Instructor Website

Instructors can log into the password-protected website through http://login.cengage.com. This site places all the teaching resources in one place. It includes the Instructor's Manual, Teaching Transparency Masters, PowerPoint® lecture presentations, Test Bank in Word format, Solutions to the spreadsheet templates, Study Guide Solutions, and the Solutions Manual in Word format.

ACKNOWLEDGEMENTS

We thank the following individuals for their helpful contributions to this revision of *College Accounting*.

Abe Qastin, *Lakeland College*
Adam Baker, *Minnesota State Community and Technical College*
Alex Gialanella, *Manhattanville College*
Alyson Crow, *Temple College*
Amanda Hardin, *Mississippi Delta Community College*
Amy Chataginer, *Mississippi Gulf Coast Community College*
Amy Smith, *Pearl River Community College*
Anna Boulware, *St. Charles Community College*
Anne Bikofsky, *College of Westchester*
Anne Borsellino, *Mclennan community college*
Barbara L. Squires, *Corning Community College*
Barbara Prince, *Anoka Ramsey Community College, Cambridge*
Barbara Squires, *Corning Community College*
Belinda Chastain, *Spartanburg Community College*
Beth Berry, *Glendale Community College*
Bhaskar Singh, *College of Menominee Nation*
Bob Urell, *Irvine Valley College*
Bonnie Hopson, *Athens Technical College*
Brad Davis, *Santa Rosa Junior College*
Brian Fink, *Danville Area Community College*
Britt Blackwell, *Central Community College*
Carol Ann Kirby, *Portland Community College*
Carol Ottaway, *Chemeketa Community College*
Cheryl Corke, *Genesee Community College*
Christy Chauvin, *Delgado Community College*
Chuck Smith, *Iowa Western Community College*
Cynthia E. Moody-Paige, *Erwin Technical Center*
Dale Walker, *Arkansas State University—Little Rock Air Force Base*
Daniel J. Kerch, *Pennsylvania Highlands Community College*
Dawn Stevens, *Northwest Mississippi Community College*
Deanna Knight, *Daytona State College*
Debbie Adkins, *University of Phoenix*
Diana Sullivan, *Portland Community College*
Dianne Henline, *Texarkana College*
Dmitriy Kalyagin, *Chabot College*
Dominique Svarc, *Harper College*
Don Williams, *Feather River College*
Dale Walker, *Arkansas State University—Little Rock Air Force Base*
Thomas Gross, *Herzing University*
Eilene LePelley, *Lane Community College*
Ellen Orr, *Seminole State College of Florida*
Eric Stadnik, *Santa Rosa Junior College*
Eugene Schneider, *ASA Institute of Business and Trechnology*
George Holder, *Cloud County Community College*
Glenn Pate, *Palm Beach State College*
Gloria Sanchez, *Mt. San Jacinto College*
Greg Lauer, *North Iowa Area Community College*
H. Gin Chong, *Prairie View A&M University*
Jackie Marshall, *Ohio Business College*
James M. Emig, *Villanova University*
Jan Hogue, *Laurel Technical Institute*
Jean Rodgers, *Wenatchee Valley College*
Jeanette Milius, *Iowa Western Community College*
Jeff Hsu, *St. Louis Community College at Meramec*

Jennifer Garcia, *Blinn College*
Jim Bauer, *Archbishop Moeller High School*
Jody Dunaway, *Herzing University*
Joe Adamo, *Cazenovia College*
John Allen Fortner, *Daytona State College*
John Fasler, *Whatcom Community College*
John Fortner, *Daytona State College*
John Nader, *Davenport University*
John Seilo, *Orange Coast College*
Johnny Howard, *Arkansas State University - Mountain Home*
Jolena Grande, *Cypress College*
Joseph M. Nicassio, *Westmoreland County Community College*
Judith Toland, *Bucks County Community College*
Judy Boozer, *Lane Community College*
Judy Hurtt, *East Central Community College*
Julia Angel, *North Arkansas College*
June Hanson, *Upper Iowa University*
Junnae Landry, *Pratt Community College*
Karen Alexander, *College of The Albemarle*
Karen M. Kydd, *Husson University*
Karen Welch, *Tennessee College of Applied Technology—Jackson*
Kathleen Fratianne, *Blackhawk Technical College*
Kathleen Smith, *Tennessee College of Applied Technology*
Kathy Beith, *Milan Institute*
Kathy Bowen, *Murray State College*
Keith Blankenship, *South College-Asheville*
Kerry Stager, *Lake Area Technical Institute*
Kim Anderson, *Elgin Community College*
Kim Hurt, *Central Community College*
Kim Potts, *North Arkansas College*
Kippi Harraid, *Trinity Valley Community College*
Kirk Canzano, *Long Beach City College*
La Vonda Ramey, *Schoolcraft College*
Laurie Gambrell, *Copiah-Lincoln Community College*
Lawrence A. Roman, *Cuyahoga Community College*
Leonia Houston, *Holmes Community College*
Leslie Schmidt, *Front Range Community College*
Linda Arndt, *LCO College*
Lingling Zhang, *American River College*
Lisa Briggs, *Columbus State Community College*
Lisa Nash, *Vincennes University*
Lisa Novak, *Mott Community College*
Lori Grady, *Bucks County Community College*
Lorna Hofer, *Lake Area Technical Institute*
Luis Plascencia, *Harold Washington College*
M. Jeff Quinlan, *Madison Area Technical College*
Mabel Machin, *Valencia College*
Marcia Shulman, *New York University*
Marilyn St. Clair, *Weatherford College*
Marina Grau, *Houston Community College*
Mark Gale, *Cosumnes River College*
Mark Wells, *Big Sandy Community and Technical College*
Meg Costello Lambert, *Oakland Community College-Auburn Hills Campus*

Melvin Williams, *College of the Mainland*
Michael Dole, *Marquette University*
Michele Wehrle, *Community College of Allegheny County*
Mike Belleman, *St Clair County Community College*
Mike Boren, *Tooele Applied Technology College*
Molly McFadden-May, *Tulsa Community College - Metro*
Monica Quattlebaum, *Phillips Community College of the University of Arkansas*
Morgan Rockett, *Moberly Area Community College*
Nancy Lee Howard, *Mt. Hood Community College*
Nelly Cintron Lorenzo, *Valencia College-West Campus*
Norma Cerpa, *Custom Training Solutions*
Nova Randolph, *Shawnee Community College*
Pam Perry, *Hinds Community College*
Patricia Worsham, *Norco College*
Patrick Borja, *Citrus College*
Perry Sellers, *Lone Star College System*
R. Stephen Holman, *Elizabethtown Community and Technical College*
Richard J. Pettit, *Mountain View College*
Rick Street, *Spokane Community College*
Robert Brooks, *San Bernardino Valley College*
Robert Derstine, *West Chester University*
Robin Fuller, *Mississippi Gulf Coast Community College*
Roger McMillian, *Mineral Area College*
Ronald Edward Camp, *Trinity Valley Community College*
Ronald Pearson, *Bay College*
Rosemary C. Garcia, *New Mexico State University, Doña Ana Community College*
Rosemary Nurre, *College Of San Mateo*
Ruth Gregory, *East Central Community College*
Sandra Sturdy, *Bay College*

Scott Birk, *Portland Community College*
Scott Wallace, *Blue Mountain Community College*
Sharon R. Morgan, *Western Nevada College*
Shawn Abbott, *College of the Siskiyous*
Sherry Laskie, *Milan Institute*
Shirley A. Montagne, *Community College of Vermont*
Sonora White, *Caddo Kiowa Technology Center*
Spencer Miller, *Eastern Idaho Technical College*
Stella Sorovigas, *Lansing Community College*
Stephanie Cox, *Louisiana Delta Community College*
Steven Ernest, *Baton Rouge Community College*
Sue Sandblom, *Scottsdale Community College*
Sue Savino, *Copiah Lincoln Community College*
Sueann Hely, *West Kentucky Community and Technical College*
Susan Davis, *Green River Community College*
Susan Greene, *Cloud County Community College*
Susan Mundy, *City University of Seattle*
Tatyana Pashnyak, *Bainbridge State College*
Teresa Worthy, *Gaston College*
Therese Rice, *North Hennepin Community College*
Tilda A. Woody, *Navajo Technical University*
Tim Green, *North Georgia Technical College*
Tim Whited, *American National University*
Tom Snare, *Southhills School of Business and Technology*
Toni Hartley, *Laurel Business Institute*
Tricia Popowsky, *Redlands Community College*
Tynia Kessler, *Lake Land College*
Vickie Boeder, *Madison Area Technical College—Watertown*
Vicky Lassiter, *Wayne Community College*
Wayne Corlis, *Mid Michigan Community College*
Wendy Eismont, *South Hills School of Business and Technology*
Whit Hunt, *South Plains College*

Special recognition goes to the following supplemental preparers for their revision work on the instructor and student materials:

Yvette J. Lazdowski, *Plymouth State University*
Vernon Richardson, *University of Arkansas*
Mark D. Sears
Domenic Tavella, *Carlow University*

We would like to thank the following individuals for their detailed verification of the homework:

Robin Browning
Erin Dischler, *Milwaukee Area Technical College*
Dr. Marina Grau, *Houston Community College*
Toni R. Hartley, *Laurel Business Institute*

We are honored to serve as the authors of the all-time and current best-selling college accounting text. As has been true for over two decades, we are delighted with the editorial and marketing support provided by Cengage Learning. Without their support and the constructive comments and suggestions made by our loyal friends using our text, this success would not have been possible. We are anxious to receive your comments on this edition, because we want to make the next one even better.

James A. Heintz
jheintz@ku.edu

Rob Parry
parry@indiana.edu

Contents

PART 2   ACCOUNTING FOR CASH AND PAYROLL

Accounting for a Service Business

PART 1

JUAN SILVA/JUPITER IMAGES

Add Some Color to Your Learning!

Throughout the text, you will be introduced to many important terms and types of accounts. To help you learn the different terms and types of accounts, we have coded many of them using the following color key in Part 1:

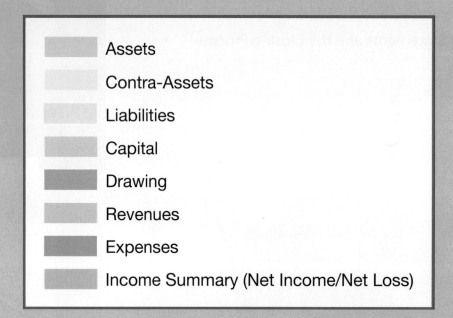

Assets

Contra-Assets

Liabilities

Capital

Drawing

Revenues

Expenses

Income Summary (Net Income/Net Loss)

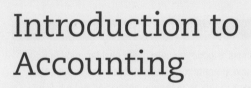

Introduction to Accounting

Need a private jet to get away for the weekend, attend a business meeting, or visit Mom? Call Jets.com. Established in 1999, Jets.com serves as a broker for private jet services. Call or go online, and its technology will automatically send your trip request/itinerary to a network of approved operators who will locate available aircraft. Operators will competitively bid for your business, resulting in significant savings and increased aircraft options for you.

In addition to a system that links customers with private jet service, Jets.com needs a system to account for its business transactions. Thus, it employs accounting professionals who understand the accounting process and generally accepted accounting principles.

Welcome to the world of accounting. We are delighted that you have decided to join us. A solid foundation in accounting concepts and techniques will serve you well. This is true whether you accept a professional position in accounting, work for or own a business, or simply seek a better understanding of your personal finances.

Oh, and what does it cost to take a private jet to the Super Bowl? Rates run from $4,300 to $10,000 per hour on one of the busiest weekends of the year.

LEARNING OBJECTIVES

Careful study of this chapter should enable you to:

LO1 Describe the purpose of accounting.

LO2 Describe the accounting process.

LO3 Define GAAP and describe the process used by FASB to develop these principles.

LO4 Define three types of business ownership structures.

LO5 Classify different types of businesses by activities.

LO6 Identify career opportunities in accounting.

A ccounting is the language of business. You must learn this language to understand the impact of economic events on a specific company. Common, everyday terms have very precise meanings when used in accounting. For example, you have probably heard terms like asset, liability, revenue, expense, and net income. Take a moment to jot down how you would define each of these terms. After reading and studying Chapter 2, compare your definitions with those developed in this text. This comparison will show whether you can trust your current understanding of accounting terms. Whether you intend to pursue a career in accounting or simply wish to understand the impact of business transactions, you need a clear understanding of this language.

THE PURPOSE OF ACCOUNTING

LO1 Describe the purpose of accounting.

The purpose of accounting is to provide financial information about the current operations and financial condition of a business to individuals, agencies, and organizations. As shown in Figure 1-1, owners, managers, creditors, and government agencies all need accounting information. Other users of accounting information include customers, clients, labor unions, stock exchanges, and financial analysts.

FIGURE 1-1   Users of Accounting Information

USER	INFORMATION NEEDED	DECISIONS MADE BY USERS
Owners—Present and future	Company's profitability and current financial condition.	If business is good, owners may consider making additional investments for growth. If business is poor, they may want to talk to management to find out why and may consider closing the business.
Managers—May or may not own business	Detailed measures of business performance.	Managers need to make operating decisions. How much and what kinds of inventory should be carried? Is business strong enough to support higher wages for employees?
Creditors—Present and future	Company's profitability, debt outstanding, and assets that could be used to secure debt.	Should a loan be granted to this business? If so, what amount of debt can the business support, and what interest rate should be charged?
Government Agencies—National, state, and local	Company's profitability, cash flows, and overall financial condition.	The IRS will decide how much income tax the business must pay. Local governments may be willing to adjust property taxes paid by the business to encourage it to stay in town.

THE ACCOUNTING PROCESS

LO2 Describe the accounting process.

Accounting is a system of gathering financial information about a business and reporting this information to users. The six major steps of the accounting process are analyzing, recording, classifying, summarizing, reporting, and interpreting (Figure 1-2). Computers are often used in the recording, classifying, summarizing, and reporting steps. Whether or not computers are used, the accounting concepts and techniques are the same. Information entered into the computer system must reflect a proper application of these concepts. Otherwise, the output will be meaningless.

FIGURE 1-2   The Accounting Process

Analyzing ➡ Recording ➡ Classifying ➡ Summarizing ➡ Reporting ➡ Interpreting

- **Analyzing** is looking at events that have taken place and thinking about how they affect the business.

- **Recording** is entering financial information about events into the accounting system. Although this can be done with paper and pencil, most businesses use computers to perform routine record-keeping operations.

- **Classifying** is sorting and grouping similar items together rather than merely keeping a simple, diary-like record of numerous events.

- **Summarizing** is the aggregation of many similar events to provide information that is easy to understand. For example, a firm may buy and sell baseballs during the year. Summarizing provides information on the total baseballs bought and sold and the change in the number of baseballs held from the beginning to the end of the period.

- **Reporting** is telling the results. In accounting, it is common to use tables of numbers to report results.

- **Interpreting** is deciding the meaning and importance of the information in various reports. This may include ratio analysis to help explain how pieces of information relate to one another.

GENERALLY ACCEPTED ACCOUNTING PRINCIPLES (GAAP)

LO3 Define GAAP and describe the process used by FASB to develop these principles.

Soon after the stock market crash of 1929, the federal government established the Securities and Exchange Commission (SEC). The purpose of this government agency is to help develop standards for reporting financial information to stockholders. The SEC currently has authority over 12,000 companies listed on the major stock exchanges (New York, American, and NASDAQ). It has the power to require these firms to follow certain rules when preparing their financial statements. These rules are referred to as generally accepted accounting principles (GAAP).

Rather than developing GAAP on its own, the SEC encouraged the creation of a private standard-setting body. It did so because it believed the private sector had better access to the resources and talent necessary to develop these standards. Since 1973, the Financial Accounting Standards Board (FASB) has filled this role. In developing accounting standards, FASB follows a specific process and relies on the advice of many organizations. When an accounting issue is identified, the following steps are followed:

1. The issue is placed on FASB's agenda. This lets everyone know that the Board plans to develop a standard addressing this issue.

2. After researching an issue, FASB issues a **Preliminary Views** document. This document identifies the pros and cons of various accounting treatments for an event and invites others to comment.

3. To gather additional views on the issue, the Board will often hold **public hearings** around the country. Interested parties are invited to express their opinions at these hearings.

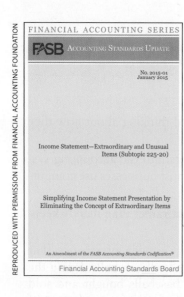

4. Following these hearings, the Board issues an **exposure draft**. This document explains the rules that FASB believes firms should follow in accounting for this event.

5. After considering feedback on the exposure draft, the Board issues a final **Accounting Standards Update** which amends the **Financial Accounting Standards Board Accounting Standards Codification**. This Codification is an electronic database that provides one authoritative source for the standards that must be followed by U.S. companies.

Throughout this process, many parties participate by testifying at public hearings or by sending letters to the Board explaining why they agree or disagree with the proposed standard. These parties include the American Institute of Certified Public Accountants (AICPA), the American Accounting Association (AAA), the Institute of Management Accountants (IMA), Financial Executives International (FEI), corporate executives and accountants, representatives from the investment community, analysts, bankers, industry associations, and the SEC and other government agencies. Clearly, FASB considers the views of a wide range of parties. By doing so, it maximizes the likelihood of developing and gaining acceptance of the most appropriate accounting and disclosure requirements.

The International Accounting Standards Board (IASB) issues accounting standards followed by many firms in countries outside the United States. These are called International Financial Reporting Standards (IFRS). In recent years, the IASB and FASB have worked together to try to minimize the differences in these standards. These standards may eventually converge into one set of standards used around the world.

THREE TYPES OF OWNERSHIP STRUCTURES

LO4 Define three types of business ownership structures.

One or more persons may own a business. Businesses are classified according to who owns them and the specific way they are organized. Three types of ownership structures are (1) sole proprietorship, (2) partnership, and (3) corporation (Figure 1-3). Accountants provide information to owners of all three types of ownership structures.

FIGURE 1-3   Types of Ownership Structures—Advantages and Disadvantages

TYPES OF OWNERSHIP STRUCTURES		
Sole Proprietorship	**Partnership**	**Corporation**
• One owner • Owner assumes all risk • Owner makes all decisions	• Two or more partners • Partners share risks • Partners may disagree on how to run business	• Stockholders • Stockholders have limited risk • Stockholders may have little influence on business decisions

Sole Proprietorship

A sole proprietorship is owned by one person. The owner is usually called a proprietor. The proprietor often manages the business. The owner assumes all risks for the business, and personal assets can be taken to pay creditors. The advantage of a sole proprietorship is that the owner can make all decisions.

Partnership

A partnership is owned by more than one person. One or more partners may manage the business. Like proprietors, partners assume the risks for the business, and their

Most businesses in the United States operate as sole proprietorships or partnerships. However, corporations earn the highest amount of revenue.

assets may be taken to pay creditors. An advantage of a partnership is that owners share risks and decision making. A disadvantage is that partners may disagree about the best way to run the business.

Corporation

The largest corporations in the United States are known as the "Fortune 500."

A **corporation** is owned by stockholders (or shareholders). Corporations may have many owners, and they usually employ professional managers. The owners' risk is usually limited to their initial investment, and they often have very little influence on the business decisions.

TYPES OF BUSINESSES

LO5 Classify different types of businesses by activities.

Businesses are classified according to the type of service or product provided. Some businesses provide a service. Others sell a product. A business that provides a service is called a **service business**. A business that buys a product from another business to sell to customers is called a **merchandising business**. A business that makes a product to sell is called a **manufacturing business**. You will learn about all three types of businesses in this book. Figure 1-4 lists examples of types of businesses organized by activity.

FIGURE 1-4   Types and Examples of Businesses Organized by Activities

SERVICE	MERCHANDISING	MANUFACTURING
Travel Agency	Department Store	Automobile Manufacturer
Computer Consultant	Pharmacy	Furniture Maker
Physician	Grocery Store	Toy Factory

A Broader View

All Kinds of Businesses Need Accounting Systems

Even small businesses like those that provide guided horseback tours of the Rocky Mountains need good accounting systems. Proper records must be maintained for the cost of the horses, feed, food served, tour guides' salaries, and office expenses. Without this information, the company would not know how much to charge and whether a profit is made on these trips.

© JACK HOLLINGSWORTH/CORBIS

CAREER OPPORTUNITIES IN ACCOUNTING

LO6 Identify career opportunities in accounting.

Accounting offers many career opportunities. The positions described below require varying amounts of education, experience, and technological skill.

Accounting Clerks

Businesses with large quantities of accounting tasks to perform daily often employ **accounting clerks** to record, sort, and file accounting information. Often, accounting clerks will specialize in cash, payroll, accounts receivable, accounts payable, inventory, or purchases. As a result, they are involved with only a small portion of the total accounting responsibilities for the firm. Accounting clerks usually have at least one year of accounting education.

Bookkeepers and Para-Accountants

Bookkeepers generally supervise the work of accounting clerks, help with daily accounting work, and summarize accounting information. In small-to-medium-sized businesses, the bookkeeper may also help managers and owners interpret the accounting information. Bookkeepers usually have one to two years of accounting education and experience as an accounting clerk.

Para-accountants provide many accounting, auditing, or tax services under the direct supervision of an accountant. A typical para-accountant has a two-year degree or significant accounting and bookkeeping experience.

Accountants

The difference between accountants and bookkeepers is not always clear, particularly in smaller companies where bookkeepers also help interpret the accounting information. In large companies, the distinction is clearer. Bookkeepers focus on the processing of accounting data. **Accountants** design the accounting information system and focus on analyzing and interpreting information. They also look for important trends in the data and study the impact of alternative decisions.

Most accountants enter the field with a college degree in accounting. In fact, since many states require 150 credit hours to sit for the CPA exam, many students are also earning a master's degree in accounting before entering the profession. Accountants are employed in public accounting, private (managerial) accounting, and governmental and not-for-profit accounting (Figure 1-5).

FIGURE 1-5 Accounting Careers

ACCOUNTING CAREERS		
Public Accounting • Auditing • Taxation • Management Advisory Services	**Private Accounting** • Accounting Information Systems • Financial Accounting • Cost Accounting • Budgeting • Tax Accounting • Internal Auditing	**Governmental and Not-for-Profit Accounting**

Public Accounting

Public accountants offer services in much the same way as doctors and lawyers. The public accountant can achieve professional recognition as a **Certified Public Accountant (CPA)**. This is done by meeting certain educational and experience requirements as determined by each state and passing a uniform examination prepared by the American Institute of Certified Public Accountants.

Many CPAs work alone, while others work for local, regional, national, or international accounting firms that vary in scope and size. The largest public accounting firms in the United States are known as the "Big Four." They are Deloitte, Ernst & Young, KPMG, and PricewaterhouseCoopers.

Services offered by public accountants are listed below.

- **Auditing.** Auditing involves the application of standard review and testing procedures to be certain that proper accounting policies and practices have been followed. The purpose of the audit is to provide an independent opinion that the financial information about a business is fairly presented in a manner consistent with generally accepted accounting principles.

- **Taxation.** Tax specialists advise on tax planning, prepare tax returns, and represent clients before governmental agencies such as the Internal Revenue Service.

- **Management Advisory Services.** Given the financial training and business experience of public accountants, many businesses seek their advice on a wide variety of managerial issues. Often, accounting firms are involved in designing computerized accounting systems.

- **Forensic Accounting.** Forensic accounting is a rapidly growing segment of accounting practice. It includes fraud detection, fraud prevention, litigation support, business valuations, expert witness services, and other investigative activities. Public accounting firms offer forensic accounting services, but forensic accountants also work for insurance companies, banks, law enforcement agencies, and other organizations. By meeting certain requirements, and passing the Certified Fraud Examiner exam, a forensic accountant may earn a **Certified Fraud Examiner (CFE)** designation.

In 2002, the **Sarbanes-Oxley Act (SOX)** was passed by Congress to help improve reporting practices of public companies. The act was in response to accounting scandals at firms like Enron, WorldCom, Cendant, Xerox, and others. Key provisions of SOX are listed below.

- The Public Company Accounting Oversight Board (PCAOB) was created to enforce SOX rules and regulations. The PCAOB also has authority to set auditing standards for public company audits and to perform inspections of auditing firms.

- For the largest companies, external auditors are required to report on the effectiveness of a public company's accounting procedures.

- Auditing firms are prohibited from offering many nonaudit services to their public audit clients.

- Auditing firms must rotate lead audit partners off audit engagements every five years.

- The CEO and CFO must personally certify that the financial statements are accurate.

It is difficult to guarantee that information provided in financial statements is always complete and accurate. These measures are a step in the right direction. If our economy and financial markets are to function properly, information provided in financial statements must be reliable.

Private (Managerial) Accounting

Many accountants are employees of private business firms. The **controller** oversees the entire accounting process and is the principal accounting officer of the company. Private or managerial accountants perform a wide variety of services for the business. These services are listed below.

- **Accounting Information Systems.** Accountants in this area design and implement manual and computerized accounting systems.

- **Financial Accounting.** Based on the accounting data prepared by the bookkeepers and accounting clerks, accountants prepare various reports and financial statements and help in analyzing operating, investing, and financing decisions.

- **Cost Accounting.** The cost of producing specific products or providing services must be measured. Further analysis is also done to determine whether the products are produced and services are provided in the most cost-effective manner.

- **Budgeting.** In the budgeting process, accountants help managers develop a financial plan.

- **Tax Accounting.** Instead of hiring a public accountant, a company may have its own accountants. They focus on tax planning, preparation of tax returns, and dealing with the Internal Revenue Service and other governmental agencies.

- **Internal Auditing.** Internal auditors review the operating and accounting control procedures adopted by management to make sure the controls are adequate and are being followed. They also monitor the accuracy and timeliness of the reports provided to management and to external parties.

A managerial accountant can achieve professional status as a **Certified Management Accountant (CMA)**. This is done by passing a uniform examination offered by the Institute of Management Accountants. An internal auditor can achieve professional recognition as a **Certified Internal Auditor (CIA)** by passing the uniform examination offered by the Institute of Internal Auditors.

Governmental and Not-for-Profit Accounting

Thousands of governmental and not-for-profit organizations (states, cities, schools, churches, and hospitals) gather and report financial information. These organizations employ a large number of accountants. Since these entities are not profit oriented, the rules are somewhat different for governmental and not-for-profit organizations. However, many accounting procedures are similar to those found in profit-seeking enterprises.

Job Opportunities

Job growth in some areas will be much greater than in others. Employment advertisements often indicate that accountants and accounting clerks are expected to have computer skills. Computer skills definitely increase the opportunities available to you in your career. Almost every business needs accountants, accounting clerks, and bookkeepers. Figure 1-6 shows the expected growth for different types of businesses. Notice that growth will be greatest in health care services. Chapters 2 through 9 introduce accounting skills that you will need to work in a service business, like health care. Chapter 10 begins the discussion of merchandising businesses. Accounting for manufacturing businesses is addressed in the last chapters of the book.

Figure 1-7 shows the expected demand for accounting skills. An 11.4% increase in demand, 205,000 new jobs, is expected for bookkeeping, accounting, and auditing clerks. These types of positions will offer the highest number of job opportunities over the next several years. The next highest demand is for accountants and auditors, and this demand is expected to increase by 167,000, or 13.1%, over the next several years.

FIGURE 1-6   Expected Growth

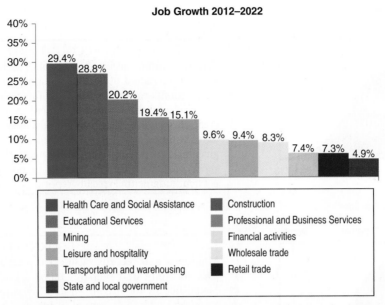

The growth in the number of new jobs from 2012 to 2022 will vary according to industry. The major areas of growth will be in health care and construction. Moderate growth is expected in educational services and business and professional services. Slower growth is expected in the remaining industries. Total employment for all industry sectors is projected to grow by 10.8% over the decade, resulting in 15.6 million new jobs.

Source: U.S. Department of Labor—Bureau of Labor Statistics News Release, Thursday December 19, 2013: Employment Projections—2012–2022. (www.bls.gov/news.release/pdf/ecopro.pdf)

FIGURE 1-7   Expected Demand

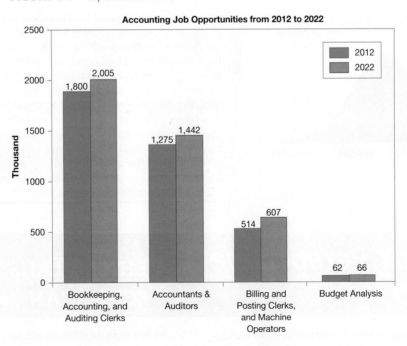

The highest number of jobs available will be for bookkeepers, accounting and auditing clerks, and accountants and auditors. The growth for each area shown from 2012 to 2022 will be as follows:

	Thousands	Percentage
Accountants and auditors	167	13.1%
Budget analysts	4	6.1%*
Bookkeeping, accounting, and auditing clerks	205	11.4%
Billing and posting clerks, and machine operators	93	18.1%*

*Difference due to rounding.

Source: Bureau of Labor Statistics, National Employment Matrix (http://data.bls.gov/oep/nioem/empiohm.jsp) as of March 12, 2015.

FIGURE 1-8   Accounting Positions according to Salary.com, 2015

Accounting Clerk I - U.S. National Averages

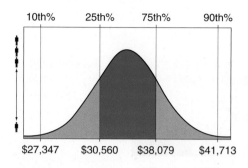

10th%	25th%	75th%	90th%
$27,347	$30,560	$38,079	$41,713

ACCOUNTING CLERK I

Performs routine accounting activities such as maintenance of the general ledger, preparation of various accounting statements and financial reports and accounts payable or receivable functions. Requires a high school diploma or its equivalent with 0–2 years of experience in the field or in a related area. Has knowledge of commonly used concepts, practices, and procedures within a particular field. Relies on instructions and pre-established guidelines to perform the functions of the job. Works under immediate supervision. Primary job functions do not typically require exercising independent judgment. Typically reports to a supervisor or manager.

Bookkeeper - U.S. National Averages

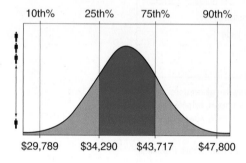

10th%	25th%	75th%	90th%
$29,789	$34,290	$43,717	$47,800

BOOKKEEPER

Maintains and records business transactions. Balances ledgers, reconciles accounts, and prepares reports. Follows bookkeeping procedures established by the organization. May require an associate's degree or its equivalent with 2–4 years of experience in the field or in a related area. Familiar with standard concepts, practices, and procedures within a particular field. Relies on experience and judgment to plan and accomplish goals. Performs a variety of tasks. Works under general supervision. A certain degree of creativity and latitude is required. Typically reports to a manager or head of a unit/department.

Budget Analyst I - U.S. National Averages

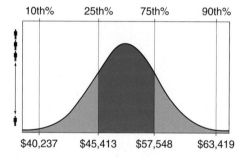

10th%	25th%	75th%	90th%
$40,237	$45,413	$57,548	$63,419

BUDGET ANALYST I

Analyzes accounting records to determine financial resources required to implement programs and makes recommendations for budget allocations to ensure conformance to budgetary limits. Also responsible for reviewing operating budgets periodically in order to analyze trends affecting budget needs. Requires a bachelor's degree and 0–2 years of experience in the field or in a related area. Has knowledge of commonly used concepts, practices, and procedures within a particular field. Relies on instructions and pre-established guidelines to perform the functions of the job. Works under immediate supervision. Primary job functions do not typically require exercising independent judgment. Typically reports to a supervisor or manager.

Your Perspective   VEHICLE EMISSIONS TECHNICIAN

If you worked in a vehicle emissions center in states such as California, Georgia, Maryland, or Illinois, you are most likely familiar with working with customers and their vehicles to ensure that all vehicle emissions are tested properly. No matter what the business is or how it is structured (sole proprietorship, partnership or corporation), accounting is needed to maintain financial data. You most likely work in a sole proprietorship business.

As you work on different cars and trucks each day, all vehicles tested as well as their costs are maintained in an accurate record. Behind the scenes of your daily duties, your manager uses the information to make important operating decisions. Accounting is the language of business and the eyes and ears of management.

Accounts Payable Manager - U.S. National Averages

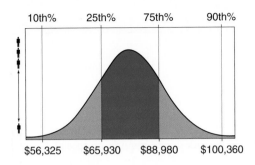

ACCOUNTS PAYABLE MANAGER

Responsible for all activities in the accounts payable function. Ensures timely payments of vendor invoices and expense vouchers and maintains accurate records and control reports. Reviews applicable accounting reports and accounts payable register to ensure accuracy. May require a bachelor's degree in a related area and at least 7 years of experience in the field. Familiar with a variety of the field's concepts, practices, and procedures. Relies on extensive experience and judgment to plan and accomplish goals. Performs a variety of tasks. Leads and directs the work of others. A wide degree of creativity and latitude is expected. Typically reports to a head of a unit/department.

Top Audit Executive - U.S. National Averages

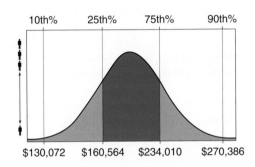

TOP AUDIT EXECUTIVE

Oversees all aspects of an organization's auditing function. Responsible for planning and directing all accounting and financial data. Requires a bachelor's degree with at least 15 years of experience in the field. Familiar with a variety of the field's concepts, practices, and procedures. Relies on extensive experience and judgment to plan and accomplish goals. Performs a variety of tasks. Leads and directs the work of others. A wide degree of creativity and latitude is expected. Typically reports to top management.

Controller - U.S. National Averages

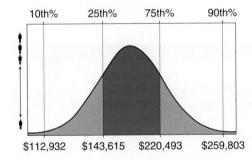

CONTROLLER

Responsible for directing an organization's accounting functions. These functions include establishing and maintaining the organization's accounting principles, practices, procedures, and initiatives. Prepares financial reports and presents findings and recommendations to top management. Requires a bachelor's degree and at least 15 years of direct experience in the field. Typically requires a CPA. Demonstrates expertise in a variety of the field's concepts, practices, and procedures. Relies on extensive experience and judgment to plan and accomplish goals. Performs a variety of tasks. Leads and directs the work of others. A wide degree of creativity and latitude is expected. Typically reports to top financial officer or CEO.

Source: Salary.com, March 2015

Regardless of the type of career you desire, writing skills are important in business and your personal life. Becoming a good writer requires practice and a strategy for the process used to prepare memos, letters, and other documents. On pages 14 and 15, Ken Davis offers an excellent approach to managing your writing. Take a moment to read Ken's tips. Then, practice his approach by completing the writing assignments as you finish each chapter.

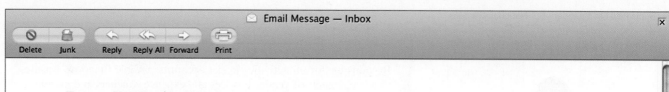

From: Ken Davis
Subject: Managing Your Writing
To: Accounting Students

Here's a secret: the business writing that you and I do—the writing that gets the world's work done—requires no special gift. It can be managed, like any other business process.

Managing writing is largely a matter of managing time. Writing is a process, and like any process it can be done efficiently or inefficiently. Unfortunately, most of us are pretty inefficient writers. That's because we try to get each word, each sentence, right the first time. Given a letter to write, we begin with the first sentence. We think about that sentence, write it, revise it, even check its spelling, before going on to the second sentence. In an hour of writing, we might spend 45 or 50 minutes doing this kind of detailed drafting. We spend only a few minutes on overall planning at the beginning and only a few minutes on overall revising at the end.

That approach to writing is like building a house by starting with the front door: planning, building, finishing—even washing the windows—before doing anything with the rest of the house. No wonder most of us have so much trouble writing.

Efficient, effective writers take better charge of their writing time. They *manage* their writing. Like building contractors, they spend time planning before they start construction. Once construction has started, they don't try to do all of the finishing touches as they go.

As the following illustration shows, many good writers break their writing process into three main stages: planning, drafting, and revising. They spend more time at the first and third stages than at the second. They also build in some "management" time at the beginning and the end, and some break time in the middle. To manage *your* writing time, try the following steps.

To Do List
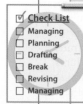 ✓ At the MANAGING stage (perhaps two or three minutes for a one-hour writing job), remind yourself that writing *can* be managed and that it's largely a matter of managing time. Plan your next hour.
At the PLANNING stage (perhaps 20 minutes out of the hour):
1. **Find the "we."** Define the community to which you and your reader belong. Then ask, "How are my reader and I alike and different?"—in knowledge, attitudes, and circumstances.
2. **Define your purpose.** Remember the advice a consultant once gave Stanley Tool executives: "You're not in the business of making drills: you're in the business of making holes." Too many of us lose sight of the difference between making drills and making holes when we write letters and memos. We focus on the piece of writing—the tool itself—not its purpose. The result: our writing often misses the chance to be as effective as it could be. When you're still at the planning stage, focus on the outcome you want, not on the means you will use to achieve it.

Check List
☑ Check List
☐ Managing
☐ Planning
☐ Drafting
☐ Break
☐ Revising
☐ Managing

3. **Get your stuff together.** Learn from those times when you've turned a one-hour home-improvement project into a three- or four-hour job by having to make repeated trips to the hardware store for tools or parts. Before you start the drafting stage of writing, collect the information you need.

4. **Get your ducks in a row.** Decide on the main points you want to make. Then, make a list or rough outline placing your points in the most logical order.

At the DRAFTING STAGE (perhaps 5 minutes out of the hour):

5. **Do it wrong the first time.** Do a "quick and dirty" draft, without editing. Think of your draft as a "prototype," written not for the end user but for your own testing and improvement. Stopping to edit while you draft breaks your train of thought and keeps you from being a good writer. (*Hint:* If you are writing at a computer, try turning off the monitor during the drafting stage.)

At the BREAK STAGE (perhaps 5 minutes):

6. **Take a break and change hats.** Get away from your draft, even if for only a few minutes. Come back with a fresh perspective—the reader's perspective.

At the REVISING STAGE (perhaps 25 minutes):

7. **Signal your turns.** Just as if you were driving a car, you're leading your reader through new territory. Use "turn signals"—*and, in addition, but, however, or, therefore, because, for example*—to guide your reader from sentence to sentence.

8. **Say what you mean.** Put the point of your sentences in the subjects and verbs. For example, revise "There are drawbacks to using this accounting method" to "This accounting method has some drawbacks." You'll be saying what you mean, and you'll be a more effective communicator.

9. **Pay by the word.** Reading your memo requires work. If your sentences are wordy and you are slow to get to the point, the reader may decide that it is not worth the effort. Pretend you are paying the reader by the word to read your memo. Then, revise your memo to make it as short and to the point as possible.

10. **Translate into English.** Keep your words simple. (Lee Iacocca put both these tips in one "commandment of good management": "Say it in English and keep it short.") Remember that you write to express, not impress.

11. **Finish the job.** Check your spelling, punctuation, and mechanics.

Finally, at the MANAGING STAGE again (2 to 3 minutes):

12. **Evaluate your writing process.** Figure out how to improve it next time.

By following these 12 steps, you can take charge of your writing time. Begin today to *manage your writing.* As a United Technologies Corporation advertisement in *The Wall Street Journal* admonished, "If you want to manage somebody, manage yourself. Do that well and you'll be ready to stop managing and start leading."

Dr. Kenneth W. Davis is Professor Emeritus of English at Indiana University, and a writing trainer and coach.

Source: Kenneth W. Davis, *The McGraw-Hill 36-Hour Course in Business Writing and Communications,* Second Edition. Copyright © 2010 by Kenneth W. Davis. Reprinted with permission of The McGraw-Hill Companies, Inc.

Self-Study

LEARNING OBJECTIVES	Key Points to Remember
LO1 Describe the purpose of accounting.	The purpose of accounting is to provide financial information about a business to individuals and organizations.
LO2 Describe the accounting process.	The six major steps of the accounting process are analyzing, recording, classifying, summarizing, reporting, and interpreting.
LO3 Define GAAP and describe the process used by FASB to develop these principles.	Generally accepted accounting principles (GAAP) are the rules that businesses must follow when preparing financial statements. FASB takes the following steps to develop an accounting standard: 1. The issue is placed on the Board's agenda. 2. After researching the issue, a discussion memorandum is issued. 3. Public hearings are held. 4. An exposure draft is issued. 5. The statement of financial accounting standards is issued.
LO4 Define three types of business ownership structures.	Three types of business ownership structures are the sole proprietorship, the partnership, and the corporation.
LO5 Classify different types of businesses by activities.	Different types of businesses classified by activities are a service business, a merchandising business, and a manufacturing business.
LO6 Identify career opportunities in accounting.	Career opportunities in accounting include work in public accounting, private accounting, and governmental and not-for-profit accounting.

KEY TERMS

accountant (8) Designs the accounting information system and focuses on analyzing and interpreting information.

accounting (4) A system of gathering financial information about a business and reporting this information to users.

accounting clerk (8) Records, sorts, and files accounting information.

accounting information systems (10) Accountants in this area design and implement manual and computerized accounting systems.

Accounting Standards Update (6) A standard issued by the Financial Accounting Standards Board. These standards must be followed when preparing financial statements. The updates are included in the FASB Accounting Standards Codification.

analyzing (5) Looking at events that have taken place and thinking about how they affect the business.

auditing (9) Reviewing and testing to be certain that proper accounting policies and practices have been followed.

bookkeeper (8)   Generally supervises the work of accounting clerks, helps with daily accounting work, and summarizes accounting information.

budgeting (10)   The process in which accountants help managers develop a financial plan.

Certified Fraud Examiner (CFE) (9)   A forensic accountant who has passed the exam offered by the Association of Certified Fraud Examiners.

Certified Internal Auditor (CIA) (10)   An internal auditor who has achieved professional recognition by passing the uniform examination offered by the Institute of Internal Auditors.

Certified Management Accountant (CMA) (10)   An accountant who has passed an examination offered by the Institute of Management Accountants.

Certified Public Accountant (CPA) (9)   A public accountant who has met certain educational and experience requirements and has passed an examination prepared by the American Institute of Certified Public Accountants.

classifying (5)   Sorting and grouping similar items together rather than merely keeping a simple, diary-like record of numerous events.

Controller (10)   The accountant who oversees the entire accounting process and is the principal accounting officer of a company.

corporation (7)   A type of ownership structure in which stockholders own the business. The owners' risk is usually limited to their initial investment, and they usually have very little influence on the business decisions.

cost accounting (10)   Determining the cost of producing specific products or providing services and analyzing for cost effectiveness.

Exposure Draft (6)   This document explains the rules that FASB believes firms should follow in accounting for a particular event. Based on the responses to the exposure draft, the Board will decide if any changes are necessary before issuing a final standard.

financial accounting (10)   Includes preparing various reports and financial statements and analyzing operating, investing, and financing decisions.

Financial Accounting Standards Board Accounting Standards Codification (6)   This Codification is an electronic database that provides one authoritative source for the standards which must be followed by U.S. companies.

forensic accounting (9)   A specialized field that combines fraud detection, fraud prevention, litigation support, expert witnessing, business valuations, and other investigative activities.

generally accepted accounting principles (GAAP) (5)   Procedures and guidelines developed by the Financial Accounting Standards Board to be followed in the accounting and reporting process.

internal auditing (10)   Reviewing the operating and accounting control procedures adopted by management to make sure the controls are adequate and being followed; assuring that accurate and timely information is provided.

interpreting (5)   Deciding the meaning and importance of the information in various reports.

management advisory services (9)   Providing advice to businesses on a wide variety of managerial issues.

manufacturing business (7)   A business that makes a product to sell.

merchandising business (7)   A business that buys products to sell.

para-accountant (8)   A paraprofessional who provides many accounting, auditing, or tax services under the direct supervision of an accountant.

partnership (6)   A type of ownership structure in which more than one person owns the business.

Preliminary Views (5)   The first document issued by FASB when developing an accounting standard. This document identifies the pros and cons of various accounting treatments for an event and invites others to comment.

public hearing (5)   Following the issuance of a discussion memorandum, public meetings are often held by FASB to gather opinions on the accounting issue.

recording (5)   Entering financial information about events affecting the company into the accounting system.

reporting (5)   Telling the results of the financial information.

Sarbanes-Oxley Act (SOX) (9)   An act passed by Congress to help improve reporting practices of public companies.

service business (7)   A business that provides a service.

sole proprietorship (6)   A type of ownership structure in which one person owns the business.

summarizing (5)   Bringing the various items of information together to determine a result.

tax accounting (10)   Services focused on tax planning, preparing tax returns, and dealing with the Internal Revenue Service and other governmental agencies.

taxation (9)   See tax accounting.

Applying Your Knowledge

REVIEW QUESTIONS

LO1	1. What is the purpose of accounting?
LO1	2. Identify four user groups normally interested in financial information about a business.
LO2	3. Identify the six major steps of the accounting process and explain each step.
LO3	4. What are generally accepted accounting principles (GAAP)?
LO3	5. Describe the steps followed by the Financial Accounting Standards Board when developing an accounting standard.
LO3	6. What is the name of the organization that issues accounting standards followed by many firms in countries outside the United States?
LO4	7. Identify the three types of ownership structures and discuss the advantages and disadvantages of each.
LO5	8. Identify three types of businesses according to activities.
LO6	9. What are the main functions of an accounting clerk?
LO6	10. Name and describe four areas of specialization for a public accountant.
LO6	11. What is the purpose of the Sarbanes-Oxley Act?
LO6	12. Name and describe six areas of specialization for a managerial accountant.

SERIES A EXERCISES

E 1-1A   (LO1)

SHOW
ME HOW

PURPOSE OF ACCOUNTING Match the following users with the information needed.

1. Owners
2. Managers
3. Creditors
4. Government agencies

a. Whether the firm can pay its bills on time
b. Detailed, up-to-date information to measure business performance (and plan for future operations)
c. To determine taxes to be paid and whether other regulations are met
d. The firm's current financial condition

E 1-2A   (LO2)

SHOW
ME HOW

ACCOUNTING PROCESS List the six major steps of the accounting process in order (1–6) and define each.

_____   Recording
_____   Summarizing
_____   Reporting
_____   Analyzing
_____   Interpreting
_____   Classifying

SERIES B EXERCISES

E 1-1B   (LO1)

SHOW
ME HOW

PURPOSE OF ACCOUNTING Describe the kind of information needed by the users listed.

Owners (present and future)
Managers
Creditors (present and future)
Government agencies

E 1-2B   (LO2)

ACCOUNTING PROCESS Match the following steps of the accounting process with their definitions.

Analyzing
Recording
Classifying
Summarizing
Reporting
Interpreting

a. Telling the results
b. Looking at events that have taken place and thinking about how they affect the business
c. Deciding the importance of the various reports
d. Aggregating many similar events to provide information that is easy to understand
e. Sorting and grouping like items together
f. Entering financial information into the accounting system

☑ **Check List**
☐ Managing
☐ Planning
☐ Drafting
☐ Break
☐ Revising
☐ Managing

MANAGING YOUR WRITING

Take a moment to think about what it would be like to run your own business. If you started a business, what would it be? Prepare a one-page memo that describes the type of business you would enjoy the most. Would it be a service, merchandising, or manufacturing business? Explain what form of ownership you would prefer and why.

Chapter 2

RICH ABRAHAMSON/FORT COLLINS COLORADOAN

LEARNING OBJECTIVES

Careful study of this chapter should enable you to:

LO1 Define the accounting elements.

LO2 Construct the accounting equation.

LO3 Analyze business transactions.

LO4 Show the effects of business transactions on the accounting equation.

LO5 Prepare and describe the purposes of a simple income statement, statement of owner's equity, and balance sheet.

LO6 Define the three basic phases of the accounting process.

Analyzing Transactions: The Accounting Equation

At Rob's Bike Courier Service in Fort Collins, Colorado, Rob believes "less is more." His small company doesn't "have a fleet of vehicles, just some pretty cool bicycles." His mission is providing successful bike delivery service, perfect for both traditional business delivery services and residential errands. Since January of 2005, Rob's Bike Courier Service has been the alternative to gas-powered vehicle delivery. Thus, besides great rates and friendly, reliable service, Rob offers earth-friendly service.

Currently, he delivers wholesale bagels from a mid-town baker to several downtown coffee shops. He does the same for another pastry chef. Rob also picks up recycling materials, offers bike towing services, and will go to a customer's home to fix flat bike tires and make repairs.

Though his company is small, Rob still needs an accounting system to maintain records of his business transactions and to prepare financial statements. Currently, he uses Quickbooks®, an accounting program used by many small companies. In Chapters 2 through 6, we learn how to account for a service business like Rob's by using an example of a similar company: Rohan's Campus Delivery.

The entire accounting process is based on one simple equation, called the accounting equation. In this chapter, you will learn how to use this equation to analyze business transactions. You will also learn how to prepare financial statements that report the effect of these transactions on the financial condition of a business.

THE ACCOUNTING ELEMENTS

LO1 Define the accounting elements.

Before the accounting process can begin, the entity to be accounted for must be defined. A **business entity** is an individual, association, or organization that engages in economic activities and controls specific economic resources. This definition allows the personal and business finances of an owner to be accounted for separately.

Three basic accounting elements exist for every business entity: assets, liabilities, and owner's equity. These elements are defined below.

Assets

Assets are items that are owned by a business and will provide future benefits. Examples of assets include cash, merchandise, furniture, fixtures, machinery, buildings, and land. Businesses may also have an asset called **accounts receivable**. This asset represents the amount of money owed to the business by its customers as a result of making sales "on account," or "on credit." Making sales on account simply means that the customers have promised to pay sometime in the future.

Liabilities

Liabilities represent something owed to another business entity. The amount owed represents a probable future outflow of assets as a result of a past event or transaction. Liabilities are debts or obligations of the business that can be paid with cash, goods, or services.

The most common liabilities are accounts payable and notes payable. An **account payable** is an unwritten promise to pay a supplier for assets purchased or services received. Acquiring assets or services by promising to make payments in the future is referred to as making a purchase "on account," or "on credit." Formal written promises to pay suppliers or lenders specified sums of money at definite future times are known as **notes payable**.

Owner's Equity

Owner's equity is the amount by which the business assets exceed the business liabilities. Other terms used for owner's equity include **net worth** and **capital**. If there are no business liabilities, the owner's equity is equal to the total assets.

The owner of a business may have business assets and liabilities as well as nonbusiness assets and liabilities. For example, the business owner probably owns a home, clothing, and a car, and perhaps owes the dentist for dental service. These are personal, nonbusiness assets and liabilities. According to the **business entity concept**, nonbusiness assets and liabilities are not included in the business entity's accounting records.

If the owner invests money or other assets in the business, the item invested is reclassified from a nonbusiness asset to a business asset. If the owner withdraws money or other assets from the business for personal use, the item withdrawn is reclassified from a business asset to a nonbusiness asset. These distinctions are important and allow the owner to make decisions based on the financial condition and results of the business apart from nonbusiness activities.

LEARNING KEY
Pay close attention to the definitions for the basic accounting elements. A clear understanding of these definitions will help you analyze even the most complex business transactions.

LEARNING KEY
The business entity's assets and liabilities are separate from the owner's nonbusiness assets and liabilities.

Checkpoint ✓

Complete Checkpoint-1 on page 41 to test your basic understanding of LO1.

© CHAMPIOFOTO/SHUTTERSTOCK.COM

A Broader View

Assets and the Cost of Products We Buy

Next time you buy something, think of all the assets a company needs to produce that product. If the product comes from a capital-intensive industry, one that requires heavy investments in assets, the company must price the product high enough to cover the cost of using the assets and replacing them when they wear out. For example, AT&T recently reported that the cost of property, plant, and equipment used for operating purposes came to over $274 billion.

THE ACCOUNTING EQUATION

LO2 Construct the accounting equation.

The relationship between the three basic accounting elements—assets, liabilities, and owner's equity—can be expressed in the form of a simple equation known as the accounting equation.

Assets	=	Liabilities	+	Owner's Equity

This equation reflects the fact that both outsiders and insiders have an interest in the assets of a business.

- Liabilities represent the outside interests of creditors.
- Owner's equity represents the inside interests of owners.

Or, viewed another way,

The left side of the equation shows the assets.   *The right side of the equation shows where the money came from to buy the assets.*

When two elements are known, the third can always be calculated. For example, assume that assets on December 31 total $60,400. On that same day, the business liabilities consist of $5,400 owed for equipment. Owner's equity is calculated by subtracting total liabilities from total assets, $60,400 – $5,400 = $55,000.

LEARNING KEY

If you know two accounting elements, you can calculate the third element.

Total assets	$60,400
Total liabilities	−5,400
Owner's equity	$55,000

Assets	=	Liabilities	+	Owner's Equity
$60,400	=	$5,400	+	$55,000
$60,400	**=**	**$60,400**		

If during the next accounting period, assets increased by $10,000 and liabilities increased by $3,000, owner's equity must have increased by $7,000 ($10,000 – $3,000) as shown on the next page.

	Assets	=	Liabilities	+	Owner's Equity
BB	$60,400		$5,400		$55,000
	+10,000	=	+3,000	+	+7,000
EB	$70,400	=	$8,400	+	$62,000
	$70,400	=		$70,400	

BB: Beginning balance
EB: Ending balance

Checkpoint ✓

Complete Checkpoint-2 on page 41 to test your basic understanding of LO2.

Note also that after computing the ending balances for assets, liabilities, and owner's equity, the accounting equation remains in balance.

ANALYZING BUSINESS TRANSACTIONS

LO3 Analyze business transactions.

A business transaction is an economic event that has a direct impact on the business. A business transaction almost always requires an exchange between the business and another outside entity. We must be able to measure this exchange in dollars. Examples of business transactions include buying goods and services, selling goods and services, buying and selling assets, making loans, and borrowing money.

All business transactions affect the accounting equation through specific accounts. An account is a separate record used to summarize changes in each asset, liability, and owner's equity of a business. Account titles provide a description of the particular type of asset, liability, or owner's equity affected by a transaction.

Three basic questions must be answered when analyzing the effects of a business transaction on the accounting equation. These questions help address the steps in the accounting process discussed in Chapter 1.

1. **What happened?**
   - Make certain you understand the event that has taken place.

2. **Which accounts are affected?**
   - Identify the accounts that are affected.
   - Classify these accounts as assets, liabilities, or owner's equity.

3. **How is the accounting equation affected?**
   - Determine which accounts have increased or decreased.
   - Make certain that the accounting equation remains in balance after the transaction has been entered.

EFFECT OF TRANSACTIONS ON THE ACCOUNTING EQUATION

LO4 Show the effects of business transactions on the accounting equation.

In Chapters 2 through 6, we will focus on learning how to account for a business similar to Rob's Bike Courier Service, discussed in the chapter opener. In these chapters, we will focus on Rohan's Campus Delivery. By studying Rohan's business transactions and accounting techniques, you will learn about business and accounting. A major advantage of studying accounting is that it helps you learn a great deal about business.

As explained previously, we must first understand the economic substance of events. Then, we must determine how that information is entered into the accounting system. If Rohan does not understand the economic events affecting his delivery business and their impact on the accounting equation, the events will not be correctly entered into the accounting system.

Each transaction affects at least two accounts and one or more of the three basic accounting elements. A transaction increases or decreases specific asset, liability, or owner's equity accounts. Assume that the following transactions occurred during June 20--, the first month of operations for Rohan's Campus Delivery.

Transaction (a): Investment by owner

An Increase in an Asset Offset by an Increase in Owner's Equity. Rohan Macsen opened a bank account with a deposit of $2,000 for his business. The new business now has $2,000 of the asset Cash. Since Rohan contributed the asset, the owner's equity element, Rohan Macsen, Capital, increases by the same amount.

> Remember, capital does not mean cash. The cash is shown in the cash account.

Assets (Items Owned)	=	Liabilities (Amounts Owed)	+	Owner's Equity (Owner's Investment)
Cash	=			Rohan Macsen, Capital
(a) $2,000	=			$2,000

Transaction (b): Purchase of an asset for cash

An Increase in an Asset Offset by a Decrease in Another Asset. Rohan decided that the fastest and easiest way to get around campus and find parking is on a motor scooter. Thus, he bought a motor scooter (delivery equipment) for $1,200 cash. Rohan exchanged one asset, cash, for another, delivery equipment. This transaction reduces Cash and creates a new asset, Delivery Equipment.

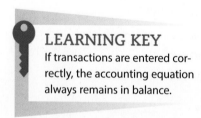

LEARNING KEY
If transactions are entered correctly, the accounting equation always remains in balance.

Assets (Items Owned)			=	Liabilities (Amounts Owed)	+	Owner's Equity (Owner's Investment)
Cash	+	Delivery Equipment	=			Rohan Macsen, Capital
$2,000						$2,000
(b) −1,200		+ $1,200				
$ 800	+	$1,200	=			$2,000
$2,000			=			$2,000

Transaction (c): Purchase of an asset on account

An Increase in an Asset Offset by an Increase in a Liability. Rohan hired a friend to work for him, which meant that a second scooter would be needed. Given Rohan's limited cash, he bought a secondhand model for $900. The seller agreed to allow Rohan to spread the payments over the next three months. This transaction increased an asset, Delivery Equipment, by $900 and increased the liability, Accounts Payable, by an equal amount.

Assets (Items Owned)		=	Liabilities (Amounts Owed)	+	Owner's Equity (Owner's Investment)
Cash +	Delivery Equipment	=	Accounts Payable	+	Rohan Macsen, Capital
(c) $800	$1,200 +900		+$900		$2,000
$800 +	$2,100	=	$900	+	$2,000
$2,900		**=**	**$2,900**		

Transaction (d): Payment on a loan

A Decrease in an Asset Offset by a Decrease in a Liability. Rohan paid the first installment on the scooter of $300 [see transaction (c)]. This payment decreased the asset, Cash, and the liability, Accounts Payable, by $300.

Assets (Items Owned)		=	Liabilities (Amounts Owed)	+	Owner's Equity (Owner's Investment)
Cash +	Delivery Equipment	=	Accounts Payable	+	Rohan Macsen, Capital
(d) $800 −300	$2,100		$900 −300		$2,000
$500 +	$2,100	=	$600	+	$2,000
$2,600		**=**	**$2,600**		

Expanding the Accounting Equation: Revenues, Expenses, and Withdrawals

In the preceding sections, three key accounting elements of every business entity were defined and explained: assets, liabilities, and owner's equity. To complete the explanation of the accounting process, three additional elements must be added to the discussion: revenues, expenses, and withdrawals.

Revenues

Revenues represent the amount a business charges customers for products sold or services performed. Customers generally pay with cash or a credit card, or they promise to pay at a later date. Most businesses recognize revenues when earned, even if cash has not yet been received. Separate accounts are used to recognize different types of revenue. Examples include Delivery Fees; Consulting Fees; Rent Revenue, if the business rents space to others; Interest Revenue, for interest earned on bank deposits; and Sales, for sales of merchandise. *Revenues increase both assets and owner's equity.*

Expenses

Expenses represent the *decrease* in assets (or *increase* in liabilities) as a result of a company's efforts to produce revenues. Common examples of expenses are rent, salaries, supplies consumed, and taxes. As with revenues, separate accounts are used to keep the accounting records for each different type of expense. Expenses are "incurred" as

- assets are consumed (such as supplies), or
- services are provided (by employees, for example) to the business.

The two main purposes of recognizing an expense are (a) to keep track of the amount and types of expenses incurred and (b) to show the reduction in owner's equity. Again, an expense can cause a reduction in assets or an increase in liabilities. Wages earned by employees is a good example.

- If paid, the expense reduces owner's equity and an asset, Cash.
- If not paid, the expense reduces owner's equity and increases a liability, Wages Payable.

Either way, owner's equity is reduced. If total revenues are greater than total expenses for the period, the excess is the **net income**, or net profit, for the period. On the other hand, if total expenses are greater than total revenues for the period, the excess is a **net loss** for the period.

Revenues	$900	Revenues	$ 300
Expenses	500	Expenses	500
Net income	$400	Net loss	$(200)

The owner can determine the time period used in the measurement of net income or net loss. It may be a month, a quarter (three months), a year, or some other time period. The concept that income determination can be made on a periodic basis is known as the **accounting period concept**. Any accounting period of 12 months is called a **fiscal year**. The fiscal year frequently coincides with the calendar year.

Withdrawals

Withdrawals, or drawing, reduce owner's equity as a result of the owner taking cash or other assets out of the business for personal use. Since earnings are expected to offset withdrawals, this reduction is viewed as temporary.

The accounting equation is expanded to include revenues, expenses, and withdrawals. Note that revenues increase owner's equity, while expenses and drawing reduce owner's equity.

Assets (Items Owned)			=	**Liabilities** (Amounts Owed)	+	**Owner's Equity**					
						(Owner's Investment)	+	(Earnings)			
Cash	+	Delivery Equipment	=	Accounts Payable	+	Rohan Macsen, Capital	− Rohan Macsen, Drawing	+	Revenues	−	Expenses
Balance $500	+	$2,100	=	$600	+	$2,000					
$2,600			=			$2,600					

Effect of Revenue, Expense, and Withdrawal Transactions on the Accounting Equation

To show the effects of revenue, expense, and withdrawal transactions, the example of Rohan's Campus Delivery will be continued. Assume that the following transactions took place in Rohan's business during June 20--.

Transaction (e): Delivery revenues earned in cash

An Increase in an Asset Offset by an Increase in Owner's Equity Resulting from Revenue. Rohan received $500 cash from clients for delivery services. This transaction increased the asset, Cash, and increased owner's equity by $500. The increase in owner's equity is shown by increasing the revenue account, Delivery Fees, by $500.

	Cash	+	Delivery Equipment	=	Accounts Payable	+	Rohan Macsen, Capital	−	Rohan Macsen, Drawing	+	Revenues	−	Expenses	Description
	$ 500		$2,100		$600		$2,000							
(e)	+ 500										+ $500			Deliv. Fees
	$1,000	+	$2,100	=	$600	+	$2,000			+	$500			

$3,100 = $3,100

Transaction (f): Paid rent for month

A Decrease in an Asset Offset by a Decrease in Owner's Equity Resulting from an Expense. Rohan rents a small office on campus. He paid $200 for office rent for June. This transaction decreased both Cash and owner's equity by $200. The decrease in owner's equity is shown by increasing an expense called Rent Expense by $200. An increase in an expense decreases owner's equity.

	Cash	+	Delivery Equipment	=	Accounts Payable	+	Rohan Macsen, Capital	−	Rohan Macsen, Drawing	+	Revenues	−	Expenses	Description
	$1,000	+	$2,100		$600		$2,000				$500			
(f)	− 200												+ $200	Rent Exp.
	$ 800	+	$2,100	=	$600	+	$2,000			+	$500	−	$200	

$2,900 = $2,900

Transaction (g): Paid phone bill

A Decrease in an Asset Offset by a Decrease in Owner's Equity Resulting from an Expense. Rohan paid $50 in cash for phone service. This transaction, like the previous one, decreased both Cash and owner's equity. This decrease in owner's equity is shown by increasing an expense called Phone Expense by $50.

	Cash	+	Delivery Equipment	=	Accounts Payable	+	Rohan Macsen, Capital	−	Rohan Macsen, Drawing	+	Revenues	−	Expenses	Description
	$800		$2,100		$600		$2,000				$500		$200	
(g)	− 50												+ 50	Phone Expense
	$750	+	$2,100	=	$600	+	$2,000			+	$500	−	$250	

$2,850 = $2,850

Transaction (h): Delivery revenues earned on account

An Increase in an Asset Offset by an Increase in Owner's Equity Resulting from Revenue. Rohan extends credit to regular customers. Often, delivery services are performed for which payment will be received later. Since revenues are recognized when earned, an increase in owner's equity must be reported by increasing the revenue account. Since no cash is received at this time, Cash cannot be increased. Instead, an increase is reported for another asset, Accounts Receivable. *The total of Accounts Receivable at any point in time reflects the amount owed to Rohan by his customers.* Deliveries made on account amounted to $600. Accounts Receivable and Delivery Fees are increased.

	Assets (Items Owned)				=	Liabilities (Amounts Owed)	+	Owner's Equity (Owner's Investment)			+	(Earnings)		
	Cash +	Accounts Receivable +	Delivery Equipment		=	Accounts Payable	+	Rohan Macsen, Capital	− Rohan Macsen, Drawing	+		Revenues	− Expenses	Description
	$750		$2,100			$600		$2,000				$ 500	$250	
(h)		+ $600										+ 600		Deliv. Fees
	$750 +	$600 +	$2,100		=	$600	+	$2,000		+		$1,100	− $250	
	$3,450				=					$3,450				

Transaction (i): Purchase of supplies

An Increase in an Asset Offset by a Decrease in an Asset. Rohan bought pens, paper, delivery envelopes, and other supplies for $80 cash. These supplies should last for several months. Since they will generate future benefits, the supplies should be recorded as an asset. The accounting equation will show an increase in an asset, Supplies, and a decrease in Cash.

	Assets (Items Owned)					=	Liabilities (Amounts Owed)	+	Owner's Equity (Owner's Investment)			+	(Earnings)		
	Cash +	Accounts Receivable +	Supplies +	Delivery Equipment		=	Accounts Payable	+	Rohan Macsen, Capital	− Rohan Macsen, Drawing	+		Revenues	− Expenses	Description
	$750	$600		$2,100			$600		$2,000				$1,100	$250	
(i)	− 80		+ $80												
	$670 +	$600 +	$80 +	$2,100		=	$600	+	$2,000		+		$1,100	− $250	
	$3,450					=					$3,450				

Transaction (j): Payment of insurance premium

An Increase in an Asset Offset by a Decrease in an Asset. Since Rohan plans to graduate and sell the business next January, he paid $200 for an eight-month liability insurance policy. Insurance is paid in advance and will provide future benefits. Thus, it is treated as an asset. We must expand the equation to include another asset, Prepaid Insurance, and show that Cash has been reduced.

Assets (Items Owned)					=	Liabilities (Amounts Owed)	+	Owner's Equity (Owner's Investment)	+	(Earnings)		
Cash +	Accounts Receivable +	Supplies +	Prepaid Insurance +	Delivery Equipment =		Accounts Payable	+	Rohan Macsen, Capital −	Rohan Macsen, Drawing +	Revenues −	Expenses	Description
$670	$600	$80		$2,100		$600		$2,000		$1,100	$250	
(j) − 200			+ $200									
$470 +	$600 +	$80 +	$200 +	$2,100 +	=	$600	+	$2,000	+	$1,100 −	$250	
		$3,450						$3,450				

Transaction (k): Cash receipts from prior sales on account

An Increase in an Asset Offset by a Decrease in an Asset. Rohan received $570 in cash for delivery services performed for customers earlier in the month [see transaction (h)]. Receipt of this cash increases the cash account and reduces the amount due from customers reported in the accounts receivable account. *Notice that owner's equity is not affected in this transaction. Owner's equity increased in transaction (h) when revenue was recognized as it was earned, rather than now when cash is received.*

As shown in transactions (i), (j), and (k), transactions do not always affect both sides of the accounting equation.

Assets (Items Owned)					=	Liabilities (Amounts Owed)	+	Owner's Equity (Owner's Investment)	+	(Earnings)		
Cash +	Accounts Receivable +	Supplies +	Prepaid Insurance +	Delivery Equipment =		Accounts Payable	+	Rohan Macsen, Capital −	Rohan Macsen, Drawing +	Revenues −	Expenses	Description
$ 470	$600	$80	$200	$2,100		$600		$2,000		$1,100	$250	
(k) + 570	− 570											
$1,040 +	$ 30 +	$80 +	$200 +	$2,100 +	=	$600	+	$2,000	+	$1,100 −	$250	
		$3,450						$3,450				

Transaction (l): Purchase of an asset on account making a partial payment

An Increase in an Asset Offset by a Decrease in an Asset and an Increase in a Liability. With business increasing, Rohan hired a second employee and bought a third motor scooter. The scooter cost $1,500. Rohan paid $300 in cash and will spread the remaining payments over the next four months. The asset Delivery Equipment increases by $1,500, Cash decreases by $300, and the liability Accounts Payable increases by $1,200. *Note that this transaction changes three accounts. Even so, the accounting equation remains in balance.*

Assets (Items Owned)					=	Liabilities (Amounts Owed)	+	Owner's Equity (Owner's Investment)	+	(Earnings)		
Cash +	Accounts Receivable +	Supplies +	Prepaid Insurance +	Delivery Equipment =		Accounts Payable	+	Rohan Macsen, Capital −	Rohan Macsen, Drawing +	Revenues −	Expenses	Description
$1,040	$30	$80	$200	$2,100		$ 600		$2,000		$1,100	$250	
(l) − 300				+ 1,500		+ 1,200						
$ 740 +	$30 +	$80 +	$200 +	$3,600 +	=	$1,800	+	$2,000	+	$1,100 −	$250	
		$4,650						$4,650				

Transaction (m): Payment of wages

A Decrease in an Asset Offset by a Decrease in Owner's Equity Resulting from an Expense. Rohan paid his part-time employees $650 in wages. This represents an additional business expense. As with other expenses, Cash is reduced and owner's equity is reduced by increasing an expense.

	Assets (Items Owned)					=	Liabilities (Amounts Owed)	+	Owner's Equity			(Earnings)		
	Cash +	Accounts Receivable +	Supplies +	Prepaid Insurance +	Delivery Equipment =		Accounts Payable	+	Rohan Macsen, Capital	− Rohan Macsen, Drawing	+ Revenues	− Expenses	Description
	$740	$30	$80	$200	$3,600		$1,800		$2,000		$1,100	$250	
(m)	− 650											+ 650	Wages Exp.
	$ 90 +	$30 +	$80 +	$200 +	$3,600 =		$1,800	+	$2,000		+ $1,100	− $900	
			$4,000			=					$4,000		

Transaction (n): Deliveries made for cash and on account

An Increase in Two Assets Offset by an Increase in Owner's Equity. Total delivery fees for the remainder of the month amounted to $1,050: $430 in cash and $620 on account. Since all of these delivery fees have been earned, the revenue account increases by $1,050. Also, Cash increases by $430 and Accounts Receivable increases by $620. Thus, revenues increase assets and owner's equity. Note, once again, that recording these revenues impacts three accounts while the equation remains in balance.

	Assets (Items Owned)					=	Liabilities (Amounts Owed)	+	Owner's Equity			(Earnings)		
	Cash +	Accounts Receivable +	Supplies +	Prepaid Insurance +	Delivery Equipment =		Accounts Payable	+	Rohan Macsen, Capital	− Rohan Macsen, Drawing	+ Revenues	− Expenses	Description
	$ 90	$ 30	$80	$200	$3,600		$1,800		$2,000		$1,100	$900	
(n)	+ 430	+ 620									+ 1,050		Deliv. Fees
	$520 +	$650 +	$80 +	$200 +	$3,600 =		$1,800	+	$2,000		+ $2,150	− $900	
			$5,050			=					$5,050		

LEARNING KEY

Withdrawals by the owner are reported in the drawing account. Withdrawals are the opposite of investments by the owner.

Transaction (o): Withdrawal of cash from business

A Decrease in an Asset Offset by a Decrease in Owner's Equity Resulting from a Withdrawal by the Owner. At the end of the month, Rohan took $150 in cash from the business to purchase books for his classes. Since the books are not business related, this is a withdrawal. Withdrawals can be viewed as the opposite of investments by the owner. Both owner's equity and Cash decrease.

	Assets (Items Owned)					=	Liabilities (Amounts Owed)	+	Owner's Equity			(Earnings)		
	Cash +	Accounts Receivable +	Supplies +	Prepaid Insurance +	Delivery Equipment =		Accounts Payable	+	Rohan Macsen, Capital	− Rohan Macsen, Drawing	+ Revenues	− Expenses	Description
	$520	$650	$80	$200	$3,600		$1,800		$2,000		$2,150	$900	
(o)	− 150									+ $150			
	$370 +	$650 +	$80 +	$200 +	$3,600 =		$1,800	+	$2,000	− $150	+ $2,150	− $900	
			$4,900			=					$4,900		

FIGURE 2-1 Summary of Transactions Illustrated

Trans-action	Cash	+ Accounts Receivable	+ Supplies	+ Prepaid Insurance	+ Delivery Equipment	= Accounts Payable	+ Rohan Macsen, Capital	− Rohan Macsen, Drawing	+ Revenues	− Expenses	Description
Balance											
(a)	2,000						2,000				
Balance	2,000						2,000				
(b)	(1,200)				1,200						
Balance	800				1,200		2,000				
(c)					900	900					
Balance	800				2,100	900	2,000				
(d)	(300)					(300)					
Balance	500				2,100	600	2,000				
(e)	500								500		Deliv. Fees
Balance	1,000				2,100	600	2,000		500		
(f)	(200)									200	Rent Exp.
Balance	800				2,100	600	2,000		500	200	
(g)	(50)									50	Phone Exp.
Balance	750				2,100	600	2,000		500	250	
(h)		600							600		Deliv. Fees
Balance	750	600			2,100	600	2,000		1,100	250	
(i)	(80)		80								
Balance	670	600	80		2,100	600	2,000		1,100	250	
(j)	(200)			200							
Balance	470	600	80	200	2,100	600	2,000		1,100	250	
(k)	570	(570)									
Balance	1,040	30	80	200	2,100	600	2,000		1,100	250	
(l)	(300)				1,500	1,200					
Balance	740	30	80	200	3,600	1,800	2,000		1,100	250	
(m)	(650)									650	Wages Exp.
Balance	90	30	80	200	3,600	1,800	2,000		1,100	900	
(n)	430	620							1,050		Deliv. Fees
Balance	520	650	80	200	3,600	1,800	2,000		2,150	900	
(o)	(150)							150			
Balance	**370** +	**650** +	**80** +	**200** +	**3,600** =	**1,800** +	**2,000** −	**150** +	**2,150** −	**900**	

Cash	$ 370	Accounts Payable	$1,800
Accounts Receivable	650	Rohan Macsen, Capital	2,000
Supplies	80	Rohan Macsen, Drawing	(150)
Prepaid Insurance	200	Delivery Fees	2,150
Delivery Equipment	3,600	Rent Expense	(200)
Total Assets	$4,900	Phone Expense	(50)
		Wages Expense	(650)
		Total Liabilities and Owner's Equity	$4,900

Amounts in ( ) are subtracted

As with the running totals in the table, the listing immediately below the table provides proof that the accounting equation is in balance.

Checkpoint ✓

Complete Checkpoint-3 on page 41 to test your basic understanding of LO3/4.

Figure 2-1 shows a summary of the transactions. Use this summary to test your understanding of transaction analysis by describing the economic event represented by each transaction. At the bottom of Figure 2-1, the asset accounts and their totals are compared with the liability and owner's equity accounts and their totals.

FINANCIAL STATEMENTS

LO5 Prepare and describe
the purposes of a
simple income
statement, statement
of owner's equity, and
balance sheet.

Three financial statements commonly prepared by a business entity are the income statement, statement of owner's equity, and balance sheet. The transaction information gathered and summarized in the accounting equation may be used to prepare these financial statements. Figure 2-2 shows the following:

1. A summary of the specific revenue and expense transactions and the ending totals for the asset, liability, capital, and drawing accounts from the accounting equation.

2. The financial statements and their linkages with the accounting equation and each other.

Note that each of the financial statements in Figure 2-2 has a heading consisting of:

HEADING FOR FINANCIAL STATEMENTS	
1. The name of the company	Rohan's Campus Delivery
2. The title of the statement	Income Statement, Statement of Owner's Equity, or Balance Sheet
3. The time period covered or the date of the statement	For Month Ended June 30, 20--, or June 30, 20--

The income statement and statement of owner's equity provide information concerning events covering a period of time, in this case, *the month ended* June 30, 20--. The balance sheet, on the other hand, offers a picture of the business on *a specific date*, June 30, 20--.

GUIDELINES FOR PREPARING FINANCIAL STATEMENTS
1. Financial statements are prepared primarily for users not associated with the company. To make a good impression and enhance understanding, financial statements must follow a standard form with careful attention to placement, spacing, and indentations.
2. All statements have a heading with the name of the company, name of the statement, and accounting period or date.
3. Single rules (underlines) indicate that the numbers above the line have been added or subtracted. Double rules (double underlines) indicate a total.
4. Dollar signs are used at the top of columns and for the first amount entered in a column beneath a ruling.
5. On the income statement, some companies list expenses from highest to lowest dollar amount, with miscellaneous expense listed last.
6. On the balance sheet, assets are listed from most liquid to least liquid. **Liquidity** measures the ease with which the asset will be converted to cash. Liabilities are listed from most current to least current.

The Income Statement

The income statement, sometimes called the profit and loss statement **or** operating statement, reports the profitability of business operations for a specific period of time.

FIGURE 2-2   Summary and Financial Statements

Trans-action	Cash	+	Accounts Receivable	+ Supplies +	Prepaid Insurance	+	Delivery Equipment	=	Accounts Payable	+	Rohan Macsen, Capital	–	Rohan Macsen, Drawing	+	Revenues	–	Expenses	Description
			Assets (Items Owned)					**=**	**Liabilities** (Amounts Owed)	**+**	**Owner's Equity** (Owner's Investment) + (Earnings)							
(e)															500			Deliv. Fees
(f)																	200	Rent Exp.
(g)																	50	Phone Exp.
(h)															600			Deliv. Fees
(m)																	650	Wages Exp.
(n)															1,050			Deliv. Fees
Balance	370	+	650	+ 80 +	200	+	3,600	=	1,800	+	2,000	–	150	+	2,150	–	900	

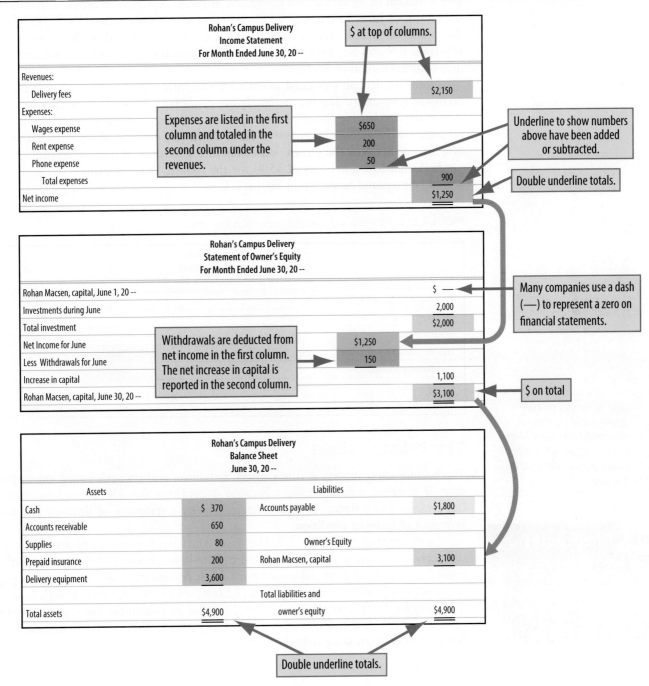

Rohan's Campus Delivery
Income Statement
For Month Ended June 30, 20 --

$ at top of columns.

Revenues:		
Delivery fees		$2,150
Expenses:		
Wages expense	$650	
Rent expense	200	
Phone expense	50	
Total expenses		900
Net income		$1,250

Expenses are listed in the first column and totaled in the second column under the revenues.

Underline to show numbers above have been added or subtracted.

Double underline totals.

Rohan's Campus Delivery
Statement of Owner's Equity
For Month Ended June 30, 20 --

Rohan Macsen, capital, June 1, 20 --		$ —
Investments during June		2,000
Total investment		$2,000
Net Income for June	$1,250	
Less Withdrawals for June	150	
Increase in capital		1,100
Rohan Macsen, capital, June 30, 20 --		$3,100

Withdrawals are deducted from net income in the first column. The net increase in capital is reported in the second column.

Many companies use a dash (—) to represent a zero on financial statements.

$ on total

Rohan's Campus Delivery
Balance Sheet
June 30, 20 --

Assets		Liabilities	
Cash	$ 370	Accounts payable	$1,800
Accounts receivable	650		
Supplies	80	Owner's Equity	
Prepaid insurance	200	Rohan Macsen, capital	3,100
Delivery equipment	3,600		
		Total liabilities and	
Total assets	$4,900	owner's equity	$4,900

Double underline totals.

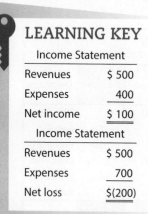
Rohan's income statement shows the revenues earned for the month of June. Next, the expenses incurred as a result of the efforts made to earn these revenues are deducted. If the revenues are greater than the expenses, net income is reported. If the expenses are greater than the revenue, a net loss is reported.

By carefully studying the income statement, it is clear that Rohan earns revenues in only one way: by making deliveries. If other types of services were offered, these revenues would also be identified on the statement. Further, the reader can see the kinds of expenses that were incurred. The reader can make a judgment as to whether these seem reasonable given the amount of revenue earned. Finally, the most important number on the statement is the net income. This is known as the "bottom line."

The Statement of Owner's Equity

The **statement of owner's equity** illustrated in Figure 2-2 reports on these activities for the month of June. Rohan started his business with an investment of $2,000. During the month of June, he earned $1,250 in net income and withdrew $150 for personal expenses. Rohan's $2,000 original investment, plus the net increase of $1,100, results in his ending capital of $3,100.

Note that Rohan's original investment and later withdrawal are taken from the accounting equation. *The net income figure could have been computed from information in the accounting equation. However, it is easier to simply transfer net income as reported on the income statement to the statement of owner's equity.* This is an important linkage between the income statement and statement of owner's equity.

If Rohan had a net loss of $500 for the month, the statement of owner's equity would be prepared as shown in Figure 2-3.

FIGURE 2-3   Statement of Owner's Equity with Net Loss

Rohan's Campus Delivery Statement of Owner's Equity For Month Ended June 30, 20 --		
Rohan Macsen, capital, June 1, 20 --		$ —
Investments during June		2,000
Total investment		$2,000
Less: Net loss for June	$500	
Withdrawals for June	150	
Decrease in capital		(650)
Rohan Macsen, capital, June 30, 20 --		$1,350

The Balance Sheet

The **balance sheet** reports a firm's assets, liabilities, and owner's equity on a specific date. It is called a balance sheet because it confirms that the accounting equation has remained in balance. It is also referred to as a **statement of financial position** or **statement of financial condition**.

As illustrated in Figure 2-2, the asset and liability accounts are taken from the accounting equation and reported on the balance sheet. *The total of Rohan's capital account on June 30 could have been computed from the owner's equity accounts in the accounting equation ($2,000 − $150 + $2,150 − $900). However, it is simpler to take the June 30, 20--, capital as computed on the statement of owner's equity and transfer it to the balance sheet.* This is an important linkage between these two statements.

Most firms also prepare a statement of cash flows. Given the complexity of this statement, we will postpone its discussion until later in this text.

Checkpoint ✓

Complete Checkpoint-4 on page 41 to test your basic understanding of LO5.

OVERVIEW OF THE ACCOUNTING PROCESS

LO6 Define the three basic phases of the accounting process.

Figure 2-4 shows the three basic phases of the accounting process in terms of input, processing, and output.

- Input. Business transactions provide the necessary *input*.
- Processing. Recognizing the effect of these transactions on the assets, liabilities, owner's equity, revenues, and expenses of a business is the *processing* function.
- Output. The financial statements are the *output*.

FIGURE 2-4   Input, Processing, and Output

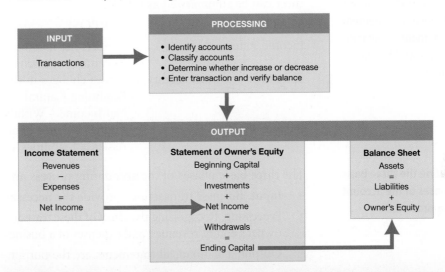

Self-Study

LEARNING OBJECTIVES	Key Points to Remember
LO1 Define the accounting elements.	The three key accounting elements are assets, liabilities, and owner's equity. Owner's equity is expanded in LO4 to include revenues, expenses, and drawing.
LO2 Construct the accounting equation.	The accounting equation is: Assets = Liabilities + Owner's Equity
LO3 Analyze business transactions.	Three questions must be answered in analyzing business transactions: 1. What happened? 2. Which accounts are affected? 3. How is the accounting equation affected?
LO4 Show the effects of business transactions on the accounting equation.	Each transaction affects at least two accounts and one or more of the three basic accounting elements. The transactions described in this chapter can be classified into five groups: 1. Increase in an asset offset by an increase in owner's equity. 2. Increase in an asset offset by a decrease in another asset.

(*continued*)

LEARNING OBJECTIVES   Key Points to Remember

	3. Increase in an asset offset by an increase in a liability.
	4. Decrease in an asset offset by a decrease in a liability.
	5. Decrease in an asset offset by a decrease in owner's equity.

LO5 Prepare and describe the purposes of a simple income statement, statement of owner's equity, and balance sheet.

The purposes of the income statement, statement of owner's equity, and balance sheet can be summarized as follows:

STATEMENT	PURPOSE
Income statement	Reports net income or loss Revenues – Expenses = Net Income or Loss
Statement of owner's equity	Shows changes in the owner's capital account Beginning Capital + Investments + Net Income – Withdrawals = Ending Capital
Balance sheet	Verifies balance of accounting equation Assets = Liabilities + Owner's Equity

LO6 Define the three basic phases of the accounting process.

The three basic phases of the accounting process are shown below.

- **Input.** Business transactions provide the necessary input.
- **Processing.** Recognizing the effect of these transactions on the assets, liabilities, owner's equity, revenues, and expenses of a business is the processing function.
- **Output.** The financial statements are the output.

DEMONSTRATION PROBLEM

Kenny Young has started his own business, Home and Away Inspections. He inspects property for buyers and sellers of real estate. Young rents office space and has a part-time assistant to answer the phone and help with inspections. The transactions for the month of September are as follows:

(a) On the first day of the month, Young invested cash by making a deposit in a bank account for the business, $15,000.

(b) Paid rent for September, $300.

(c) Bought a used truck for cash, $8,000.

(d) Purchased tools on account from Crafty Tools, $3,000.

(e) Paid electricity bill, $50.

(f) Paid two-year premium for liability insurance on truck, $600.

(g) Received cash from clients for services performed, $2,000.

(h) Paid part-time assistant (wages) for first half of month, $200.

(i) Performed inspection services for clients on account, $1,000.

(j) Paid phone bill, $35.

(k) Bought office supplies costing $300. Paid $100 cash and will pay the balance next month, $200.

(l) Received cash from clients for inspections performed on account in (i), $300.

(m) Paid part-time assistant (wages) for last half of month, $250.

(n) Made partial payment on tools bought in (d), $1,000.

(o) Earned additional revenues amounting to $2,000: $1,400 in cash and $600 on account.

(p) Young withdrew cash at the end of the month for personal expenses, $500.

REQUIRED

1. Enter the transactions in an accounting equation similar to the one illustrated below.

	Assets (Items Owned)						=	Liabilities (Amounts Owed)	+	Owner's Equity (Owner's Investment) + (Earnings)				
Cash +	Accounts Receivable	+ Supplies +	Prepaid Insurance	+ Tools	+ Truck =			Accounts Payable	+	Kenny Young, Capital	– Kenny Young, Drawing	+ Revenues	– Expenses	Description

2. Compute the ending balances for all accounts.

3. Prepare an income statement for Home and Away Inspections for the month of September 20--.

4. Prepare a statement of owner's equity for Home and Away Inspections for the month of September 20--.

5. Prepare a balance sheet for Home and Away Inspections as of September 30, 20--.

Solution 1, 2.

	Cash +	Accounts Receivable +	Supplies +	Prepaid Insurance +	Tools +	Truck =	Accounts Payable	+ Kenny Young, Capital	– Kenny Young, Drawing	+ Revenues	– Expenses	Description
(a)	15,000							15,000				
(b)	(300)										300	Rent Exp.
(c)	(8,000)				8,000							
(d)					3,000		3,000					
(e)	(50)										50	Utilities Exp.
(f)	(600)		600									
(g)	2,000									2,000		Inspect. Fees
(h)	(200)										200	Wages Exp.
(i)		1,000								1,000		Inspect. Fees
(j)	(35)										35	Phone Exp.
(k)	(100)		300				200					
(l)	300	(300)										
(m)	(250)										250	Wages Exp.
(n)	(1,000)						(1,000)					
(o)	1,400	600								2,000		Inspect. Fees
(p)	(500)								500			
Bal.	7,665 +	1,300 +	300 +	600 +	3,000 +	8,000 =	2,200	+ 15,000 –	500	+ 5,000	– 835	

3.

Home and Away Inspections Income Statement For Month Ended September 30, 20 --		
Revenues:		
Inspection fees		$ 5,000
Expenses:		
Wages expense	$450	
Rent expense	300	
Utilities expense	50	
Phone expense	35	
Total expenses		835
Net income		$ 4,165

4.

Home and Away Inspections Statement of Owner's Equity For Month Ended September 30, 20 --		
Kenny Young, capital, September 1, 20 --		$ ——
Investment during September		15,000
Total investment		$15,000
Net income for September	$4,165	
Less withdrawals for September	500	
Increase in capital		3,665
Kenny Young, capital, September 30, 20 --		$18,665

5.

Home and Away Inspections Balance Sheet September 30, 20 --			
Assets		**Liabilities**	
Cash	$ 7,665	Accounts payable	$ 2,200
Accounts receivable	1,300		
Supplies	300	**Owner's Equity**	
Prepaid insurance	600	Kenny Young, capital	18,665
Tools	3,000		
Truck	8,000		
		Total liabilities and	
Total assets	$20,865	owner's equity	$20,865

KEY TERMS

account (23)   A separate record used to summarize changes in each asset, liability, and owner's equity of a business.

account title (23)   Provides a description of the particular type of asset, liability, owner's equity, revenue, or expense.

accounting equation (22)   The accounting equation consists of the three basic accounting elements: Assets = Liabilities + Owner's Equity.

accounting period concept (26)   The concept that income determination can be made on a periodic basis.

accounts payable (21)   An unwritten promise to pay a supplier for assets purchased or services received.

accounts receivable (21)   An amount owed to a business by its customers as a result of the sale of goods or services.

asset (21)   An item that is owned by a business and will provide future benefits.

balance sheet (34)   Reports assets, liabilities, and owner's equity on a specific date. It is called a balance sheet because it confirms that the accounting equation is in balance.

business entity (21)   An individual, association, or organization that engages in economic activities and controls specific economic resources.

business entity concept (21)   The concept that nonbusiness assets and liabilities are not included in the business entity's accounting records.

business transaction (23)   An economic event that has a direct impact on the business.

capital (21)   Another term for owner's equity, the amount by which the business assets exceed the business liabilities.

drawing (26)   Withdrawals that reduce owner's equity as a result of the owner taking cash or other assets out of the business for personal use.

expenses (25)   The decrease in assets (or increase in liabilities) as a result of efforts to produce revenues.

fiscal year (26)   Any accounting period of 12 months' duration.

income statement (32)   Reports the profitability of business operations for a specific period of time.

input (35)   Business transactions provide the necessary input for the accounting information system.

liability (21)   Something owed to another business entity.

liquidity (32)   A measure of the ease with which an asset will be converted to cash.

net income (26)   The excess of total revenues over total expenses for the period.

net loss (26)   The excess of total expenses over total revenues for the period.

net worth (21)   Another term for owner's equity, the amount by which the business assets exceed the business liabilities.

notes payable (21)   A formal written promise to pay a supplier or lender a specified sum of money at a definite future time.

operating statement (32)   Another name for the income statement, which reports the profitability of business operations for a specific period of time.

output (35)   The financial statements are the output of the accounting information system.

owner's equity (21)   The amount by which the business assets exceed the business liabilities.

processing (35)   Recognizing the effect of transactions on the assets, liabilities, owner's equity, revenues, and expenses of a business.

profit and loss statement (32)   Another name for the income statement, which reports the profitability of business operations for a specific period of time.

revenues (25) The amount a business charges customers for products sold or services performed.

statement of financial condition (34) Another name for the balance sheet, which reports assets, liabilities, and owner's equity on a specific date.

statement of financial position (34) Another name for the balance sheet, which reports assets, liabilities, and owner's equity on a specific date.

statement of owner's equity (34) Reports beginning capital plus net income less withdrawals to compute ending capital.

withdrawals (26) Reduce owner's equity as a result of the owner taking cash or other assets out of the business for personal use.

SELF-STUDY TEST QUESTIONS

True/False

1. **LO1** Assets are items that are owned by the business and are expected to provide future benefits.

2. **LO1** Accounts Payable is an example of an asset account.

3. **LO1** According to the business entity concept, nonbusiness assets and liabilities are not included in the business's accounting records.

4. **LO2** The accounting equation (Assets = Liabilities + Owner's Equity) must always be in balance.

5. **LO2** When an asset increases, a liability must also increase.

6. **LO3** Expenses represent outflows of assets or increases in liabilities as a result of efforts to produce revenues.

7. **LO5** When total revenues exceed total expenses, the difference is called net loss.

Multiple Choice

1. **LO4** An increase to which of these accounts will increase owner's equity?

   (a) Accounts Payable   (c) Client Fees
   (b) Drawing   (d) Rent Expense

2. **LO4** When delivery revenue is earned in cash, which accounts increase or decrease?

   (a) Cash increases; Revenue increases.
   (b) Cash decreases; Revenue increases.
   (c) Cash decreases; Revenue decreases.
   (d) Cash does not change; owner's equity increases.

3. **LO4**   When delivery revenue is earned on account, which accounts increase or decrease?

   (a) Cash increases; Revenue increases.
   (b) Accounts Receivable increases; Revenue increases.
   (c) Accounts Receivable increases; Revenue decreases.
   (d) Accounts Receivable decreases; Revenue decreases.

4. **LO4**   When payment is made on an existing debt, which accounts increase or decrease?

   (a) Cash increases; Accounts Receivable increases.
   (b) Cash decreases; Accounts Payable increases.
   (c) Cash increases; Accounts Payable increases.
   (d) Cash decreases; Accounts Payable decreases.

5. **LO5**   Which of the following accounts does not appear on the income statement?

   (a) Delivery Fees   (c) Drawing
   (b) Wages Expense   (d) Rent Expense

Checkpoint Exercises

1. **LO1**   Label each of the following accounts as an asset (A), a liability (L), or owner's equity (OE), using the following format:

Account	Classification
Accounts Receivable	_____
Accounts Payable	_____
Judy Smith, Capital	_____

2. **LO2**   What is missing from the accounting equation below?

   _____?_____ = Liabilities + Owner's Equity

3. **LO3/4**   What are the effects of the following transactions on the accounting equation? Indicate an increase (+) or decrease (–) under the appropriate asset, liability, and owner's equity headings.

Transaction	Assets	Liabilities	Owner's Equity
a. Purchase of an asset on account.	_____	_____	_____
b. Made payment on account for transaction (a).	_____	_____	_____

4. **LO5**   Classify the following accounts as assets (A), liabilities (L), owner's equity (OE), revenue (R), or expense (E). Indicate the financial statement on which the account belongs—income statement (IS), statement of owner's equity (SOE), or balance sheet (BS).

Account	Classification	Financial Statement
Accounts Payable	_____	_____
Peggy Welsch, Drawing	_____	_____
Rent Expense	_____	_____
Sales	_____	_____
Equipment	_____	_____

   The answers to the Self-Study Test Questions are at the end of the chapter (page 49).

Applying Your Knowledge

REVIEW QUESTIONS

LO1	1.	Why is it necessary to distinguish between business assets and liabilities and nonbusiness assets and liabilities of a single proprietor?
LO1/4	2.	Name and define the six major elements of the accounting equation.
LO3	3.	List the three basic questions that must be answered when analyzing the effects of a business transaction on the accounting equation.
LO5	4.	What is the function of an income statement?
LO5	5.	What is the function of a statement of owner's equity?
LO5	6.	What is the function of a balance sheet?
LO6	7.	What are the three basic phases of the accounting process?

SERIES A EXERCISES

E 2-1A (LO1)

ACCOUNTING ELEMENTS Label each of the following accounts as an asset (A), a liability (L), or owner's equity (OE), using the following format:

Item	Account	Classification
Money in bank	Cash	
Office supplies	Supplies	
Money owed	Accounts Payable	
Office chairs	Office Furniture	
Net worth of owner	John Smith, Capital	
Money withdrawn by owner	John Smith, Drawing	
Money owed by customers	Accounts Receivable	

E 2-2A (LO2)

THE ACCOUNTING EQUATION Using the accounting equation, compute the missing elements.

Assets	=	Liabilities	+	Owner's Equity
_____	=	$27,000	+	$17,000
$32,000	=	$18,000	+	_____
$27,000	=	_____	+	$20,000

E 2-3A (LO3/4)

✓ Assets following (d): $32,200

SHOW
ME HOW

EFFECTS OF TRANSACTIONS (BALANCE SHEET ACCOUNTS) John Sullivan started a business. During the first month (February 20--), the following transactions occurred. Show the effect of each transaction on the accounting equation: *Assets = Liabilities + Owner's Equity.* After each transaction, show the new totals.

(a) Invested cash in the business, $27,000.

(b) Bought office equipment on account, $7,500.

(c) Bought office equipment for cash, $1,600.

(d) Paid cash on account to supplier in transaction (b), $2,300.

E 2-4A   (LO3/4)

✓ Assets following (k): $31,586

SHOW
ME HOW

EFFECTS OF TRANSACTIONS (REVENUE, EXPENSE, WITHDRAWALS) This exercise is an extension of Exercise 2-3A. Assume John Sullivan completed the following additional transactions during February. Show the effect of each transaction on the basic elements of the expanded accounting equation: *Assets = Liabilities + Owner's Equity (Capital – Drawing + Revenues – Expenses)*. After transaction (k), report the totals for each element. Demonstrate that the accounting equation has remained in balance.

(e) Received cash from a client for professional services, $1,500.

(f) Paid office rent for February, $600.

(g) Paid February phone bill, $64.

(h) Withdrew cash for personal use, $1,000.

(i) Performed services for clients on account, $750.

(j) Paid wages to part-time employee, $1,200.

(k) Received cash for services performed on account in transaction (i), $400.

E 2-5A   (LO1/5)

FINANCIAL STATEMENT ACCOUNTS Label each of the following accounts as an asset (A), liability (L), owner's equity (OE), revenue (R), or expense (E). Indicate the financial statement on which the account belongs—income statement (IS), statement of owner's equity (SOE), or balance sheet (BS)—in a format similar to the following.

Account	Classification	Financial Statement
Cash		
Rent Expense		
Accounts Payable		
Service Fees		
Supplies		
Wages Expense		
Ramon Martinez, Drawing		
Ramon Martinez, Capital		
Prepaid Insurance		
Accounts Receivable		

E 2-6A   (LO5)

✓ Capital, 6/30: $22,000

STATEMENT OF OWNER'S EQUITY REPORTING NET INCOME Betsy Ray started an accounting service on June 1, 20--, by investing $20,000. Her net income for the month was $10,000, and she withdrew $8,000. Prepare a statement of owner's equity for the month of June.

E 2-7A   (LO5)

✓ Capital, 6/30: $9,000

STATEMENT OF OWNER'S EQUITY REPORTING NET LOSS Based on the information provided in Exercise 2-6A, prepare a statement of owner's equity assuming Ray had a net loss of $3,000.

SERIES A PROBLEMS

P 2-8A   (LO1/2)
✓ 3: $32,040 = $12,910 + $19,130

SHOW
ME HOW

THE ACCOUNTING EQUATION Dr. John Salvaggi is a chiropractor. As of December 31, he owned the following property that related to his professional practice.

Cash	$ 3,500
Office Equipment	6,400
X-ray Equipment	10,220
Laboratory Equipment	6,840

He also owes the following business suppliers:

Chateau Gas Company	$ 3,430
Aloe Medical Supply Company	4,120

REQUIRED

1. From the preceding information, compute the accounting elements and enter them in the accounting equation shown as follows.

Assets	=	Liabilities	+	Owner's Equity
_____	=	_____	+	_____

2. During January, the assets increase by $8,540, and the liabilities increase by $3,360. Compute the resulting accounting equation.

3. During February, the assets decrease by $3,460, and the liabilities increase by $2,000. Compute the resulting accounting equation.

P 2-9A   (LO3/4)
✓ Total cash following (g): $12,950

EFFECT OF TRANSACTIONS ON ACCOUNTING EQUATION Jay Pembroke started a business. During the first month (April 20--), the following transactions occurred.

(a) Invested cash in business, $18,000.
(b) Bought office supplies for $4,600: $2,000 in cash and $2,600 on account.
(c) Paid one-year insurance premium, $1,200.
(d) Earned revenues totaling $3,300: $1,300 in cash and $2,000 on account.
(e) Paid cash on account to the company that supplied the office supplies in transaction (b), $2,300.
(f) Paid office rent for the month, $750.
(g) Withdrew cash for personal use, $100.

REQUIRED

Show the effect of each transaction on the individual accounts of the expanded accounting equation: *Assets = Liabilities + Owner's Equity (Capital – Drawing + Revenues – Expenses)*. After transaction (g), report the totals for each element. Demonstrate that the accounting equation has remained in balance.

P 2-10A   (LO5)
✓ Net income: $2,550

SHOW
ME HOW

INCOME STATEMENT Based on Problem 2-9A, prepare an income statement for Jay Pembroke for the month of April 20--.

P 2-11A   (LO5)
✓ Capital, 4/30: $20,450

SHOW
ME HOW

STATEMENT OF OWNER'S EQUITY Based on Problem 2-9A, prepare a statement of owner's equity for Jay Pembroke for the month of April 20--.

P 2-12A   (LO5)
✓ Total assets, 4/30: $20,750

CLGL
SHOW
ME HOW

BALANCE SHEET Based on Problem 2-9A, prepare a balance sheet for Jay Pembroke as of April 30, 20--.

SERIES B EXERCISES

E 2-1B   (LO1)

ACCOUNTING ELEMENTS Label each of the following accounts as an asset (A), liability (L), or owner's equity (OE) using the following format.

Account	Classification
Cash	
Accounts Payable	
Supplies	
Bill Jones, Drawing	
Prepaid Insurance	
Accounts Receivable	
Bill Jones, Capital	

E 2-2B   (LO2)

THE ACCOUNTING EQUATION Using the accounting equation, compute the missing elements.

Assets	=	Liabilities	+	Owner's Equity
_____	=	$20,000	+	$ 5,000
$30,000	=	$15,000	+	_____
$20,000	=	_____	+	$10,000

E 2-3B   (LO3/4)
✓ Assets following (d): $32,500

SHOW
ME HOW

EFFECTS OF TRANSACTIONS (BALANCE SHEET ACCOUNTS) Jon Wallace started a business. During the first month (March 20--), the following transactions occurred. Show the effect of each transaction on the accounting equation: *Assets = Liabilities + Owner's Equity*. After each transaction, show the new account totals.

(a) Invested cash in the business, $30,000.
(b) Bought office equipment on account, $4,500.
(c) Bought office equipment for cash, $1,600.
(d) Paid cash on account to supplier in transaction (b), $2,000.

E 2-4B   (LO3/4)
✓ Assets following (k): $34,032

SHOW
ME HOW

EFFECTS OF TRANSACTIONS (REVENUE, EXPENSE, WITHDRAWALS) This exercise is an extension of Exercise 2-3B. Assume Jon Wallace completed the following additional transactions during March. Show the effect of each transaction on the basic elements of the expanded accounting equation: *Assets = Liabilities + Owner's Equity (Capital – Drawing + Revenues – Expenses)*. After transaction (k), report the totals for each element. Demonstrate that the accounting equation has remained in balance.

(e) Performed services and received cash, $3,000.
(f) Paid rent for March, $1,000.
(g) Paid March phone bill, $68.
(h) Jon Wallace withdrew cash for personal use, $800.

(*continued*)

(i) Performed services for clients on account, $900.

(j) Paid wages to part-time employee, $500.

(k) Received cash for services performed on account in transaction (i), $500.

E 2-5B   (LO1/5)

FINANCIAL STATEMENT ACCOUNTS Label each of the following accounts as an asset (A), liability (L), owner's equity (OE), revenue (R), or expense (E). Indicate the financial statement on which the account belongs—income statement (IS), statement of owner's equity (SOE), or balance sheet (BS)—in a format similar to the following.

Account	Classification	Financial Statement
Cash		
Rent Expense		
Accounts Payable		
Service Fees		
Supplies		
Wages Expense		
Amanda Wong, Drawing		
Amanda Wong, Capital		
Prepaid Insurance		
Accounts Receivable		

E 2-6B   (LO5)
✓ Capital, 6/30: $14,000

STATEMENT OF OWNER'S EQUITY REPORTING NET INCOME Efran Lopez started a financial consulting service on June 1, 20--, by investing $15,000. His net income for the month was $6,000, and he withdrew $7,000 for personal use. Prepare a statement of owner's equity for the month of June.

E 2-7B   (LO5)
✓ Capital, 6/30: $6,000

STATEMENT OF OWNER'S EQUITY REPORTING NET LOSS Based on the information provided in Exercise 2-6B, prepare a statement of owner's equity assuming Lopez had a net loss of $2,000.

SERIES B PROBLEMS

P 2-8B   (LO1/2)
✓ 3: $25,235 = $10,165 + $15,070

SHOW
ME HOW

THE ACCOUNTING EQUATION Dr. Patricia Parsons is a dentist. As of January 31, Parsons owned the following property that related to her professional practice:

Cash	$3,560
Office Equipment	4,600
X-ray Equipment	8,760
Laboratory Equipment	5,940

She also owes the following business suppliers:

Cupples Gas Company	$1,815
Swan Dental Lab	2,790

REQUIRED

1. From the preceding information, compute the accounting elements and enter them in the accounting equation as shown below.

Assets	=	Liabilities	+	Owner's Equity
_____	=	_____	+	_____

2. During February, the assets increase by $4,565, and the liabilities increase by $3,910. Compute the resulting accounting equation.

3. During March, the assets decrease by $2,190, and the liabilities increase by $1,650. Compute the resulting accounting equation.

P 2-9B   (LO3/4)

✓ Total cash following (g): $11,300

EFFECT OF TRANSACTIONS ON ACCOUNTING EQUATION David Segal started a business. During the first month (October 20--), the following transactions occurred.

(a) Invested cash in the business, $15,000.

(b) Bought office supplies for $3,800: $1,800 in cash and $2,000 on account.

(c) Paid one-year insurance premium, $1,000.

(d) Earned revenues amounting to $2,700: $1,700 in cash and $1,000 on account.

(e) Paid cash on account to the company that supplied the office supplies in transaction (b), $1,800.

(f) Paid office rent for the month, $650.

(g) Withdrew cash for personal use, $150.

REQUIRED

Show the effect of each transaction on the individual accounts of the expanded accounting equation: *Assets = Liabilities + Owner's Equity (Capital – Drawing + Revenues – Expenses)*. After transaction (g), report the totals for each element. Demonstrate that the accounting equation has remained in balance.

P 2-10B   (LO5)

✓ Net income: $2,050

SHOW
ME HOW

INCOME STATEMENT Based on Problem 2-9B, prepare an income statement for David Segal for the month of October 20--.

P 2-11B   (LO5)

✓ Capital, 10/31: $16,900

SHOW
ME HOW

STATEMENT OF OWNER'S EQUITY Based on Problem 2-9B, prepare a statement of owner's equity for David Segal for the month of October 20--.

P 2-12B   (LO5)

✓ Total assets, 10/31: $17,100

SHOW
ME HOW

BALANCE SHEET Based on Problem 2-9B, prepare a balance sheet for David Segal as of October 31, 20--.

MANAGING YOUR WRITING

Write a brief memo that explains the differences and similarities between expenses and withdrawals.

Check List
☑ Managing
☐ Planning
☐ Drafting
☐ Break
☐ Revising
☐ Managing

MASTERY PROBLEM

✓ Cash following (p): $3,105
✓ Revenue following (p): $2,100

Lisa Vozniak started her own business, We Do Windows. She offers interior and exterior window cleaning for local area residents. Lisa rents a garage to store her tools and cleaning supplies and has a part-time assistant to answer the phone and handle third-story work. (Lisa is afraid of heights.) The transactions for the month of July are as follows:

(a) On the first day of the month, Vozniak invested cash by making a deposit in a bank account for the business, $8,000.

(b) Paid rent for July, $150.

(c) Purchased a used van for cash, $5,000.

(d) Purchased tools on account from Clean Tools, $600.

(e) Purchased cleaning supplies that cost $300. Paid $200 cash and will pay the balance next month, $100.

(f) Paid part-time assistant (wages) for first half of month, $100.

(g) Paid for advertising, $75.

(h) Paid two-year premium for liability insurance on van, $480.

(i) Received cash from clients for services performed, $800.

(j) Performed cleaning services for clients on account, $500.

(k) Paid phone bill, $40.

(l) Received cash from clients for window cleaning performed on account in transaction (j), $200.

(m) Paid part-time assistant (wages) for last half of month, $150.

(n) Made partial payment on tools purchased in transaction (d), $200.

(o) Earned additional revenues amounting to $800: $600 in cash and $200 on account.

(p) Vozniak withdrew cash at the end of the month for personal expenses, $100.

REQUIRED

1. Enter the above transactions in an accounting equation similar to the one illustrated below.

Assets (Items Owned)						=	Liabilities (Amounts Owed)	+	Owner's Equity				
									(Owner's Investment) +		(Earnings)		
Cash +	Accounts Receivable +	Supplies +	Prepaid Insurance +	Tools +	Van	=	Accounts Payable	+	Lisa Vozniak Capital –	Lisa Vozniak Drawing	+ Revenues	– Expenses	Description

2. After transaction (p), compute the balance of each account.

3. Prepare an income statement for We Do Windows for the month of July 20--.

4. Prepare a statement of owner's equity for We Do Windows for the month of July 20--.

5. Prepare a balance sheet for We Do Windows as of July 31, 20--.

This problem challenges you to apply your cumulative accounting knowledge to move a step beyond the material in the chapter.

✓ Cash difference: $2,165

CHALLENGE PROBLEM

In this chapter, you learned about three important financial statements: the income statement, statement of owner's equity, and balance sheet. As mentioned in the margin note on page 34, most firms also prepare a statement of cash flows. Part of this statement reports the **cash received** from customers and **cash paid** for goods and services.

REQUIRED

Take another look at the Demonstration Problem for Kenny Young's "Home and Away Inspections." Note that when revenues are measured based on the amount earned, and expenses are measured based on the amount incurred, net income for the period was $4,165. Now, compute the difference between cash received from customers and cash paid to suppliers of goods and services by completing the form provided below. Are these measures different? Which provides a better measure of profitability?

Cash from customers	_____
Cash paid for wages	_____
Cash paid for rent	_____
Cash paid for utilities	_____
Cash paid for insurance	_____
Cash paid for supplies	_____
Cash paid for phone	_____
Total cash paid for operating items	_____
Difference between cash received from customers and cash paid for goods and services	_____

Answers to Self-Study Test Questions

True/False

1. T

2. F (Accounts Payable is a liability.)

3. T

4. T

5. F (Other changes could occur: capital could increase, revenue could increase, etc.)

6. T

7. F (net income)

Multiple Choice

1. c   2. a   3. b   4. d   5. c

Checkpoint Exercises

1.
Account	Classification
Accounts Receivable	A
Accounts Payable	L
Judy Smith, Capital	OE

2. Assets = Liabilities + Owner's Equity

3.
Transaction	Assets	Liabilities	Owner's Equity
a. Purchase of an asset on account.	+	+	_____
b. Made payment on account for transaction (a).	−	−	_____

4.
Account	Classification	Financial Statement
Accounts Payable	L	BS
Peggy Welsch, Drawing	OE	SOE
Rent Expense	E	IS
Sales	R	IS
Equipment	A	BS

Chapter 3

The Double-Entry Framework

Tired of receiving spam e-mail messages? Or, are you worried about your computer picking up a virus? Businesses have the same concerns. Computer viruses can cause serious financial damage to a business. In response to demand for e-mail and Web security, AppRiver was founded in April of 2002 to provide simple, yet powerful protection from Internet-based threats to businesses of any size. The company is based in Gulf Breeze, Florida, and maintains multiple data centers at secure locations in the United States, Europe, and Asia. AppRiver's 200 employees protect more than 47,000 companies around the world from spam, viruses, and Internet pollution.

Just as Internet security is important to you in your personal life and to businesses, the same can be said about accounting. A solid understanding of financial accounting will help you manage your personal finances and help you understand business transactions in your professional life. In this chapter, you will learn about the double-entry framework used by businesses to enter transactions into an accounting system. You could use the same concepts for your personal transactions or for a business you might start.

The terms asset, liability, owner's equity, revenue, and expense were explained in Chapter 2. Examples showed how individual business transactions change one or more of these basic accounting elements. Each transaction had a dual effect. An increase or decrease in any asset, liability, owner's equity, revenue, or expense was *always* accompanied by an offsetting change within the basic accounting elements. The fact that each transaction has a dual effect upon the accounting elements provides the basis for what is called **double-entry accounting**. To understand double-entry accounting, it is important to learn how T accounts work and the role of debits and credits in accounting.

THE T ACCOUNT

LO1   Define the parts of a T account.

The assets of a business may consist of a number of items, such as cash, accounts receivable, equipment, buildings, and land. The liabilities may consist of one or more items, such as accounts payable and notes payable. Similarly, owner's equity may consist of the owner's investments and various revenue and expense items. A separate account is used to record the increases and decreases in each type of asset, liability, owner's equity, revenue, and expense.

The T account gets its name from the fact that it resembles the letter T. The three major parts of an account are as follows:

1. the title,
2. the debit, or left side, and
3. the credit, or right side.

Title	
Debit = Left	Credit = Right

LEARNING KEY

Debit means left and credit means right.

The debit side is always on the left, and the credit side is always on the right. This is true for all types of asset, liability, owner's equity, revenue, and expense accounts.

Sometimes new accounting students think that a debit is bad because it sounds like "debt." Similarly, credit sounds like a good thing, especially when the bank says they will credit your account. Please clear your mind of these thoughts. *In accounting, debit simply means left and credit means right.*

BALANCING A T ACCOUNT

LO2   Foot and balance a T account

To determine the balance of a T account at any time, simply total the dollar amounts on the debit and credit sides. These totals are known as footings. The difference between the footings is called the balance of the account. This amount is then written on the side with the larger footing.

In Chapter 2, the accounting equation was used to analyze business transactions. This required columns in which to record the increases and decreases in various accounts. Let's compare this approach with the use of a T account for the transactions affecting cash. When a T account is used, increases in cash are recorded on the debit side and decreases are recorded on the credit side. Transactions for Rohan's Campus Delivery are shown in Figure 3-1.

FIGURE 3-1 Cash T Account

COLUMNAR SUMMARY (From Chapter 2, page 31)		T ACCOUNT FORM				
Transaction	Cash		Cash			
(a)	2,000		(a)	2,000	(b)	1,200
(b)	(1,200)		(e)	500	(d)	300
(d)	(300)		(k)	570	(f)	200
(e)	500		(n)	430	(g)	50
(f)	(200)	footing ⟶		3,500	(i)	80
(g)	(50)				(j)	200
(i)	(80)				(l)	300
(j)	(200)				(m)	650
(k)	570				(o)	150
(l)	(300)	Balance ⟶	370		3,130	⟵ footing
(m)	(650)					
(n)	430					
(o)	(150)					
Balance	370					

Checkpoint ✓

Complete Checkpoint-1 on page 74 to test your basic understanding of LO2.

DEBITS AND CREDITS

LO3 Describe the effects of debits and credits on specific types of accounts.

To debit an account means to enter an amount on the left or debit side of the account. To credit an account means to enter an amount on the right or credit side of the account. *Debits may increase or decrease the balances of specific accounts. This is also true for credits. To learn how to use debits and credits, it is best to focus on the accounting equation.*

Abbreviations: Often debit and credit are abbreviated as: Dr. = Debit, Cr. = Credit (based on the Latin terms "debere" and "credere")

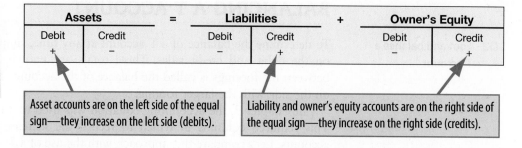

Assets		=	Liabilities		+	Owner's Equity	
Debit +	Credit –		Debit –	Credit +		Debit –	Credit +

Asset accounts are on the left side of the equal sign—they increase on the left side (debits).

Liability and owner's equity accounts are on the right side of the equal sign—they increase on the right side (credits).

ASSETS

Assets are on the left side of the accounting equation. Therefore, increases are entered on the left (debit) side of an asset account, and decreases are entered on the right (credit) side.

Liabilities and Owner's Equity

Liabilities and owner's equity are on the right side of the equation. Therefore, increases are entered on the right (credit) side, and decreases are entered on the left (debit) side.

The Owner's Equity Umbrella

Owner's equity includes four types of accounts: Owner's Capital, Revenues, Expenses, and Drawing. Expanding the accounting equation helps illustrate the use of debits and credits. Since these accounts affect owner's equity, they are shown under the "umbrella" of owner's equity in the accounting equation in Figure 3-2. It is helpful to think of the Owner's Capital account as hovering over the revenue, expense, and drawing accounts like an umbrella. Since revenues increase Owner's Capital, the revenue account is shown under the credit side of Owner's Capital. Since expenses and drawing reduce Owner's Capital, they are shown under the debit side of Owner's Capital.

FIGURE 3-2 The Accounting Equation and the Owner's Equity Umbrella

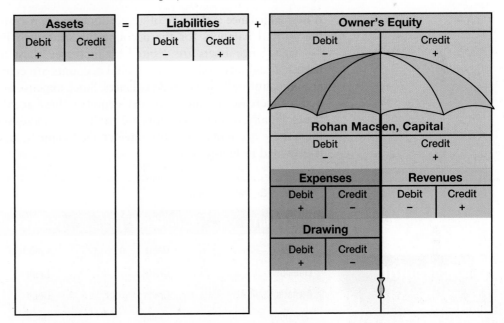

Owner's Capital

The owner's capital account, Rohan Macsen, Capital, in Figure 3-2 reports the amount the owner has invested in the business. These investments increase the owner's equity and are credited to the owner's capital account.

Revenues

Revenues increase owner's equity. Revenues could be recorded directly on the credit side of the owner's capital account. However, readers of financial statements are interested in the specific types of revenues earned. Therefore, specific revenue accounts, like Delivery Fees, Sales, and Service Fees, are used. These specific accounts are credited when revenue is earned.

LEARNING KEY

You could credit the owner's capital account for revenues and debit the capital account for expenses and withdrawals. However, this is not a good idea. Using specific accounts provides additional information about why owner's equity increased or decreased.

Remember: An increase in an expense decreases owner's equity.

Expenses

Expenses decrease owner's equity. Expenses could be recorded on the debit side of the owner's capital account. However, readers of financial statements want to see the types of expenses incurred during the accounting period. Thus, specific expense accounts are maintained for items like rent, wages, advertising, and utilities. These specific accounts are debited as expenses are incurred.

Drawing

Withdrawals of cash and other assets by the owner for personal reasons decrease owner's equity. Withdrawals could be debited directly to the owner's capital account. However, readers of financial statements want to know the amount of withdrawals for the accounting period. Thus, as shown in Figure 3-2, withdrawals are debited to a separate account, Drawing.

Normal Balances

A normal balance is the side of an account that is used to increase the account. Thus, the normal balances for the accounts illustrated in Figure 3-2 are shown with a "+" sign. Since assets are debited for increases, these accounts normally have debit balances. Liability and owner's capital accounts are credited for increases; thus, these accounts normally have credit balances. Since expense and drawing accounts are debited for increases (reducing owner's equity), these accounts normally have debit balances. Finally, revenue accounts are credited for increases (increasing owner's equity); thus, these accounts normally have credit balances. A summary of normal balances is provided in Figure 3-3.

FIGURE 3-3   Normal Balances

ACCOUNT	INCREASE	DECREASE	NORMAL BALANCE
Assets	Debit	Credit	Debit
Liabilities	Credit	Debit	Credit
Owner's Capital	Credit	Debit	Credit
Revenues	Credit	Debit	Credit
Expenses	Debit	Credit	Debit
Drawing	Debit	Credit	Debit

Checkpoint ✓

Complete Checkpoint-2 on page 74 to test your basic understanding of LO3.

LO4   Use T accounts to analyze transactions.

LEARNING KEY

Since the accounting equation must stay in balance, there must be at least one debit and at least one credit for each transaction.

TRANSACTION ANALYSIS

In Chapter 2, you learned how to analyze transactions by using the accounting equation. Here, we continue to use the accounting equation, but add debits and credits by using T accounts. As shown in Figure 3-4, the three basic questions that must be answered when analyzing a transaction are essentially the same but are expanded slightly to address the use of the owner's equity umbrella and T accounts. You must determine the location of the account within the accounting equation and/or the owner's equity umbrella. You must also determine whether the accounts should be debited or credited.

FIGURE 3-4   Steps in Transaction Analysis

1. **What happened?**
   Be sure you understand the event that has taken place.

2. **Which accounts are affected?**
   Once you understand what happened, you must:

   - Identify the accounts that are affected.
   - Classify these accounts as assets, liabilities, owner's equity, revenues, or expenses.
   - Identify the location of the accounts in the accounting equation and/or the owner's equity umbrella—left or right.

3. **How is the accounting equation affected?**

   - Determine whether the accounts have increased or decreased.
   - Determine whether the accounts should be debited or credited.
   - Make certain the accounting equation remains in balance after the transaction has been entered.
     (1) Assets = Liabilities + Owner's Equity.
     (2) Debits = Credits for every transaction.

Debits and Credits: Asset, Liability, and Owner's Equity Accounts

Transactions (a) through (d) from Rohan's Campus Delivery (Chapter 2) demonstrate the double-entry process for transactions affecting asset, liability, and owner's equity accounts.

As you study each transaction, answer the three questions: (1) What happened? (2) Which accounts are affected? and (3) How is the accounting equation affected? The transaction statement tells you what happened. The analysis tells which accounts are affected. The illustration shows you how the accounting equation is affected.

Transaction (a): Investment by owner

Rohan Macsen, opened a bank account with a deposit of $2,000 for his business (Figure 3-5).

Analysis. As a result of this transaction, the business acquired an asset, Cash. In exchange for the asset, the business gave Rohan Macsen, owner's equity. The owner's equity account is called Rohan Macsen, Capital. The transaction is entered as an increase in an asset and an increase in owner's equity. Debit Cash and credit Rohan Macsen, Capital for $2,000.

FIGURE 3-5   Transaction (a): Investment by Owner

Assets		=	Liabilities		+	Owner's Equity	
Debit +	Credit −		Debit −	Credit +		Debit −	Credit +
Cash						**Rohan Macsen, Capital**	
(a) 2,000							(a) 2,000
$2,000		=	$0		+	$2,000	
$2,000		=		$2,000			

Transaction (b): Purchase of an asset for cash

Rohan bought a motor scooter (delivery equipment) for $1,200 cash (Figure 3-6).

Analysis. Rohan exchanged one asset, Cash, for another, Delivery Equipment. Debit Delivery Equipment and credit Cash for $1,200. Notice that the total assets are still $2,000 as they were following transaction (a). Transaction (b) shifted assets from cash to delivery equipment, but total assets remained the same.

FIGURE 3-6   Transaction (b): Purchase of an Asset for Cash

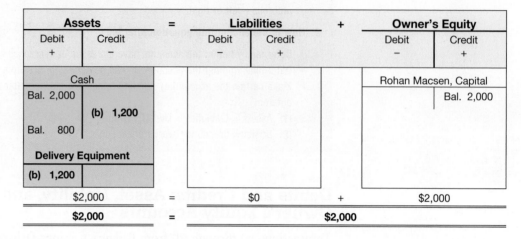

Transaction (c): Purchase of an asset on account

Rohan bought a second motor scooter on account for $900 (Figure 3-7). Recall from Chapter 2 that "on account" means Rohan will pay for the asset later.

Analysis. The asset, Delivery Equipment, increases by $900 and the liability, Accounts Payable, increases by the same amount. Thus, debit Delivery Equipment and credit Accounts Payable for $900.

FIGURE 3-7   Transaction (c): Purchase of an Asset on Account

Assets		=	Liabilities		+	Owner's Equity	
Debit +	Credit −		Debit −	Credit +		Debit −	Credit +
Cash			**Accounts Payable**			**Rohan Macsen, Capital**	
Bal. 800				(c) 900			Bal. 2,000
Delivery Equipment							
Bal. 1,200							
(c) 900							
Bal. 2,100							
$2,900		=	$900		+	$2,000	
$2,900		=		**$2,900**			

Transaction (d): Payment on account

Rohan made the first $300 payment on the scooter purchased in transaction (c) (Figure 3-8).

Analysis. This payment decreases the asset, Cash, and decreases the liability, Accounts Payable. Debit Accounts Payable and credit Cash for $300.

FIGURE 3-8   Transaction (d): Payment on Account

Assets		=	Liabilities		+	Owner's Equity	
Debit +	Credit −		Debit −	Credit +		Debit −	Credit +
Cash			**Accounts Payable**			Rohan Macsen, Capital	
Bal. 800				Bal. 900			Bal. 2,000
	(d) 300		(d) 300				
Bal. 500				Bal. 600			
Delivery Equipment							
Bal. 2,100							
$2,600		=	$600		+	$2,000	
$2,600		=	$2,600				

Notice that for transactions (a) through (d), the debits equal credits and the accounting equation is in balance. Review transactions (a) through (d). Again, identify the accounts that were affected and how they were classified (assets, liabilities, or owner's equity). Finally, note each account's location within the accounting equation.

Debits and Credits: Including Revenues, Expenses, and Drawing

Transactions (a) through (d) involved only assets, liabilities, and the owner's capital account. To complete the illustration of Rohan's Campus Delivery, the equation is expanded to include revenues, expenses, and drawing. Remember, revenues increase owner's equity and are shown under the credit side of the capital account. Expenses and drawing decrease owner's equity and are shown under the debit side of the capital account. The expanded equation is shown in Figure 3-9.

> **LEARNING KEY**
> Credits increase the capital account. Revenues increase capital. Thus, revenues are shown under the credit side of the capital account. Debits decrease the capital account. Expenses and drawing reduce owner's equity. Thus, they are shown under the debit side of the capital account.

FIGURE 3-9   The Expanded Accounting Equation

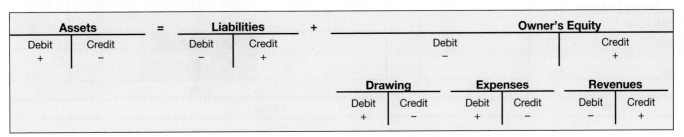

Transaction (e): Delivery revenues earned in cash

Rohan made deliveries and received $500 cash from clients (Figure 3-10).

Analysis. The asset, Cash, and the revenue, Delivery Fees, increase. Debit Cash and credit Delivery Fees for $500.

FIGURE 3-10   Transaction (e): Delivery Revenues Earned in Cash

Assets		=	Liabilities		+	Owner's Equity	
Debit +	Credit −		Debit −	Credit +		Debit −	Credit +

Cash
Bal. 500	
(e) 500	
Bal. 1,000	

Accounts Payable
	Bal. 600

Rohan Macsen, Capital
	Bal. 2,000

Delivery Equipment
Bal. 2,100	

Drawing		Expenses		Revenues	
Debit +	Credit −	Debit +	Credit −	Debit −	Credit +

Delivery Fees
	(e) 500

$3,100	=	$600	+	$2,500
$3,100	=		**$3,100**	

Transaction (f): Paid rent for month

Rohan paid $200 for office rent for June (Figure 3-11).

Analysis. Rent Expense increases and Cash decreases. Debit **Rent Expense** and credit **Cash** for $200.

A debit to an expense account *increases* that expense and *decreases* owner's equity. Notice that the placement of the plus and minus signs for expenses is opposite the placement of the signs for owner's equity. Note also that expenses are located on the left (debit) side of the owner's equity umbrella.

FIGURE 3-11   Transaction (f): Paid Rent for Month

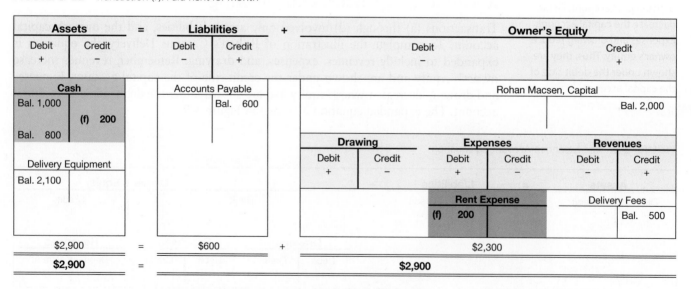

Assets		=	Liabilities		+	Owner's Equity	
Debit +	Credit −		Debit −	Credit +		Debit −	Credit +

Cash
Bal. 1,000	
	(f) 200
Bal. 800	

Accounts Payable
	Bal. 600

Rohan Macsen, Capital
	Bal. 2,000

Delivery Equipment
Bal. 2,100	

Drawing		Expenses		Revenues	
Debit +	Credit −	Debit +	Credit −	Debit −	Credit +

Rent Expense
(f) 200	

Delivery Fees
	Bal. 500

$2,900	=	$600	+	$2,300
$2,900	=		**$2,900**	

Transaction (g): Paid phone bill

Rohan paid for phone service, $50 (Figure 3-12).

Analysis. This transaction, like the previous one, increases an expense and decreases an asset. Debit **Phone Expense** and credit **Cash** for $50.

FIGURE 3-12   Transaction (g): Paid Phone Bill

Assets		=	Liabilities		+	Owner's Equity			
Debit +	Credit –		Debit –	Credit +		Debit –		Credit +	

Cash			Accounts Payable			Rohan Macsen, Capital	
Bal. 800				Bal. 600			Bal. 2,000
	(g) 50						
Bal. 750							

Delivery Equipment	
Bal. 2,100	

Drawing		Expenses		Revenues	
Debit +	Credit –	Debit +	Credit –	Debit –	Credit +

Rent Expense		Delivery Fees	
Bal. 200			Bal. 500

Phone Expense	
(g) 50	

$2,850	=	$600	+	$2,250
$2,850	=			**$2,850**

Transaction (h): Delivery revenues earned on account

Rohan made deliveries on account for $600 (Figure 3-13).

Analysis. As discussed in Chapter 2, delivery services are performed for which payment will be received later. This is called offering services "on account" or "on credit." Instead of receiving cash, Rohan receives a promise that his customers will pay cash in the future. Therefore, the asset, Accounts Receivable, increases. Since revenues are recognized when earned, the revenue account, Delivery Fees, also increases. Debit Accounts Receivable and credit Delivery Fees for $600.

FIGURE 3-13   Transaction (h): Delivery Revenues Earned on Account

Assets		=	Liabilities		+	Owner's Equity		
Debit +	Credit –		Debit –	Credit +		Debit –		Credit +

Cash			Accounts Payable			Rohan Macsen, Capital	
Bal. 750				Bal. 600			Bal. 2,000

Accounts Receivable	
(h) 600	

Delivery Equipment	
Bal. 2,100	

Drawing		Expenses		Revenues	
Debit +	Credit –	Debit +	Credit –	Debit –	Credit +

Rent Expense		Delivery Fees	
Bal. 200			Bal. 500
			(h) 600
			Bal. 1,100

Phone Expense	
Bal. 50	

$3,450	=	$600	+	$2,850
$3,450	=			**$3,450**

Review transactions (e) through (h). Note the following:

- Expense and revenue transactions do not always affect cash.
- The debits equal credits, and the accounting equation is in balance after each transaction.

Upcoming transactions (i) and (j) both involve an exchange of cash for another asset. As you analyze these two transactions, you may wonder why prepaid insurance and supplies are assets while the rent and phone bill in transactions (f) and (g) are expenses. Prepaid insurance and supplies are assets because they will provide benefits for more than one month. Rohan pays his rent and his phone bill each month so they are classified as expenses. If Rohan paid his rent only once every three months, he would need to set up an asset account called Prepaid Rent. He would debit this account when he paid the rent.

Transaction (i): Purchase of supplies

Rohan bought pens, paper, delivery envelopes, and other supplies for $80 cash (Figure 3-14).

Analysis. These supplies will last for several months. Since they will generate future benefits, the supplies should be recorded as an asset. An asset, Supplies, increases, and an asset, Cash, decreases. Debit Supplies and credit Cash for $80.

FIGURE 3-14   Transaction (i): Purchase of Supplies

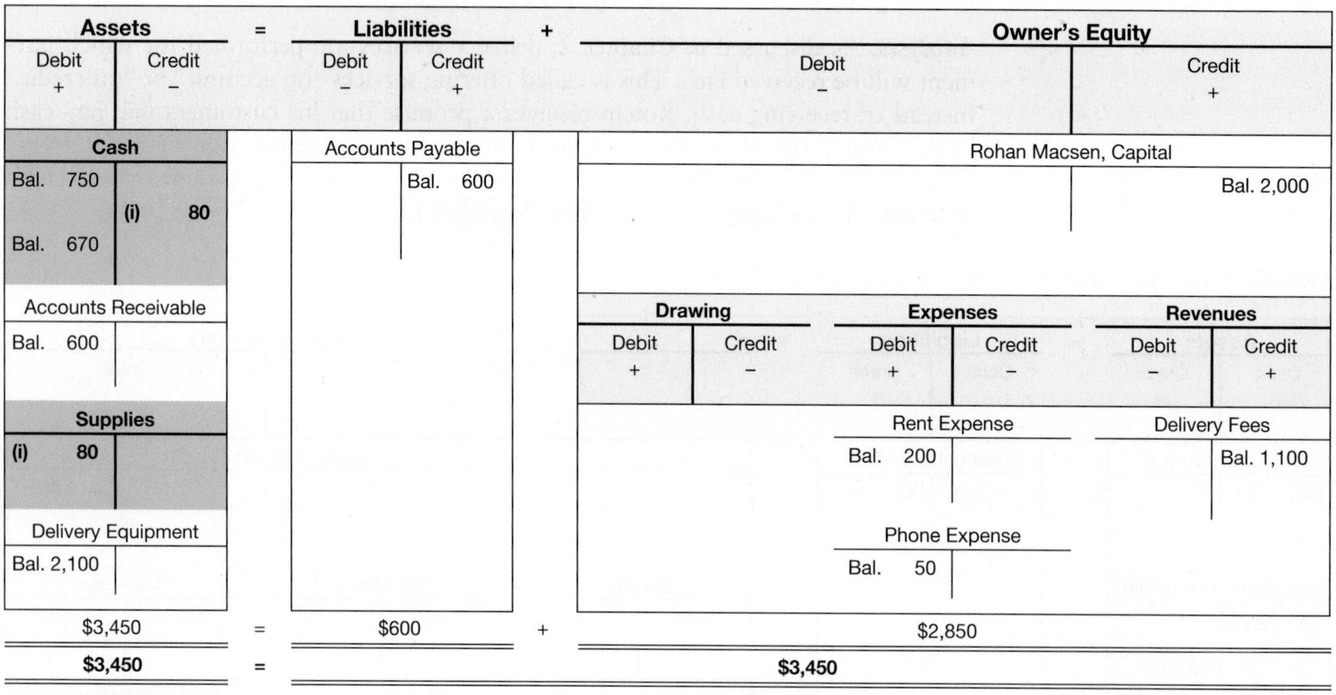

A Broader View

Supplies—Asset or Expense?

When businesses buy office supplies from Staples or other suppliers, the supplies are initially recorded as assets. This is done because the supplies will provide future benefits. Those still remaining in inventory at the end of the accounting period are reported on the balance sheet as assets. Supplies actually used during the period are recognized as an expense on the income statement. We will discuss how to account for the expense in Chapter 5.

CONVERY FLOWERS/ALAMY

Transaction (j): Payment of insurance premium

Rohan paid $200 for an eight-month liability insurance policy (Figure 3-15).

Analysis. Since insurance is paid in advance and will provide future benefits, it is treated as an asset. Therefore, one asset, Prepaid Insurance, increases and another, Cash, decreases. Debit Prepaid Insurance and credit Cash for $200.

FIGURE 3-15   Transaction (j): Payment of Insurance Premium

Assets		=	Liabilities		+	Owner's Equity	
Debit +	Credit −		Debit −	Credit +		Debit −	Credit +

Cash

Bal.	670		
		(j)	200
Bal.	470		

Accounts Payable

	Bal.	600

Rohan Macsen, Capital

	Bal. 2,000

Accounts Receivable

Bal.	600	

Drawing		Expenses		Revenues	
Debit +	Credit −	Debit +	Credit −	Debit −	Credit +

Supplies

Bal.	80	

Rent Expense

Bal.	200	

Delivery Fees

	Bal. 1,100

Prepaid Insurance

(j)	200	

Phone Expense

Bal.	50	

Delivery Equipment

Bal. 2,100	

$3,450	=	$600	+	$2,850
$3,450	=			$3,450

Transaction (k): Cash receipts from prior sales on account

Rohan received $570 in cash for delivery services performed for customers earlier in the month [see transaction (h)] (Figure 3-16).

Analysis. This transaction increases Cash and reduces the amount due from customers reported in Accounts Receivable. Debit Cash and credit Accounts Receivable $570.

As you analyze transaction (k), notice which accounts are affected and the location of these accounts in the accounting equation. Rohan received cash, but this transaction did not affect revenue. The revenue was recorded in transaction (h). Transaction (k) is an exchange of one asset (Accounts Receivable) for another asset (Cash).

FIGURE 3-16   Transaction (k): Cash Receipts from Prior Sales on Account

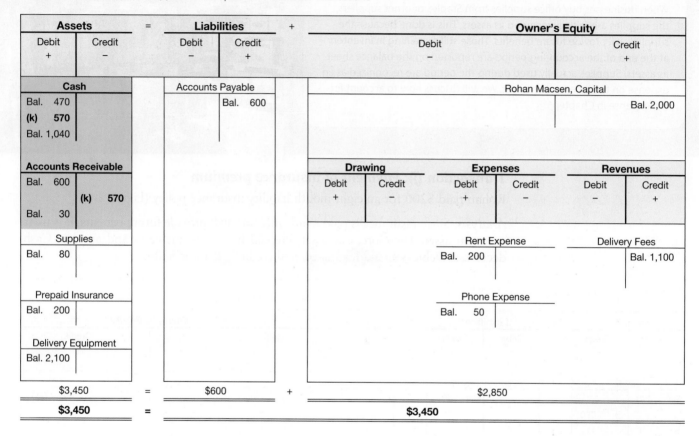

As you analyze transactions (l) through (o), make certain that you understand what has happened in each transaction. Identify the accounts that are affected and the locations of these accounts within the accounting equation. Notice that the accounting equation remains in balance after every transaction and debits equal credits for each transaction.

Transaction (l): Purchase of an asset on credit making a partial payment

Rohan bought a third motor scooter for $1,500. Rohan made a down payment of $300 and spread the remaining payments over the next four months (Figure 3-17).

Analysis. The asset, Delivery Equipment, increases by $1,500, Cash decreases by $300, and the liability, Accounts Payable, increases by $1,200. Thus, debit Delivery Equipment for $1,500, credit Cash for $300, and credit Accounts Payable for $1,200. This transaction requires one debit and two credits. Even so, total debits ($1,500) equal the total credits ($1,200 + $300) and the accounting equation remains in balance.

Transaction (m): Payment of wages

Rohan paid his part-time employees $650 in wages (Figure 3-18).

Analysis. This is an additional business expense. Wages Expense increases and Cash decreases. Debit Wages Expense and credit Cash for $650.

FIGURE 3-17 Transaction (l): Purchase of an Asset on Credit Making a Partial Payment

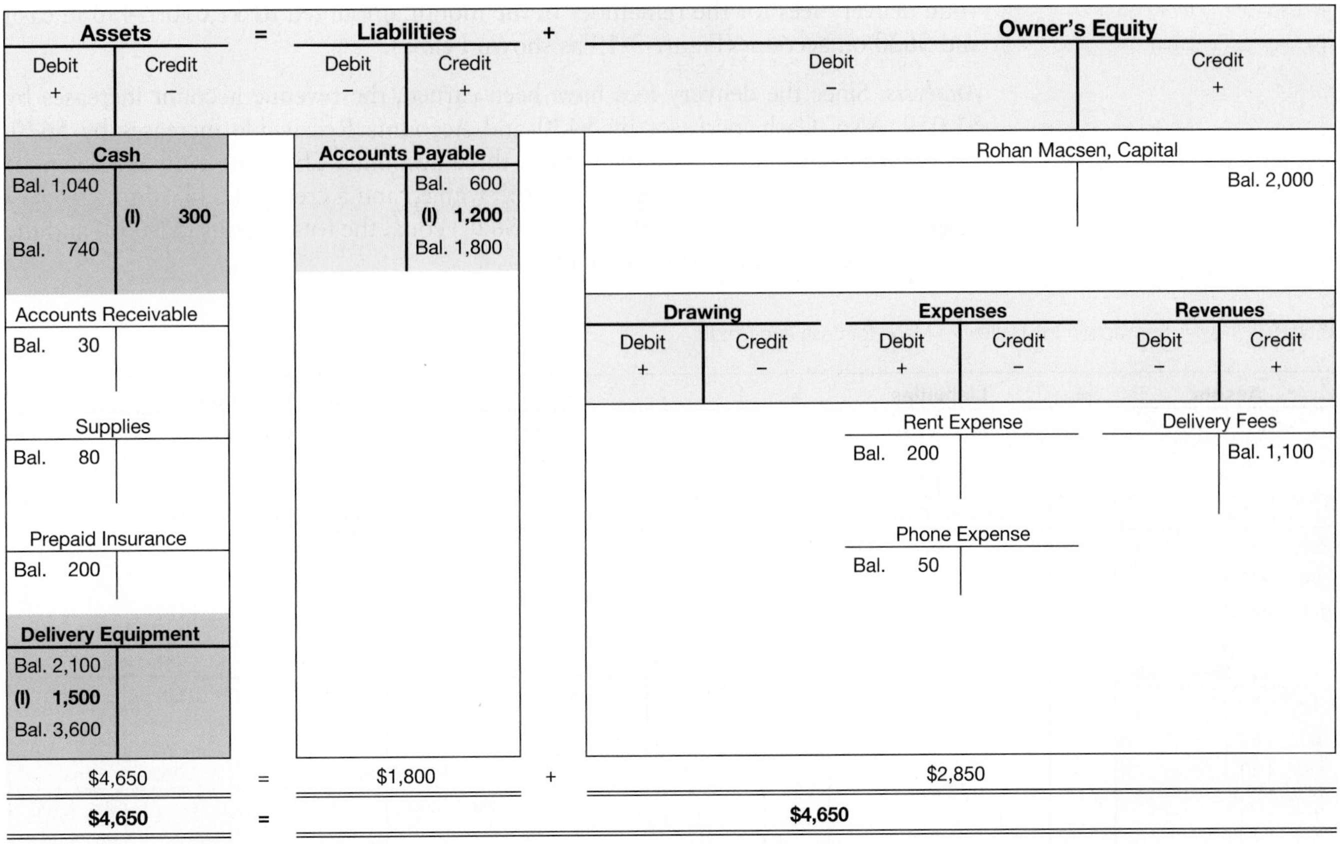

Assets		=	Liabilities		+	Owner's Equity	
Debit +	Credit –		Debit –	Credit +		Debit –	Credit +

Cash
Bal. 1,040
(l) 300
Bal. 740

Accounts Receivable
Bal. 30

Supplies
Bal. 80

Prepaid Insurance
Bal. 200

Delivery Equipment
Bal. 2,100
(l) 1,500
Bal. 3,600

Accounts Payable
Bal. 600
(l) 1,200
Bal. 1,800

Rohan Macsen, Capital
Bal. 2,000

Drawing		Expenses		Revenues	
Debit +	Credit –	Debit +	Credit –	Debit –	Credit +

Rent Expense
Bal. 200

Phone Expense
Bal. 50

Delivery Fees
Bal. 1,100

$4,650 = $1,800 + $2,850

$4,650 = $4,650

FIGURE 3-18 Transaction (m): Payment of Wages

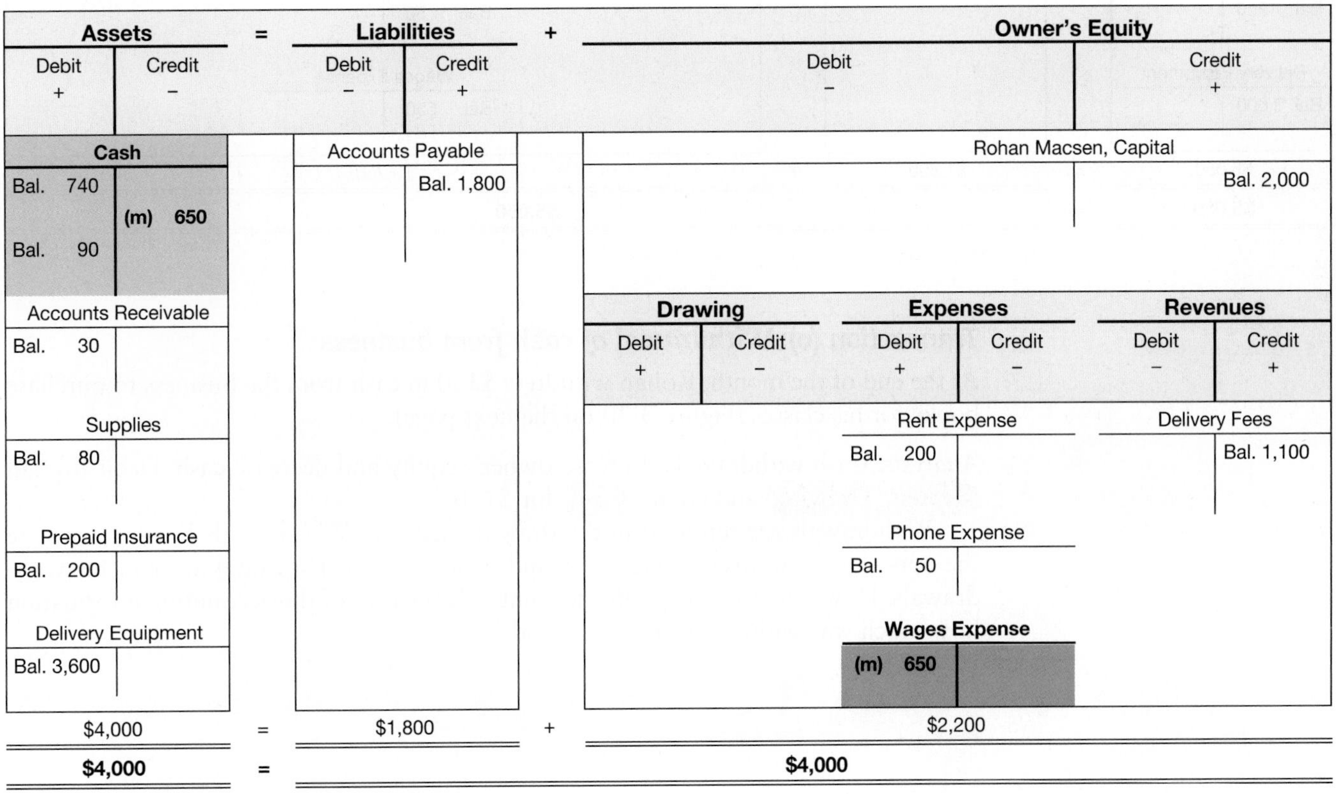

Assets		=	Liabilities		+	Owner's Equity	
Debit +	Credit –		Debit –	Credit +		Debit –	Credit +

Cash
Bal. 740
(m) 650
Bal. 90

Accounts Receivable
Bal. 30

Supplies
Bal. 80

Prepaid Insurance
Bal. 200

Delivery Equipment
Bal. 3,600

Accounts Payable
Bal. 1,800

Rohan Macsen, Capital
Bal. 2,000

Drawing		Expenses		Revenues	
Debit +	Credit –	Debit +	Credit –	Debit –	Credit +

Rent Expense
Bal. 200

Phone Expense
Bal. 50

Wages Expense
(m) 650

Delivery Fees
Bal. 1,100

$4,000 = $1,800 + $2,200

$4,000 = $4,000

Transaction (n): Deliveries made for cash and credit

Total delivery fees for the remainder of the month amounted to $1,050: $430 in cash and $620 on account (Figure 3-19 as shown below).

Analysis. Since the delivery fees have been earned, the revenue account increases by $1,050. Also, Cash increases by $430 and Accounts Receivable increases by $620. Note once again that one event impacts three accounts. This time we have debits of $430 to Cash and $620 to Accounts Receivable, and a credit of $1,050 to Delivery Fees. As before, the total debits ($430 + $620) equal the total credits ($1,050) and the accounting equation remains in balance.

FIGURE 3-19   Transaction (n): Deliveries Made for Cash and Credit

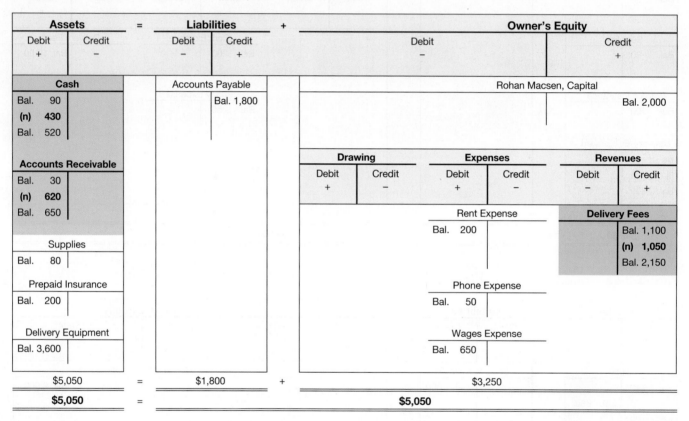

Transaction (o): Withdrawal of cash from business

At the end of the month, Rohan withdrew $150 in cash from the business to purchase books for his classes (Figure 3-20 on the next page).

Analysis. Cash withdrawals decrease owner's equity and decrease cash. Debit Rohan Macsen, Drawing and credit Cash for $150.

Withdrawals are reported in the drawing account. Withdrawals by an owner are the opposite of an investment. You could debit the owner's capital account for withdrawals. However, using a specific account tells the user of the accounting information how much was withdrawn for the period.

FIGURE 3-20   Transaction (o): Withdrawal of Cash from Business

Assets		=	Liabilities		+	Owner's Equity	
Debit +	Credit −		Debit −	Credit +		Debit −	Credit +

Cash			Accounts Payable			Rohan Macsen, Capital	
Bal. 520				Bal. 1,800			Bal. 2,000
	(o) 150						
Bal. 370							

				Drawing		Expenses		Revenues	
				Debit +	Credit −	Debit +	Credit −	Debit −	Credit +

Accounts Receivable		
Bal. 650		

Rohan Macsen, Drawing		Rent Expense		Delivery Fees	
(o) 150		Bal. 200			Bal. 2,150

Supplies	
Bal. 80	

Phone Expense	
Bal. 50	

Prepaid Insurance	
Bal. 200	

Wages Expense	
Bal. 650	

Delivery Equipment	
Bal. 3,600	

$4,900	=	$1,800	+	$3,100
$4,900	=			**$4,900**

Summary of Transactions

In illustrating transactions (a) through (o), each T account for Rohan's Campus Delivery shows a balance before and after each transaction. To focus your attention on the transaction being explained, only a single entry was shown. In practice, this is not done. Instead, each account gathers all transactions for a period. Rohan's accounts, with all transactions listed, are shown in Figure 3-21. Note the following four items:

1. The footings are directly under the debit (left) and credit (right) sides of the T account for those accounts with more than one debit or credit.
2. The balance is shown on the side with the larger footing.
3. The footing serves as the balance for accounts with entries on only one side of the account.
4. If an account has only a single entry, it is not necessary to enter a footing or balance.

Checkpoint ✓

Complete Checkpoint-3 on page 74 to test your basic understanding of LO4.

FIGURE 3-21   Summary of Transactions (a) Through (o)

Assets		=	Liabilities		+	Owner's Equity	
Debit +	Credit −		Debit −	Credit +		Debit −	Credit +

Cash

(a)	2,000	(b)	1,200
(e)	500	(d)	300
(k)	570	(f)	200
(n)	430	(g)	50
	3,500	(i)	80
		(j)	200
		(l)	300
		(m)	650
		(o)	150
			3,130
Bal.	370		

Accounts Receivable

(h)	600	(k)	570
(n)	620		
	1,220		
Bal.	650		

Supplies

(i)	80

Prepaid Insurance

(j)	200

Delivery Equipment

(b)	1,200
(c)	900
(l)	1,500
Bal.	3,600

Accounts Payable

(d)	300	(c)	900
		(l)	1,200
			2,100
		Bal.	1,800

Rohan Macsen, Capital

(a)	2,000

Drawing		Expenses		Revenues	
Debit +	Credit −	Debit +	Credit −	Debit −	Credit +

Rohan Macsen, Drawing

(o)	150

Rent Expense

(f)	200

Phone Expense

(g)	50

Wages Expense

(m)	650

Delivery Fees

(e)	500
(h)	600
(n)	1,050
Bal.	2,150

$4,900	=	$1,800	+	$3,100
$4,900	=			**$4,900**

THE TRIAL BALANCE

LO5 Prepare a trial balance and explain its purposes and linkages with the financial statements.

Recall the following two very important rules in double-entry accounting:

1. The sum of the debits must equal the sum of the credits.

At least two accounts are affected by each transaction. This rule is so important that many computer accounting programs will not permit a transaction to be entered into the accounting system unless the debits equal the credits.

2. The accounting equation must remain in balance.

In illustrating the transactions for Rohan's Campus Delivery, the equality of the accounting equation was verified after each transaction. Because of the large number of transactions entered each day, this is not done in practice. Instead, a trial balance is prepared periodically to determine the equality of the debits and credits. A **trial balance** is a list of all accounts showing the title and balance of each account. By totaling the debits and credits, their equality can be tested.

A trial balance of Rohan's accounts, taken on June 30, 20--, is shown in Figure 3-22. This date is shown on the third line of the heading. The trial balance shows that the debit and credit totals are equal in amount. This is proof that (1) in entering transactions (a) through (o), the total of the debits was equal to the total of the credits, and (2) the accounting equation has remained in balance.

A trial balance is not a formal statement or report. Normally, only the accountant sees it. As shown in Figure 3-23, a trial balance can be used as an aid in preparing the financial statements.

FIGURE 3-22   Trial Balance

Rohan's Campus Delivery
Trial Balance
June 30, 20 --

ACCOUNT TITLE	DEBIT BALANCE	CREDIT BALANCE
Cash	3 7 0 00	
Accounts Receivable	6 5 0 00	
Supplies	8 0 00	
Prepaid Insurance	2 0 0 00	
Delivery Equipment	3 6 0 0 00	
Accounts Payable		1 8 0 0 00
Rohan Macsen, Capital		2 0 0 0 00
Rohan Macsen, Drawing	1 5 0 00	
Delivery Fees		2 1 5 0 00
Rent Expense	2 0 0 00	
Phone Expense	5 0 00	
Wages Expense	6 5 0 00	
	5 9 5 0 00	5 9 5 0 00

FIGURE 3-23   Linkages Between the Trial Balance and Financial Statements

Rohan's Campus Delivery
Trial Balance
June 30, 20 --

ACCOUNT TITLE	DEBIT BALANCE	CREDIT BALANCE
Cash	3 7 0 00	
Accounts Receivable	6 5 0 00	
Supplies	8 0 00	
Prepaid Insurance	2 0 0 00	
Delivery Equipment	3 6 0 0 00	
Accounts Payable		1 8 0 0 00
Rohan Macsen, Capital		2 0 0 0 00
Rohan Macsen, Drawing	1 5 0 00	
Delivery Fees		2 1 5 0 00
Rent Expense	2 0 0 00	
Phone Expense	5 0 00	
Wages Expense	6 5 0 00	
	5 9 5 0 00	5 9 5 0 00

(continued)

FIGURE 3-23   Linkages Between the Trial Balance and Financial Statements (*concluded*)

If the beginning capital balance was $2,000 and Rohan made no additional investments, the statement would be prepared as follows:

Rohan's Campus Delivery
Statement of Owner's Equity
For Month Ended June 30, 20 --

Rohan Macsen, capital, June 1, 20 --		$2,000
Net income for June	$1,250	
Less withdrawals for June	150	
Increase in capital		1,100
Rohan Macsen, Capital, June 30, 20 --		$3,100

Rohan's Campus Delivery
Income Statement
For Month Ended June 30, 20 --

Revenue:		
Delivery fees		$2,150
Expenses:		
Wages expense	$650	
Rent expense	200	
Phone expense	50	
Total expenses		900
Net income		$1,250

Rohan's Campus Delivery
Statement of Owner's Equity
For Month Ended June 30, 20 --

Rohan Macsen, capital, June 1, 20 --		$ —
Investments during June		2,000
Total investment		$2,000
Net income for June	$1,250	
Less withdrawals for June	150	
Increase in capital		1,100
Rohan Macsen, capital, June 30, 20 --		$3,100

Checkpoint ✓

Complete Checkpoint-4 on page 74 to test your basic understanding of LO5.

Rohan's Campus Delivery
Balance Sheet
June 30, 20 --

Assets		Liabilities	
Cash	$ 370	Accounts payable	$1,800
Accounts receivable	650		
Supplies	80	Owner's Equity	
Prepaid insurance	200	Rohan Macsen, capital	3,100
Delivery equipment	3,600		
Total assets	$4,900	Total liabilities and owner's equity	$4,900

Self-Study

LEARNING OBJECTIVES	Key Points to Remember
LO1 **Define the parts of a T account.**	The parts of a T account are: 1. the title, 2. the debit or left side, and 3. the credit or right side.

Title	
Debit = Left	Credit = Right

| LEARNING OBJECTIVES | **Key Points to Remember** |

| **LO2** Foot and balance a T account. | Rules for footing and balancing T accounts are: |

1. The footings are directly under the debit (left) and credit (right) sides of the T account for those accounts with more than one debit or credit.
2. The balance is shown on the side with the larger footing.
3. The footing serves as the balance for accounts with entries on only one side of the account.
4. If an account has only a single entry, it is not necessary to enter a footing or balance.

| **LO3** Describe the effects of debits and credits on specific types of accounts. | Rules for debits and credits. (See illustration below.) |

1. Assets are on the left side of the accounting equation. Therefore, increases are entered on the left (debit) side of an asset account and decreases are entered on the right (credit) side.
2. Liabilities and owner's equity are on the right side of the accounting equation. Therefore, increases are entered on the right (credit) side and decreases are entered on the left (debit) side.
3. Revenues increase owner's equity. Therefore, increases are entered on the right (credit) side and decreases are entered on the left (debit) side.
4. Expenses and drawing decrease owner's equity. Therefore, increases are entered on the left (debit) side and decreases are entered on the right (credit) side.

Accounting Equation with Owner's Equity Umbrella

| **LO4** Use T accounts to analyze transactions. | Picture the accounting equation in your mind as you analyze transactions. When entering transactions in T accounts: |

1. The sum of the debits must equal the sum of the credits.
2. At least two accounts are affected by each transaction.
3. When finished, the accounting equation must remain in balance.

| **LO5** Prepare a trial balance and explain its purposes and linkages with the financial statements. | A trial balance shows that the debit and credit totals are equal. A trial balance also can be used in preparing the financial statements. |

DEMONSTRATION PROBLEM

Celia Pints opened We-Buy, You-Pay Shopping Services. For a fee that is based on the amount of research and shopping time required, Pints and her associates will shop for almost anything from groceries to home furnishings. Business is particularly heavy around Christmas and in early summer. The business operates from a rented store front. The associates receive a commission based on the revenues they produce and a mileage reimbursement for the use of their personal automobiles for shopping trips. Pints decided to use the following accounts to record transactions.

Assets	Owner's Equity
Cash	Celia Pints, Capital
Accounts Receivable	Celia Pints, Drawing
Office Equipment	Revenue
Computer Equipment	Shopping Fees
Liabilities	Expenses
Accounts Payable	Rent Expense
Notes Payable	Phone Expense
	Commissions Expense
	Utilities Expense
	Travel Expense

The following transactions are for the month of December 20--.

(a) Pints invested cash in the business, $30,000.

(b) Bought office equipment for $10,000. Paid $2,000 in cash and promised to pay the balance over the next four months.

(c) Paid rent for December, $500.

(d) Provided shopping services for customers on account, $5,200.

(e) Paid phone bill, $90.

(f) Borrowed cash from the bank by signing a note payable, $5,000.

(g) Bought a computer and printer, $4,800.

(h) Collected cash from customers for services performed on account, $4,000.

(i) Paid commissions to associates for revenues generated during the first half of the month, $3,500.

(j) Paid utility bill, $600.

(k) Paid cash on account for the office equipment purchased in transaction (b), $2,000.

(l) Earned shopping fees of $13,200: $6,000 in cash and $7,200 on account.

(m) Paid commissions to associates for last half of month, $7,000.

(n) Paid mileage reimbursements for the month, $1,500.

(o) Paid cash on note payable to bank, $1,000.

(p) Pints withdrew cash for personal use, $2,000.

REQUIRED

1. Enter the transactions for December in T accounts. Use the accounting equation as a guide for setting up the T accounts.

2. Foot the T accounts and determine their balances as necessary.

3. Prepare a trial balance of the accounts as of December 31 of the current year.

4. Prepare an income statement for the month ended December 31 of the current year.

5. Prepare a statement of owner's equity for the month ended December 31 of the current year.

6. Prepare a balance sheet as of December 31 of the current year.

Solution 1, 2.

Assets		=	Liabilities		+	Owner's Equity	
Debit +	**Credit** −		**Debit** −	**Credit** +		**Debit** −	**Credit** +

Assets

Cash

(a) 30,000	(b) 2,000
(f) 5,000	(c) 500
(h) 4,000	(e) 90
(l) 6,000	(g) 4,800
45,000	(i) 3,500
	(j) 600
	(k) 2,000
	(m) 7,000
	(n) 1,500
	(o) 1,000
	(p) 2,000
	24,990
Bal. 20,010	

Accounts Receivable

(d) 5,200	(h) 4,000
(l) 7,200	
12,400	
Bal. 8,400	

Office Equipment

(b) 10,000	

Computer Equipment

(g) 4,800	

Liabilities

Accounts Payable

(k) 2,000	(b) 8,000
	Bal. 6,000

Notes Payable

(o) 1,000	(f) 5,000
	Bal. 4,000

Owner's Equity

Celia Pints, Capital

	(a) 30,000

Drawing		Expenses		Revenues	
Debit +	**Credit** −	**Debit** +	**Credit** −	**Debit** −	**Credit** +

Celia Pints, Drawing

(p) 2,000	

Rent Expense

(c) 500	

Shopping Fees

	(d) 5,200
	(l) 13,200
	Bal. 18,400

Phone Expense

(e) 90	

Commissions Expense

(i) 3,500	
(m) 7,000	
Bal. 10,500	

Utilities Expense

(j) 600	

Travel Expense

(n) 1,500	

$43,210	=	$10,000	+	$33,210
$43,210	=			**$43,210**

3.

We-Buy, You-Pay Shopping Services
Trial Balance
December 31, 20 --

ACCOUNT TITLE	DEBIT BALANCE	CREDIT BALANCE
Cash	20 0 1 0 00	
Accounts Receivable	8 4 0 0 00	
Office Equipment	10 0 0 0 00	
Computer Equipment	4 8 0 0 00	
Accounts Payable		6 0 0 0 00
Notes Payable		4 0 0 0 00
Celia Pints, Capital		30 0 0 0 00
Celia Pints, Drawing	2 0 0 0 00	
Shopping Fees		18 4 0 0 00
Rent Expense	5 0 0 00	
Phone Expense	9 0 00	
Commissions Expense	10 5 0 0 00	
Utilities Expense	6 0 0 00	
Travel Expense	1 5 0 0 00	
	58 4 0 0 00	58 4 0 0 00

4.

We-Buy, You-Pay Shopping Services		
Income Statement		
For Month Ended December 31, 20 --		
Revenue:		
Shopping fees		$18,400
Expenses:		
Commissions expense	$10,500	
Travel expense	1,500	
Utilities expense	600	
Rent expense	500	
Phone expense	90	
Total expenses		13,190
Net income		$ 5,210

5.

We-Buy, You-Pay Shopping Services		
Statement of Owner's Equity		
For Month Ended December 31, 20 - -		
Celia Pints, capital, December 1, 20 --		$ —
Investments during December		30,000
Total investment		$30,000
Net income for December	$5,210	
Less withdrawals for December	2,000	
Increase in capital		3,210
Celia Pints, capital, December 31, 20 --		$33,210

6.

We-Buy, You-Pay Shopping Services				
Balance Sheet				
December 31, 20 - -				
Assets		Liabilities		
Cash	$20,010	Accounts payable		$ 6,000
Accounts receivable	8,400	Notes payable		4,000
Office equipment	10,000	Total liabilities		$10,000
Computer equipment	4,800			
		Owner's Equity		
		Celia Pints, capital		33,210
Total assets	$43,210	Total liabilities and owner's equity		$43,210

KEY TERMS

balance (51)   The difference between the footings of an account.

credit (52)   To enter an amount on the right side of an account.

credit balance (54)   The normal balance of liability, owner's equity, and revenue accounts.

debit (52)   To enter an amount on the left side of an account.

debit balance (54)   The normal balance of asset, expense, and drawing accounts.

double-entry accounting (51)   A system in which each transaction has a dual effect on the accounting elements.

footings (51)   The total dollar amounts on the debit and credit sides of an account.

normal balance (54)   The side of an account that is increased.

trial balance (66)   A list of all accounts, showing the title and balance of each account, used to prove that the sum of the debits equals the sum of the credits.

SELF-STUDY TEST QUESTIONS

True/False

1. **LO3**   To debit an account is to enter an amount on the left side of the account.

2. **LO3**   Liability accounts normally have debit balances.

3. **LO3**   Increases in owner's equity are entered as credits.

4. **LO3**   Revenue accounts normally have debit balances.

5. **LO3**   To credit an account is to enter an amount on the right side of the account.

6. **LO3**   A debit to an asset account will decrease it.

Multiple Choice

1. **LO3**   A common example of an asset is

   (a) Professional Fees.
   (b) Rent Expense.
   (c) Accounts Receivable.
   (d) Accounts Payable.

2. **LO3**   The accounting equation may be expressed as

   (a) Assets = Liabilities − Owner's Equity.
   (b) Assets = Liabilities + Owner's Equity.
   (c) Liabilities = Owner's Equity − Assets.
   (d) all of the above.

3. **LO3**   Liability, owner's equity, and revenue accounts normally have

   (a) debit balances.
   (b) large balances.
   (c) negative balances.
   (d) credit balances.

4. **LO4**   To record the payment of rent expense, an accountant would

   (a) debit Cash; credit Rent Expense.
   (b) debit Rent Expense; debit Cash.
   (c) debit Rent Expense; credit Cash.
   (d) credit Rent Expense; credit Cash.

5. **LO4**   An investment of cash by the owner will

   (a) increase assets and owner's equity.
   (b) increase assets and liabilities.
   (c) increase liabilities and owner's equity.
   (d) increase owner's equity and decrease liabilities.

Checkpoint ✓

Checkpoint Exercises

1. **LO2**   Foot and balance the accounts receivable T account shown below.

Accounts Receivable	
100	50
200	30

2. **LO3**   Complete the following questions using either "debit" or "credit":

(a) The asset account Supplies is increased with a _____.
(b) The owner's capital account is increased with a _____.
(c) The rent expense account is increased with a _____.

3. **LO4**   Analyze the following transaction using the T accounts provided below. Robb Todd purchased equipment for $300 cash.

Cash		Equipment	

4. **LO5**   The following accounts have normal balances. Prepare a trial balance. Accounts Payable, $20; Accounts Receivable, $90; Capital, $40; Sales, $200; Cash, $100; Rent Expense, $70.

The answers to the Self-Study Test Questions are at the end of the chapter (page 84).

Applying Your Knowledge

REVIEW QUESTIONS

LO1	1.	What are the three major parts of a T account?
LO1	2.	What is the left side of the T account called? the right side?
LO2	3.	What is a footing?
LO3	4.	What is the relationship between the revenue and expense accounts and the owner's equity account?
LO5	5.	What is the function of the trial balance?

SERIES A EXERCISES

E 3-1A   (LO2)
✓ Cash bal.: $1,200 (Dr.)

FOOT AND BALANCE A T ACCOUNT Foot and balance the cash T account shown below.

Cash	
500	100
400	200
600	

E 3-2A   (LO3)

DEBIT AND CREDIT ANALYSIS Complete the following statements using either "debit" or "credit":

(a) The cash account is increased with a _____.

(b) The owner's capital account is increased with a _____.

(c) The delivery equipment account is increased with a _____.

(d) The cash account is decreased with a _____.

(e) The liability account Accounts Payable is increased with a _____.

(f) The revenue account Delivery Fees is increased with a _____.

(g) The asset account Accounts Receivable is increased with a _____.

(h) The rent expense account is increased with a _____.

(i) The owner's drawing account is increased with a _____.

E 3-3A   (LO2/3/4)

✓ Cash bal. after (c): $3,100 (Dr.)

SHOW
ME HOW

ANALYSIS OF T ACCOUNTS Richard Gibbs began a business called Richard's Shoe Repair.

1. Create T accounts for Cash; Supplies; Richard Gibbs, Capital; and Utilities Expense. Identify the following transactions by letter and place them on the proper side of the T accounts:

    (a) Invested cash in the business, $6,500.

    (b) Purchased supplies for cash, $700.

    (c) Paid utility bill, $2,700.

2. Foot the T account for cash and enter the ending balance.

E 3-4A   (LO3)

NORMAL BALANCE OF ACCOUNT Indicate the normal balance (debit or credit) for each of the following accounts:

1. Cash
2. Wages Expense
3. Accounts Payable
4. Owner's Drawing
5. Supplies
6. Owner's Capital
7. Equipment

E 3-5A   (LO4)

TRANSACTION ANALYSIS Linda Kipp started a business on May 1, 20--. Analyze the following transactions for the first month of business using T accounts. Label each T account with the title of the account affected and then place the transaction letter and the dollar amount on the debit or credit side.

(a) Invested cash in the business, $5,000.

(b) Bought equipment for cash, $700.

(c) Bought equipment on account, $600.

(d) Paid cash on account for equipment purchased in transaction (c), $400.

(e) Withdrew cash for personal use, $900.

E 3-6A   (LO2)

✓ Cash bal. after (e): $3,000 (Dr.)

FOOT AND BALANCE T ACCOUNTS Foot and balance the T accounts prepared in Exercise 3-5A if necessary.

E 3-7A   (LO2/4)

✓ Cash bal. after (k): $24,400 (Dr.)

SHOW
ME HOW

ANALYSIS OF TRANSACTIONS Charles Chadwick opened a business called Charlie's Detective Service in January 20--. Set up T accounts for the following accounts: Cash; Accounts Receivable; Office Supplies; Computer Equipment; Office Furniture; Accounts Payable; Charles Chadwick, Capital; Charles Chadwick, Drawing; Professional Fees; Rent Expense; and Utilities Expense.

The following transactions occurred during the first month of business. Record these transactions in T accounts. After all transactions are recorded, foot and balance the accounts if necessary.

(a) Invested cash in the business, $30,000.
(b) Bought office supplies for cash, $300.
(c) Bought office furniture for cash, $5,000.
(d) Purchased computer and printer on account, $8,000.
(e) Received cash from clients for services, $3,000.
(f) Paid cash on account for computer and printer purchased in transaction (d), $4,000.
(g) Earned professional fees on account during the month, $9,000.
(h) Paid cash for office rent for January, $1,500.
(i) Paid utility bills for the month, $800.
(j) Received cash from clients billed in transaction (g), $6,000.
(k) Withdrew cash for personal use, $3,000.

E 3-8A (LO5)

✓ Trial bal. total debits: $46,000

SHOW ME HOW

TRIAL BALANCE Based on the transactions recorded in Exercise 3-7A, prepare a trial balance for Charlie's Detective Service as of January 31, 20--.

E 3-9A (LO5)

✓ Trial bal. total debits: $42,800

TRIAL BALANCE The following accounts have normal balances. Prepare a trial balance for Kenny's Lawn Service as of September 30, 20--.

Cash	$10,000
Accounts Receivable	6,000
Supplies	1,600
Prepaid Insurance	1,200
Delivery Equipment	16,000
Accounts Payable	4,000
Kenny Young, Capital	20,000
Kenny Young, Drawing	2,000
Delivery Fees	18,800
Wages Expense	4,200
Rent Expense	1,800

E 3-10A, E 3-11A, E 3-12A

Provided below is a trial balance for Juanita's Delivery Service. **Use this trial balance for Exercises 3-10A, 3-11A, and 3-12A.**

Juanita's Delivery Service
Trial Balance
September 30, 20 --

ACCOUNT TITLE	DEBIT BALANCE	CREDIT BALANCE
Cash	5 0 0 0 00	
Accounts Receivable	3 0 0 0 00	
Supplies	8 0 0 00	
Prepaid Insurance	6 0 0 00	
Delivery Equipment	8 0 0 0 00	
Accounts Payable		2 0 0 0 00
Juanita Raye, Capital		10 0 0 0 00
Juanita Raye, Drawing	1 0 0 0 00	
Delivery Fees		9 4 0 0 00
Wages Expense	2 1 0 0 00	
Rent Expense	9 0 0 00	
	21 4 0 0 00	21 4 0 0 00

E 3-10A   (LO5)
✓ Net income: $6,400

INCOME STATEMENT From the information in the trial balance presented above, prepare an income statement for Juanita's Delivery Service for the month ended September 30, 20--.

E 3-11A   (LO5)
✓ Capital, 9/30: $15,400

STATEMENT OF OWNER'S EQUITY From the information in the trial balance presented above, prepare a statement of owner's equity for Juanita's Delivery Service for the month ended September 30, 20--.

E 3-12A   (LO5)
✓ Total assets, 9/30: $17,400

SHOW
ME HOW

BALANCE SHEET From the information in the trial balance presented for Juanita's Delivery Service on page 76, prepare a balance sheet for Juanita's Delivery Service as of September 30, 20--.

SERIES A PROBLEMS

P 3-13A   (LO2/4/5)
✓ Cash bal. after (p): $21,805 (Dr.)
✓ Trial bal. total debits: $44,900

SHOW
ME HOW

T ACCOUNTS AND TRIAL BALANCE Wilhelm Kohl started a business in May 20-- called Kohl's Home Repair. Kohl hired a part-time college student as an assistant. Kohl has decided to use the following accounts for recording transactions:

Assets
   Cash
   Accounts Receivable
   Office Supplies
   Prepaid Insurance
   Equipment
   Van
Liabilities
   Accounts Payable

Owner's Equity
   Wilhelm Kohl, Capital
   Wilhelm Kohl, Drawing
Revenue
   Service Fees
Expenses
   Rent Expense
   Wages Expense
   Phone Expense
   Gas and Oil Expense

The following transactions occurred during May:

(a) Invested cash in the business, $25,000.
(b) Purchased a used van for cash, $6,000.
(c) Purchased equipment on account, $4,000.
(d) Received cash for services rendered, $7,500.
(e) Paid cash on account owed from transaction (c), $2,300.
(f) Paid rent for the month, $850.
(g) Paid phone bill, $230.
(h) Earned revenue on account, $4,500.
(i) Purchased office supplies for cash, $160.
(j) Paid wages to an assistant, $800.
(k) Purchased a one-year insurance policy, $1,100.
(l) Received cash from services performed in transaction (h), $3,400.
(m) Paid cash for gas and oil expense on the van, $155.
(n) Purchased additional equipment for $4,200, paying $1,500 cash and spreading the remaining payments over the next 10 months.
(o) Earned service fees for the remainder of the month of $3,500: $1,900 in cash and $1,600 on account.
(p) Withdrew cash at the end of the month, $2,900.

1. Enter the transactions in T accounts, identifying each transaction with its corresponding letter.

2. Foot and balance the accounts where necessary.

3. Prepare a trial balance as of May 31, 20--.

P 3-14A   (LO5)

✓ Net income: $13,465

✓ Owner's equity, 5/31: $35,565

✓ Total assets, 5/31: $39,965

NET INCOME AND CHANGE IN OWNER'S EQUITY Refer to the trial balance of Kohl's Home Repair in Problem 3-13A to determine the following information. Use the format provided below.

1. a. Total revenue for the month   _____

   b. Total expenses for the month   _____

   c. Net income for the month   _____

2. a. Wilhelm Kohl's original investment

       in the business   _____

       + Net income for the month   _____

       – Owner's drawing   _____

       Increase (decrease) in capital   _____

       = Ending owner's equity   _____

   b. End of month accounting equation:

Assets	=	Liabilities	+	Owner's Equity
_____	=	_____	+	_____

P 3-15A   (LO5)

✓ NI: $13,465

✓ Capital, 5/31/20--: $35,565

✓ Total assets 5/31/20--: $39,965

FINANCIAL STATEMENTS Refer to the trial balance in Problem 3-13A and to the analysis of the change in owner's equity in Problem 3-14A.

1. Prepare an income statement for Kohl's Home Repair for the month ended May 31, 20--.

2. Prepare a statement of owner's equity for Kohl's Home Repair for the month ended May 31, 20--.

3. Prepare a balance sheet for Kohl's Home Repair as of May 31, 20--.

SERIES B EXERCISES

E 3-1B   (LO2)

✓ Accts. Pay: $400 (Cr.)

FOOT AND BALANCE A T ACCOUNT Foot and balance the accounts payable T account shown below.

Accounts Payable	
300	450
250	350
	150

E 3-2B   (LO3)

DEBIT AND CREDIT ANALYSIS Complete the following statements using either "debit" or "credit":

(a) The asset account Prepaid Insurance is increased with a _____.

(b) The owner's drawing account is increased with a _____.

(c) The asset account Accounts Receivable is decreased with a _____.

(d) The liability account Accounts Payable is decreased with a _____.

(e) The owner's capital account is increased with a _____.

(f) The revenue account Professional Fees is increased with a _____.

(g) The expense account Repair Expense is increased with a _____.

(h) The asset account Cash is decreased with a _____.

(i) The asset account Delivery Equipment is decreased with a _____.

E 3-3B   (LO2/3/4)

✓ Cash bal. after (c): $3,900 (Dr.)

SHOW
ME HOW

ANALYSIS OF T ACCOUNTS Roberto Alvarez began a business called Roberto's Fix-It Shop.

1. Create T accounts for Cash; Supplies; Roberto Alvarez, Capital; and Utilities Expense. Identify the following transactions by letter and place them on the proper side of the T accounts:

   (a) Invested cash in the business, $6,000.

   (b) Purchased supplies for cash, $1,200.

   (c) Paid utility bill, $900.

2. Foot the T account for cash and enter the ending balance.

E 3-4B   (LO3)

NORMAL BALANCE OF ACCOUNT Indicate the normal balance (debit or credit) for each of the following accounts:

1. Cash

2. Rent Expense

3. Notes Payable

4. Owner's Drawing

5. Accounts Receivable

6. Owner's Capital

7. Tools

E 3-5B   (LO4)

TRANSACTION ANALYSIS George Atlas started a business on June 1, 20--. Analyze the following transactions for the first month of business using T accounts. Label each T account with the title of the account affected and then place the transaction letter and the dollar amount on the debit or credit side.

(a) Invested cash in the business, $7,000.

(b) Purchased equipment for cash, $900.

(c) Purchased equipment on account, $1,500.

(d) Paid cash on account for equipment purchased in transaction (c), $800.

(e) Withdrew cash for personal use, $1,100.

E 3-6B   (LO2)

✓ Cash bal. after (e): $4,200 (Dr.)

FOOT AND BALANCE T ACCOUNTS Foot and balance the T accounts prepared in Exercise 3-5B if necessary.

E 3-7B   (LO2/4)

✓ Cash bal. after (k): $9,000 (Dr.)

SHOW
ME HOW

ANALYSIS OF TRANSACTIONS Nicole Lawrence opened a business called Nickie's Neat Ideas in January 20--. Set up T accounts for the following accounts: Cash; Accounts Receivable; Office Supplies; Computer Equipment; Office Furniture; Accounts Payable; Nicole Lawrence, Capital; Nicole Lawrence, Drawing; Professional Fees; Rent Expense; and Utilities Expense.

The following transactions occurred during the first month of business. Record these transactions in T accounts. After all transactions have been recorded, foot and balance the accounts if necessary.

(a) Invested cash in the business, $18,000.

(b) Purchased office supplies for cash, $500.

(c) Purchased office furniture for cash, $8,000.

(d) Purchased computer and printer on account, $5,000.

(e) Received cash from clients for services, $4,000.

(f) Paid cash on account for computer and printer purchased in transaction (d), $2,000.

(g) Earned professional fees on account during the month, $7,000.

(h) Paid office rent for January, $900.

(i) Paid utility bills for the month, $600.

(j) Received cash from clients that were billed previously in transaction (g), $3,000.

(k) Withdrew cash for personal use, $4,000.

E 3-8B   (LO5)
✓ Trial bal. total debits: $32,000

SHOW ME HOW

TRIAL BALANCE Based on the transactions recorded in Exercise 3-7B, prepare a trial balance for Nickie's Neat Ideas as of January 31, 20--.

E 3-9B   (LO5)
✓ Trial bal. total debits: $55,000

TRIAL BALANCE The following accounts have normal balances. Prepare a trial balance for Betty's Cleaning Service as of September 30, 20--.

Cash	$14,000	Betty Par, Capital	$24,000
Accounts Receivable	8,000	Betty Par, Drawing	4,000
Supplies	1,200	Delivery Fees	25,000
Prepaid Insurance	1,800	Wages Expense	6,000
Delivery Equipment	18,000	Rent Expense	2,000
Accounts Payable	6,000		

E 3-10B, E 3-11B, E 3-12B

Provided below is a trial balance for Bill's Delivery Service. **Use this trial balance for Exercises 3-10B, 3-11B, and 3-12B.**

Bill's Delivery Service
Trial Balance
September 30, 20 --

ACCOUNT TITLE	DEBIT BALANCE	CREDIT BALANCE
Cash	7 0 0 0 00	
Accounts Receivable	4 0 0 0 00	
Supplies	6 0 0 00	
Prepaid Insurance	9 0 0 00	
Delivery Equipment	9 0 0 0 00	
Accounts Payable		3 0 0 0 00
Bill Swift, Capital		12 0 0 0 00
Bill Swift, Drawing	2 0 0 0 00	
Delivery Fees		12 5 0 0 00
Wages Expense	3 0 0 0 00	
Rent Expense	1 0 0 0 00	
	27 5 0 0 00	27 5 0 0 00

E 3-10B   (LO5)
✓ Net income: $8,500

SHOW
ME HOW

INCOME STATEMENT From the information in the trial balance presented above, prepare an income statement for Bill's Delivery Service for the month ended September 30, 20--.

E 3-11B   (LO5)
✓ Capital, 9/30: $18,500

SHOW
ME HOW

STATEMENT OF OWNER'S EQUITY From the information in the trial balance presented above, prepare a statement of owner's equity for Bill's Delivery Service for the month ended September 30, 20--.

E 3-12B   (LO5)
✓ Total assets, 9/30: $21,500

SHOW
ME HOW

BALANCE SHEET From the information in the trial balance presented for Bill's Delivery Service on page 80, prepare a balance sheet for Bill's Delivery Service as of September 30, 20--.

SERIES B PROBLEMS

P 3-13B   (LO2/4/5)
✓ Cash bal. after (p): $20,200 (Dr.)
✓ Trial bal. total debits: $44,300

CLGL

SHOW
ME HOW

T ACCOUNTS AND TRIAL BALANCE Sue Jantz started a business in August 20-- called Jantz Plumbing Service. Jantz hired a part-time college student as an administrative assistant. Jantz has decided to use the following accounts:

Assets
  Cash
  Accounts Receivable
  Office Supplies
  Prepaid Insurance
  Plumbing Equipment
  Van
Liabilities
  Accounts Payable

Owner's Equity
  Sue Jantz, Capital
  Sue Jantz, Drawing
Revenue
  Service Fees
Expenses
  Rent Expense
  Wages Expense
  Phone Expense
  Advertising Expense

The following transactions occurred during August:

(a) Invested cash in the business, $30,000.
(b) Purchased a used van for cash, $8,000.
(c) Purchased plumbing equipment on account, $4,000.
(d) Received cash for services rendered, $3,000.
(e) Paid cash on account owed from transaction (c), $1,000.
(f) Paid rent for the month, $700.
(g) Paid phone bill, $100.
(h) Earned revenue on account, $4,000.
(i) Purchased office supplies for cash, $300.
(j) Paid wages to student, $500.
(k) Purchased a one-year insurance policy, $800.
(l) Received cash from services performed in transaction (h), $3,000.
(m) Paid cash for advertising expense, $2,000.
(n) Purchased additional plumbing equipment for $2,000, paying $500 cash and spreading the remaining payments over the next six months.
(o) Earned revenue from services for the remainder of the month of $2,800: $1,100 in cash and $1,700 on account.
(p) Withdrew cash at the end of the month, $3,000.

REQUIRED

1. Enter the transactions in T accounts, identifying each transaction with its corresponding letter.

2. Foot and balance the accounts where necessary.

3. Prepare a trial balance as of August 31, 20--.

P 3-14B   (LO5)

✓ Net income: $6,500

✓ Owner's equity, 8/31: $33,500

✓ Total assets, 8/31: $38,000

NET INCOME AND CHANGE IN OWNER'S EQUITY Refer to the trial balance of Jantz Plumbing Service in Problem 3-13B to determine the following information. Use the format provided below.

1. a. Total revenue for the month   _____

    b. Total expenses for the month   _____

    c. Net income for the month   _____

2. a. Sue Jantz's original investment in the business   _____

        + Net income for the month   _____

        – Owner's drawing   _____   _____

        Increase (decrease) in capital   _____

        = Ending owner's equity   _____

    b. End of month accounting equation:

Assets	=	Liabilities	+	Owner's Equity
_____	=	_____	+	_____

P 3-15B   (LO5)

✓ NI: $6,500

✓ Capital, 8/31/20--: $33,500

✓ Total assets, 8/31/20--: $38,000

FINANCIAL STATEMENTS Refer to the trial balance in Problem 3-13B and to the analysis of the change in owner's equity in Problem 3-14B.

REQUIRED

1. Prepare an income statement for Jantz Plumbing Service for the month ended August 31, 20--.

2. Prepare a statement of owner's equity for Jantz Plumbing Service for the month ended August 31, 20--.

3. Prepare a balance sheet for Jantz Plumbing Service as of August 31, 20--.

MANAGING YOUR WRITING

Write a one-page memo to your instructor explaining how you could use the double-entry system to maintain records of your personal finances. What types of accounts would you use for the accounting elements?

MASTERY PROBLEM

☑ **Check List**

☐ Managing

☐ Planning

☐ Drafting

☐ Break

☐ Revising

☐ Managing

✓ Cash bal. after (p): $1,980 (Dr.)

✓ Trial bal. debit total: $5,840

✓ Net income: $500

✓ Total assets: $4,300

Craig Fisher started a lawn service called Craig's Quick Cut to earn money over the summer months. Fisher has decided to use the following accounts for recording transactions:

(continued)

Assets
    Cash
    Accounts Receivable
    Mowing Equipment
    Lawn Tools
Liabilities
    Accounts Payable
    Notes Payable
Owner's Equity
    Craig Fisher, Capital
    Craig Fisher, Drawing

Revenue
    Lawn Fees
Expenses
    Rent Expense
    Wages Expense
    Phone Expense
    Gas and Oil Expense
    Transportation Expense

Transactions for the month of June are listed below.

(a) Invested cash in the business, $3,000.

(b) Bought mowing equipment for $1,000: paid $200 in cash and promised to pay the balance over the next four months.

(c) Paid garage rent for June, $50.

(d) Provided lawn services for customers on account, $520.

(e) Paid phone bill, $30.

(f) Borrowed cash from the bank by signing a note payable, $500.

(g) Bought lawn tools, $480.

(h) Collected cash from customers for services performed on account in transaction (d), $400.

(i) Paid associates for lawn work done during the first half of the month, $350.

(j) Paid for gas and oil for the equipment, $60.

(k) Paid cash on account for the mowing equipment purchased in transaction (b), $200.

(l) Earned lawn fees of $1,320: $600 in cash and $720 on account.

(m) Paid associates for last half of month, $700.

(n) Reimbursed associates for costs incurred using their own vehicles for transportation, $150.

(o) Paid on note payable to bank, $100.

(p) Withdrew cash for personal use, $200.

REQUIRED

1. Enter the transactions for June in T accounts. Use the accounting equation as a guide for setting up the T accounts.

2. Foot and balance the T accounts where necessary.

3. Prepare a trial balance of the accounts as of June 30, 20--.

4. Prepare an income statement for the month ended June 30, 20--.

5. Prepare a statement of owner's equity for the month ended June 30, 20--.

6. Prepare a balance sheet as of June 30, 20--.

CHALLENGE PROBLEM

This problem challenges you to apply your cumulative accounting knowledge to move a step beyond the material in the chapter.

✓ Capital, 8/31/20--: $600

Your friend Chris Stevick started a part-time business in June and has been keeping her own accounting records. She has been preparing monthly financial statements. At the end of August, she stopped by to show you her performance for the most recent month. She prepared the following income statement and balance sheet:

Income Statement		Balance Sheet	End of Month	Beginning of Month
Revenues	$500	Cash	$600	$400
Expenses	200	Capital	600	400
Net income	$300			

Chris has also heard that there is a statement of owner's equity, but she is not familiar with that statement. She asks if you can help her prepare one. After confirming that she has no assets other than cash, no liabilities, and made no additional investments in the business in August, you agree.

REQUIRED

1. Prepare the statement of owner's equity for your friend's most recent month.
2. What suggestions might you give to Chris that would make her income statement more useful?

Answers to Self-Study Test Questions

True/False

1. T
2. F (Liability accounts normally have credit balances.)
3. T
4. F (credit balances)
5. T
6. F (increase)

Multiple Choice

1. c   2. b   3. d   4. c   5. a

Checkpoint Exercises

1.
Accounts Receivable	
100	50
200	30
300	**80**
Bal. 220	

2. (a) The asset account Supplies is increased with a <u>debit</u>.
   (b) The owner's capital account is increased with a <u>credit</u>.
   (c) The rent expense account is increased with a <u>debit</u>.

3.
Cash		Equipment	
	300	300	

4.
Trial Balance		
Cash	100	
Accounts Receivable	90	
Accounts Payable		20
Capital		40
Sales		200
Rent Expense	70	
	260	260

ANDRE JENNY/ALAMY

Chapter 4

Journalizing and Posting Transactions

Campus Advantage (CA) provides a comprehensive range of student residential services in the following areas: management, development, acquisition, and consulting. It specializes in the creation of modern, full-service facilities that are secure, private, and equipped with all of the tools that today's students need for success. Its communities are no-hassle alternatives to dorm living with full dining service options. CA has facilities across the country, but each student residence reflects the unique identity of the school and community it serves. University Crossing, CA furnished, luxury, student apartments in Manhattan, Kansas, are just minutes from Kansas State University.

As with all businesses, CA relies on an accounting system to maintain a record of transactions from the source document through the preparation of the trial balance and financial statements. In this chapter, we discuss source documents, the chart of accounts, and the process used to journalize and post transactions. And, just in case an error is made, we address how to find and correct errors.

LEARNING OBJECTIVES

Careful study of this chapter should enable you to:

LO1 Describe the flow of data from source documents to the trial balance.

LO2 Describe and explain the purpose of source documents.

LO3 Describe the chart of accounts as a means of classifying financial information.

LO4 Journalize transactions.

LO5 Post to the general ledger and prepare a trial balance.

LO6 Explain how to find and correct errors.

The double-entry framework of accounting was explained and illustrated in Chapter 3. To demonstrate the use of debits and credits, business transactions were entered directly into T accounts. Now we will take a more detailed look at the procedures used to account for business transactions.

FLOW OF DATA

LO1 Describe the flow of data from source documents to the trial balance.

This chapter traces the flow of financial data from the source documents through the accounting information system. This process includes the following steps:

1. Analyze what happened by using information from source documents and the firm's chart of accounts.
2. Enter business transactions in the general journal in the form of journal entries.
3. Post these journal entries to the accounts in the general ledger.
4. Prepare a trial balance.

The flow of data from the source documents through the preparation of a trial balance is shown in Figure 4-1.

FIGURE 4-1   Flow of Data from Source Documents through Trial Balance

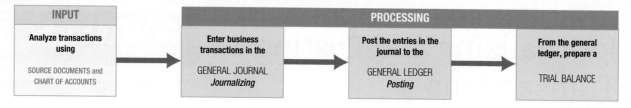

INPUT	PROCESSING		
Analyze transactions using SOURCE DOCUMENTS and CHART OF ACCOUNTS	**Enter business transactions in the** GENERAL JOURNAL *Journalizing*	**Post the entries in the journal to the** GENERAL LEDGER *Posting*	**From the general ledger, prepare a** TRIAL BALANCE

SOURCE DOCUMENTS

LO2 Describe and explain the purpose of source documents.

Almost any document that provides information about a business transaction can be called a source document. A source document triggers the analysis of what happened. It begins the process of entering transactions in the accounting system. Examples of source documents are shown in Figure 4-2. These source documents provide information that is useful in determining the effect of business transactions on specific accounts.

In addition to serving as input for transaction analysis, source documents serve as objective evidence of business transactions. If anyone questions the accounting records, these documents may be used as objective, verifiable evidence of the accuracy of the accounting records. For this reason, source documents are filed for possible future reference. *Having objective, verifiable evidence that a transaction occurred is an important accounting concept.*

FIGURE 4-2   Source Documents

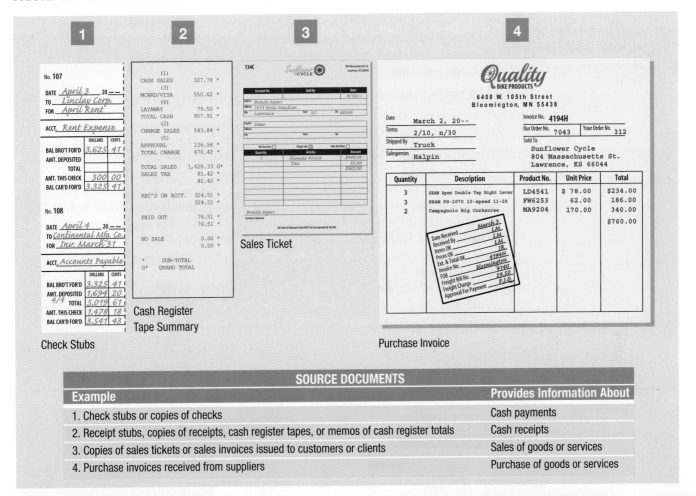

Check Stubs

Cash Register
Tape Summary

Sales Ticket

Purchase Invoice

SOURCE DOCUMENTS	
Example	**Provides Information About**
1. Check stubs or copies of checks	Cash payments
2. Receipt stubs, copies of receipts, cash register tapes, or memos of cash register totals	Cash receipts
3. Copies of sales tickets or sales invoices issued to customers or clients	Sales of goods or services
4. Purchase invoices received from suppliers	Purchase of goods or services

A Broader View

Electronic Source Documents

With the ability to go shopping in cyberspace, more transactions are being initiated electronically. This means that more and more "source documents" will be in an electronic form.

SCOTT OLSON/GETTY IMAGES

Checkpoint ✓

Complete Checkpoint-1 on page 113 to test your basic understanding of LO2.

THE CHART OF ACCOUNTS

LO3 Describe the chart of accounts as a means of classifying financial information.

You learned in Chapters 2 and 3 that there are three basic questions that must be answered when analyzing transactions.

1. What happened?
2. Which accounts are affected?
3. How is the accounting equation affected?

To determine which accounts are affected (step 2), the accountant must know the accounts being used by the business. A list of all accounts used by a business is called a chart of accounts.

The chart of accounts includes the account titles in numeric order for all assets, liabilities, owner's equity, revenues, and expenses. The numbering should follow a consistent pattern. In Rohan's Campus Delivery, asset accounts begin with "1," liability accounts begin with "2," owner's equity accounts begin with "3," revenue accounts begin with "4," and expense accounts begin with "5." Rohan uses three-digit numbers for all accounts.

A chart of accounts for Rohan's Campus Delivery is shown in Figure 4-3. Rohan would not need many accounts initially because the business is new. Additional accounts can easily be added as needed. Note that the accounts are arranged according to the accounting equation.

FIGURE 4-3   Chart of Accounts

ROHAN'S CAMPUS DELIVERY CHART OF ACCOUNTS			
Assets	**(100–199)**	**Revenues**	**(400–499)**
101	Cash	401	Delivery Fees
122	Accounts Receivable		
141	Supplies	**Expenses**	**(500–599)**
145	Prepaid Insurance	511	Wages Expense
185	Delivery Equipment	521	Rent Expense
		525	Phone Expense
Liabilities	**(200–299)**		
202	Accounts Payable		
Owner's Equity	**(300–399)**		
311	Rohan Macsen, Capital		
312	Rohan Macsen, Drawing		

Assets begin with 1

Liabilities begin with 2

Owner's Equity begin with 3

Revenues begin with 4

Expenses begin with 5

THE GENERAL JOURNAL

LO4 Journalize
        transactions.

LEARNING KEY

A journal provides a day-by-day listing of all transactions completed by the business.

A day-by-day listing of the transactions of a business is called a journal. The purpose of a journal is to provide a record of all transactions completed by the business. The journal shows the date of each transaction, titles of the accounts to be debited and credited, and the amounts of the debits and credits.

A journal is commonly referred to as a **book of original entry** because it is here that the first formal accounting record of a transaction is made. Although many types of journals are used in business, the simplest journal form is a two-column general journal (Figure 4-4). Any kind of business transaction may be entered into a general journal.

A **two-column general journal** is so-named because it has only two amount columns, one for debit amounts and one for credit amounts. Journal pages are numbered in the upper right-hand corner. The five column numbers in Figure 4-4 are explained in Figure 4-5.

FIGURE 4-4   Two-Column General Journal

	DATE	DESCRIPTION	POST. REF.	DEBIT	CREDIT	
1	20-- **1**	**2**	**3**	**4**	**5**	1
2						2
3						3

GENERAL JOURNAL   PAGE 1

FIGURE 4-5   The Columns in a Two-Column General Journal

Column **1** Date	The year is entered in small figures at the top of the column immediately below the column heading. The year is repeated only at the top of each new page. The month is entered for the first entry on the page and for the first transaction of the month. The day of the month is recorded for every transaction, even if it is the same as the prior entry.
Column **2** Description	The *Description* or *Explanation* column is used to enter the titles of the accounts affected by each transaction and to provide a very brief description of the transaction. Each transaction affects two or more accounts. The account(s) to be debited are entered first at the extreme left of the column. The account(s) to be credited are listed after the debits and indented. The description should be entered immediately following the last credit entry with an additional indentation.
Column **3** Posting Reference	No entries are made in the *Posting Reference* column during journalizing. Entries are made in this column when the debits and credits are copied to the proper accounts in the ledger. This process will be explained in detail later in this chapter.
Column **4** Debit Amount	The *Debit amount column* is used to enter the amount to be debited to an account. The amount should be entered on the same line as the title of that account.
Column **5** Credit Amount	The *Credit amount column* is used to enter the amount to be credited to an account. The amount should be entered on the same line as the title of that account.

LEARNING KEY

When journalizing, the exact account titles shown in the chart of accounts must be used. Refer to the chart of accounts in Figure 4-3 as you review the entries for Rohan's Campus Delivery.

Journalizing

Entering the transactions day-by-day in a journal is called **journalizing**. For every transaction, the entry should include the date, the title of each account affected, the amounts, and a brief description.

To illustrate the journalizing process, transactions for the first month of operations of Rohan's Campus Delivery will be journalized. The transactions are listed in Figure 4-6. Since you analyzed these transactions in Chapters 2 and 3, the journalizing process should be easier to understand. Let's start with a close look at the steps followed when journalizing the first transaction, Rohan's initial investment of $2,000.

FIGURE 4-6   Summary of Transactions

	SUMMARY OF TRANSACTIONS ROHAN'S CAMPUS DELIVERY	
Transaction		
(a)	June 1	Rohan Macsen invested cash in his business, $2,000.
(b)	3	Bought delivery equipment for cash, $1,200.
(c)	5	Bought delivery equipment on account from Big Red Scooters, $900.
(d)	6	Paid first installment from transaction (c) to Big Red Scooters, $300.
(e)	6	Received cash for delivery services rendered, $500.
(f)	7	Paid cash for June office rent, $200.
(g)	15	Paid phone bill, $50.
(h)	15	Made deliveries on account for a total of $600: Accounting Department ($400) and the School of Music ($200).
(i)	16	Bought supplies for cash, $80.
(j)	18	Paid cash for an eight-month liability insurance policy, $200. Coverage began on June 1.
(k)	20	Received $570 in cash for services performed in transaction (h): $400 from the Accounting Department and $170 from the School of Music.
(l)	25	Bought a third scooter from Big Red Scooters, $1,500. Paid $300 cash, with the remaining payments expected over the next four months.
(m)	27	Paid wages of part-time employees, $650.
(n)	30	Earned delivery fees for the remainder of the month amounting to $1,050: $430 in cash and $620 on account. Deliveries on account: Accounting Department ($250) and Athletic Ticket Office ($370).
(o)	30	Rohan withdrew cash for personal use, $150.

Transaction (a)

June 1   Rohan Macsen opened a bank account with a deposit of $2,000 for his business.

STEP 1   **Enter the date.** Since this is the first entry on the journal page, the year is entered on the first line of the Date column (in small print at the top of the line). The month and day are entered on the same line, below the year, in the Date column.

	GENERAL JOURNAL				PAGE 1
	DATE	DESCRIPTION	POST. REF.	DEBIT	CREDIT
1	20-- June 1				1
2					2

STEP 2 **Enter the debit.** Cash is entered on the first line at the extreme left of the Description column. The amount of the debit, $2,000, is entered on the same line in the Debit column. Since this is not a formal financial statement, dollar signs are not used.

In Chapter 3, we simply debited the T account.

Cash

(a) 2,000

	DATE		DESCRIPTION	POST. REF.	DEBIT	CREDIT	
			GENERAL JOURNAL			PAGE 1	
1	20-- June	1	Cash		2 0 0 0 00		1
2							2

STEP 3 **Enter the credit.** The title of the account to be credited, Rohan Macsen, Capital, is entered on the second line, **indented one-half inch from the left side of the Description column**. The amount of the credit, $2,000, is entered on the same line in the Credit column.

In Chapter 3, we simply credited the T account.

Rohan Macsen, Capital

(a) 2,000

	DATE		DESCRIPTION	POST. REF.	DEBIT	CREDIT	
			GENERAL JOURNAL			PAGE 1	
1	20-- June	1	Cash		2 0 0 0 00		1
2			Rohan Macsen, Capital			2 0 0 0 00	2

STEP 4 **Enter the explanation.** The explanation of the entry is entered on the next line, **indented an additional one-half inch.** The second line of the explanation, if needed, is also indented the same distance as the first.

	DATE		DESCRIPTION	POST. REF.	DEBIT	CREDIT	
			GENERAL JOURNAL			PAGE 1	
1	20-- June	1	Cash		2 0 0 0 00		1
2			Rohan Macsen, Capital			2 0 0 0 00	2
3			Owner's original investment in				3
4			delivery business				4

Enter the next transaction. To enter transaction (b), the purchase of a motor scooter for $1,200 cash, we skip a line and follow the same four steps. Note that the month and year do not need to be repeated. The day of the month must, however, be entered.

	DATE		DESCRIPTION	POST. REF.	DEBIT	CREDIT	
			GENERAL JOURNAL			PAGE 1	
1	20-- June	1	Cash		2 0 0 0 00		1
2			Rohan Macsen, Capital			2 0 0 0 00	2
3			Owner's original investment in				3
4			delivery business				4
5							5
6		3	Delivery Equipment		1 2 0 0 00		6
7			Cash			1 2 0 0 00	7
8			Purchased delivery equipment for cash				8

Skip a line

The journal entries for the month of June are shown in Figure 4-7. Note that the entries on June 25 and June 30 affect more than two accounts. Entries requiring more than one debit and/or one credit are called compound entries. The entry on June 25 has two credits. The credits are listed after the debit, indented and listed one under the other. The entry on June 30 has two debits. They are aligned with the left margin of the Description column and listed one under the other. In both cases, the debits equal the credits.

FIGURE 4-7 General Journal Entries

	DATE		DESCRIPTION	POST. REF.	DEBIT	CREDIT	
1	20-- June	1	Cash ← List debits first.		2 0 0 0 00		1
2			Rohan Macsen, Capital			2 0 0 0 00	2
3			Owner's original investment in ← Explanation is third and indented.				3
4			delivery business				4
5							5
6		3	Delivery Equipment		1 2 0 0 00		6
7			Cash			1 2 0 0 00	7
8			Purchased delivery equipment for cash				8
9							9
10		5	Delivery Equipment		9 0 0 00		10
11			Accounts Payable			9 0 0 00	11
12			Purchased delivery equipment on account				12
13			from Big Red Scooters				13
14							14
15		6	Accounts Payable		3 0 0 00		15
16			Cash			3 0 0 00	16
17			Made partial payment to Big Red Scooters				17
18							18
19		6	Cash		5 0 0 00		19
20			Delivery Fees			5 0 0 00	20
21			Received cash for delivery services				21
22							22
23		7	Rent Expense		2 0 0 00		23
24			Cash			2 0 0 00	24
25			Paid office rent for June				25
26							26
27		15	Phone Expense		5 0 00		27
28			Cash			5 0 00	28
29			Paid phone bill for June				29
30							30
31		15	Accounts Receivable		6 0 0 00		31
32			Delivery Fees			6 0 0 00	32
33			Deliveries made on account for Accounting				33
34			Department ($400) and School of Music ($200)				34
35							35

GENERAL JOURNAL PAGE 1

List credits second and indented.

Space to make entries easier to read. To prevent improper changes to entries, the extra spacing might not be used in practice.

(continued)

FIGURE 4-7   General Journal Entries (*concluded*)

	DATE		DESCRIPTION	POST. REF.	DEBIT	CREDIT	
			GENERAL JOURNAL			PAGE 2	
1	20-- June	16	Supplies		8 0 0 00		1
2			Cash			8 0 0 00	2
3			Purchased supplies for cash				3
4							4
5		18	Prepaid Insurance		2 0 0 0 00		5
6			Cash			2 0 0 0 00	6
7			Paid premium for eight-month				7
8			insurance policy				8
9							9
10		20	Cash		5 7 0 00		10
11			Accounts Receivable			5 7 0 00	11
12			Received cash on account from Accounting				12
13			Department ($400) and School of Music ($170)				13
14							14
15		25	Delivery Equipment		1 5 0 0 00		15
16			Accounts Payable			1 2 0 0 00	16
17			Cash			3 0 0 00	17
18			Purchased scooter with down payment;				18
19			balance on account with Big Red Scooters				19
20							20
21		27	Wages Expense		6 5 0 00		21
22			Cash			6 5 0 00	22
23			Paid employees				23
24							24
25		30	Cash		4 3 0 00		25
26			Accounts Receivable		6 2 0 00		26
27			Delivery Fees			1 0 5 0 00	27
28			Deliveries made for cash and on account to				28
29			Accounting Department ($250) and				29
30			Athletic Ticket Office ($370)				30
31							31
32		30	Rohan Macsen, Drawing		1 5 0 00		32
33			Cash			1 5 0 00	33
34			Owner's withdrawal				34

Annotations on figure: Line up credits → (lines 15–17); Compound entry; Debits = Credits. Line up debits → (lines 25–27); Compound entry; Debits = Credits.

Checkpoint ✓

Complete Checkpoint-2 on page 113 to test your basic understanding of LO4.

THE GENERAL LEDGER

LO5 Post to the general ledger and prepare a trial balance.

The journal provides a day-by-day record of business transactions. To determine the current balance of specific accounts, however, the information in the journal must be transferred to accounts similar to the T accounts illustrated in Chapter 3. This process is called posting.

LEARNING KEY

While the *journal* provides a day-by-day record of business transactions, the *ledger* provides a record of the transactions entered in each account.

A three-column account with just one column for the normal balance also may be used.

A complete set of all the accounts used by a business is known as the **general ledger**. The general ledger accumulates a complete record of the debits and credits made to each account as a result of entries made in the journal. The accounts are numbered and arranged in the same order as the chart of accounts. That is, accounts are numbered and grouped by classification: assets, liabilities, owner's equity, revenues, and expenses.

General Ledger Account

For purposes of illustration, the T account was introduced in Chapter 3. In practice, businesses are more likely to use a version of the account called the **general ledger account**. Figure 4-8 compares the cash T account from Chapter 3 for Rohan's Campus Delivery and a general ledger account summarizing the same cash transactions.

A four-column general ledger account contains columns for the debit or credit transaction and columns for the debit or credit running balance. In addition, there are columns for the date, description of the item, and posting reference.

The Item column is used to provide descriptions of special entries. For example, "Balance" is written in this column when the balance of an account is transferred to a new page. In addition, "Correcting," "Adjusting," "Closing," or "Reversing" may be written in this column when these types of entries are made. Correcting entries are described later in the chapter. Adjusting, closing, and reversing entries are illustrated in Chapters 5, 6, and 15, respectively.

The Posting Reference (Post. Ref.) column is used to indicate the journal page from which an entry was posted, or a check mark (✓) is inserted to indicate that no posting was required.

As shown in Figure 4-8, the primary advantage of the T account is that the debit and credit sides of the account are easier to identify. Thus, for demonstration purposes

FIGURE 4-8   Comparison of T Account and General Ledger Account

Cash

(a)	2,000	(b)	1,200
(e)	500	(d)	300
(k)	570	(f)	200
(n)	430	(g)	50
	3,500	(i)	80
		(j)	200
		(l)	300
		(m)	650
		(o)	150
Bal.	370		*3,130*

GENERAL LEDGER

ACCOUNT: Cash   ACCOUNT NO. 101

DATE	ITEM	POST. REF.	DEBIT	CREDIT	BALANCE DEBIT	BALANCE CREDIT
20-- June 1			2 0 0 0 00		2 0 0 0 00	
3				1 2 0 0 00	8 0 0 00	
6				3 0 0 00	5 0 0 00	
6			5 0 0 00		1 0 0 0 00	
7				2 0 0 00	8 0 0 00	
15				5 0 00	7 5 0 00	
16				8 0 00	6 7 0 00	
18				2 0 0 00	4 7 0 00	
20			5 7 0 00		1 0 4 0 00	
25				3 0 0 00	7 4 0 00	
27				6 5 0 00	9 0 00	
30			4 3 0 00		5 2 0 00	
30				1 5 0 00	3 7 0 00	

└── Transaction Amount ──┘ └── Running Balance ──┘

LEARNING KEY

Although similar to a T account, the general ledger account keeps a running balance.

LEARNING KEY

Posting is simply the process of copying the exact dates and dollar amounts from the journal to the correct ledger accounts.

and analyzing what happened, T accounts are very helpful. However, computing the balance of a T account is cumbersome. The primary advantage of the general ledger account is that it maintains a running balance.

Note that the heading for the general ledger account has the account title and an account number. The account number is taken from the chart of accounts and is used in the posting process.

Posting to the General Ledger

The process of copying the debits and credits from the journal to the ledger accounts is known as posting. All amounts entered in the journal must be posted to the general ledger accounts. Posting from the journal to the ledger is done daily or at frequent intervals.

To illustrate the posting process, the first journal entry for Rohan's Campus Delivery will be posted step by step. There are five steps in the process of posting each debit and credit. First, let's post the debit to Cash (Figure 4-9).

FIGURE 4-9 Posting a Debit

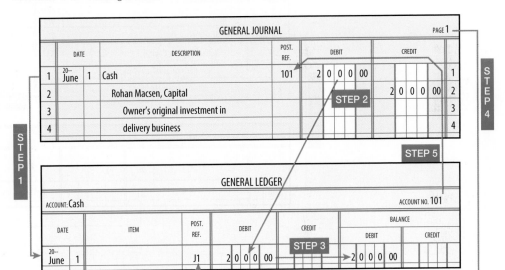

In the ledger account:

STEP 1 **Enter the date of the transaction in the Date column.** Enter the year, "20--," the month, "June," and the day, "1," in the Date column of the cash account.

STEP 2 **Enter the debit.** Copy the $2,000 debit to Cash in the journal to the Debit column of the ledger. Since this is not a formal financial statement, dollar signs are not used.

STEP 3 **Enter the balance of the account.** Enter the $2,000 balance in the Balance columns under Debit. (If the balance of the account is zero, draw a line through the Debit and Credit columns.)

STEP 4 **Enter the journal page in the Posting Reference column.** Enter "J1" in the Posting Reference column since the posting came from page 1 of the journal.

The Item column is left blank, except for special reasons such as indicating the beginning balance, adjusting, correcting, closing, or reversing entries.

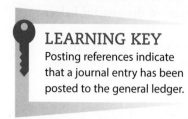

In the journal:

STEP 5 **Enter the ledger account number in the Posting Reference column.** Enter the account number for Cash, 101 (see chart of accounts in Figure 4-3 on page 88), in the Posting Reference column of the journal on the same line as the debit to Cash for $2,000.

Step 5 is the last step in the posting process. After this step is completed, the posting references will indicate which journal entries have been posted to the ledger accounts. This is very helpful, particularly if you are interrupted during the posting process. The information in the Posting Reference columns of the journal and ledger provides a link between the journal and ledger known as a cross-reference.

Now let's post the credit portion of the first entry (Figure 4-10).

FIGURE 4-10 Posting a Credit

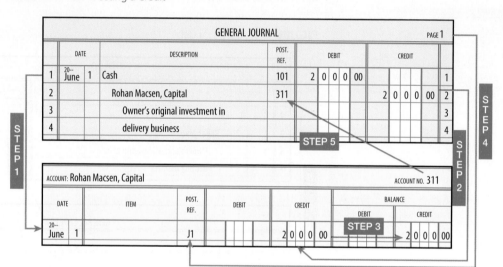

In the ledger account:

STEP 1 **Enter the date of the transaction in the Date column.** Enter the year, "20--," the month, "June," and the day, "1," in the Date column of the account Rohan Macsen, Capital.

STEP 2 **Enter the credit.** Copy the $2,000 credit to Rohan Macsen, Capital in the journal to the Credit column in the ledger.

STEP 3 **Enter the balance of the account.** Enter the $2,000 balance in the Balance columns under Credit. (If the balance of the account is zero, draw a line through the Debit and Credit columns.)

STEP 4 **Enter the journal page in the Posting Reference column.** Enter "J1" in the Posting Reference column since the posting came from page 1 of the journal.

The Item column is left blank, except for special reasons such as indicating the beginning balance, adjusting, correcting, closing, or reversing entries.

In the journal:

STEP 5   **Enter the ledger account number in the Posting Reference column.** Enter the account number for Rohan Macsen, Capital, 311, in the Posting Reference column. Again, this last step indicates that the credit has been posted to the general ledger.

After posting the journal entries for Rohan's Campus Delivery for the month of June, the general journal and general ledger should appear as illustrated in Figures 4-11 and 4-12 on pages 97–100. *Note that the Posting Reference column of the journal has been filled in because the entries have been posted.*

FIGURE 4-11   General Journal After Posting

	DATE		DESCRIPTION	POST. REF.	DEBIT					CREDIT					
1	20-- June	1	Cash	101	2	0	0	0	00						1
2			Rohan Macsen, Capital	311						2	0	0	0	00	2
3			Owner's original investment in												3
4			delivery business												4
5															5
6		3	Delivery Equipment	185	1	2	0	0	00						6
7			Cash	101						1	2	0	0	00	7
8			Purchased delivery equipment for cash												8
9															9
10		5	Delivery Equipment	185		9	0	0	00						10
11			Accounts Payable	202							9	0	0	00	11
12			Purchased delivery equipment on account												12
13			from Big Red Scooters												13
14															14
15		6	Accounts Payable	202		3	0	0	00						15
16			Cash	101							3	0	0	00	16
17			Made partial payment to Big Red Scooters												17
18															18
19		6	Cash	101		5	0	0	00						19
20			Delivery Fees	401							5	0	0	00	20
21			Received cash for delivery services												21
22															22
23		7	Rent Expense	521		2	0	0	00						23
24			Cash	101							2	0	0	00	24
25			Paid office rent for June												25
26															26
27		15	Phone Expense	525			5	0	00						27
28			Cash	101								5	0	00	28
29			Paid phone bill for June												29
30															30
31		15	Accounts Receivable	122		6	0	0	00						31
32			Delivery Fees	401							6	0	0	00	32
33			Deliveries made on account for Accounting												33
34			Department ($400) and School of Music ($200)												34
35															35

GENERAL JOURNAL   PAGE 1

FIGURE 4-11 General Journal After Posting *(concluded)*

	DATE		DESCRIPTION	POST. REF.	DEBIT					CREDIT					
1	20— June	16	Supplies	141		8	0	00				8	0	00	1
2			Cash	101								8	0	00	2
3			Purchased supplies for cash												3
4															4
5		18	Prepaid Insurance	145	2	0	0	00							5
6			Cash	101						2	0	0	00		6
7			Paid premium for eight-month												7
8			insurance policy												8
9															9
10		20	Cash	101	5	7	0	00							10
11			Accounts Receivable	122						5	7	0	00		11
12			Received cash on account from Accounting												12
13			Department ($400) and School of Music ($170)												13
14															14
15		25	Delivery Equipment	185	1	5	0	0	00						15
16			Accounts Payable	202						1	2	0	0	00	16
17			Cash	101							3	0	0	00	17
18			Purchased scooter with down payment;												18
19			balance on account with Big Red Scooters												19
20															20
21		27	Wages Expense	511	6	5	0	00							21
22			Cash	101							6	5	0	00	22
23			Paid employees												23
24															24
25		30	Cash	101	4	3	0	00							25
26			Accounts Receivable	122	6	2	0	00							26
27			Delivery Fees	401						1	0	5	0	00	27
28			Deliveries made for cash and on account to												28
29			Accounting Department ($250) and												29
30			Athletic Ticket Office ($370)												30
31															31
32		30	Rohan Macsen, Drawing	312	1	5	0	00							32
33			Cash	101							1	5	0	00	33
34			Owner's withdrawal												34
35															35

GENERAL JOURNAL — PAGE 2

FIGURE 4-12 General Ledger After Posting

For asset, expense, and drawing accounts, a running balance is maintained by adding the debit or subtracting the credit from the previous balance.

GENERAL LEDGER

ACCOUNT: Cash   ACCOUNT NO. 101

DATE		ITEM	POST. REF.	DEBIT	CREDIT	BALANCE DEBIT	BALANCE CREDIT
20-- June	1		J1	2 0 0 0 00		2 0 0 0 00	
	3		J1		1 2 0 0 00	8 0 0 00	
	6		J1		3 0 0 00	5 0 0 00	
	6		J1	5 0 0 00		1 0 0 0 00	
	7		J1		2 0 0 00	8 0 0 00	
	15		J1		5 0 00	7 5 0 00	
	16		J2		8 0 00	6 7 0 00	
	18		J2		2 0 0 00	4 7 0 00	
	20		J2	5 7 0 00		1 0 4 0 00	
	25		J2		3 0 0 00	7 4 0 00	
	27		J2		6 5 0 00	9 0 00	
	30		J2	4 3 0 00		5 2 0 00	
	30		J2		1 5 0 00	3 7 0 00	

ACCOUNT: Accounts Receivable   ACCOUNT NO. 122

DATE		ITEM	POST. REF.	DEBIT	CREDIT	BALANCE DEBIT	BALANCE CREDIT
20-- June	15		J1	6 0 0 00		6 0 0 00	
	20		J2		5 7 0 00	3 0 00	
	30		J2	6 2 0 00		6 5 0 00	

ACCOUNT: Supplies   ACCOUNT NO. 141

DATE		ITEM	POST. REF.	DEBIT	CREDIT	BALANCE DEBIT	BALANCE CREDIT
20-- June	16		J2	8 0 00		8 0 00	

ACCOUNT: Prepaid Insurance   ACCOUNT NO. 145

DATE		ITEM	POST. REF.	DEBIT	CREDIT	BALANCE DEBIT	BALANCE CREDIT
20-- June	18		J2	2 0 0 00		2 0 0 00	

ACCOUNT: Delivery Equipment   ACCOUNT NO. 185

DATE		ITEM	POST. REF.	DEBIT	CREDIT	BALANCE DEBIT	BALANCE CREDIT
20-- June	3		J1	1 2 0 0 00		1 2 0 0 00	
	5		J1	9 0 0 00		2 1 0 0 00	
	25		J2	1 5 0 0 00		3 6 0 0 00	

FIGURE 4-12 General Ledger After Posting *(concluded)*

ACCOUNT: Accounts Payable — ACCOUNT NO. 202

DATE		ITEM	POST. REF.	DEBIT	CREDIT	BALANCE DEBIT	BALANCE CREDIT
20-- June	5		J1		9 0 0 00		9 0 0 00
	6		J1	3 0 0 00			6 0 0 00
	25		J2		1 2 0 0 00		1 8 0 0 00

ACCOUNT: Rohan Macsen, Capital — ACCOUNT NO. 311

DATE		ITEM	POST. REF.	DEBIT	CREDIT	BALANCE DEBIT	BALANCE CREDIT
20-- June	1		J1		2 0 0 0 00		2 0 0 0 00

ACCOUNT: Rohan Macsen, Drawing — ACCOUNT NO. 312

DATE		ITEM	POST. REF.	DEBIT	CREDIT	BALANCE DEBIT	BALANCE CREDIT
20-- June	30		J2	1 5 0 00		1 5 0 00	

ACCOUNT: Delivery Fees — ACCOUNT NO. 401

DATE		ITEM	POST. REF.	DEBIT	CREDIT	BALANCE DEBIT	BALANCE CREDIT
20-- June	6		J1		5 0 0 00		5 0 0 00
	15		J1		6 0 0 00		1 1 0 0 00
	30		J2		1 0 5 0 00		2 1 5 0 00

ACCOUNT: Wages Expense — ACCOUNT NO. 511

DATE		ITEM	POST. REF.	DEBIT	CREDIT	BALANCE DEBIT	BALANCE CREDIT
20-- June	27		J2	6 5 0 00		6 5 0 00	

ACCOUNT: Rent Expense — ACCOUNT NO. 521

DATE		ITEM	POST. REF.	DEBIT	CREDIT	BALANCE DEBIT	BALANCE CREDIT
20-- June	7		J1	2 0 0 00		2 0 0 00	

ACCOUNT: Phone Expense — ACCOUNT NO. 525

DATE		ITEM	POST. REF.	DEBIT	CREDIT	BALANCE DEBIT	BALANCE CREDIT
20-- June	15		J1	5 0 00		5 0 00	

For liability, revenue, and capital accounts, a running balance is maintained by adding the credit or subtracting the debit from the previous balance.

The Trial Balance

In Chapter 3, a trial balance was used to prove that the totals of the debit and credit balances in the T accounts were equal. In this chapter, a trial balance is used to prove the equality of the debits and credits in the ledger accounts. A trial balance can be prepared daily, weekly, monthly, or whenever desired. Before preparing a trial balance, all transactions should be journalized and posted so that the effect of all transactions will be reflected in the ledger accounts.

The trial balance for Rohan's Campus Delivery shown in Figure 4-13 was prepared from the balances in the general ledger in Figure 4-12. The accounts are listed in the order used in the chart of accounts. This order is also often used when preparing financial statements. In Chapter 2, we pointed out that many firms list expenses from highest to lowest amounts. Some firms list expenses according to the chart of accounts, which is the method we will follow.

LEARNING KEY
The chart of accounts determines the order for listing accounts in the general ledger and trial balance. This order may also be used when preparing financial statements.

FIGURE 4-13   Trial Balance

ACCOUNT TITLE	ACCOUNT NO.	DEBIT BALANCE	CREDIT BALANCE
Rohan's Campus Delivery			
Trial Balance			
June 30, 20 - -			
Cash	101	3 7 0 00	
Accounts Receivable	122	6 5 0 00	
Supplies	141	8 0 00	
Prepaid Insurance	145	2 0 0 00	
Delivery Equipment	185	3 6 0 0 00	
Accounts Payable	202		1 8 0 0 00
Rohan Macsen, Capital	311		2 0 0 0 00
Rohan Macsen, Drawing	312	1 5 0 00	
Delivery Fees	401		2 1 5 0 00
Wages Expense	511	6 5 0 00	
Rent Expense	521	2 0 0 00	
Phone Expense	525	5 0 00	
		5 9 5 0 00	5 9 5 0 00

Checkpoint ✓

Complete Checkpoint-3 on page 113 to test your basic understanding of LO5.

Even though the trial balance indicates that the ledger is in balance, the ledger can still contain errors. For example, if a journal entry was made debiting or crediting the wrong accounts, or if an item was posted to the wrong account, the ledger will still be in balance. It is important, therefore, to be very careful in preparing the journal entries and in posting them to the ledger accounts.

FINDING AND CORRECTING ERRORS IN THE TRIAL BALANCE

LO6 Explain how to find and correct errors.

Tips are available to help if your trial balance has an error. Figure 4-14 offers hints for finding the error when your trial balance does not balance.

FIGURE 4-14   Tips for Finding Errors in the Trial Balance

1. Double check your addition. Review balances to see if they are too large or small, relative to other accounts, or entered in the wrong column.

2. Find the difference between the debits and the credits.

   a. If the difference is equal to the amount of a specific transaction, perhaps you forgot to post the debit or credit portion of this transaction.

   b. Divide the difference by 2. If the difference is evenly divisible by 2, you may have posted two debits or two credits for a transaction. If a debit was posted as a credit, it would mean that one transaction had two credits and no debits. The difference between the total debits and credits would be twice the amount of the debit that was posted as a credit.

   c. Divide the difference by 9. If the difference is evenly divisible by 9, you may have committed a **slide error** or a **transposition error**. A slide occurs when debit or credit amounts "slide" a digit or two to the left or right when entered. For example, if *$250* was entered as *$25*:

$250	−	$25	=	$225	
$225	÷	9	=	$25	

   The difference is evenly divisible by 9.

   A transposition occurs when two digits are reversed. For example, if *$250* was entered as *$520*:

$520	−	$250	=	$270	
$270	÷	9	=	$30	

   Again, the difference is evenly divisible by 9.

If the tips in Figure 4-14 don't work, you must retrace your steps through the accounting process. Double check your addition for the ledger accounts. Also trace all postings. Be patient as you search for your error. Use this process as an opportunity to reinforce your understanding of the flow of information through the accounting system. Much can be learned while looking for an error.

Once you have found an error, there are two methods of making the correction. Although you may want to erase when correcting your homework, this is not acceptable in practice. An erasure may suggest that you are trying to hide something. You should use the ruling method or make a correcting entry instead.

Ruling Method

The ruling method should be used to correct two types of errors.

1. When an incorrect journal entry has been made, but not yet posted.

2. When a proper entry has been made but posted to the wrong account or for the wrong amount.

When using the ruling method, draw a single line through the incorrect account title or amount and write the correct information directly above the line. Corrections should be initialed by someone authorized to make such changes. This is done so the source and reason for the correction can be traced. This type of correction may be made in the journal or ledger accounts, as shown in Figure 4-15.

FIGURE 4-15   Ruling Method of Making a Correction

	DATE		DESCRIPTION	POST. REF.	DEBIT	CREDIT	
			GENERAL JOURNAL			PAGE 2	
1	20-- Sept.	17	~~Wages Expense MP~~ ~~Entertainment Expense~~		6 5 0 00		1
2			Cash			6 5 0 00	2
3			Paid employees				3
4							4
5		18	Prepaid Insurance		MP 2 0 0 00 ~~2 0 00~~	MP 2 0 0 00 ~~2 0 00~~	5
6			Cash				6
7			Paid premium for eight-month				7
8			insurance policy				8
9							9

Slide

	DATE	ITEM	POST. REF.	DEBIT	CREDIT	BALANCE DEBIT	BALANCE CREDIT
		GENERAL LEDGER					
ACCOUNT: Accounts Payable							ACCOUNT NO. 202
20-- Sept.	8		J1		7 0 0 00		7 0 0 00
	15		J1	2 0 0 00			5 0 0 00
	25		J2	~~1 2 0 0 00~~ MP ~~2 1 0 0 00~~			MP 1 7 0 0 00 ~~2 6 0 0 00~~

Transposition

Correcting Entry Method

If an incorrect entry has been journalized and posted to the wrong account, a **correcting entry** should be made. For example, assume that a $400 payment for Rent Expense was incorrectly debited to Repair Expense and correctly credited to Cash. This requires a correcting entry and explanation as shown in Figure 4-16. Figure 4-17 shows the effects of the correcting entry on the ledger accounts. Generally, "Correcting" is written in the Item column of the general ledger account.

When using a computerized accounting system, the journal entries are automatically posted to the ledger. To correct an error, the correcting entry method should be used.

FIGURE 4-16   Correcting Entry Method

	DATE		DESCRIPTION	POST. REF.	DEBIT	CREDIT	
			GENERAL JOURNAL			PAGE 6	
1	20-- Sept.	25	Rent Expense	521	4 0 0 00		1
2			Repair Expense	537		4 0 0 00	2
3			To correct error in which payment for rent				3
4			was debited to Repair Expense				4
5							5

FIGURE 4-17   Effects of Correcting Entry on Ledger Accounts

GENERAL LEDGER											
ACCOUNT: Rent Expense										ACCOUNT NO. 521	
DATE		ITEM	POST. REF.	DEBIT		CREDIT		BALANCE			
								DEBIT		CREDIT	
20-- Sept.	25	Correcting	J6	4 0 0 00				4 0 0 00			

GENERAL LEDGER											
ACCOUNT: Repair Expense										ACCOUNT NO. 537	
DATE		ITEM	POST. REF.	DEBIT		CREDIT		BALANCE			
								DEBIT		CREDIT	
20-- Sept.	10		J5	5 0 00				5 0 00			
	15		J5	4 0 0 00				4 5 0 00			
	25	Correcting	J6			4 0 0 00		5 0 00			

Checkpoint ✓

Complete Check-
point-4 on page 113
to test your basic
understanding of LO6

Self-Study

LEARNING OBJECTIVES   Key Points to Remember

LO1 Describe the flow of data from source documents to the trial balance.

The flow of data from the source documents to the trial balance is as follows:

1. Analyze business transactions.
2. Journalize transactions in the general journal.
3. Post journal entries to the general ledger.
4. Prepare a trial balance.

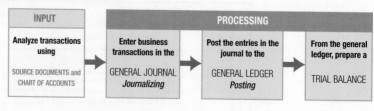

INPUT	PROCESSING		
Analyze transactions using	**Enter business transactions in the**	**Post the entries in the journal to the**	**From the general ledger, prepare a**
SOURCE DOCUMENTS and CHART OF ACCOUNTS	GENERAL JOURNAL *Journalizing*	GENERAL LEDGER *Posting*	TRIAL BALANCE

(continued)

LEARNING OBJECTIVES	Key Points to Remember
LO2 Describe and explain the purpose of source documents.	Source documents trigger the analysis of business transactions and the entries into the accounting system.
LO3 Describe the chart of accounts as a means of classifying financial information.	The chart of accounts includes the account titles in numerical order for all assets, liabilities, owner's equity, revenues, and expenses. The chart of accounts is used in classifying information about transactions.
LO4 Journalize transactions.	A journal provides a day-by-day listing of transactions. The journal shows the date, titles of the accounts to be debited or credited, and the amounts of the debits and credits. The steps in the journalizing process are as follows: 1. Enter the date. 2. Enter the debit. Accounts to be debited are entered first. 3. Enter the credit. Accounts to be credited are entered after the debits and are indented one-half inch. 4. Enter the explanation. A brief explanation of the transaction should be entered in the description column on the line following the last credit. The explanation should be indented an additional one-half inch.
LO5 Post to the general ledger and prepare a trial balance.	The general ledger is a complete set of all accounts used by the business. The steps in posting from the general journal to the general ledger are as follows: In the general ledger: 1. Enter the date of each transaction. 2. Enter the amount of each debit or credit in the Debit or Credit column. 3. Enter the new balance. 4. Enter the journal page number from which each transaction is posted in the Posting Reference column. In the journal: 5. Enter the account number to which each transaction is posted in the Posting Reference column. The trial balance provides a check to make sure the total of all debit balances in the ledger accounts equals the total of all credit balances in the ledger accounts.
LO6 Explain how to find and correct errors.	Errors may be found by verifying your addition, by dividing the difference between the debits and credits by 2 or 9, and by retracing your steps through the accounting process. Use the ruling method or the correcting entry method to correct the error.

DEMONSTRATION PROBLEM

George Fielding is a financial planning consultant. He provides budgeting, estate planning, tax planning, and investing advice for professional golfers. He developed the following chart of accounts for his business:

Assets		Revenues	
101	Cash	401	Professional Fees
142	Office Supplies		
		Expenses	
Liabilities		511	Wages Expense
202	Accounts Payable	521	Rent Expense
		525	Phone Expense
Owner's Equity		533	Utilities Expense
311	George Fielding, Capital	534	Charitable Contributions Expense
312	George Fielding, Drawing	538	Automobile Expense

The following transactions took place during the month of December of the current year:

Dec. 1   Fielding invested cash to start the business, $20,000.

    3   Paid Bollhorst Real Estate for December office rent, $1,000.

    4   Received cash from Aaron Patton, a client, for services, $2,500.

    6   Paid T. Z. Anderson Electric for December heating and light, $75.

    7   Received cash from Andrew Conder, a client, for services, $2,000.

   12   Paid Fichter's Super Service for gasoline and oil purchases for the company car, $60.

   14   Paid Hillenburg Staffing for temporary secretarial services during the past two weeks, $600.

   17   Bought office supplies from Bowers Office Supply on account, $280.

   20   Paid Mitchell Phone Co. for business calls during the past month, $100.

   21   Fielding withdrew cash for personal use, $1,100.

   24   Made donation to the National Multiple Sclerosis Society, $100.

   27   Received cash from Billy Walters, a client, for services, $2,000.

   28   Paid Hillenburg Staffing for temporary secretarial services during the past two weeks, $600.

   29   Made payment on account to Bowers Office Supply, $100.

REQUIRED

1. Record the preceding transactions in a general journal.

2. Post the entries to the general ledger.

3. Prepare a trial balance.

4. Prepare an income statement, statement of owner's equity, and balance sheet for the month of December.

(continued)

Solution 1, 2.

	DATE		DESCRIPTION	POST. REF.	DEBIT					CREDIT					
	GENERAL JOURNAL													PAGE 1	
1	20-- Dec.	1	Cash	101	20	0	0	0	00						1
2			George Fielding, Capital	311						20	0	0	0	00	2
3			Owner's original investment in												3
4			consulting business												4
5															5
6		3	Rent Expense	521	1	0	0	0	00						6
7			Cash	101						1	0	0	0	00	7
8			Paid rent for December												8
9															9
10		4	Cash	101	2	5	0	0	00						10
11			Professional Fees	401						2	5	0	0	00	11
12			Received cash for services rendered												12
13															13
14		6	Utilities Expense	533			7	5	00						14
15			Cash	101								7	5	00	15
16			Paid utilities												16
17															17
18		7	Cash	101	2	0	0	0	00						18
19			Professional Fees	401						2	0	0	0	00	19
20			Received cash for services rendered												20
21															21
22		12	Automobile Expense	538			6	0	00						22
23			Cash	101								6	0	00	23
24			Paid for gas and oil												24
25															25
26		14	Wages Expense	511		6	0	0	00						26
27			Cash	101							6	0	0	00	27
28			Paid temporary secretaries												28
29															29
30		17	Office Supplies	142		2	8	0	00						30
31			Accounts Payable	202							2	8	0	00	31
32			Purchased office supplies on account from												32
33			Bowers Office Supply												33
34															34
35															35

	DATE		DESCRIPTION	POST. REF.	DEBIT					CREDIT					
			GENERAL JOURNAL											PAGE 2	
1	20-- Dec.	20	Phone Expense	525		1	0	0	00						1
2			Cash	101							1	0	0	00	2
3			Paid phone bill												3
4															4
5		21	George Fielding, Drawing	312	1	1	0	0	00						5
6			Cash	101						1	1	0	0	00	6
7			Owner's withdrawal												7
8															8
9		24	Charitable Contributions Expense	534		1	0	0	00						9
10			Cash	101							1	0	0	00	10
11			Contribution to National Multiple												11
12			Sclerosis Society												12
13															13
14		27	Cash	101	2	0	0	0	00						14
15			Professional Fees	401						2	0	0	0	00	15
16			Received cash for services rendered												16
17															17
18		28	Wages Expense	511		6	0	0	00						18
19			Cash	101							6	0	0	00	19
20			Paid temporary secretaries												20
21															21
22		29	Accounts Payable	202		1	0	0	00						22
23			Cash	101							1	0	0	00	23
24			Payment on account to Bowers Office Supply												24

2.

GENERAL LEDGER

ACCOUNT: Cash   ACCOUNT NO. 101

DATE		ITEM	POST. REF.	DEBIT						CREDIT					BALANCE DEBIT					BALANCE CREDIT				
20-- Dec.	1		J1	20	0	0	0	00							20	0	0	0	00					
	3		J1							1	0	0	0	00	19	0	0	0	00					
	4		J1	2	5	0	0	00							21	5	0	0	00					
	6		J1								7	5	00		21	4	2	5	00					
	7		J1	2	0	0	0	00							23	4	2	5	00					
	12		J1								6	0	00		23	3	6	5	00					
	14		J1							6	0	0	00		22	7	6	5	00					
	20		J2							1	0	0	00		22	6	6	5	00					
	21		J2							1	1	0	0	00	21	5	6	5	00					
	24		J2							1	0	0	00		21	4	6	5	00					
	27		J2	2	0	0	0	00							23	4	6	5	00					
	28		J2							6	0	0	00		22	8	6	5	00					
	29		J2							1	0	0	00		22	7	6	5	00					

(continued)

ACCOUNT: Office Supplies   ACCOUNT NO. 142

DATE		ITEM	POST. REF.	DEBIT	CREDIT	BALANCE	
						DEBIT	CREDIT
20-- Dec.	17		J1	2 8 0 00		2 8 0 00	

ACCOUNT: Accounts Payable   ACCOUNT NO. 202

DATE		ITEM	POST. REF.	DEBIT	CREDIT	BALANCE	
						DEBIT	CREDIT
20-- Dec.	17		J1		2 8 0 00		2 8 0 00
	29		J2	1 0 0 00			1 8 0 00

ACCOUNT: George Fielding, Capital   ACCOUNT NO. 311

DATE		ITEM	POST. REF.	DEBIT	CREDIT	BALANCE	
						DEBIT	CREDIT
20-- Dec.	1		J1		20 0 0 0 00		20 0 0 0 00

ACCOUNT: George Fielding, Drawing   ACCOUNT NO. 312

DATE		ITEM	POST. REF.	DEBIT	CREDIT	BALANCE	
						DEBIT	CREDIT
20-- Dec.	21		J2	1 1 0 0 00		1 1 0 0 00	

ACCOUNT: Professional Fees   ACCOUNT NO. 401

DATE		ITEM	POST. REF.	DEBIT	CREDIT	BALANCE	
						DEBIT	CREDIT
20-- Dec.	4		J1		2 5 0 0 00		2 5 0 0 00
	7		J1		2 0 0 0 00		4 5 0 0 00
	27		J2		2 0 0 0 00		6 5 0 0 00

ACCOUNT: Wages Expense   ACCOUNT NO. 511

DATE		ITEM	POST. REF.	DEBIT	CREDIT	BALANCE	
						DEBIT	CREDIT
20-- Dec.	14		J1	6 0 0 00		6 0 0 00	
	28		J2	6 0 0 00		1 2 0 0 00	

ACCOUNT: Rent Expense   ACCOUNT NO. 521

DATE		ITEM	POST. REF.	DEBIT	CREDIT	BALANCE	
						DEBIT	CREDIT
20-- Dec.	3		J1	1 0 0 0 00		1 0 0 0 00	

ACCOUNT: Phone Expense   ACCOUNT NO. 525

DATE	ITEM	POST. REF.	DEBIT	CREDIT	BALANCE DEBIT	BALANCE CREDIT
20-- Dec. 20		J2	1 0 0 00		1 0 0 00	

ACCOUNT: Utilities Expense   ACCOUNT NO. 533

DATE	ITEM	POST. REF.	DEBIT	CREDIT	BALANCE DEBIT	BALANCE CREDIT
20-- Dec. 6		J1	7 5 00		7 5 00	

ACCOUNT: Charitable Contributions Expense   ACCOUNT NO. 534

DATE	ITEM	POST. REF.	DEBIT	CREDIT	BALANCE DEBIT	BALANCE CREDIT
20-- Dec. 24		J2	1 0 0 00		1 0 0 00	

ACCOUNT: Automobile Expense   ACCOUNT NO. 538

DATE	ITEM	POST. REF.	DEBIT	CREDIT	BALANCE DEBIT	BALANCE CREDIT
20-- Dec. 12		J1	6 0 00		6 0 00	

3.

George Fielding, Financial Planning Consultant Trial Balance December 31, 20 --			
ACCOUNT TITLE	ACCOUNT NO.	DEBIT BALANCE	CREDIT BALANCE
Cash	101	22 7 6 5 00	
Office Supplies	142	2 8 0 00	
Accounts Payable	202		1 8 0 00
George Fielding, Capital	311		20 0 0 0 00
George Fielding, Drawing	312	1 1 0 0 00	
Professional Fees	401		6 5 0 0 00
Wages Expense	511	1 2 0 0 00	
Rent Expense	521	1 0 0 0 00	
Phone Expense	525	1 0 0 00	
Utilities Expense	533	7 5 00	
Charitable Contributions Expense	534	1 0 0 00	
Automobile Expense	538	6 0 00	
		26 6 8 0 00	26 6 8 0 00

(continued)

4.

George Fielding, Financial Planning Consultant Income Statement For Month Ended December 31, 20 --		
Revenue:		
Professional fees		$6,500
Expenses:		
Wages expense	$1,200	
Rent expense	1,000	
Phone expense	100	
Utilities expense	75	
Charitable contributions expense	100	
Automobile expense	60	
Total expenses		2,535
Net income		$3,965

George Fielding, Financial Planning Consultant Statement of Owner's Equity For Month Ended December 31, 20 --		
George Fielding, capital, December 1, 20 --		$ —
Investments during December		20,000
Total investment		$20,000
Net income for December	$3,965	
Less withdrawals for December	1,100	
Increase in capital		2,865
George Fielding, Capital, December 31, 20 --		$22,865

George Fielding, Financial Planning Consultant Balance Sheet December 31, 20 --			
Assets		Liabilities	
Cash	$22,765	Accounts payable	$ 180
Office Supplies	280	Owner's equity	
		George Fielding, capital	22,865
Total assets	$23,045	Total liabilities and owner's equity	$23,045

KEY TERMS

book of original entry (89)   The journal or the first formal accounting record of a transaction.

chart of accounts (88)   A list of all accounts used by a business.

compound entry (92)   A general journal entry that affects more than two accounts.

correcting entry (103)   An entry to correct an incorrect entry that has been journalized and posted to the wrong account.

cross-reference (96)   The information in the Posting Reference columns of the journal and ledger that provides a link between the journal and ledger.

general ledger (94)   A complete set of all the accounts used by a business. The general ledger accumulates a complete record of the debits and credits made to each account as a result of entries made in the journal.

general ledger account (94)   An account with columns for the debit or credit transaction and columns for the debit or credit running balance.

journal (89)   A day-by-day listing of the transactions of a business.

journalizing (89)   Entering the transactions in a journal.

posting (95)   Copying the debits and credits from the journal to the ledger accounts.

ruling method (102)   A method of correcting an entry in which a line is drawn through the error and the correct information is placed above it.

slide error (102)   An error that occurs when debit or credit amounts "slide" a digit or two to the left or right.

source document (86)   Any document that provides information about a business transaction.

transposition error (102)   An error that occurs when two digits are reversed.

trial balance (101)   A list used to prove that the totals of the debit and credit balances in the ledger accounts are equal.

two-column general journal (89)   A journal with only two amount columns, one for debit amounts and one for credit amounts.

SELF-STUDY TEST QUESTIONS

True/False

1. **LO2**   Source documents serve as historical evidence of business transactions.

2. **LO3**   The chart of accounts lists capital accounts first, followed by liabilities, assets, expenses, and revenue.

3. **LO4**   No entries are made in the Posting Reference column at the time of journalizing.

4. **LO4**   When entering the credit item in a general journal, it should be listed after all debits and indented.

5. **LO6**   When an incorrect entry has been journalized and posted to the wrong account, a correcting entry should be made.

Multiple Choice

1. **LO2**   Which of the following is not a source document?

   (a) Check stub
   (b) Cash register tape
   (c) Journal entry
   (d) Purchase invoice

2. **LO3**   A revenue account will begin with the number _____ in the chart of accounts.

   (a) 1   (c) 3
   (b) 2   (d) 4

3. **LO4**   To purchase an asset such as office equipment on account, you would credit which account?

    (a) Cash
    (b) Accounts Receivable

    (c) Accounts Payable
    (d) Capital

4. **LO4**   When fees are earned and the customer promises to pay later, which account is debited?

    (a) Cash
    (b) Accounts Receivable

    (c) Accounts Payable
    (d) Capital

5. **LO6**   When the correct numbers are used but are in the wrong order, the error is called a

    (a) transposition.
    (b) slide.

    (c) ruling.
    (d) correcting entry.

Checkpoint Exercises

1. **LO2**   A check stub serves as a source document for what kind of transaction?

2. **LO4**   Indicate the information that would be entered for each of the lettered items in the general journal provided below.

		GENERAL JOURNAL					PAGE
	DATE	DESCRIPTION	POST. REF.	DEBIT		CREDIT	
1	A B	C D	G	H			1
2		E	J			I	2
3		F					3
4							4
5							5

3. **LO5**   Indicate the information that would be entered for each of the lettered items in the general ledger account provided below.

		GENERAL LEDGER						
ACCOUNT: A						ACCOUNT NO. B		
						BALANCE		
DATE	ITEM	POST. REF.	DEBIT	CREDIT		DEBIT	CREDIT	
C D	E	F	G	H	I	J	K	

4. **LO6**   Dunkin Company made the following entry for the payment of $500 cash for rent expense:

    Rent Expense   500
        Rent Payable   500

Prepare a correcting entry.

The answers to the Self-Study Test Questions are at the end of the chapter (pages 128–129).

Applying Your Knowledge

REVIEW QUESTIONS

LO1   1. Trace the flow of accounting information through the accounting system.

LO2   2. Name a source document that provides information about each of the following types of business transactions:

        a. Cash payment
        b. Cash receipt
        c. Sale of goods or services
        d. Purchase of goods or services

LO3   3. Explain the purpose of a chart of accounts.

LO3   4. Name the five types of financial statement classifications for which it is ordinarily desirable to keep separate accounts.

LO4   5. Where is the first formal accounting record of a business transaction usually made?

LO4   6. Describe the four steps required to journalize a business transaction in a general journal.

LO5   7. In what order are the accounts customarily placed in the ledger?

LO5   8. Explain the primary advantage of a general ledger account.

LO5   9. Explain the five steps required when posting the journal to the ledger.

LO5   10. What information is entered in the Posting Reference column of the journal as an amount is posted to the proper account in the ledger?

LO6   11. Explain why the ledger can still contain errors even though the trial balance is in balance. Give examples of two such types of errors.

LO6   12. What is a slide error?

LO6   13. What is a transposition error?

LO6   14. What is the ruling method of correcting an error?

LO6   15. What is the correcting entry method?

SERIES A EXERCISES

E 4-1A   (LO2)

SOURCE DOCUMENTS Source documents trigger the analysis of events requiring an accounting entry. Match the following source documents with the type of information they provide.

1. Check stubs or check register
2. Purchase invoice from suppliers (vendors)
3. Sales tickets or invoices to customers
4. Receipts or cash register tapes

a. A good or service has been sold.
b. Cash has been received by the business.
c. Cash has been paid by the business.
d. Goods or services have been purchased by the business.

E 4-2A   (LO4)

SHOW
ME HOW

GENERAL JOURNAL ENTRIES For each of the following transactions, list the account to be debited and the account to be credited in the general journal.

1. Invested cash in the business, $5,000.
2. Paid office rent, $500.
3. Purchased office supplies on account, $300.
4. Received cash for services rendered (fees), $400.
5. Paid cash on account, $50.
6. Rendered services on account, $300.
7. Received cash for an amount owed by a customer, $100.

E 4-3A   (LO5)

✓ Final Cash bal.: $4,950

SHOW
ME HOW

GENERAL LEDGER ACCOUNTS Set up T accounts for each of the general ledger accounts needed for Exercise 4-2A and post debits and credits to the accounts. Foot the accounts and enter the balances. Prove that total debits equal total credits.

E 4-4A   (LO4)

SHOW
ME HOW

GENERAL JOURNAL ENTRIES Diane Bernick has opened Bernick's Consulting. Journalize the following transactions that occurred during January of the current year. Use the following journal pages: January 1–10, page 1, and January 11–29, page 2. Use the following chart of accounts:

Chart of Accounts

Assets
101   Cash
142   Office Supplies
181   Office Equipment

Liabilities
202   Accounts Payable

Owner's Equity
311   Diane Bernick, Capital
312   Diane Bernick, Drawing

Revenues
401   Consulting Fees

Expenses
511   Wages Expense
521   Rent Expense
525   Phone Expense
533   Utilities Expense
549   Miscellaneous Expense

Jan. 1   Bernick invested cash in the business, $12,000.
2   Paid office rent, $750.
3   Purchased office equipment on account, $1,300.
5   Received cash for services rendered, $950.
8   Paid phone bill, $85.
10   Paid for a magazine subscription (miscellaneous expense), $20.
11   Purchased office supplies on account, $250.
15   Made a payment on account (see Jan. 3 transaction), $200.
18   Paid part-time employee, $600.
21   Received cash for services rendered, $800.
25   Paid utilities bill, $105.
27   Bernick withdrew cash for personal use, $400.
29   Paid part-time employee, $600.

E 4-5A   (LO5)

✓ Final Cash bal.: $10,990

✓ Trial bal. total debits:
   $15,100

SHOW
ME HOW

GENERAL LEDGER ACCOUNTS; TRIAL BALANCE Set up general ledger accounts using the chart of accounts provided in Exercise 4-4A. Post the transactions from Exercise 4-4A to the general ledger accounts and prepare a trial balance.

E 4-6A   (LO5)

✓ Total assets, Jan. 31: $12,540

FINANCIAL STATEMENTS From the information in Exercises 4-4A and 4-5A, prepare an income statement, a statement of owner's equity, and a balance sheet.

E 4-7A   (LO5)

✓ Total assets, July 31: $7,100

FINANCIAL STATEMENTS From the following trial balance taken after one month of operation, prepare an income statement, a statement of owner's equity, and a balance sheet.

					TJ's Paint Service							
					Trial Balance							
					July 31, 20 - -							

ACCOUNT TITLE	ACCOUNT NO.	DEBIT BALANCE	CREDIT BALANCE
Cash	101	4 3 0 0 00	
Accounts Receivable	122	1 1 0 0 00	
Supplies	141	8 0 0 00	
Paint Equipment	183	9 0 0 00	
Accounts Payable	202		2 1 5 0 00
TJ Ulza, Capital	311		3 2 0 5 00
TJ Ulza, Drawing	312	5 0 0 00	
Painting Fees	401		3 6 0 0 00
Wages Expense	511	9 0 0 00	
Rent Expense	521	2 5 0 00	
Phone Expense	525	5 0 00	
Transportation Expense	526	6 0 00	
Utilities Expense	533	7 0 00	
Miscellaneous Expense	549	2 5 00	
		8 9 5 5 00	8 9 5 5 00

E 4-8A   (LO6)

FINDING AND CORRECTING ERRORS Joe Adams bought $500 worth of office supplies on account. The following entry was recorded on May 17. Find the error(s) and correct it (them) using the ruling method.

14						14
15	20-- May	17	Office Equipment	4 0 0 00		15
16			Cash		4 0 0 00	16
17			Purchased copy paper			17

On May 25, after the transactions had been posted, Adams discovered that the following entry contains an error. The cash received represents a collection on account, rather than new service fees. Correct the error in the general journal using the correcting entry method.

22							22
23	20-- May	23	Cash	101	1 0 0 0 00		23
24			Service Fees	401		1 0 0 0 00	24
25			Received cash for services previously earned				25

SERIES A PROBLEMS

P 4-9A   (LO4/5)

✓ Cash bal., Jan. 31: $10,021
✓ Trial bal. total debits: $13,460

JOURNALIZING AND POSTING TRANSACTIONS Annette Creighton opened Creighton Consulting. She rented a small office and paid a part-time worker to answer the phone and make deliveries. Her chart of accounts is as follows:

Chart of Accounts

Assets		Revenues	
101	Cash	401	Consulting Fees
142	Office Supplies		
181	Office Equipment	**Expenses**	
		511	Wages Expense
Liabilities		512	Advertising Expense
202	Accounts Payable	521	Rent Expense
		525	Phone Expense
Owner's Equity		526	Transportation Expense
311	Annette Creighton, Capital	533	Utilities Expense
312	Annette Creighton, Drawing	549	Miscellaneous Expense

Creighton's transactions for the first month of business are as follows:

Jan.	1	Creighton invested cash in the business, $10,000.
	1	Paid rent, $500.
	2	Purchased office supplies on account, $300.
	4	Purchased office equipment on account, $1,500.
	6	Received cash for services rendered, $580.
	7	Paid phone bill, $42.
	8	Paid utilities bill, $38.
	10	Received cash for services rendered, $360.
	12	Made payment on account, $50.
	13	Paid for car rental while visiting an out-of-town client (transportation expense), $150.
	15	Paid part-time worker, $360.
	17	Received cash for services rendered, $420.
	18	Creighton withdrew cash for personal use, $100.
	20	Paid for a newspaper ad, $26.
	22	Reimbursed part-time employee for cab fare incurred delivering materials to clients (transportation expense), $35.
	24	Paid for books on consulting practices (miscellaneous expense), $28.
	25	Received cash for services rendered, $320.
	27	Made payment on account for office equipment purchased, $150.
	29	Paid part-time worker, $360.
	30	Received cash for services rendered, $180.

(continued)

REQUIRED

1. Set up general ledger accounts from the chart of accounts.

2. Journalize the transactions for January in a two-column general journal. Use the following journal page numbers: January 1–10, page 1; January 12–24, page 2; January 25–30, page 3.

3. Post the transactions to the general ledger.

4. Prepare a trial balance.

5. Prepare an income statement and a statement of owner's equity for the month of January and a balance sheet as of January 31, 20--.

P 4-10A **(LO4/5)**

✓ Cash bal., June 30: $3,958

✓ Trial bal. total debits: $22,358

JOURNALIZING AND POSTING TRANSACTIONS Jim Andrews opened a delivery business in March. He rented a small office and has a part-time assistant. His trial balance shows accounts for the first three months of business.

ACCOUNT TITLE	ACCOUNT NO.	DEBIT BALANCE	CREDIT BALANCE
Jim's Quick Delivery Trial Balance May 31, 20 - -			
Cash	101	3 8 2 6 00	
Accounts Receivable	122	1 2 1 2 00	
Office Supplies	142	6 4 8 00	
Office Equipment	181	2 1 0 0 00	
Delivery Truck	185	8 0 0 0 00	
Accounts Payable	202		6 0 0 0 00
Jim Andrews, Capital	311		4 4 7 8 00
Jim Andrews, Drawing	312	1 8 0 0 00	
Delivery Fees	401		9 8 8 0 00
Wages Expense	511	1 2 0 0 00	
Advertising Expense	512	9 0 00	
Rent Expense	521	9 0 0 00	
Phone Expense	525	1 2 6 00	
Electricity Expense	533	9 8 00	
Charitable Contributions Expense	534	6 0 00	
Gas and Oil Expense	538	1 8 6 00	
Miscellaneous Expense	549	1 1 2 00	
		20 3 5 8 00	20 3 5 8 00

Andrews' transactions for the month of June are as follows:

June 1 Paid rent, $300.

   2 Performed delivery services for $300: $100 in cash and $200 on account.

   4 Paid for newspaper advertising, $15.

   6 Purchased office supplies on account, $180.

   7 Received cash for delivery services rendered, $260.

   9 Paid cash on account (truck payment), $200.

   10 Purchased a copier (office equipment) for $700: paid $100 in cash and put $600 on account.

June 11   Made a contribution to the Red Cross (charitable contributions), $20.

12   Received cash for delivery services rendered, $380.

13   Received cash on account for services previously rendered, $100.

15   Paid a part-time worker, $200.

16   Paid electric bill, $36.

18   Paid phone bill, $46.

19   Received cash on account for services previously rendered, $100.

20   Andrews withdrew cash for personal use, $200.

21   Paid for gas and oil, $32.

22   Made payment on account (for office supplies), $40.

24   Received cash for services rendered, $340.

26   Paid for a magazine subscription (miscellaneous expense), $15.

27   Received cash for services rendered, $180.

27   Received cash on account for services previously rendered, $100.

29   Paid for gasoline, $24.

30   Paid a part-time worker, $200.

REQUIRED

1. Set up general ledger accounts by entering the balances as of June 1.

2. Journalize the transactions for June in a two-column general journal. Use the following journal pages: June 1–10, page 7; June 11–20, page 8; June 21–30, page 9.

3. Post the entries to the general ledger.

4. Prepare a trial balance.

P 4-11A   (LO6)

CORRECTING ERRORS Assuming that all entries have been posted, prepare correcting entries for each of the following errors.

1. The following entry was made to record the purchase of $700 in supplies on account:

Supplies	142	700	
Cash	101		700

2. The following entry was made to record the payment of $450 in wages:

Rent Expense	521	450	
Cash	101		450

3. The following entry was made to record a $300 payment to a supplier on account:

Supplies	142	100	
Cash	101		100

SERIES B EXERCISES

E 4-1B   **(LO2)**

SOURCE DOCUMENTS What type of information is found on each of the following source documents?

1. Cash register tape
2. Sales ticket (issued to customer)
3. Purchase invoice (received from supplier or vendor)
4. Check stub

E 4-2B   **(LO4)**

SHOW
ME HOW

GENERAL JOURNAL ENTRIES For each of the following transactions, list the account to be debited and the account to be credited in the general journal.

1. Invested cash in the business, $1,000.
2. Performed services on account, $200.
3. Purchased office equipment on account, $500.
4. Received cash on account for services previously rendered, $200.
5. Made a payment on account, $100.

E 4-3B   **(LO5)**

✓ Final Cash bal.: $1,100

SHOW
ME HOW

GENERAL LEDGER ACCOUNTS Set up T accounts for each of the general ledger accounts needed for Exercise 4-2B and post debits and credits to the accounts. Foot the accounts and enter the balances. Prove that total debits equal total credits.

E 4-4B   **(LO4)**

SHOW
ME HOW

GENERAL JOURNAL ENTRIES Sengel Moon opened The Bike Doctor. Journalize the following transactions that occurred during the month of October of the current year. Use the following journal pages: October 1–12, page 1, and October 14–29, page 2. Use the following chart of accounts:

Chart of Accounts

Assets	Revenues
101 Cash	401 Repair Fees
141 Bicycle Parts	
142 Office Supplies	Expenses
	511 Wages Expense
Liabilities	521 Rent Expense
202 Accounts Payable	525 Phone Expense
	533 Utilities Expense
Owner's Equity	549 Miscellaneous Expense
311 Sengel Moon, Capital	
312 Sengel Moon, Drawing	

Oct.   1   Moon invested cash in the business, $15,000.
      2   Paid shop rental for the month, $300.
      3   Purchased bicycle parts on account, $2,000.
      5   Purchased office supplies on account, $250.
      8   Paid phone bill, $38.

Oct. 9   Received cash for services, $140.

11   Paid a sports magazine subscription (miscellaneous expense), $15.

12   Made payment on account (see Oct. 3 transaction), $100.

14   Paid part-time employee, $300.

15   Received cash for services, $350.

16   Paid utilities bill, $48.

19   Received cash for services, $250.

23   Moon withdrew cash for personal use, $50.

25   Made payment on account (see Oct. 5 transaction), $50.

29   Paid part-time employee, $300.

E 4-5B   (LO5)
✓ Final Cash bal.: $14,539
✓ Trial bal. total debits: $17,840   SHOW ME HOW

GENERAL LEDGER ACCOUNTS; TRIAL BALANCE Set up general ledger accounts using the chart of accounts provided in Exercise 4-4B. Post the transactions from Exercise 4-4B to the general ledger accounts and prepare a trial balance.

E 4-6B   (LO5)
✓ Total assets, Oct. 31: $16,789

FINANCIAL STATEMENTS From the information in Exercises 4-4B and 4-5B, prepare an income statement, a statement of owner's equity, and a balance sheet.

E 4-7B   (LO5)
✓ Total assets, Mar. 31: $11,900

FINANCIAL STATEMENTS From the following trial balance taken after one month of operation, prepare an income statement, a statement of owner's equity, and a balance sheet.

AT Speaker's Bureau Trial Balance March 31, 20 - -													
ACCOUNT TITLE	ACCOUNT NO.	DEBIT BALANCE					CREDIT BALANCE						
Cash	101	6	6	0	0	00							
Accounts Receivable	122	2	8	0	0	00							
Office Supplies	142	1	0	0	0	00							
Office Equipment	181	1	5	0	0	00							
Accounts Payable	202							3	0	0	0	00	
AT Speaker, Capital	311							6	0	9	8	00	
AT Speaker, Drawing	312		8	0	0	00							
Speaking Fees	401							4	8	0	0	00	
Wages Expense	511		4	0	0	00							
Rent Expense	521		2	0	0	00							
Phone Expense	525			3	5	00							
Travel Expense	526		4	5	0	00							
Utilities Expense	533			8	8	00							
Miscellaneous Expense	549			2	5	00							
		13	8	9	8	00		13	8	9	8	00	

E 4-8B   (LO6)

FINDING AND CORRECTING ERRORS Mary Smith purchased $350 worth of office equipment on account. The following entry was recorded on April 6. Find the error(s) and correct it (them) using the ruling method.

7															7
8	20-- Apr.	6	Office Supplies			5	3	0	00						8
9			Cash								5	3	0	00	9
10			Purchased office equipment												10

(continued)

On April 25, after the transactions had been posted, Smith discovered the following entry contains an error. When her customer received services, Cash was debited, but no cash was received. Correct the error in the journal using the correcting entry method.

27																	27
28	20-- Apr.	21	Cash		101	3	0	0	00								28
29			Service Fees		401						3	0	0	00			29
30			Revenue earned from services														30
31			previously rendered														31

SERIES B PROBLEMS

P 4-9B   (LO4/5)
✓ Cash bal., May 31: $4,500
✓ Trial bal. total debits: $8,790

JOURNALIZING AND POSTING TRANSACTIONS Benito Mendez opened Mendez Appraisals. He rented office space and has a part-time secretary to answer the phone and make appraisal appointments. His chart of accounts is as follows:

Chart of Accounts

Assets
101   Cash
122   Accounts Receivable
142   Office Supplies
181   Office Equipment

Liabilities
202   Accounts Payable

Owner's Equity
311   Benito Mendez, Capital
312   Benito Mendez, Drawing

Revenues
401   Appraisal Fees

Expenses
511   Wages Expense
512   Advertising Expense
521   Rent Expense
525   Phone Expense
526   Transportation Expense
533   Electricity Expense
549   Miscellaneous Expense

Mendez's transactions for the first month of business are as follows:

May 1   Mendez invested cash in the business, $5,000.
     2   Paid rent, $500.
     3   Purchased office supplies, $100.
     4   Purchased office equipment on account, $2,000.
     5   Received cash for services rendered, $280.
     8   Paid phone bill, $38.
     9   Paid electric bill, $42.
     10   Received cash for services rendered, $310.
     13   Paid part-time employee, $500.
     14   Paid car rental for out-of-town trip, $200.
     15   Paid for newspaper ad, $30.
     18   Received cash for services rendered, $620.

May 19   Paid mileage reimbursement for part-time employee's use of personal car for business deliveries (transportation expense), $22.

21   Mendez withdrew cash for personal use, $50.

23   Made payment on account for office equipment purchased earlier, $200.

24   Earned appraisal fee, which will be paid in a week, $500.

26   Paid for newspaper ad, $30.

27   Paid for local softball team sponsorship (miscellaneous expense), $15.

28   Paid part-time employee, $500.

29   Received cash on account, $250.

30   Received cash for services rendered, $280.

31   Paid cab fare (transportation expense), $13.

REQUIRED

1. Set up general ledger accounts from the chart of accounts.

2. Journalize the transactions for May in a two-column general journal. Use the following journal page numbers: May 1–10, page 1; May 13–24, page 2; May 26–31, page 3.

3. Post the transactions to the general ledger.

4. Prepare a trial balance.

5. Prepare an income statement and a statement of owner's equity for the month of May, and a balance sheet as of May 31, 20--.

P 4-10B   (LO4/5)
✓ Cash bal., Nov. 30: $7,012
✓ Trial bal. total debits: $16,105

JOURNALIZING AND POSTING TRANSACTIONS Ann Taylor owns a suit tailoring shop. She opened business in September. She rented a small work space and has an assistant to receive job orders and process claim tickets. Her trial balance shows her account balances for the first two months of business.

Taylor Tailoring **Trial Balance** **October 31, 20 --**													
ACCOUNT TITLE	ACCOUNT NO.		DEBIT BALANCE					CREDIT BALANCE					
Cash	101	6	2	1	1	00							
Accounts Receivable	122		4	8	4	00							
Tailoring Supplies	141	1	0	0	0	00							
Tailoring Equipment	183	3	8	0	0	00							
Accounts Payable	202							4	1	2	5	00	
Ann Taylor, Capital	311							6	1	3	0	00	
Ann Taylor, Drawing	312		8	0	0	00							
Tailoring Fees	401							3	6	0	0	00	
Wages Expense	511		8	0	0	00							
Advertising Expense	512			3	4	00							
Rent Expense	521		6	0	0	00							
Phone Expense	525			6	0	00							
Electricity Expense	533			4	4	00							
Miscellaneous Expense	549			2	2	00							
		13	8	5	5	00		13	8	5	5	00	

(continued)

Taylor's transactions for November are as follows:

Nov. 1   Paid rent, $300.

2   Purchased tailoring supplies on account, $150.

3   Purchased a new button hole machine on account, $300.

5   Earned first week's revenue, $400: $100 in cash and $300 on account.

8   Paid for newspaper advertising, $13.

9   Paid phone bill, $28.

10   Paid electric bill, $21.

11   Received cash on account from customers, $200.

12   Earned second week's revenue, $450: $200 in cash and $250 on account.

15   Paid assistant, $400.

16   Made payment on account, $100.

17   Paid for magazine subscription (miscellaneous expense), $12.

19   Earned third week's revenue, $450: $300 in cash, $150 on account.

23   Received cash on account from customers, $300.

24   Paid for newspaper advertising, $13.

26   Paid for postage (miscellaneous expense), $12.

27   Earned fourth week's revenue, $600: $200 in cash and $400 on account.

30   Received cash on account from customers, $400.

REQUIRED

1. Set up general ledger accounts by entering the balances as of November 1, 20--.

2. Journalize the transactions for November in a two-column general journal. Use the following journal page numbers: November 1–11, page 7; November 12–24, page 8; November 26–30, page 9.

3. Post the entries to the general ledger.

4. Prepare a trial balance.

P 4-11B   (LO6)   **CORRECTING ERRORS** Assuming that all entries have been posted, prepare correcting entries for each of the following errors.

1. The following entry was made to record the purchase of $400 in equipment on account:

Supplies	142	400	
Cash	101		400

2. The following entry was made to record the payment of $200 for advertising:

Repair Expense	537	200	
Cash	101		200

3. The following entry was made to record a $600 payment to a supplier on account:

Prepaid Insurance	145	400	
Cash	101		400

MANAGING YOUR WRITING

Check List

- ☑ Check List
- ☐ Managing
- ☐ Planning
- ☐ Drafting
- ☐ Break
- ☐ Revising
- ☐ Managing

You are a public accountant with many small business clients. During a recent visit to a client's business, the bookkeeper approached you with a problem. The columns of the trial balance were not equal. You helped the bookkeeper find and correct the error, but believe you should go one step further. Write a memo to all of your clients that explains the purpose of the double-entry framework, the importance of maintaining the equality of the accounting equation, the errors that might cause an inequality, and suggestions for finding the errors.

MASTERY PROBLEM

✓ Cash bal., June 30: $45,495
✓ Trial bal. total debits: $96,200

CLGL

Barry Bird opened the Barry Bird Basketball Camp for children ages 10 through 18. Campers typically register for one week in June or July, arriving on Sunday and returning home the following Saturday. College players serve as cabin counselors and assist the local college and high school coaches who run the practice sessions. The registration fee includes a room, meals at a nearby restaurant, and basketball instruction. In the off-season, the facilities are used for weekend retreats and coaching clinics. Bird developed the following chart of accounts for his service business:

Chart of Accounts

Assets
101   Cash
142   Office Supplies
183   Athletic Equipment
184   Basketball Facilities

Liabilities
202   Accounts Payable

Owner's Equity
311   Barry Bird, Capital
312   Barry Bird, Drawing

Revenues
401   Registration Fees

Expenses
511   Wages Expense
512   Advertising Expense
524   Food Expense
525   Phone Expense
533   Utilities Expense
536   Postage Expense

(*continued*)

The following transactions took place during the month of June:

June 1   Bird invested cash in the business, $10,000.

1   Purchased basketballs and other athletic equipment, $3,000.

2   Paid Hite Advertising for flyers that had been mailed to prospective campers, $5,000.

2   Collected registration fees, $15,000.

2   Rogers Construction completed work on a new basketball court that cost $12,000. Arrangements were made to pay the bill in July.

5   Purchased office supplies on account from Gordon Office Supplies, $300.

6   Received bill from Magic's Restaurant for meals served to campers on account, $5,800.

7   Collected registration fees, $16,200.

10   Paid wages to camp counselors, $500.

14   Collected registration fees, $13,500.

14   Received bill from Magic's Restaurant for meals served to campers on account, $6,200.

17   Paid wages to camp counselors, $500.

18   Paid postage, $85.

21   Collected registration fees, $15,200.

22   Received bill from Magic's Restaurant for meals served to campers on account, $6,500.

24   Paid wages to camp counselors, $500.

28   Collected registration fees, $14,000.

30   Received bill from Magic's Restaurant for meals served to campers on account, $7,200.

30   Paid wages to camp counselors, $500.

30   Paid Magic's Restaurant on account, $25,700.

30   Paid utility bill, $500.

30   Paid phone bill, $120.

30   Bird withdrew cash for personal use, $2,000.

REQUIRED

1. Enter the transactions in a general journal. Use the following journal pages: June 1–6, page 1; June 7–22, page 2; June 24–30, page 3.

2. Post the entries to the general ledger.

3. Prepare a trial balance.

CHALLENGE PROBLEM

This problem challenges you to apply your cumulative accounting knowledge to move a step beyond the material in the chapter.

✓ Total debits: $19,150

Journal entries and a trial balance for Fred Phaler Consulting follow. As you will note, the trial balance does not balance, suggesting that there are errors. Recall that the chapter offers tips on identifying individual posting errors. These techniques are not as effective when there are two or more errors. Thus, you will need to first carefully inspect the trial balance to see if you can identify any obvious errors due to amounts that either look out of proportion or are simply reported in the wrong place. Then, you will need to carefully evaluate the other amounts by using the techniques offered in the text, or tracing the journal entries to the amounts reported on the trial balance. (*Hint*: Four errors were made in the posting process and preparation of the trial balance.)

	DATE		DESCRIPTION	POST. REF.	DEBIT	CREDIT	
1	20-- June	1	Cash	101	10 0 0 0 00		1
2			Fred Phaler, Capital	311		10 0 0 0 00	2
3							3
4		2	Rent Expense	521	5 0 0 00		4
5			Cash	101		5 0 0 00	5
6							6
7		3	Cash	101	4 0 0 0 00		7
8			Professional Fees	401		4 0 0 0 00	8
9							9
10		4	Utilities Expense	533	1 0 0 00		10
11			Cash	101		1 0 0 00	11
12							12
13		7	Cash	101	3 0 0 0 00		13
14			Professional Fees	401		3 0 0 0 00	14
15							15
16		12	Automobile Expense	526	5 0 00		16
17			Cash	101		5 0 00	17
18							18
19		14	Wages Expense	511	5 0 0 00		19
20			Cash	101		5 0 0 00	20
21							21
22		14	Office Supplies	142	2 5 0 00		22
23			Accounts Payable	202		2 5 0 00	23
24							24
25		20	Phone Expense	525	1 0 0 00		25
26			Cash	101		1 0 0 00	26
27							27
28		21	Fred Phaler, Drawing	312	1 2 0 0 00		28
29			Cash	101		1 2 0 0 00	29
30							30
31		24	Accounts Receivable	122	2 0 0 0 00		31
32			Professional Fees	401		2 0 0 0 00	32
33							33
34		25	Accounts Payable	202	1 0 0 00		34
35			Cash	101		1 0 0 00	35
36							36
37		30	Wages Expense	511	3 0 0 00		37
38			Cash	101		3 0 0 00	38

GENERAL JOURNAL   PAGE 1

(*continued*)

Fred Phaler Consulting Trial Balance June 30, 20 - -											
ACCOUNT TITLE	ACCOUNT NO.	DEBIT BALANCE					CREDIT BALANCE				
Cash	101						13	9	0	0	00
Accounts Receivable	122	2	0	0	0	00					
Office Supplies	142		2	5	0	00					
Accounts Payable	202		1	0	0	00					
Fred Phaler, Capital	311						10	0	0	0	00
Fred Phaler, Drawing	312	2	1	0	0	00					
Professional Fees	401						9	0	0	0	00
Wages Expense	511		8	0	0	00					
Rent Expense	521		5	0	0	00					
Phone Expense	525		1	0	0	00					
Automobile Expense	526	50	0	0	0	00					
Utilities Expense	533		1	0	0	00					
		55	9	5	0	00	32	9	0	0	00

REQUIRED

1. Find the errors.
2. Explain what caused the errors.
3. Prepare a corrected trial balance.

Answers to Self-Study Test Questions

True/False

1. T
2. F (A, L, OE, R, E)
3. T
4. T
5. T

Multiple Choice

1. c   2. d   3. c   4. b   5. a

Checkpoint Exercises

1. A   cash payment.
2. A   Year in which entry was made. (Needed for first transaction on this page.)

B   Month in which entry was made. (Needed for first transaction on this page.)

C   Day of the month entry was made. (Needed for every transaction.)

D   Account debited.

E   Account credited.

F   Description of transaction.

G   Account number for account debited to indicate the debit has been posted.

H   Amount for account debited.

I   Amount for account credited.

J   Account number for account credited to indicate the credit has been posted.

3. **A** Account title.

  B Account number.

  C Year of transaction. (Needed for first transaction on this page.)

  D Month of transaction. (Needed for first transaction on this page.)

  E Day of month transaction was made. (Needed for every transaction.)

  F Generally left blank, except for special reasons such as indicating the beginning balance, adjusting, correcting, closing, or reversing entries.

  G Journal page from which entry was posted.

  H Dollar amount of debit.

  I Dollar amount of credit.

  J Balance if account has a debit balance.

  K Balance if account has a credit balance.

4.

	DATE	DESCRIPTION	POST. REF.	DEBIT	CREDIT	
			GENERAL JOURNAL		PAGE 1	
1		Rent Payable		5 0 0 00		1
2		Cash			5 0 0 00	2
3		To correct error in which payment for rent				3
4		was credited to Rent Payable rather than Cash.				4
5						5

Chapter 5

Adjusting Entries and the Work Sheet

LEARNING OBJECTIVES

Careful study of this chapter should enable you to:

LO1 Prepare end-of-period adjustments.

LO2 Post adjusting entries to the general ledger.

LO3 Prepare a work sheet.

LO4 Describe methods for finding errors on the work sheet.

LO5 Journalize adjusting entries from the work sheet.

LO6 Explain the cash, modified cash, and accrual bases of accounting.

Floyd's 99 Barbershop, founded in 2001, is a contemporary full-service barbershop/hair-care concept offering haircuts, coloring, styling, and shaves. In a setting where *Hard Rock* meets haircuts, customers listen to custom designed Floyd's 99 Radio, watch TV, surf the internet, and get a signature shoulder massage and hot lather neck shave all as a part of their overall haircut experience. About 80% of Floyd's 99 customers are male. Headquartered in Greenwood Village, Colorado, Floyd's 99 has 85 shops in 12 states, primarily Colorado, California, Texas, and Illinois.

As a rapidly growing company, Floyd's 99 uses the accrual basis of accounting, which requires making end-of-period adjusting entries. In this chapter, you will learn why adjusting entries are important, how they are made, and how they affect the financial statements. In addition, you will learn how to use a work sheet to help in the preparation of adjusting entries and the financial statements.

U p to this point, you have learned how to journalize business transactions, post to the ledger, and prepare a trial balance. Now it is time to learn how to make end-of-period adjustments to the accounts listed in the trial balance. This chapter explains the need for adjustments and illustrates how they are made with or without the use of a work sheet.

END-OF-PERIOD ADJUSTMENTS

LO1 Prepare end-of-period adjustments.

Throughout the accounting period, business transactions are entered in the accounting system. These transactions are based on exchanges between the business and other companies and individuals. During the accounting period, other changes occur that affect the business's financial condition. For example, equipment is wearing out, prepaid insurance and supplies are being used up, and employees are earning wages that have not yet been paid. Since these events have not been entered into the accounting system, **adjusting entries** must be made prior to the preparation of financial statements.

LEARNING KEY

Transactions are entered as they occur throughout the year. Adjustments are made at the end of the accounting period for items that do not involve exchanges with an outside party.

These adjustments are guided by three important principles. The **revenue recognition principle** states that revenues should be recognized when earned, regardless of when cash is received from the customer. Revenues are considered earned when a service is provided or a product is sold. Similarly, the **expense recognition principle** states that expenses should be recognized when incurred, regardless of when cash is paid. Expenses are generally considered incurred when services are received or assets are consumed. The proper matching of revenues earned during an accounting period with the expenses incurred to produce the revenues is often referred to as the **matching principle**. This approach offers the best measure of net income. The income statement reports earnings for a specific period of time, and the balance sheet reports the assets, liabilities, and owner's equity on a specific date. Thus, to follow these three principles, the accounts must be brought up to date before financial statements are prepared. This requires adjusting some of the accounts listed in the trial balance. Figure 5-1 lists reasons to adjust the trial balance.

FIGURE 5-1   Reasons to Adjust the Trial Balance

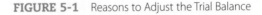

1. To report all revenues earned during the accounting period.

2. To report all expenses incurred to produce the revenues earned in the accounting period.

3. To accurately report the assets on the balance sheet date. Some assets may have been used up during the accounting period.

4. To accurately report the liabilities on the balance sheet date. Expenses may have been incurred but not yet paid.

LEARNING KEY

Matching revenues earned with expenses incurred to produce those revenues offers the best measure of net income.

Generally, adjustments are made and financial statements prepared at the end of a 12-month period called a **fiscal year**. This period does not need to be the same as a calendar year. In fact, many businesses schedule their fiscal year-end for a time when business is slow. In this chapter, we continue the illustration of Rohan's Campus Delivery and will prepare adjustments at the end of the first month of operations. We will focus on the following accounts: Supplies, Prepaid Insurance, Wages Expense, and Delivery Equipment.

ROSAIRENEBETANCOURT 4/ALAMY

A Broader View

Adjusting Entries

Are adjusting entries important? The Walt Disney Company and Mattel, Inc., probably think so. The Walt Disney Company granted Mattel, Inc., the right to make and sell toys based on Disney characters. In return, Mattel agreed to make payments to Disney as the toys were sold. One of the issues in a court case was whether Mattel should have made an adjusting entry when it fell behind on these payments. The entry would have been:

Royalty Expense	17,000,000	
Accounts Payable (Disney)		17,000,000

This adjusting entry would have reduced Mattel's fourth-quarter earnings for that year by more than 15%. Following an investigation by the Securities and Exchange Commission, Mattel eventually agreed to make an adjustment to later financial statements.

Supplies

During June, Rohan purchased supplies consisting of paper, pens, and delivery envelopes for $80. *Since these supplies were expected to provide future benefits, Supplies, an asset, was debited at the time of the purchase.* No other entries were made to the supplies account during June. As reported on the trial balance in Figure 5-2, the $80 balance remains in the supplies account at the end of the month.

FIGURE 5-2   Trial Balance

ACCOUNT TITLE	ACCOUNT NO	DEBIT BALANCE	CREDIT BALANCE
		Rohan's Campus Delivery Trial Balance June 30, 20 - -	
Cash	101	3 7 0 00	
Accounts Receivable	122	6 5 0 00	
Supplies	141	8 0 00	
Prepaid Insurance	145	2 0 0 00	
Delivery Equipment	185	3 6 0 0 00	
Accounts Payable	202		1 8 0 0 00
Rohan Macsen, Capital	311		2 0 0 0 00
Rohan Macsen, Drawing	312	1 5 0 00	
Delivery Fees	401		2 1 5 0 00
Wages Expense	511	6 5 0 00	
Rent Expense	521	2 0 0 00	
Phone Expense	525	5 0 00	
		5 9 5 0 00	5 9 5 0 00

LEARNING KEY

Since it is not practical to make a journal entry for supplies expense each time supplies are used, one adjusting entry is made at the end of the accounting period.

As supplies are used, an expense is incurred. However, it is not practical to make a journal entry to recognize this expense and the reduction in the supplies account every time someone uses an envelope. It is more efficient to wait until the end of the accounting period to make one adjusting entry to reflect the expense incurred for the use of supplies for the entire month.

At the end of the month, an inventory, or physical count, of the remaining supplies is taken. The inventory shows that supplies costing $20 were still unused at the end of June. Since Rohan bought supplies costing $80, and only $20 worth remain, supplies costing $60 must have been used ($80 − $20 = $60). Thus, supplies expense for the month is $60.

Since $60 worth of supplies have been used, Supplies Expense is debited and Supplies (asset) is credited for $60. This entry is illustrated in Figure 5-3 in T account and general journal form. Thus, as shown in Figure 5-4, supplies with a cost of $20 will be reported as an asset on the balance sheet and a supplies expense of $60 will be reported on the income statement. The adjusting entry affected an income statement account (Supplies Expense) and a balance sheet account (Supplies).

FIGURE 5-3   Adjustment for Supplies

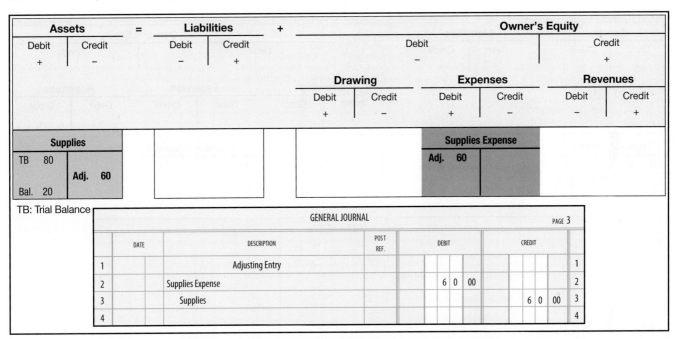

FIGURE 5-4   Effect of Adjusting Entry for Supplies on Financial Statements

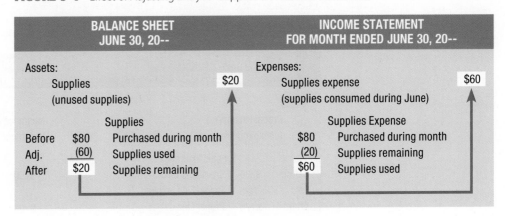

Prepaid Insurance

On June 18, Rohan paid $200 for an eight-month liability insurance policy with coverage beginning on June 1. *Prepaid Insurance, an asset, was debited because the insurance policy is expected to provide future benefits in the form of insurance coverage, or a cash refund if the policy is canceled.* The $200 balance is reported on the trial balance. As the insurance policy expires with the passage of time, the asset should be reduced and an expense recognized.

Since the $200 premium covers eight months, the cost of the expired coverage for June is $25 ($200 ÷ 8 months). As shown in Figure 5-5, the adjusting entry is to debit Insurance Expense for $25 and credit Prepaid Insurance for $25. Figure 5-6 shows that the unexpired portion of the insurance premium will be reported on the balance sheet as Prepaid Insurance of $175. The expired portion will be reported on the income statement as Insurance Expense of $25.

FIGURE 5-5   Adjustment for Expired Insurance

Assets		=	Liabilities		+	Owner's Equity			
Debit	Credit		Debit	Credit		Debit		Credit	
+	–		–	+		–		+	

			Drawing		Expenses		Revenues	
			Debit	Credit	Debit	Credit	Debit	Credit
			+	–	+	–	–	+

Prepaid Insurance						Insurance Expense	
TB 200						Adj. 25	
	Adj. 25						
Bal. 175							

	DATE	DESCRIPTION	POST REF.	DEBIT	CREDIT	
			GENERAL JOURNAL		PAGE 3	
1		Adjusting Entry				1
5		Insurance Expense		2 5 00		5
6		Prepaid Insurance			2 5 00	6
7						7

FIGURE 5-6   Effect of Adjusting Entry for Prepaid Insurance on Financial Statements

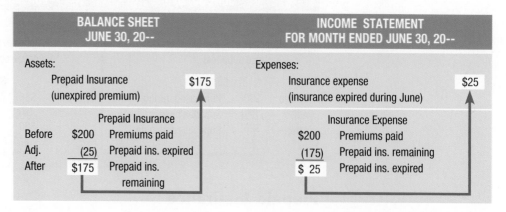

BALANCE SHEET JUNE 30, 20--			INCOME STATEMENT FOR MONTH ENDED JUNE 30, 20--		
Assets:			Expenses:		
Prepaid Insurance (unexpired premium)		$175	Insurance expense (insurance expired during June)		$25
	Prepaid Insurance			Insurance Expense	
Before	$200	Premiums paid		$200	Premiums paid
Adj.	(25)	Prepaid ins. expired		(175)	Prepaid ins. remaining
After	$175	Prepaid ins. remaining		$ 25	Prepaid ins. expired

Wages Expense

Rohan paid his part-time employees $650 on June 27. Since then, they have earned an additional $50, but have not yet been paid. The additional wages expense must be recognized.

Since the employees have not been paid, Wages Payable, a liability, should be established. Thus, Wages Expense is debited and Wages Payable is credited for $50 in Figure 5-7. Note in Figure 5-8 that Wages Expense of $700 is reported on the income statement and Wages Payable of $50 is reported on the balance sheet.

FIGURE 5-7   Adjustment for Unpaid Wages

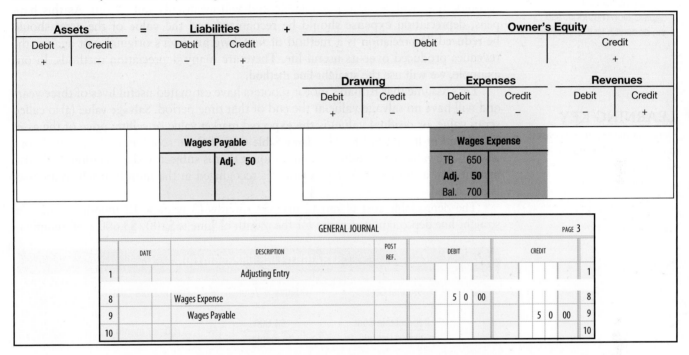

FIGURE 5-8   Effect of Adjusting Entry for Wages on Financial Statements

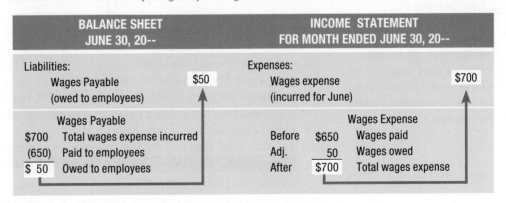

Depreciation Expense

During the month of June, Rohan purchased three motor scooters. Since the scooters will provide future benefits, they were recorded as assets in the delivery equipment account. Under the **historical cost principle**, assets are recorded at their actual cost, in this case $3,600. This cost remains on the books as long as the business owns the asset. No adjustments are made for changes in the market value of the asset. It does not matter whether the firm got a "good buy" or paid "too much" when the asset was purchased.

The period of time that an asset is expected to help produce revenues is called its **useful life**. The asset's useful life expires as a result of wear and tear or because it no longer satisfies the needs of the business. For example, as miles are added to the scooters, they will become less reliable and will eventually fail to run. As this happens, depreciation expense should be recognized and the value of the asset should be reduced. **Depreciation** is a method of *matching* an asset's original cost against the revenues produced over its useful life. There are many depreciation methods. In our example, we will use the **straight-line method**.

Let's assume that Rohan's motor scooters have estimated useful lives of three years and will have no salvage value at the end of that time period. **Salvage value** (also called scrap value, or residual value) is the expected **market value** or selling price of the asset at the end of its useful life. The **depreciable cost** of these scooters is the original cost, less salvage value, or $3,600. It is this amount that is subject to depreciation. Let's also assume that a full month's depreciation is recognized in the month in which an asset is purchased.

The depreciable cost is spread over 36 months (3 years × 12 months). Thus, the straight-line depreciation expense for the month of June is $100 ($3,600 ÷ 36 months).

STRAIGHT-LINE DEPRECIATION					
Original Cost	−	Salvage Value	=	Depreciable Cost	
$\dfrac{\text{Depreciable Cost}}{\text{Estimated Useful Life}}$	=	$\dfrac{\$3,600}{36 \text{ months}}$	=	$100 per month	

When we made adjustments for supplies and prepaid insurance, the asset accounts were credited to show that they had been consumed. Assets of a durable nature that are expected to provide benefits over several years or more, called **plant assets**, require a different approach. The business maintains a record of the original cost and the amount of depreciation taken since the asset was acquired. By comparing these two amounts, the reader can estimate the relative age of the assets. Thus, instead of crediting Delivery Equipment for the amount of depreciation, a contra-asset account, Accumulated Depreciation—Delivery Equipment, is credited. "Contra" means opposite or against. Thus, a **contra-asset** has a credit balance (the opposite of an asset) and is deducted from the related asset account on the balance sheet.

As shown in Figure 5-9, the appropriate adjusting entry consists of a debit to Depreciation Expense—Delivery Equipment and a credit to Accumulated Depreciation—Delivery Equipment. Note the position of the accumulated depreciation account in the accounting equation. It is shown in the assets section, directly beneath Delivery Equipment. Contra-asset accounts should always be shown along with the related asset account. Therefore, Delivery Equipment and Accumulated Depreciation—Delivery Equipment are shown together.

FIGURE 5-9   Adjustment for Depreciation of Delivery Equipment

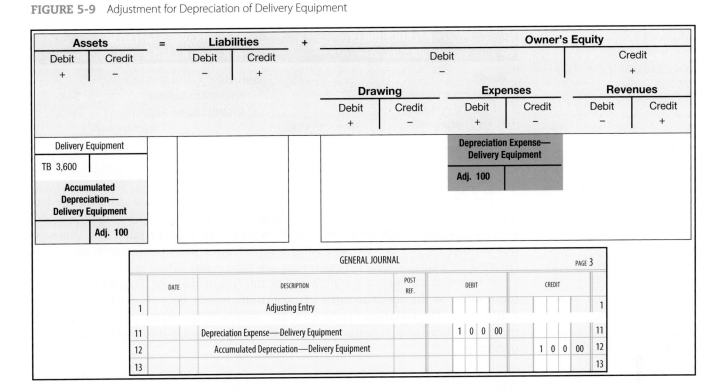

The same concept is used on the balance sheet. Note in Figure 5-10 that Accumulated Depreciation is reported immediately beneath Delivery Equipment as a deduction. The difference between these accounts is known as the **book value**, or **undepreciated cost**, of the delivery equipment. Book value simply means the value carried on the books or in the accounting records. It does *not* represent the market value, or selling price, of the asset.

LEARNING KEY

There is no individual account that reports book value. It must be computed.

    Cost of Plant Assets
  − Accumulated Depreciation
  = Book Value

FIGURE 5-10   Effect of Adjusting Entry for Depreciation on Financial Statements for June

BALANCE SHEET JUNE 30, 20--		INCOME STATEMENT FOR MONTH ENDED JUNE 30, 20--	
Assets:		Expenses:	
Delivery equipment	$3,600	Depreciation expense (Expired cost for June)	$100
Less: Accumulated depreciation	100		
	$3,500 (Book value)		

If no delivery equipment is bought or sold during the next month, the same adjusting entry would be made at the end of July. If an income statement for the month of July and a balance sheet as of July 31 were prepared, the amounts shown in Figure 5-11 would be reported for the delivery equipment.

FIGURE 5-11 Effect of Adjusting Entry for Depreciation on Financial Statements for July

BALANCE SHEET JULY 31, 20--			INCOME STATEMENT FOR MONTH ENDED JULY 31, 20--	
Assets:			Expenses:	
Delivery equipment	$3,600		Depreciation expense	$100
Less: Accumulated			(Expired cost for July)	
depreciation	200	$3,400		
		(Book value)		

The cost ($3,600) remains unchanged, but the accumulated depreciation has increased to $200. This represents *the depreciation that has accumulated* since the delivery equipment was purchased ($100 in June and $100 in July). The depreciation expense for July is $100, the same as reported for June. Depreciation expense is reported for a specific time period. It does not accumulate across reporting periods.

If financial statements are prepared at the end of the year, December 31, 20--, the results for the seven months of operations would be presented as shown in Figure 5-12. Depreciation expense for the year is $700 ($100 × 7 months), and the accumulated depreciation would be the same because this is the first year of operation.

Cost	$3,600 / 36 months = $100
Useful life	
Dep./month	$100
Months in service	× 7
Dep. June–Dec.	$700

FIGURE 5-12 Straight-Line Depreciation for Seven Months

BALANCE SHEET DECEMBER 31, 20--			INCOME STATEMENT FOR YEAR ENDED DECEMBER 31, 20--	
Assets:			Expenses:	
Delivery equipment	$3,600		Depreciation expense	$700
Less: Accumulated			(Expired cost from June	
depreciation	700	$2,900	through December)	
		(Book value)		

Expanded Chart of Accounts

Checkpoint ✓

Complete Checkpoint-1 on page 158 to test your basic understanding of LO1.

Several new accounts were needed to make the adjusting entries. New accounts are easily added to the chart of accounts, as shown in Figure 5-13. Note the close relationship between assets and contra-assets in the numbering of the accounts. Contra-accounts carry the same number as the related asset account with a ".1" suffix. For example, Delivery Equipment is account number 185 and the contra-asset account, Accumulated Depreciation—Delivery Equipment, is account number 185.1.

POSTING ADJUSTING ENTRIES

LO2 Post adjusting entries to the general ledger.

Adjusting entries are posted to the general ledger in the same manner as all other entries, except that "*Adjusting*" is written in the Item column of the general ledger. Figure 5-14 shows the posting of the adjusting entries. The posting reference numbers are inserted as each entry is posted.

FIGURE 5-13 Expanded Chart of Accounts

ROHAN'S CAMPUS DELIVERY CHART OF ACCOUNTS			
Assets		**Revenues**	
101	Cash	401	Delivery Fees
122	Accounts Receivable		
141	Supplies	**Expenses**	
145	Prepaid Insurance	511	Wages Expense
185	Delivery Equipment	521	Rent Expense
185.1	Accumulated Depr.—	523	Supplies Expense
	Delivery Equipment	525	Phone Expense
		535	Insurance Expense
Liabilities		541	Depr. Expense —
202	Accounts Payable		Delivery Equipment
219	Wages Payable		
Owner's Equity			
311	Rohan Macsen, Capital		
312	Rohan Macsen, Drawing		

FIGURE 5-14 Posting the Adjusting Entries

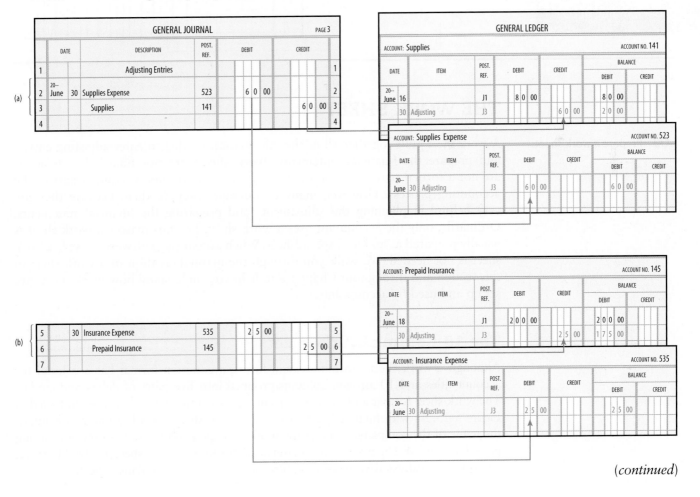

(continued)

FIGURE 5-14 Posting the Adjusting Entries (*concluded*)

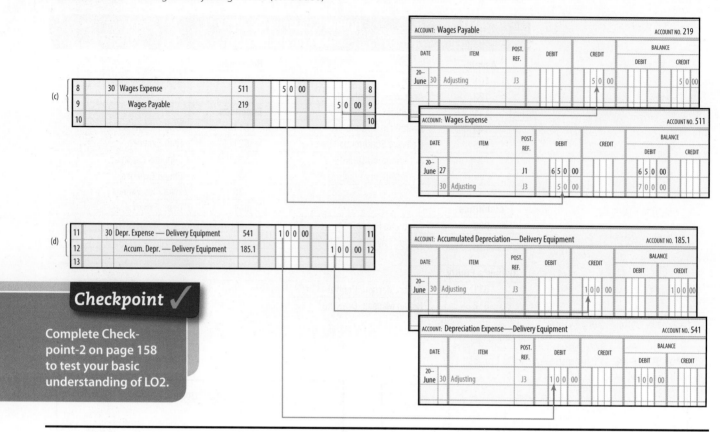

Checkpoint ✓

Complete Checkpoint-2 on page 158 to test your basic understanding of LO2.

THE WORK SHEET

LO3 Prepare a work sheet.

A work sheet pulls together all of the information needed to enter adjusting entries and prepare the financial statements. Work sheets are not financial statements, are not a formal part of the accounting system, and are not a required part of the accounting process. However, many accountants prepare them because they are very helpful in planning the adjustments and preparing the financial statements. Ordinarily, only the accountant uses a work sheet. For this reason, a work sheet is usually prepared as an Excel spreadsheet. When accounting software is used, a work sheet is not needed. We walk you through the manual creation of a work sheet in this section and throughout Chapter 6 to help you understand how work sheets are set up and used by accountants.

The 10-Column Work Sheet

Although a work sheet can take several forms, a common format has a column for account titles and 10 amount columns grouped into five pairs of debits and credits. The work sheet format and the five steps in preparing the work sheet are illustrated in Figure 5-15. As with financial statements, the work sheet has a heading consisting of the name of the company, name of the working paper, and the date of the accounting period just ended. The five major column headings for the work sheet are Trial Balance, Adjustments, Adjusted Trial Balance, Income Statement, and Balance Sheet.

FIGURE 5-15   Steps In Preparing The Work Sheet

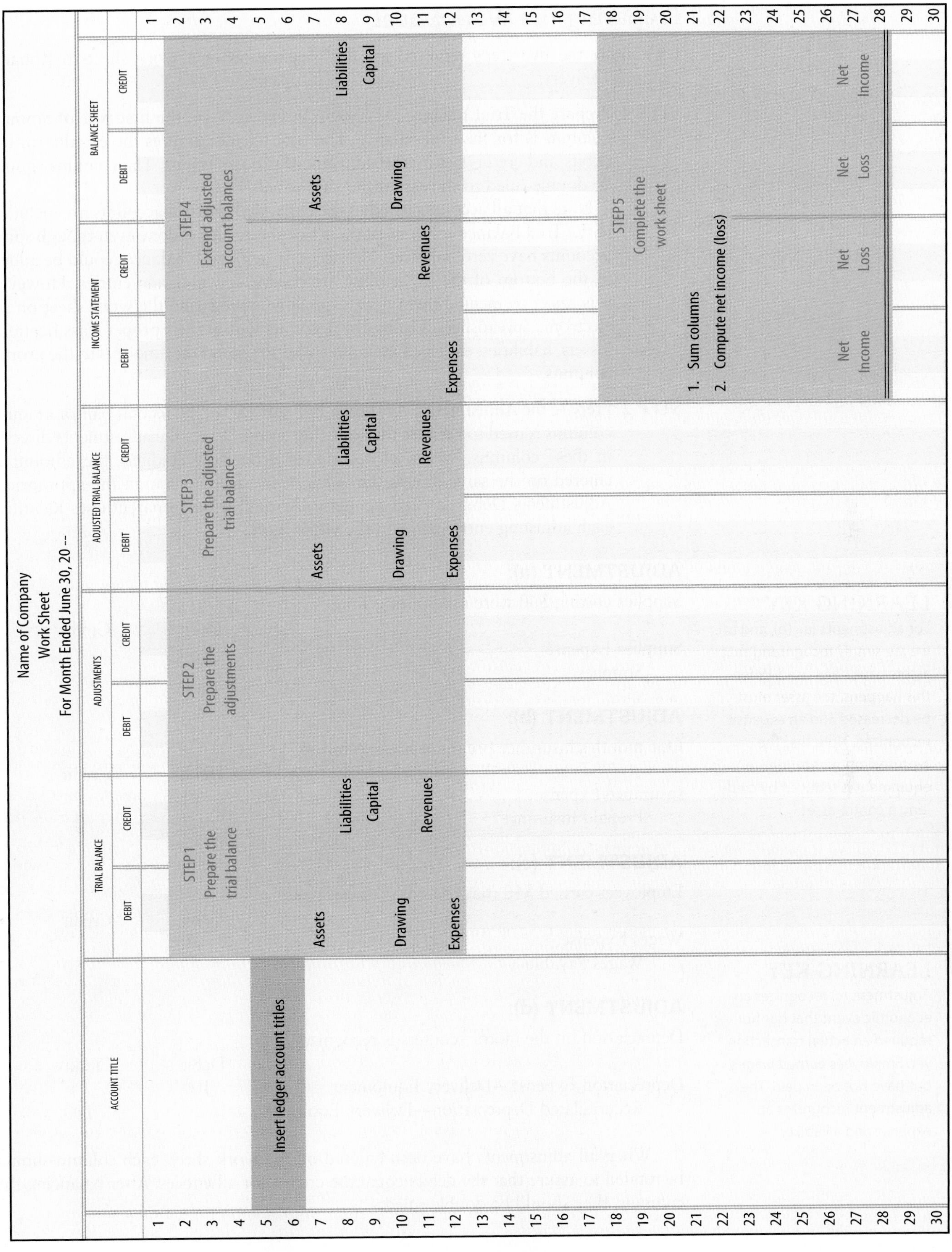

Name of Company
Work Sheet
For Month Ended June 30, 20 --

ACCOUNT TITLE	TRIAL BALANCE		ADJUSTMENTS		ADJUSTED TRIAL BALANCE		INCOME STATEMENT		BALANCE SHEET	
	DEBIT	CREDIT	DEBIT	CREDIT	DEBIT	CREDIT	DEBIT	CREDIT	DEBIT	CREDIT

Insert ledger account titles

STEP1
Prepare the trial balance

Assets

Drawing

Expenses

Liabilities
Capital
Revenues

STEP2
Prepare the adjustments

STEP3
Prepare the adjusted trial balance

Assets

Drawing

Expenses

Liabilities
Capital
Revenues

STEP4
Extend adjusted account balances

Assets

Drawing

Revenues

Expenses

Liabilities
Capital

STEP5
Complete the work sheet
1. Sum columns
2. Compute net income (loss)

Net Income   Net Loss   Net Loss   Net Income

Preparing the Work Sheet

Let's apply the five steps required for the preparation of a work sheet to Rohan's Campus Delivery.

STEP 1 **Prepare the Trial Balance.** As shown in Figure 5-16, the first pair of amount columns is for the trial balance. The trial balance assures the equality of the debits and credits before the adjustment process begins. The columns should be double ruled to show that they are equal.

Note that all accounts listed in the expanded chart of accounts are included in the Trial Balance columns of the work sheet. This is done even though some accounts have zero balances. The accounts with zero balances could be added to the bottom of the list as they are needed for adjusting entries. However, it is easier to include them now, especially if preparing the work sheet on an electronic spreadsheet. Listing the accounts within their proper classifications (assets, liabilities, etc.) also makes it easier to extend the amounts to the proper columns.

STEP 2 **Prepare the Adjustments.** As shown in Figure 5-16, the second pair of amount columns is used to prepare the adjusting entries. Enter the adjustments directly in these columns. When an account is debited or credited, the amount is entered on the same line as the name of the account and in the appropriate Adjustments Debit or Credit column. A small letter in parentheses identifies each adjusting entry made on the work sheet.

ADJUSTMENT (a):

Supplies costing $60 were used during June.

	Debit	Credit
Supplies Expense	60	
Supplies		60

ADJUSTMENT (b):

One month's insurance premium has expired.

	Debit	Credit
Insurance Expense	25	
Prepaid Insurance		25

ADJUSTMENT (c):

Employees earned $50 that has not yet been paid.

	Debit	Credit
Wages Expense	50	
Wages Payable		50

ADJUSTMENT (d):

Depreciation on the motor scooters is recognized.

	Debit	Credit
Depreciation Expense—Delivery Equipment	100	
Accumulated Depreciation—Delivery Equipment		100

When all adjustments have been entered on the work sheet, each column should be totaled to assure that the debits equal the credits for all entries. After balancing the columns, they should be double ruled.

FIGURE 5-16   Step 1: Prepare the Trial Balance; Step 2: Prepare the Adjustments

Rohan's Campus Delivery
Work Sheet
For Month Ended June 30, 20 - -

	ACCOUNT TITLE	TRIAL BALANCE DEBIT	TRIAL BALANCE CREDIT	ADJUSTMENT DEBIT	ADJUSTMENT CREDIT	ADJUSTED TRIAL BALANCE DEBIT	ADJUSTED TRIAL BALANCE CREDIT	INCOME STATEMENT DEBIT	INCOME STATEMENT CREDIT	BALANCE SHEET DEBIT	BALANCE SHEET CREDIT
1	Cash	3 7 0 00									
2	Accounts Receivable	6 5 0 00									
3	Supplies	8 0 00			(a) 6 0 00						
4	Prepaid Insurance	2 0 0 00			(b) 2 5 00						
5	Delivery Equipment	3 6 0 0 00									
6	Accum. Depr.—Delivery Equipment				(d) 1 0 0 00						
7	Accounts Payable		1 8 0 0 00								
8	Wages Payable				(c) 5 0 00						
9	Rohan Macsen, Capital		2 0 0 0 00								
10	Rohan Macsen, Drawing	1 5 0 00									
11	Delivery Fees		2 1 5 0 00								
12	Wages Expense	6 5 0 00		(c) 5 0 00							
13	Rent Expense	2 0 0 00									
14	Supplies Expense			(a) 6 0 00							
15	Phone Expense	5 0 00									
16	Insurance Expense			(b) 2 5 00							
17	Depr. Expense—Delivery Equipment			(d) 1 0 0 00							
18		5 9 5 0 00	5 9 5 0 00	2 3 5 00	2 3 5 00						
19	Net income										
20											

STEP 1

Step 1 Prepare the Trial Balance.
- Write the heading, account titles, and the debit and credit amounts from the general ledger.
- Place a single rule across the Trial Balance columns and total the debit and credit amounts.
- Place a double rule under the totals for each column.
- Total debits must equal total credits.

STEP 2

Step 2 Prepare the Adjustments.
- Record the adjustments.
  Hint: Make certain that each adjustment is on the same line as the account name and in the appropriate column.
  Hint: Identify each adjusting entry by a letter in parentheses.
- Rule the Adjustments columns.
- Total the Debit and Credit columns and double rule the columns.
- Total debits must equal total credits.

STEP 3 **Prepare the Adjusted Trial Balance.** As shown in Figure 5-17, the third pair of amount columns on the work sheet is the **Adjusted Trial Balance columns.**

- When an account balance is not affected by entries in the Adjustments columns, the amount in the Trial Balance columns is extended directly to the Adjusted Trial Balance columns.

- *When affected by an entry in the Adjustments columns, the account balance to be entered in the Adjusted Trial Balance columns increases or decreases by the amount of the adjusting entry.*

For example, in Rohan Macsen's business, Supplies is listed in the Trial Balance Debit column as $80. Since the entry of $60 is in the Adjustments Credit column, the amount extended to the Adjusted Trial Balance Debit column is $20 ($80 − $60).

Wages Expense is listed in the Trial Balance Debit column as $650. Since $50 is in the Adjustments Debit column, the amount extended to the Adjusted Trial Balance Debit column is $700 ($650 + $50).

After all extensions have been made, the Adjusted Trial Balance columns are totaled to prove the equality of the debits and the credits. Once balanced, the columns are double ruled.

STEP 4 **Extend Adjusted Balances to the Income Statement and Balance Sheet Columns.** As shown in Figure 5-18, each account listed in the Adjusted Trial Balance must be extended to either the Income Statement or Balance Sheet columns. The **Income Statement columns** show the amounts that will be reported in the income statement. All revenue accounts are extended to the Income Statement Credit column and expense accounts are extended to the Income Statement Debit column.

The asset, liability, drawing, and capital accounts are extended to the **Balance Sheet columns.** Although called the Balance Sheet columns, these columns of the work sheet show the amounts that will be reported in the balance sheet and the statement of owner's equity. The asset and drawing accounts are extended to the Balance Sheet Debit column. The liability and owner's capital accounts are extended to the Balance Sheet Credit column.

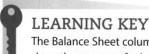

LEARNING KEY
The Balance Sheet columns show the amounts for both the balance sheet and the statement of owner's equity.

STEP 5 **Complete the Work Sheet.** To complete the work sheet, first total the Income Statement columns. If the total of the credits (revenues) exceeds the total of the debits (expenses), the difference represents net income. If the total of the debits exceeds the total of the credits, the difference represents a net loss.

The Income Statement columns of Rohan's work sheet in Figure 5-18 show total credits of $2,150 and total debits of $1,135. The difference, $1,015, is the net income for the month of June. This amount should be added to the Debit column to balance the Income Statement columns. "Net Income" should be written on the same line in the Account Title column. If the business had a net loss, the amount of the loss would be added to the Income Statement Credit column and the words "Net Loss" would be written in the Account Title column. Once balanced, the columns should be double ruled.

LEARNING KEY
In the Balance Sheet columns of the work sheet, total debits minus total credits equals net *income* if greater than zero and equals net *loss* if less than zero.

Finally, the Balance Sheet columns are totaled. The difference between the totals of these columns also is the amount of net income or net loss for the accounting period. If the total debits exceed the total credits, the difference is net income. If the total credits exceed the total debits, the difference is a net loss. This difference should be the same as the difference we found for the Income Statement columns.

FIGURE 5-17   Step 3: Prepare the Adjusted Trial Balance

Rohan's Campus Delivery
Work Sheet
For Month Ended June 30, 20--

	TRIAL BALANCE DEBIT	TRIAL BALANCE CREDIT	ADJUSTMENT DEBIT	ADJUSTMENT CREDIT	ADJUSTED TRIAL BALANCE DEBIT	ADJUSTED TRIAL BALANCE CREDIT	INCOME STATEMENT DEBIT	INCOME STATEMENT CREDIT	BALANCE SHEET DEBIT	BALANCE SHEET CREDIT	
1 Cash	3 7 0 00				3 7 0 00						1
2 Accounts Receivable	6 5 0 00				6 5 0 00						2
3 Supplies	8 0 00			(a) 6 0 00	2 0 00						3
4 Prepaid Insurance	2 0 0 00			(b) 2 5 00	1 7 5 00						4
5 Delivery Equipment	3 6 0 0 00				3 6 0 0 00						5
6 Accum. Depr.—Delivery Equipment				(d) 1 0 0 00		1 0 0 00					6
7 Accounts Payable		1 8 0 0 00				1 8 0 0 00					7
8 Wages Payable				(c) 5 0 00		5 0 00					8
9 Rohan Macsen, Capital		2 0 0 0 00				2 0 0 0 00					9
10 Rohan Macsen, Drawing	1 5 0 00				1 5 0 00						10
11 Delivery Fees		2 1 5 0 00				2 1 5 0 00					11
12 Wages Expense	6 5 0 00		(c) 5 0 00		7 0 0 00						12
13 Rent Expense	2 0 0 00				2 0 0 00						13
14 Supplies Expense			(a) 6 0 00		6 0 00						14
15 Phone Expense	5 0 00				5 0 00						15
16 Insurance Expense			(b) 2 5 00		2 5 00						16
17 Depr. Expense—Delivery Equipment			(d) 1 0 0 00		1 0 0 00						17
18	5 9 5 0 00	5 9 5 0 00	2 3 5 00	2 3 5 00	6 1 0 0 00	6 1 0 0 00					18
19 Net income											19

STEP 1   STEP 2   STEP 3

Callout boxes:
- No adjustment: simply extend balance to appropriate column.
- A debit and a credit: subtract.
- A single debit or credit: extend to appropriate column.
- Two debits: add.
- When columns are balanced, use double ruling.

Step 3 Prepare the Adjusted Trial Balance.
- Extend those debits and credits that are not adjusted directly to the appropriate Adjusted Trial Balance column.
- Enter the adjusted balances in the appropriate Adjusted Trial Balance column.
  Hint: If an account has a debit and a credit, subtract the adjustment. If an account has two debits or two credits, add the adjustment.
- Single rule the Adjusted Trial Balance columns. Total and double rule the Debit and Credit columns.
- Total debits must equal total credits.

FIGURE 5-18 Step 4: Extend Adjusted Balances to the Inc. Stmt. & Balance Sheet Columns; Step 5: Complete the Work Sheet

Rohan's Campus Delivery
Work Sheet
For Month Ended June 30, 20 - -

	ACCOUNT TITLE	TRIAL BALANCE DEBIT	TRIAL BALANCE CREDIT	ADJUSTMENT DEBIT	ADJUSTMENT CREDIT	ADJUSTED TRIAL BALANCE DEBIT	ADJUSTED TRIAL BALANCE CREDIT	INCOME STATEMENT DEBIT	INCOME STATEMENT CREDIT	BALANCE SHEET DEBIT	BALANCE SHEET CREDIT	
1	Cash	3 7 0 00				3 7 0 00				3 7 0 00		1
2	Accounts Receivable	6 5 0 00				6 5 0 00				6 5 0 00		2
3	Supplies	8 0 00			(a) 6 0 00	2 0 00				2 0 00		3
4	Prepaid Insurance	2 0 0 00			(b) 2 5 00	1 7 5 00				1 7 5 00		4
5	Delivery Equipment	3 6 0 0 00				3 6 0 0 00				3 6 0 0 00		5
6	Accum. Depr.—Delivery Equipment				(d) 1 0 0 00		1 0 0 00				1 0 0 00	6
7	Accounts Payable		1 8 0 0 00				1 8 0 0 00				1 8 0 0 00	7
8	Wages Payable				(c) 5 0 00		5 0 00				5 0 00	8
9	Rohan Macsen, Capital		2 0 0 0 00				2 0 0 0 00				2 0 0 0 00	9
10	Rohan Macsen, Drawing	1 5 0 00				1 5 0 00				1 5 0 00		10
11	Delivery Fees		2 1 5 0 00				2 1 5 0 00		2 1 5 0 00			11
12	Wages Expense	6 5 0 00		(c) 5 0 00		7 0 0 00		7 0 0 00				12
13	Rent Expense	2 0 0 00				2 0 0 00		2 0 0 00				13
14	Supplies Expense			(a) 6 0 00		6 0 00		6 0 00				14
15	Phone Expense	5 0 00				5 0 00		5 0 00				15
16	Insurance Expense			(b) 2 5 00		2 5 00		2 5 00				16
17	Depr. Expense—Delivery Equipment			(d) 1 0 0 00		1 0 0 00		1 0 0 00				17
18		5 9 5 0 00	5 9 5 0 00	2 3 5 00	2 3 5 00	6 1 0 0 00	6 1 0 0 00	1 1 3 5 00	2 1 5 0 00	4 9 6 5 00	3 9 5 0 00	18
19	Net income							1 0 1 5 00			1 0 1 5 00	19
20								2 1 5 0 00	2 1 5 0 00	4 9 6 5 00	4 9 6 5 00	20

STEP 1   STEP 2   STEP 3   STEPS 4 AND 5

Step 4 Extend Adjusted Balances to the Income Statement and Balance Sheet Columns.
- Extend all revenue accounts to the Income Statement Credit column.
- Extend all expense accounts to the Income Statement Debit column.
- Extend the asset and drawing accounts to the Balance Sheet Debit column.
- Extend the liability and owner's capital accounts to the Balance Sheet Credit columns.

Step 5 Complete the Work Sheet.
- Rule and total the Income Statement and Balance Sheet columns.
- Calculate the difference between the Income Statement Debit and Credit columns.
- Calculate the difference between the Balance Sheet Debit and Credit columns.
  Hint: If the Income Statement credits exceed debits, net income has occurred; otherwise a net loss has occurred. If the Balance Sheet debits exceed the credits, the difference is net income; otherwise a net loss has occurred.
  Hint: The difference between the Balance Sheet columns should be the same as the difference between the Income Statement columns.
- Add the net income to the Income Statement Debit column or add the net loss to the Income Statement Credit column. Add the net income to the Balance Sheet Credit column or the net loss to the Balance Sheet Debit column. Write "Net income" or "Net Loss" in the Account Title column.
- Total and double rule the columns.

Checkpoint ✓

Complete Check-
point-3 on page 158
to test your basic
understanding of LO3.

The Balance Sheet columns of Rohan's work sheet show total debits of $4,965 and total credits of $3,950. The difference of $1,015 represents the amount of net income for the month. This amount is added to the Credit column to balance the Balance Sheet columns. If the business had a net loss, this amount would be added to the Balance Sheet Debit column. Once balanced, the columns should be double ruled.

A trick for remembering the appropriate placement of the net income and net loss is the following: Net Income *apart*; Net Loss *together*. Figure 5-19 illustrates this learning aid.

FIGURE 5-19   Net Income Apart, Net Loss Together

FINDING ERRORS ON THE WORK SHEET

LO4   Describe methods for finding errors on the work sheet.

If any of the columns on the work sheet do not balance, you must find the error before you continue. Once you are confident that the work sheet is accurate, you are ready to journalize the adjusting entries and prepare financial statements. Figure 5-20 offers tips for finding errors on the work sheet.

FIGURE 5-20   Finding Errors on the Work Sheet

TIPS FOR FINDING ERRORS ON THE WORK SHEET
1. Check the addition of all columns.
2. Check the addition and subtraction required when extending to the Adjusted Trial Balance columns.
3. Make sure the adjusted account balances have been extended to the appropriate columns.
4. Make sure that the net income or net loss has been added to the appropriate columns.

Checkpoint ✓

Complete Check-
point-4 on page 158
to test your basic
understanding of LO4.

JOURNALIZING ADJUSTING ENTRIES FROM THE WORK SHEET

LO5   Journalize adjusting entries from the work sheet.

Keep in mind that the work sheet simply helps the accountant organize the end-of-period work. *Writing the adjustments on the work sheet has no effect on the ledger accounts in the accounting system. The only way to change the balance of a ledger account is to make a journal entry.* Once the work sheet has been completed, simply copy the adjustments from the work sheet to the journal, as shown in Figure 5-21.

FIGURE 5-21   Journalizing Adjusting Entries from the Work Sheet

Rohan's Campus Delivery
Work Sheet (Partial)
For Month Ended June 30, 20--

	ACCOUNT TITLE	TRIAL BALANCE DEBIT	TRIAL BALANCE CREDIT	ADJUSTMENTS DEBIT	ADJUSTMENTS CREDIT
1	Cash	3 7 0 00			
2	Accounts Receivable	6 5 0 00			
3	Supplies	8 0 00			(a) 6 0 00
4	Prepaid Insurance	2 0 0 00			(b) 2 5 00
5	Delivery Equipment	3 6 0 0 00			
6	Accum. Depr.—Delivery Equipment				(d) 1 0 0 00
7	Accounts Payable		1 8 0 0 00		
8	Wages Payable				(c) 5 0 00
9	Rohan Macsen, Capital		2 0 0 0 00		
10	Rohan Macsen, Drawing	1 5 0 00			
11	Delivery Fees		2 1 5 0 00		
12	Wages Expense	6 5 0 00		(c) 5 0 00	
13	Rent Expense	2 0 0 00			
14	Supplies Expense			(a) 6 0 00	
15	Phone Expense	5 0 00			
16	Insurance Expense			(b) 2 5 00	
17	Depr. Expense—Delivery Equipment			(d) 1 0 0 00	
18		5 9 5 0 00	5 9 5 0 00	2 3 5 00	2 3 5 00

GENERAL JOURNAL   PAGE 3

	DATE		DESCRIPTION	POST. REF.	DEBIT	CREDIT	
1			Adjusting Entries				1
(a) 2	20-- June	30	Supplies Expense	523	6 0 00		2
3			Supplies	141		6 0 00	3
4							4
(b) 5		30	Insurance Expense	535	2 5 00		5
6			Prepaid Insurance	145		2 5 00	6
7							7
(c) 8		30	Wages Expense	511	5 0 00		8
9			Wages Payable	219		5 0 00	9
10							10
(d) 11		30	Depr. Expense—Delivery Equipment	541	1 0 0 00		11
12			Accum. Depr.—Delivery Equipment	185.1		1 0 0 00	12

Checkpoint ✓

Complete Check-point-5 on page 159 to test your basic understanding of LO5.

Rohan's adjusting entries are illustrated in Figure 5-21 as they would appear in a general journal. Note that the last day of the accounting period, June 30, has been entered in the date column and "*Adjusting Entries*" is written in the Description column prior to the first adjusting entry. No explanation is required in the Description column for individual adjusting entries. We simply label them as adjusting entries.

METHODS OF ACCOUNTING: CASH, MODIFIED CASH, AND ACCRUAL

LO6 Explain the cash, modified cash, and accrual bases of accounting.

The accrual basis of accounting offers the best matching of revenues and expenses and is required under generally accepted accounting principles. GAAP financial statements prepared using the accrual method are particularly important when major businesses want to raise large amounts of money. Investors and creditors expect GAAP financial statements and generally will not invest or make loans without them.

However, many small professional service organizations are not concerned with raising large amounts of money from investors and creditors. These organizations include CPAs, doctors, dentists, lawyers, engineers, and architects. Since these organizations do not need to prepare GAAP financial statements, they often use the cash or modified cash basis. If one of these organizations needs to borrow money from a bank that requires GAAP financial statements, an accountant can convert the financial statements to the accrual basis.

Under the **accrual basis of accounting**, revenues are recorded when earned. Revenues are considered earned when a service is provided or a product is sold, regardless of when cash is received from the customer. If cash is not received, a receivable is set up.

The accrual basis also assumes that expenses are recorded when incurred. Expenses are incurred when a service is received or an asset consumed, regardless of when cash is paid. If cash is not paid when a service is received, a payable is set up. When assets are consumed, prepaid assets are decreased or long-term assets are depreciated. Since the accrual basis accounts for long-term assets, prepaid assets, receivables, and payables, it is the most comprehensive system and best method of measuring income for the vast majority of businesses.

LEARNING KEY

Accrual Basis

Accounting for: Revenues and Expenses	Accounting for: Assets and Liabilities	
Record revenue when earned.	Accounts receivable:	Yes
Record expenses when incurred.	Accounts payable:	Yes
	Prepaid assets:	Yes
	Long-term assets:	Yes

Under the **cash basis of accounting**, revenues are recorded when cash is received and expenses are recorded when cash is paid. This method will provide results that are similar to the accrual basis if there are few receivables, payables, and assets. However, as shown in Figure 5-22, the cash and accrual bases can result in very different measures of net income if a business has significant amounts of receivables, payables, and assets.

LEARNING KEY

Cash Basis

Accounting for: Revenues and Expenses	Accounting for: Assets and Liabilities	
Record revenue when cash is received.	Accounts receivable:	No
Record expenses when cash is paid.	Accounts payable:	No
	Prepaid assets:	No
	Long-term assets:	No

FIGURE 5-22   Cash versus Accrual Accounting

RECOGNITION OF REVENUES AND EXPENSES: ACCRUAL BASIS VS. CASH BASIS				
	Method of Accounting			
	Accrual Basis		**Cash Basis**	
Transaction	**Expense**	**Revenue**	**Expense**	**Revenue**
(a) Provided services on account, $600.		$600		
(b) Paid wages earned this period, $300	$300		$300	
(c) Received cash for services performed on account last month, $200				$ 200
(d) Received cleaning bill for month, $250	250			
(e) Paid on account for last month's advertising, $100			100	
(f) Purchase of supplies, $50			50	
(g) Supplies used during month, $40	40			
	$590	$600	$450	$ 200
Revenue		$600		$ 200
Expense		590		450
Net Income (Loss)		$ 10		$(250)
Revenues are recognized when:		earned		cash is received
Expenses are recognized when:		incurred		cash is paid

> The modified cash basis is the same as the accrual basis, except receivables and payables are not recognized for revenues and operating expenses.

A third method of accounting combines aspects of the cash and accrual methods. With the **modified cash basis**, a business uses the cash basis for recording revenues and most expenses. Exceptions are made when cash is paid for assets with useful lives greater than one accounting period. For example, under a strict cash basis, if cash is paid for equipment, buildings, supplies, or insurance, the amount is immediately recorded as an expense. This approach could cause major distortions when measuring net income. Under the modified cash basis, cash payments like these are recorded as assets, and adjustments are made each period as under the accrual basis. Liabilities associated with the acquisition of these assets are also recognized.

Although similar to the accrual basis, the modified cash basis does not account for receivables or for payables for services received. Thus, the modified cash basis is a combination of the cash and accrual methods of accounting. The differences and similarities among the cash, modified cash, and accrual methods of accounting are demonstrated in Figure 5-23.

LEARNING KEY

Modified Cash Basis

Accounting for:
Revenues and Expenses

Record revenue when cash is received.
Record expenses when cash is paid, except
  for assets with useful lives greater than
  one accounting period. Accrual accounting
  is used for prepaid assets (insurance and
  supplies) and long-term assets.

Accounting for:
Assets and Liabilities

Accounts receivable:	No
Accounts payable	
for purchase of assets:	Yes
for services received:	No
Prepaid assets:	Yes
Long-term assets:	Yes

FIGURE 5-23 Comparison of Cash, Modified Cash, and Accrual Methods

ENTRIES MADE UNDER EACH ACCOUNTING METHOD			
Event	**Cash**	**Modified Cash**	**Accrual**

Revenues:
Perform services for cash
	Cash
	   Professional Fees
		Cash
		   Professional Fees
			Cash
			   Professional Fees

Perform services on account	No entry	No entry	Accounts Receivable Professional Fees

Expenses:
Pay cash for operating expenses:
wages, advertising, rent,
phone, etc.
	Expense
	   Cash
		Expense
		   Cash
			Expense
			   Cash

Pay cash for prepaid items:
insurance, supplies, etc.
	Expense
	   Cash
		Prepaid Asset
		   Cash
			Prepaid Asset
			   Cash

Pay cash for property, plant, and
equipment (PP&E)
	Expense
	   Cash
		PP&E Asset
		   Cash
			PP&E Asset
			   Cash

Receive bill for services received	No entry	No entry	Expense Accounts Payable
End-of-period adjustments: Wages earned by employees but not paid	No entry	No entry	Wages Expense Wages Payable

Prepaid items used	No entry	Expense
		   Prepaid Asset
			Expense
			   Prepaid Asset

Depreciation on property,
plant, and equipment
	No entry	Depreciation Expense
		   Accumulated Depreciation
			Depreciation Expense
			   Accumulated Depreciation

Other:
Purchase of assets
on account
	No entry	Asset
		   Accounts Payable
			Asset
			   Accounts Payable

Payments for assets
purchased on account
	Expense
	   Cash
		Accounts Payable
		   Cash
			Accounts Payable
			   Cash

LEARNING KEY

The shaded areas in Figure 5-23 show that sometimes the modified cash basis is the same as the cash basis and sometimes it is the same as the accrual basis. For some transactions, all methods are the same.

Checkpoint ✓

Complete Checkpoint-6 on page 159 to test your basic understanding of LO6.

If all businesses were the same, only one method of accounting would be needed. However, businesses vary in their need for major assets like buildings and equipment, the amount of customer receivables, and payables to suppliers. For example, if a business were rather small with no major assets, receivables, or payables, it would be simpler to use the cash basis of accounting. In addition, under these circumstances, the difference in net income under the accrual and cash bases of accounting would be small. Most individuals fit this description and use the cash basis on their tax returns.

Businesses with buildings and equipment, but few receivables and payables, might use the modified cash basis. Again, the accounting would be a little simpler and differences between net income computed under the modified cash and accrual bases would be small. Finally, businesses with buildings and equipment, and receivables and payables, should use the accrual basis of accounting to achieve the best matching of revenues and expenses.

Self-Study

Key Points to Remember

LO1	Prepare end-of-period adjustments.	End-of-period adjustments are necessary to bring the general ledger accounts up to date prior to preparing financial statements. Reasons to adjust the trial balance are as follows: 1. To report all revenues earned during the accounting period. 2. To report all expenses incurred to produce the revenues during the accounting period. 3. To accurately report the assets on the balance sheet. Some assets may have expired, depreciated, or been used up during the accounting period. 4. To accurately report the liabilities on the balance sheet date. Expenses may have been incurred, but not yet paid.
LO2	Post adjusting entries to the general ledger.	Adjusting entries are posted to the general ledger in the same manner as all other entries, except that "Adjusting" is written in the Item column of the general ledger.
LO3	Prepare a work sheet.	Steps in preparing the work sheet are as follows: 1. Prepare the trial balance. 2. Prepare the adjustments. 3. Prepare the adjusted trial balance. 4. Extend the adjusted account balances to the Income Statement and Balance Sheet columns. 5. Total the Income Statement and Balance Sheet columns to compute the net income or net loss.
LO4	Describe methods for finding errors on the work sheet.	Tips for finding errors on the work sheet include the following: 1. Check the addition of all columns. 2. Check the addition and subtraction required when extending to the Adjusted Trial Balance columns. 3. Make sure the adjusted account balances have been extended to the appropriate columns. 4. Make sure that the net income or net loss has been added to the appropriate columns.
LO5	Journalize adjusting entries from the work sheet.	The adjustments are copied from the work sheet to the journal. The last day of the accounting period is entered in the Date column and "Adjusting Entries" is written in the Description column.
LO6	Explain the cash, modified cash, and accrual bases of accounting.	Cash Basis—Record revenues when cash is received and expenses when cash is paid. Accrual Basis—Record revenues when earned and expenses as incurred. Modified Cash Basis—Same as accrual, except no accounts receivable and no accounts payable for operating expenses.

DEMONSTRATION PROBLEM

Justin Park is a lawyer specializing in corporate tax law. He began his practice on January 1. A chart of accounts and trial balance taken on December 31, 20--, are provided on below and on page 154.

Information for year-end adjustments is as follows:

(a) Office supplies on hand at year-end amounted to $300.

(b) On January 1, 20--, Park purchased office equipment costing $15,000 with an expected life of five years and no salvage value.

(c) Computer equipment costing $6,000 with an expected life of three years and no salvage value was purchased on July 1, 20--. Assume that Park computes depreciation to the nearest full month.

(d) A premium of $1,200 for a one-year insurance policy was paid on December 1, 20--.

(e) Wages earned by Park's part-time secretary, which have not yet been paid, amount to $300.

REQUIRED

1. Prepare the work sheet for the year ended December 31, 20--.

2. Prepare adjusting entries in a general journal.

JUSTIN PARK LEGAL SERVICES CHART OF ACCOUNTS			
Assets		**Revenue**	
101	Cash	401	Client Fees
142	Office Supplies		
145	Prepaid Insurance	**Expenses**	
181	Office Equipment	511	Wages Expense
181.1	Accumulated Depr.—	521	Rent Expense
	Office Equipment	523	Office Supplies Expense
187	Computer Equipment	525	Phone Expense
187.1	Accumulated Depr.—	533	Utilities Expense
	Computer Equipment	535	Insurance Expense
Liabilities		541	Depr. Expense—
201	Notes Payable		Office Equipment
202	Accounts Payable	542	Depr. Expense—
219	Wages Payable		Computer Equipment
Owner's Equity			
311	Justin Park, Capital		
312	Justin Park, Drawing		

(*continued*)

Justin Park Legal Services
Trial Balance
December 31, 20 --

ACCOUNT TITLE	ACCOUNT NO.	DEBIT BALANCE					CREDIT BALANCE				
Cash	101	7	0	0	0	00					
Office Supplies	142		8	0	0	00					
Prepaid Insurance	145	1	2	0	0	00					
Office Equipment	181	15	0	0	0	00					
Computer Equipment	187	6	0	0	0	00					
Notes Payable	201						5	0	0	0	00
Accounts Payable	202						5	0	0	0	00
Justin Park, Capital	311						11	4	0	0	00
Justin Park, Drawing	312	5	0	0	0	00					
Client Fees	401						40	0	0	0	00
Wages Expense	511	12	0	0	0	00					
Rent Expense	521	5	0	0	0	00					
Phone Expense	525	1	0	0	0	00					
Utilities Expense	533	3	9	0	0	00					
		56	9	0	0	00	56	9	0	0	00

The solution to part (1) is found on page 155.

2.

	DATE		DESCRIPTION	POST. REF.	DEBIT					CREDIT					
	GENERAL JOURNAL												PAGE 11		
1			**Adjusting Entries**												1
2	20-- Dec.	31	Office Supplies Expense			5	0	0	00						2
3			Office Supplies								5	0	0	00	3
4															4
5		31	Depr. Expense—Office Equipment		3	0	0	0	00						5
6			Accum. Depr.—Office Equipment							3	0	0	0	00	6
7															7
8		31	Depr. Expense—Computer Equipment		1	0	0	0	00						8
9			Accum. Depr.—Computer Equipment							1	0	0	0	00	9
10															10
11		31	Insurance Expense			1	0	0	00						11
12			Prepaid Insurance								1	0	0	00	12
13															13
14		31	Wages Expense			3	0	0	00						14
15			Wages Payable								3	0	0	00	15

SOLUTION 1.

Justin Park Legal Services
Work Sheet
For Year Ended December 31, 20--

#	ACCOUNT TITLE	TRIAL BALANCE DEBIT	TRIAL BALANCE CREDIT	ADJUSTMENTS DEBIT	ADJUSTMENTS CREDIT	ADJUSTED TRIAL BALANCE DEBIT	ADJUSTED TRIAL BALANCE CREDIT	INCOME STATEMENT DEBIT	INCOME STATEMENT CREDIT	BALANCE SHEET DEBIT	BALANCE SHEET CREDIT
1	Cash	7 0 0 0 00				7 0 0 0 00				7 0 0 0 00	
2	Office Supplies	8 0 0 00			(a) 5 0 0 00	3 0 0 00				3 0 0 00	
3	Prepaid Insurance	1 2 0 0 00			(d) 1 0 0 00	1 1 0 0 00				1 1 0 0 00	
4	Office Equipment	15 0 0 0 00				15 0 0 0 00				15 0 0 0 00	
5	Accum. Depr.—Office Equip.				(b) 3 0 0 0 00		3 0 0 0 00				3 0 0 0 00
6	Computer Equipment	6 0 0 0 00				6 0 0 0 00				6 0 0 0 00	
7	Accum. Depr.—Computer Equip.				(c) 1 0 0 0 00		1 0 0 0 00				1 0 0 0 00
8	Notes Payable		5 0 0 0 00				5 0 0 0 00				5 0 0 0 00
9	Accounts Payable		5 0 0 00				5 0 0 00				5 0 0 00
10	Wages Payable				(e) 3 0 0 00		3 0 0 00				3 0 0 00
11	Justin Park, Capital		11 4 0 0 00				11 4 0 0 00				11 4 0 0 00
12	Justin Park, Drawing	5 0 0 0 00				5 0 0 0 00				5 0 0 0 00	
13	Client Fees		40 0 0 0 00				40 0 0 0 00		40 0 0 0 00		
14	Wages Expense	12 0 0 0 00		(e) 3 0 0 00		12 3 0 0 00		12 3 0 0 00			
15	Rent Expense	5 0 0 0 00				5 0 0 0 00		5 0 0 0 00			
16	Office Supplies Expense			(a) 5 0 0 00		5 0 0 00		5 0 0 00			
17	Phone Expense	1 0 0 0 00				1 0 0 0 00		1 0 0 0 00			
18	Utilities Expense	3 9 0 0 00				3 9 0 0 00		3 9 0 0 00			
19	Insurance Expense			(d) 1 0 0 00		1 0 0 00		1 0 0 00			
20	Depr. Expense—Office Equip.			(b) 3 0 0 0 00		3 0 0 0 00		3 0 0 0 00			
21	Depr. Expense—Computer Equip.			(c) 1 0 0 0 00		1 0 0 0 00		1 0 0 0 00			
22		56 9 0 0 00	56 9 0 0 00	4 9 0 0 00	4 9 0 0 00	61 2 0 0 00	61 2 0 0 00	26 8 0 0 00	40 0 0 0 00	34 4 0 0 00	21 2 0 0 00
23	Net Income							13 2 0 0 00			13 2 0 0 00
24								40 0 0 0 00	40 0 0 0 00	34 4 0 0 00	34 4 0 0 00
25											
26											
27											
28											
29											
30											

KEY TERMS

accrual basis of accounting (149) A method of accounting under which revenues are recorded when earned and expenses are recorded when incurred.

Adjusted Trial Balance columns (144) The third pair of amount columns on the work sheet. They are used to prove the equality of the debits and credits in the general ledger accounts after making all end-of-period adjustments.

adjusting entries (131) Journal entries made at the end of an accounting period to reflect changes in account balances that are not the direct result of an exchange with an outside party.

Balance Sheet columns (144) The work sheet columns that show the amounts that will be reported in the balance sheet and the statement of owner's equity.

book value (137) The difference between the asset account and its related accumulated depreciation account. The value reflected by the accounting records.

cash basis of accounting (149) A method of accounting under which revenues are recorded when cash is received and expenses are recorded when cash is paid.

contra-asset (136) An account with a credit balance that is deducted from the related asset account on the balance sheet.

depreciable cost (136) The cost of an asset that is subject to depreciation.

depreciation (136) A method of matching an asset's original cost against the revenues produced over its useful life.

expense recognition principle (131) Expenses should be recognized when incurred, regardless of when cash is paid. Expenses are generally considered to be incurred when services are received or assets consumed.

fiscal year (131) A 12-month period for which financial reports are prepared.

historical cost principle (136) A principle that requires assets to be recorded at their actual cost.

Income Statement columns (144) The work sheet columns that show the amounts that will be reported in the income statement.

market value (136) The amount an item can be sold for under normal economic conditions.

matching principle (131) The proper matching of revenues earned during an accounting period with the expenses incurred to produce the revenues is often referred to as the matching principle.

modified cash basis (150) A method of accounting that combines aspects of the cash and accrual methods. It uses the cash basis for recording revenues and most expenses. Exceptions are made when cash is paid for assets with useful lives greater than one accounting period.

plant assets (136) Assets of a durable nature that will be used for operations over several years. Examples include buildings and equipment.

revenue recognition principle (131) Revenues should be recognized when earned, regardless of when cash is received from the customer. Revenues are considered earned when a service is provided or a product is sold.

salvage value (136) The expected market value of an asset at the end of its useful life.

straight-line method (136) A depreciation method in which the depreciable cost is divided by the estimated useful life.

undepreciated cost (137) The difference between the asset account and its related accumulated depreciation account. Also known as book value.

useful life (136)   The period of time that an asset is expected to help produce revenues.

work sheet (140)   A form used to pull together all of the information needed to enter adjusting entries and prepare the financial statements.

SELF-STUDY TEST QUESTIONS

True/False

1. **LO1**   The matching principle in accounting requires the matching of debits and credits.

2. **LO1**   Adjusting entries are required at the end of the accounting period because of mistakes in the journal and ledger.

3. **LO1**   As part of the adjustment of supplies, an expense account is debited and Supplies is credited for the amount of supplies used during the accounting period.

4. **LO1**   Depreciable cost is the difference between the original cost of the asset and its accumulated depreciation.

5. **LO1**   The purpose of depreciation is to record the asset's market value in the accounting records.

Multiple Choice

1. **LO1**   The purpose of depreciation is to

   (a) spread the cost of an asset over its useful life.
   (b) show the current market value of an asset.
   (c) set up a reserve fund to purchase a new asset.
   (d) expense the asset in the year it was purchased.

2. **LO1**   Depreciable cost is the

   (a) difference between original cost and accumulated depreciation.
   (b) difference in actual cost and true market value.
   (c) difference between original cost and estimated salvage value.
   (d) difference between estimated salvage value and the actual salvage value.

3. **LO1**   Book value is the

   (a) difference between market value and estimated value.
   (b) difference between market value and historical cost.
   (c) difference between original cost and salvage value.
   (d) difference between original cost and accumulated depreciation.

4. **LO1**   The adjustment for wages earned by employees but not yet paid is

   (a) debit Wages Payable and credit Wages Expense.
   (b) debit Wages Expense and credit Cash.
   (c) debit Wages Expense and credit Wages Payable.
   (d) debit Wages Expense and credit Accounts Receivable.

5. **LO3**   The first step in preparing a work sheet is to

   (a) prepare the trial balance.
   (b) prepare the adjustments.
   (c) prepare the adjusted trial balance.
   (d) extend the amounts from the Adjusted Trial Balance to the Income Statement and Balance Sheet columns.

Checkpoint Exercises

1. **LO1**   On December 31, the trial balance indicates that the supplies account has a balance, prior to the adjusting entry, of $100. A physical count of the supplies inventory shows that $70 of supplies remain. What adjustment should be made to the supplies account?

2. **LO2**   When posting adjusting entries to the general ledger, what is written in the Item column?

3. **LO3**   Indicate the heading for the columns of the work sheet A through F below.

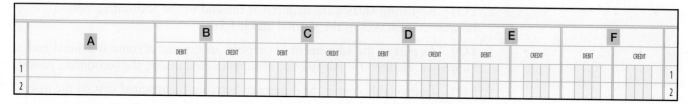

A	B		C		D		E		F	
	DEBIT	CREDIT	DEBIT	CREDIT	DEBIT	CREDIT	DEBIT	CREDIT	DEBIT	CREDIT
1										
2										

4. **LO4**   Find the error(s) in the work sheet below.

	ACCOUNT TITLE	TRIAL BALANCE		ADJUSTMENTS		ADJUSTED TRIAL BALANCE		INCOME STATEMENT		BALANCE SHEET	
		DEBIT	CREDIT	DEBIT	CREDIT	DEBIT	CREDIT	DEBIT	CREDIT	DEBIT	CREDIT
1	Cash	3 7 0 00				3 7 0 00				3 7 0 00	
2	Accounts Receivable	6 5 0 00				6 5 0 00				6 5 0 00	
3	Supplies	8 0 00			(a) 6 0 00	1 4 0 00				1 4 0 00	
4	Prepaid Insurance	2 0 0 00			(b) 2 5 00	1 7 5 00				1 7 5 00	
5	Delivery Equipment	3 6 0 0 00				3 6 0 0 00				3 6 0 0 00	
6	Accum. Depr.—Delivery Equipment			(d) 1 0 0 00			1 0 0 00				1 0 0 00
7	Accounts Payable		1 8 0 0 00				1 8 0 0 00				1 8 0 0 00
8	Wages Payable				(c) 5 0 00		5 0 00				5 0 00
9	Rohan Macsen, Capital		2 0 0 0 00				2 0 0 0 00				2 0 0 0 00
10	Rohan Macsen, Drawing	1 5 0 00				1 5 0 00				1 5 0 00	
11	Delivery Fees		2 1 5 0 00				2 1 5 0 00		2 1 5 0 00		
12	Wages Expense	6 5 0 00		(c) 5 0 00		7 0 0 00		7 0 0 00			
13	Rent Expense	2 0 0 00				2 0 0 00		2 0 0 00			
14	Supplies Expense			(a) 6 0 00		6 0 00		6 0 00			
15	Phone Expense	5 0 00				5 0 00		5 0 00			
16	Insurance Expense			(b) 2 5 00		2 5 00		2 5 00			
17	Depr. Expense—Delivery Equipment			(d) 1 0 0 00		1 0 0 00		1 0 0 00			
18		5 9 5 0 00	5 9 5 0 00	2 3 5 00	2 3 5 00	6 2 2 0 00	6 1 0 0 00	1 1 3 5 00	2 1 5 0 00	5 0 8 5 00	3 9 5 0 00
19								1 0 1 5 00			1 1 3 5 00
20								2 1 5 0 00	2 1 5 0 00	5 0 8 5 00	5 0 8 5 00
21											
22											
23											
24											

5. **LO5** Using the following partial work sheet prepared on December 31, 20--, journalize the adjusting entry.

	ACCOUNT TITLE	TRIAL BALANCE		ADJUSTMENTS	
		DEBIT	CREDIT	DEBIT	CREDIT
1	Cash	3 7 0 00			
2	Accounts Receivable	6 5 0 00			
3	Supplies	8 0 00			
4	Prepaid Insurance	2 0 0 00			(b) 5 0 00
5	Delivery Equipment	3 6 0 0 00			
6	Accum. Depr.—Delivery Equipment				
7	Accounts Payable		1 8 0 0 00		
8	Wages Payable				
9	Rohan Macsen, Capital		2 0 0 0 00		
10	Rohan Macsen, Drawing	1 5 0 00			
11	Delivery Fees		2 1 5 0 00		
12	Wages Expense	6 5 0 00			
13	Rent Expense	2 0 0 00			
14	Supplies Expense				
15	Phone Expense	5 0 00			
16	Insurance Expense			(b) 5 0 00	
17	Depr. Expense—Delivery Equipment				
18		5 9 5 0 00	5 9 5 0 00	5 0 00	5 0 00
19					

6. **LO6** Bill Roberts provided legal advice to a client for $500 on account. Roberts paid a legal assistant $50 for research on this engagement and used office supplies costing $10. If these are the only transactions for the period, compute net income under the cash, accrual, and modified cash bases.

The answers to the Self-Study Test Questions are at the end of the chapter (pages 177–178).

Applying Your Knowledge

REVIEW QUESTIONS

LO1   1. Explain the revenue recognition principle.

LO1   2. Explain the expense recognition principle.

LO1   3. Explain the matching principle.

LO1   4. Explain the historical cost principle.

LO1   5. Describe a plant asset.

LO1   6. What is a contra-asset?

LO1   7. What is the useful life of an asset?

LO1   8. What is the purpose of depreciation?

LO1   9. What is an asset's depreciable cost?

LO1   10. What is the book value of an asset?

LO3   11. Explain the purpose of the work sheet.

LO3   12. Identify the five major column headings on a work sheet.

LO3   13. List the five steps taken in preparing a work sheet.

LO4   14. Describe four tips for finding errors on the work sheet.

LO6   15. Explain when revenues are recorded under the cash basis, modified cash basis, and accrual basis of accounting.

LO6   16. Explain when expenses are recorded under the cash basis, modified cash basis, and accrual basis of accounting.

SERIES A EXERCISES

E 5-1A (LO1)

ADJUSTMENT FOR SUPPLIES On December 31, the trial balance indicates that the supplies account has a balance, prior to the adjusting entry, of $320. A physical count of the supplies inventory shows that $90 of supplies remain. Analyze this adjustment for supplies using T accounts, and then formally enter this adjustment in the general journal.

E 5-2A (LO1)

ADJUSTMENT FOR INSURANCE On December 1, a six-month liability insurance policy was purchased for $900. Analyze the required adjustment as of December 31 using T accounts, and then formally enter this adjustment in the general journal.

E 5-3A (LO1)

SHOW
ME HOW

ADJUSTMENT FOR WAGES On December 31, the trial balance shows wages expense of $600. An additional $200 of wages was earned by the employees, but has not yet been paid. Analyze this adjustment for wages using T accounts, and then formally enter this adjustment in the general journal.

E 5-4A (LO1)

SHOW
ME HOW

ADJUSTMENT FOR DEPRECIATION OF ASSET On December 1, delivery equipment was purchased for $7,200. The delivery equipment has an estimated useful life of four years (48 months) and no salvage value. Using the straight-line depreciation method, analyze the necessary adjusting entry as of December 31 (one month) using T accounts, and then formally enter this adjustment in the general journal.

E 5-5A (LO1)

CALCULATION OF BOOK VALUE On June 1, 20--, a depreciable asset was acquired for $6,840. The asset has an estimated useful life of six years (72 months) and no salvage value. Using the straight-line depreciation method, calculate the book value as of December 31, 20--.

E 5-6A   (LO1)

SHOW
ME HOW

ANALYSIS OF ADJUSTING ENTRY FOR SUPPLIES Analyze each situation and indicate the correct dollar amount for the adjusting entry. (Trial balance is abbreviated as TB.)

1. Ending inventory of supplies is $260.

(Balance Sheet) Supplies		(Income Statement) Supplies Expense	
TB	580		
Bal. _____			

2. Amount of supplies used is $230.

(Balance Sheet) Supplies		(Income Statement) Supplies Expense	
TB	435		
Bal. _____			

E 5-7A   (LO1)

ANALYSIS OF ADJUSTING ENTRY FOR INSURANCE Analyze each situation and indicate the correct dollar amount for the adjusting entry.

1. Amount of insurance expired is $970.

(Balance Sheet) Prepaid Insurance		(Income Statement) Insurance Expense	
TB	1,450		
Bal. _____			

2. Amount of unexpired insurance is $565.

(Balance Sheet) Prepaid Insurance		(Income Statement) Insurance Expense	
TB	1,350		
Bal. _____			

E 5-8A   (LO2)

POSTING ADJUSTING ENTRIES Two adjusting entries are in the following general journal. Post these adjusting entries to the four general ledger accounts. The following account numbers were taken from the chart of accounts: 141, Supplies; 219, Wages Payable; 511, Wages Expense; and 523, Supplies Expense. If you are not using the working papers that accompany this text, enter the following balances before posting the entries: Supplies, $200 Dr.; Wages Expense, $1,200 Dr.

(continued)

GENERAL JOURNAL							PAGE 9
	DATE	DESCRIPTION	POST. REF.	DEBIT	CREDIT		
1		Adjusting Entries					1
2	20-- Dec. 31	Supplies Expense		8 5 00			2
3		Supplies			8 5 00		3
4							4
5	31	Wages Expense		2 2 0 00			5
6		Wages Payable			2 2 0 00		6

E 5-9A   (LO3)

✓ Adjustments col. total: $1,550

WORK SHEET AND ADJUSTING ENTRIES A partial work sheet for Jim Jacobs' Furniture Repair is shown as follows. Indicate by letters (a) through (d) the four adjustments in the Adjustments columns of the work sheet, properly matching each debit and credit. Complete the Adjustments columns.

Jim Jacobs' Furniture Repair
Work Sheet (Partial)
For Year Ended December 31, 20 - -

	ACCOUNT TITLE	TRIAL BALANCE		ADJUSTMENTS		ADJUSTED TRIAL BALANCE		
		DEBIT	CREDIT	DEBIT	CREDIT	DEBIT	CREDIT	
1	Cash	1 0 0 00				1 0 0 00		1
2	Supplies	8 5 0 00				2 0 0 00		2
3	Prepaid Insurance	9 0 0 00				3 0 0 00		3
4	Delivery Equipment	3 6 0 0 00				3 6 0 0 00		4
5	Accum. Depr.—Delivery Equipment		6 0 0 00				8 0 0 00	5
6	Wages Payable						1 0 0 00	6
7	Jim Jacobs, Capital		4 0 0 0 00				4 0 0 0 00	7
8	Repair Fees		1 6 5 0 00				1 6 5 0 00	8
9	Wages Expense	6 0 0 00				7 0 0 00		9
10	Advertising Expense	2 0 0 00				2 0 0 00		10
11	Supplies Expense					6 5 0 00		11
12	Insurance Expense					6 0 0 00		12
13	Depr. Expense—Delivery Equipment					2 0 0 00		13
14		6 2 5 0 00	6 2 5 0 00			6 5 5 0 00	6 5 5 0 00	14

E 5-10A   (LO5)

SHOW
ME HOW

JOURNALIZING ADJUSTING ENTRIES From the adjustments columns in Exercise 5-9A, journalize the four adjusting entries, as of December 31, in proper general journal format.

E 5-11A   (LO3)

EXTENDING ADJUSTED BALANCES TO THE INCOME STATEMENT AND BALANCE SHEET COLUMNS Indicate with an "X" whether each account total should be extended to the Income Statement Debit or Credit or to the Balance Sheet Debit or Credit columns on the work sheet.

	Income Statement Debit	Credit	Balance Sheet Debit	Credit
Cash	_____	_____	_____	_____
Accounts Receivable	_____	_____	_____	_____
Supplies	_____	_____	_____	_____
Prepaid Insurance	_____	_____	_____	_____
Delivery Equipment	_____	_____	_____	_____
Accum. Depr.—Delivery Equipment	_____	_____	_____	_____
Accounts Payable	_____	_____	_____	_____
Wages Payable	_____	_____	_____	_____
Owner, Capital	_____	_____	_____	_____
Owner, Drawing	_____	_____	_____	_____
Delivery Fees	_____	_____	_____	_____
Wages Expense	_____	_____	_____	_____
Rent Expense	_____	_____	_____	_____
Supplies Expense	_____	_____	_____	_____
Insurance Expense	_____	_____	_____	_____
Depr. Exp.—Delivery Equipment	_____	_____	_____	_____

E 5-12A   (LO3)

ANALYSIS OF NET INCOME OR NET LOSS ON THE WORK SHEET Indicate with an "X" in which columns, Income Statement Debit or Credit or Balance Sheet Debit or Credit, a net income or a net loss would appear on a work sheet.

	Income Statement Debit	Credit	Balance Sheet Debit	Credit
Net Income	_____	_____	_____	_____
Net Loss	_____	_____	_____	_____

E 5-13A   (LO6)

✓ See Figure 5-23 in text

CASH, MODIFIED CASH, AND ACCRUAL BASES OF ACCOUNTING Prepare the entry for each of the following transactions, using the (a) cash basis, (b) modified cash basis, and (c) accrual basis of accounting.

1. Purchase supplies on account.
2. Make payment on asset previously purchased.
3. Purchase supplies for cash.
4. Purchase insurance for cash.
5. Pay cash for wages.
6. Pay cash for phone expense.
7. Pay cash for new equipment.

End-of-Period Adjusting Entries:

8. Wages earned but not paid.
9. Prepaid item purchased, partly used.
10. Depreciation on long-term assets.

SERIES A PROBLEMS

P 5-14A (LO1/3)

✓ Adjustments col. total: $2,145
✓ Net income: $810

SHOW
ME HOW

ADJUSTMENTS AND WORK SHEET SHOWING NET INCOME The trial balance after one month of operation for Mason's Delivery Service as of September 30, 20--, is shown below. Data to complete the adjustments are as follows:

(a) Supplies inventory as of September 30, $90.

(b) Insurance expired (used), $650.

(c) Depreciation on delivery equipment, $600.

(d) Wages earned by employees but not paid as of September 30, $350.

REQUIRED

1. Enter the adjustments in the Adjustments columns of the work sheet.
2. Complete the work sheet.

Mason's Delivery Service
Work Sheet (Partial)
For Month Ended September 30, 20 - -

	ACCOUNT TITLE	TRIAL BALANCE DEBIT	TRIAL BALANCE CREDIT	ADJUSTMENTS DEBIT	ADJUSTMENTS CREDIT	
1	Cash	1 6 0 0 00				1
2	Accounts Receivable	9 4 0 00				2
3	Supplies	6 3 5 00				3
4	Prepaid Insurance	1 2 0 0 00				4
5	Delivery Equipment	6 4 0 0 00				5
6	Accum. Depr.—Delivery Equipment					6
7	Accounts Payable		1 2 2 0 00			7
8	Wages Payable					8
9	Jill Mason, Capital		8 0 0 0 00			9
10	Jill Mason, Drawing	1 4 0 0 00				10
11	Delivery Fees		6 2 0 0 00			11
12	Wages Expense	1 5 0 0 00				12
13	Advertising Expense	4 6 0 00				13
14	Rent Expense	8 0 0 00				14
15	Supplies Expense					15
16	Phone Expense	1 6 5 00				16
17	Insurance Expense					17
18	Repair Expense	2 3 0 00				18
19	Oil and Gas Expense	9 0 00				19
20	Depr. Expense—Delivery Equipment					20
21		15 4 2 0 00	15 4 2 0 00			21

P 5-15A (LO1/3)

✓ Adjustments col. total: $1,380
✓ Net loss: $2,495

ADJUSTMENTS AND WORK SHEET SHOWING A NET LOSS Jason Armstrong started a business called Campus Delivery Service. After the first month of operations, the trial balance as of November 30, 20--, is as shown on the next page.

REQUIRED

1. Analyze the following adjustments and enter them on the work sheet.

   (a) Ending inventory of supplies on November 30, $185.

   (b) Unexpired (remaining) insurance as of November 30, $800.

   (c) Depreciation expense on van, $300.

   (d) Wages earned but not paid as of November 30, $190.

2. Complete the work sheet.

		TRIAL BALANCE		ADJUSTMENTS		
	ACCOUNT TITLE	DEBIT	CREDIT	DEBIT	CREDIT	
1	Cash	9 8 0 00				1
2	Accounts Receivable	5 9 0 00				2
3	Supplies	5 7 5 00				3
4	Prepaid Insurance	1 3 0 0 00				4
5	Van	5 8 0 0 00				5
6	Accum. Depr.—Van					6
7	Accounts Payable		9 6 0 00			7
8	Wages Payable					8
9	Jason Armstrong, Capital		10 0 0 0 00			9
10	Jason Armstrong, Drawing	6 0 0 00				10
11	Delivery Fees		2 6 0 0 00			11
12	Wages Expense	1 8 0 0 00				12
13	Advertising Expense	3 8 0 00				13
14	Rent Expense	9 0 0 00				14
15	Supplies Expense					15
16	Phone Expense	2 2 0 00				16
17	Insurance Expense					17
18	Repair Expense	3 1 5 00				18
19	Oil and Gas Expense	1 0 0 00				19
20	Depr. Expense—Van					20
21		13 5 6 0 00	13 5 6 0 00			21

Campus Delivery Service
Work Sheet (Partial)
For Month Ended November 30, 20 - -

P 5-16A **(LO2/5)**

CLGL

JOURNALIZE AND POST ADJUSTING ENTRIES FROM THE WORK SHEET
Refer to Problem 5-15A and the following additional information:

Account Name	Account Number	Balance in Account Before Adjusting Entry
Supplies	141	$ 575
Prepaid Insurance	145	1,300
Accum. Depr.—Van	185.1	0
Wages Payable	219	0
Wages Expense	511	1,800
Supplies Expense	523	0
Insurance Expense	535	0
Depr. Expense—Van	541	0

(*continued*)

1. Journalize the adjusting entries on page 5 of the general journal.

2. Post the adjusting entries to the general ledger. (If you are not using the working papers that accompany this text, enter the balances provided in this problem before posting the adjusting entries.)

P 5-17A   (LO4)

✓ Adjustments col. total: $1,160

✓ Net income: $1,575

CORRECTING WORK SHEET WITH ERRORS A beginning accounting student tried to complete a work sheet for Joyce Lee's Tax Service. The following adjusting entries were to have been analyzed and entered onto the work sheet. The work sheet is shown on page 167.

(a) Ending inventory of supplies as of March 31, $160.

(b) Unexpired insurance as of March 31, $520.

(c) Depreciation of office equipment, $275.

(d) Wages earned, but not paid as of March 31, $110.

REQUIRED

The accounting student made a number of errors. Review the work sheet for addition mistakes, transpositions, and other errors and make all necessary corrections.

SERIES B EXERCISES

E 5-1B   (LO1)

ADJUSTMENT FOR SUPPLIES On July 31, the trial balance indicates that the supplies account has a balance, prior to the adjusting entry, of $430. A physical count of the supplies inventory shows that $120 of supplies remain. Analyze the adjustment for supplies using T accounts, and then formally enter this adjustment in the general journal.

E 5-2B   (LO1)

ADJUSTMENT FOR INSURANCE On July 1, a six-month liability insurance policy was purchased for $750. Analyze the required adjustment as of July 31 using T accounts, and then formally enter this adjustment in the general journal.

E 5-3B   (LO1)

SHOW
ME HOW

ADJUSTMENT FOR WAGES On July 31, the trial balance shows wages expense of $800. An additional $150 of wages was earned by the employees but has not yet been paid. Analyze the required adjustment using T accounts, and then formally enter this adjustment in the general journal.

E 5-4B   (LO1)

SHOW
ME HOW

ADJUSTMENT FOR DEPRECIATION OF ASSET On July 1, delivery equipment was purchased for $4,320. The delivery equipment has an estimated useful life of three years (36 months) and no salvage value. Using the straight-line depreciation method, analyze the necessary adjusting entry as of July 31 (one month) using T accounts, and then formally enter this adjustment in the general journal.

E 5-5B   (LO1)

CALCULATION OF BOOK VALUE On January 1, 20--, a depreciable asset was acquired for $5,760. The asset has an estimated useful life of four years (48 months) and no salvage value. Use the straight-line depreciation method to calculate the book value as of July 1, 20--.

PROBLEM 5-17A

Joyce Lee's Tax Service
Work Sheet
For Month Ended March 31, 20--

#	ACCOUNT TITLE	TB Debit	TB Credit	Adj. Debit	Adj. Credit	ATB Debit	ATB Credit	IS Debit	IS Credit	BS Debit	BS Credit
1	Cash	1 7 2 5 00				1 7 2 5 00				1 7 5 2 00	
2	Accounts Receivable	9 6 0 00				9 6 0 00				9 6 00	
3	Supplies	5 2 5 00			(a) 1 6 0 00	3 6 5 00				3 6 5 00	
4	Prepaid Insurance	9 3 0 00			(b) 4 1 0 00	5 4 0 00				5 4 0 00	
5	Office Equipment	5 4 5 0 00			(c) 2 7 5 00	5 1 7 5 00				5 1 7 5 00	
6	Accum. Depr.–Office Equipment										
7	Accounts Payable		4 8 0 00				4 8 0 00				4 8 0 00
8	Wages Payable				(d) 1 1 0 00		1 1 0 00				1 1 0 00
9	Joyce Lee, Capital		7 5 0 0 00				7 5 0 0 00				7 5 0 0 00
10	Joyce Lee, Drawing	1 1 2 5 00				1 1 2 5 00		1 1 2 5 00			
11	Professional Fees		5 7 0 0 00				5 7 0 0 00		5 7 0 0 00		
12	Wages Expense	1 4 2 0 00		(d) 1 1 0 00		1 4 2 0 00		1 4 2 0 00			
13	Advertising Expense	3 5 0 00				3 5 0 00		3 5 0 00			
14	Rent Expense	7 0 0 00				7 0 0 00		7 0 0 00			
15	Supplies Expense			(a) 1 6 0 00		1 6 0 00		1 6 0 00			
16	Phone Expense	1 3 0 00				1 3 0 00		1 3 0 00			
17	Utilities Expense	1 9 0 00				1 9 0 00		1 9 0 00			
18	Insurance Expense			(b) 4 1 0 00		4 1 0 00		4 1 0 00			
19	Depr. Expense–Office Equipment			(c) 2 7 5 00		2 7 5 00		2 7 5 00			
20	Miscellaneous Expense	1 7 5 00				1 7 5 00		1 7 5 00			
21											
22		13 6 8 0 00	13 6 8 0 00	9 5 5 00	9 5 5 00	13 1 6 0 00	13 7 9 0 00	4 5 6 6 00	5 8 1 0 00	9 5 0 8 00	7 9 8 0 00
23								1 2 4 4 00			1 5 2 8 00
24								5 8 1 0 00	5 8 1 0 00	9 5 0 8 00	9 5 0 8 00

Contains Errors

This work sheet contains errors.

E 5-6B **(LO1)**

SHOW
ME HOW

ANALYSIS OF ADJUSTING ENTRY FOR SUPPLIES Analyze each situation and indicate the correct dollar amount for the adjusting entry.

1. Ending inventory of supplies is $95.

(Balance Sheet) Supplies		(Income Statement) Supplies Expense	
TB	540		
Bal. _____			

2. Amount of supplies used is $280.

(Balance Sheet) Supplies		(Income Statement) Supplies Expense	
TB	330		
Bal. _____			

E 5-7B **(LO1)**

ANALYSIS OF ADJUSTING ENTRY FOR INSURANCE Analyze each situation and indicate the correct dollar amount for the adjusting entry.

1. Amount of insurance expired (used) is $830.

(Balance Sheet) Prepaid Insurance		(Income Statement) Insurance Expense	
TB	960		
Bal. _____			

2. Amount of unexpired (remaining) insurance is $340.

(Balance Sheet) Prepaid Insurance		(Income Statement) Insurance Expense	
TB	1,135		
Bal. _____			

E 5-8B **(LO2)**

POSTING ADJUSTING ENTRIES Two adjusting entries are shown in the following general journal. Post these adjusting entries to the four general ledger accounts. The following account numbers were taken from the chart of accounts: 145, Prepaid Insurance; 183.1, Accumulated Depreciation—Cleaning Equipment; 541, Depreciation Expense—Cleaning Equipment; and 535, Insurance Expense. If you are not using the working papers that accompany this text, enter the following balances before posting the entries: Prepaid Insurance, $960 Dr.; Accumulated Depreciation—Cleaning Equipment, $870 Cr.

		GENERAL JOURNAL				PAGE 7		
	DATE	DESCRIPTION	POST. REF.	DEBIT		CREDIT		
1		Adjusting Entries						1
2	20-- July 31	Insurance Expense		3 2 0 00				2
3		Prepaid Insurance				3 2 0 00		3
4								4
5	31	Depr. Expense—Cleaning Equipment		1 4 5 00				5
6		Accum. Depr.—Cleaning Equipment				1 4 5 00		6

E 5-9B (LO3)

✓ Adjustments col. total: $1,530

WORK SHEET AND ADJUSTING ENTRIES A partial work sheet for Jasmine Kah's Auto Detailing is shown below. Indicate by letters (a) through (d) the four adjustments in the Adjustments columns of the work sheet, properly matching each debit and credit. Complete the Adjustments columns.

Jasmine Kah's Auto Detailing
Work Sheet (Partial)
For Month Ended June 30, 20 - -

	ACCOUNT TITLE	TRIAL BALANCE		ADJUSTMENTS		ADJUSTED TRIAL BALANCE		
		DEBIT	CREDIT	DEBIT	CREDIT	DEBIT	CREDIT	
1	Cash	1 5 0 00				1 5 0 00		1
2	Supplies	5 2 0 00				9 0 00		2
3	Prepaid Insurance	7 5 0 00				2 0 0 00		3
4	Cleaning Equipment	5 4 0 0 00				5 4 0 0 00		4
5	Accum. Depr.— Cleaning Equipment		8 5 0 00				1 1 5 0 00	5
6	Wages Payable						2 5 0 00	6
7	Jasmine Kah, Capital		4 6 0 0 00				4 6 0 0 00	7
8	Detailing Fees		2 2 2 0 00				2 2 2 0 00	8
9	Wages Expense	7 0 0 00				9 5 0 00		9
10	Advertising Expense	1 5 0 00				1 5 0 00		10
11	Supplies Expense					4 3 0 00		11
12	Insurance Expense					5 5 0 00		12
13	Depr. Expense—Cleaning Equipment					3 0 0 00		13
14		7 6 7 0 00	7 6 7 0 00			8 2 2 0 00	8 2 2 0 00	14

E 5-10B (LO5)

SHOW ME HOW

JOURNALIZING ADJUSTING ENTRIES From the Adjustments columns in Exercise 5-9B, journalize the four adjusting entries as of June 30, in proper general journal format.

E 5-11B (LO3)

EXTENDING ADJUSTED BALANCES TO THE INCOME STATEMENT AND BALANCE SHEET COLUMNS Indicate with an "X" whether each account total should be extended to the Income Statement Debit or Credit or to the Balance Sheet Debit or Credit columns on the work sheet.

(*continued*)

	Income Statement		Balance Sheet	
	Debit	Credit	Debit	Credit
Cash				
Accounts Receivable				
Supplies				
Prepaid Insurance				
Automobile				
Accum. Depr.—Automobile				
Accounts Payable				
Wages Payable				
Owner, Capital				
Owner, Drawing				
Service Fees				
Wages Expense				
Supplies Expense				
Utilities Expense				
Insurance Expense				
Depr. Exp.—Automobile				

E 5-12B   (LO3)

ANALYSIS OF NET INCOME OR NET LOSS ON THE WORK SHEET Insert the dollar amounts where the net income or net loss would appear on the work sheet.

	Income Statement		Balance Sheet	
	Debit	Credit	Debit	Credit
Net Income: $2,500				
Net Loss: $1,900				

E 5-13B   (LO6)
✓ See Figure 5-23 in text

CASH, MODIFIED CASH, AND ACCRUAL BASES OF ACCOUNTING For each journal entry shown below, indicate the accounting method(s) for which the entry would be appropriate. If the journal entry is not appropriate for a particular accounting method, explain the proper accounting treatment for that method.

1. Office Equipment
    Cash
        Purchased equipment for cash

2. Office Equipment
    Accounts Payable
        Purchased equipment on account

3. Cash
    Revenue
        Cash receipts for week

4. Accounts Receivable
    Revenue
        Services performed on account

5. Prepaid Insurance
    Cash
        Purchased prepaid asset

6. Supplies
    Accounts Payable
        Purchased prepaid asset

7. Phone Expense
    Cash
        Paid phone bill

8. Wages Expense
    Cash
        Paid wages for month

9. Accounts Payable
    Cash
        Made payment on account

Adjusting Entries:

10. Supplies Expense
    Supplies

11. Wages Expense
    Wages Payable

12. Depreciation Expense—Office Equipment
    Accumulated Depreciation—Office Equipment

SERIES B PROBLEMS

P 5-14B (LO1/3)
✓ Adjustments col. total: $805
✓ Net income: $2,410

SHOW
ME HOW

ADJUSTMENTS AND WORK SHEET SHOWING NET INCOME Louie Long started a business called Louie's Lawn Service. The trial balance as of March 31, after the first month of operation, is as follows:

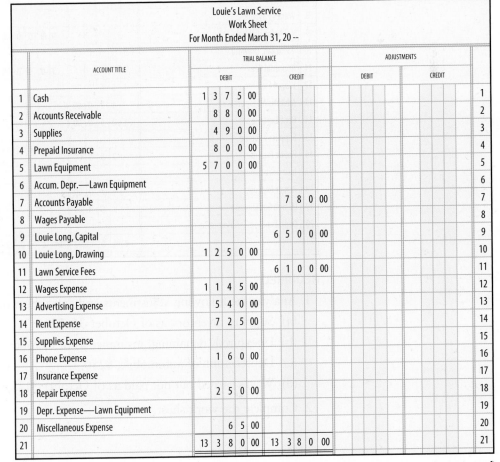

	ACCOUNT TITLE	TRIAL BALANCE DEBIT	TRIAL BALANCE CREDIT	ADJUSTMENTS DEBIT	ADJUSTMENTS CREDIT	
1	Cash	1 3 7 5 00				1
2	Accounts Receivable	8 8 0 00				2
3	Supplies	4 9 0 00				3
4	Prepaid Insurance	8 0 0 00				4
5	Lawn Equipment	5 7 0 0 00				5
6	Accum. Depr.—Lawn Equipment					6
7	Accounts Payable		7 8 0 00			7
8	Wages Payable					8
9	Louie Long, Capital		6 5 0 0 00			9
10	Louie Long, Drawing	1 2 5 0 00				10
11	Lawn Service Fees		6 1 0 0 00			11
12	Wages Expense	1 1 4 5 00				12
13	Advertising Expense	5 4 0 00				13
14	Rent Expense	7 2 5 00				14
15	Supplies Expense					15
16	Phone Expense	1 6 0 00				16
17	Insurance Expense					17
18	Repair Expense	2 5 0 00				18
19	Depr. Expense—Lawn Equipment					19
20	Miscellaneous Expense	6 5 00				20
21		13 3 8 0 00	13 3 8 0 00			21

(continued)

REQUIRED

1. Analyze the following adjustments and enter them on a work sheet.
   (a) Ending supplies inventory as of March 31, $165.
   (b) Insurance expired (used), $100.
   (c) Depreciation of lawn equipment, $200.
   (d) Wages earned but not paid as of March 31, $180.

2. Complete the work sheet.

P 5-15B   (LO1/3)
✓ Adjustments col. total: $990
✓ Net loss: $1,625

ADJUSTMENTS AND WORK SHEET SHOWING A NET LOSS Val Nolan started a business called Nolan's Home Appraisals. The trial balance as of October 31, after the first month of operations, is as follows:

Nolan's Home Appraisals
Work Sheet
For Month Ended October 31, 20 - -

	ACCOUNT TITLE	TRIAL BALANCE DEBIT	TRIAL BALANCE CREDIT	ADJUSTMENTS DEBIT	ADJUSTMENTS CREDIT	
1	Cash	8 3 0 00				1
2	Accounts Receivable	7 6 0 00				2
3	Supplies	6 2 5 00				3
4	Prepaid Insurance	9 5 0 00				4
5	Automobile	6 5 0 0 00				5
6	Accum. Depr.—Automobile					6
7	Accounts Payable		1 5 0 0 00			7
8	Wages Payable					8
9	Val Nolan, Capital		9 9 0 0 00			9
10	Val Nolan, Drawing	1 1 0 0 00				10
11	Appraisal Fees		3 0 0 0 00			11
12	Wages Expense	1 5 6 0 00				12
13	Advertising Expense	4 2 0 00				13
14	Rent Expense	1 0 5 0 00				14
15	Supplies Expense					15
16	Phone Expense	2 5 5 00				16
17	Insurance Expense					17
18	Repair Expense	2 7 0 00				18
19	Oil and Gas Expense	8 0 00				19
20	Depr. Expense—Automobile					20
21		14 4 0 0 00	14 4 0 0 00			21

REQUIRED

1. Analyze the following adjustments and enter them on the work sheet.
   (a) Supplies inventory as of October 31, $210.
   (b) Unexpired (remaining) insurance as of October 31, $800.
   (c) Depreciation of automobile, $250.
   (d) Wages earned but not paid as of October 31, $175.

2. Complete the work sheet.

P 5-16B   (LO2/5)

JOURNALIZE AND POST ADJUSTING ENTRIES FROM THE WORK SHEET

Refer to Problem 5-15B and the following additional information:

Account Name	Account Number	Balance in Account Before Adjusting Entry
Supplies	141	$ 625
Prepaid Insurance	145	950
Accum. Depr.—Automobile	185.1	0
Wages Payable	219	0
Wages Expense	511	1,560
Supplies Expense	523	0
Insurance Expense	535	0
Depr. Expense—Automobile	541	0

REQUIRED

1. Journalize the adjusting entries on page 3 of the general journal.

2. Post the adjusting entries to the general ledger. (If you are not using the working papers that accompany this text, enter the balances provided in this problem before posting the adjusting entries.)

P 5-17B   (LO4)

✓ Adjustments col. total: $1,640
✓ Net income: $1,405

CORRECTING WORK SHEET WITH ERRORS

A beginning accounting student tried to complete a work sheet for Dick Ady's Bookkeeping Service. The following adjusting entries were to have been analyzed and entered in the work sheet:

(a) Ending inventory of supplies on July 31, $130.

(b) Unexpired insurance on July 31, $420.

(c) Depreciation of office equipment, $325.

(d) Wages earned, but not paid as of July 31, $95.

REQUIRED

Review the work sheet shown on page 174 for addition mistakes, transpositions, and other errors and make all necessary corrections.

MANAGING YOUR WRITING

Delia Alvarez, owner of Delia's Lawn Service, wants to borrow money to buy new lawn equipment. A local bank has asked for financial statements. Alvarez has asked you to prepare financial statements for the year ended December 31, 20--. You have been given the unadjusted trial balance on page 175 and suspect that Alvarez expects you to base your statements on this information. You are concerned, however, that some of the account balances may need to be adjusted. Write a memo to Alvarez explaining what additional information you need before you can prepare the financial statements. Alvarez is not familiar with accounting issues. Therefore, explain in your memo why you need this information, the potential impact of this information on the financial statements, and the importance of making these adjustments before approaching the bank for a loan.

(*continued*)

PROBLEM 5-17B

Dick Ady's Bookkeeping Service
Work Sheet
For Month Ended July 31, 20--

ACCOUNT TITLE	TRIAL BALANCE Debit	TRIAL BALANCE Credit	ADJUSTMENTS Debit	ADJUSTMENTS Credit	ADJUSTED TRIAL BALANCE Debit	ADJUSTED TRIAL BALANCE Credit	INCOME STATEMENT Debit	INCOME STATEMENT Credit	BALANCE SHEET Debit	BALANCE SHEET Credit	
1 Cash	1 3 6 5 00				1 3 6 5 00				1 3 5 6 00		1
2 Accounts Receivable	8 4 5 00				8 4 5 00			8 4 5 00			2
3 Supplies	6 2 0 00			(a) 4 9 0 00	1 3 0 00				1 3 0 00		3
4 Prepaid Insurance	1 1 5 0 00			(b) 4 2 0 00	7 3 0 00				7 3 0 00		4
5 Office Equipment	6 4 0 0 00			(c) 3 2 5 00	6 7 2 5 00				6 7 2 5 00		5
6 Accum. Depr.—Office Equipment											6
7 Accounts Payable		7 3 5 00				7 3 5 00				7 3 5 00	7
8 Wages Payable				(d) 9 5 00		9 5 00				5 9 00	8
9 Dick Ady, Capital		7 8 0 0 00				7 8 0 0 00				7 8 0 0 00	9
10 Dick Ady, Drawing	1 2 0 0 00				1 2 0 0 00				1 2 0 0 00		10
11 Professional Fees		6 3 5 0 00				6 3 5 0 00		6 3 5 0 00			11
12 Wages Expense	1 4 9 5 00		(d) 9 5 00		1 5 9 0 00		1 5 9 0 00				12
13 Advertising Expense	3 8 0 00				3 8 0 00		3 8 0 00				13
14 Rent Expense	8 5 0 00				8 5 0 00		8 5 0 00				14
15 Supplies Expense			(a) 4 9 0 00		4 9 0 00		4 9 0 00				15
16 Phone Expense	2 0 5 00				2 0 5 00		2 5 0 00				16
17 Utilities Expense	2 8 5 00				2 8 5 00		2 8 5 00				17
18 Insurance Expense			(b) 4 2 0 00		4 2 0 00		4 2 0 00				18
19 Depr. Expense—Office Equipment			(c) 3 2 5 00		3 2 5 00		3 2 5 00				19
20 Miscellaneous Expense	9 0 0 00				9 0 0 00		9 0 0 00				20
21	14 8 8 5 00	14 8 8 5 00	1 3 3 0 00	1 3 3 0 00	15 6 3 0 00	14 9 8 0 00	4 8 8 0 00	7 1 9 5 00	10 1 4 1 00	8 5 9 4 00	21
22 Net Income							2 3 1 5 00			1 5 4 7 00	22
23							7 1 9 5 00	7 1 9 5 00	10 1 4 1 00	10 1 4 1 00	23

Contains Errors

This work sheet contains errors.

Delia's Lawn Service Trial Balance December 31, 20 - -												
ACCOUNT TITLE	**ACCOUNT NO.**	\multicolumn{4}{c}{**DEBIT BALANCE**}				\multicolumn{5}{c}{**CREDIT BALANCE**}				
Cash	101		7	7	0	00						
Accounts Receivable	122	1	7	0	0	00						
Supplies	142		2	8	0	00						
Prepaid Insurance	145		4	0	0	00						
Lawn Equipment	183	13	8	0	0	00						
Accounts Payable	202							2	2	0	0	00
Delia Alvarez, Capital	311							3	0	0	0	00
Delia Alvarez, Drawing	312		3	5	0	00						
Lawn Cutting Fees	401							52	4	0	0	00
Wages Expense	511	35	8	5	0	00						
Rent Expense	521	1	2	0	0	00						
Gas and Oil Expense	538	3	2	5	0	00						
		57	6	0	0	00		57	6	0	0	00

✓ **Adjusted Trial Bal. total: $58,500**
✓ **Net income: $13,630**

MASTERY PROBLEM

Kristi Williams offers family counseling services specializing in financial and marital problems. A chart of accounts and a trial balance taken on December 31, 20--, follow.

\multicolumn{4}{c}{**KRISTI WILLIAMS FAMILY COUNSELING SERVICES** **CHART OF ACCOUNTS**}			
\multicolumn{2}{l}{**Assets**}	\multicolumn{2}{l}{**Revenue**}
101	Cash	401	Client Fees
142	Office Supplies		
145	Prepaid Insurance	\multicolumn{2}{l}{**Expenses**}
181	Office Equipment	511	Wages Expense
181.1	Accumulated Depr.—	521	Rent Expense
	Office Equipment	523	Office Supplies Expense
187	Computer Equipment	533	Utilities Expense
187.1	Accumulated Depr.—	535	Insurance Expense
	Computer Equipment	541	Depr. Expense—
\multicolumn{2}{l}{**Liabilities**}		Office Equipment
201	Notes Payable	542	Depr. Expense—
202	Accounts Payable		Computer Equipment
		549	Miscellaneous Expense
\multicolumn{2}{l}{**Owner's Equity**}		
311	Kristi Williams, Capital		
312	Kristi Williams, Drawing		

(*continued*)

Kristi Williams Family Counseling Services Trial Balance December 31, 20 - -												
ACCOUNT TITLE	ACCOUNT NO.	DEBIT BALANCE					CREDIT BALANCE					
Cash	101	8	7	3	0	00						
Office Supplies	142		7	0	0	00						
Prepaid Insurance	145		6	0	0	00						
Office Equipment	181	18	0	0	0	00						
Computer Equipment	187	6	0	0	0	00						
Notes Payable	201						8	0	0	0	00	
Accounts Payable	202							5	0	0	00	
Kristi Williams, Capital	311						11	4	0	0	00	
Kristi Williams, Drawing	312	3	0	0	0	00						
Client Fees	401						35	8	0	0	00	
Wages Expense	511	9	5	0	0	00						
Rent Expense	521	6	0	0	0	00						
Utilities Expense	533	2	1	7	0	00						
Miscelleneous Expense	549	1	0	0	0	00						
		55	7	0	0	00	55	7	0	0	00	

Information for year-end adjustments is as follows:

(a) Office supplies on hand at year-end amounted to $100.

(b) On January 1, 20--, Williams purchased office equipment that cost $18,000. It has an expected useful life of 10 years and no salvage value.

(c) On July 1, 20--, Williams purchased computer equipment costing $6,000. It has an expected useful life of three years and no salvage value. Assume that Williams computes depreciation to the nearest full month.

(d) On December 1, 20--, Williams paid a premium of $600 for a six-month insurance policy.

REQUIRED

1. Prepare the work sheet for the year ended December 31, 20--.
2. Prepare adjusting entries in a general journal.

CHALLENGE PROBLEM

This problem challenges you to apply your cumulative accounting knowledge to move a step beyond the material in the chapter.

CLGL

Your friend, Diane Kiefner, teaches elementary school and operates her own wilderness kayaking tours in the summers. She thinks she has been doing fine financially, but has never really measured her profits. Until this year, her business has always had more money at the end of the summer than at the beginning. She enjoys kayaking and as long as she came out a little ahead, that was fine. Unfortunately, Diane had to dip into her savings to make up for "losses" on her kayaking tours this past summer. Hearing that you have been studying accounting, she brought a list of cash receipts and expenditures and would like you to try to figure out what happened.

Cash balance beginning of summer		$15,000
Cash receipts from kayakers over the summer	$10,000	
Cash expenditures over the summer	13,500	
Amount taken from savings		(3,500)
Cash balance end of summer		$11,500

When asked for more details on the expenditures and the kayaking gear that you saw in her garage, Diane provided the following information:

Expenditures were made on the following items:
Brochures used to advertise her services (Diane only
   used about 1/4 of them and plans to use the
   remainder over the next three summers.) $1,000
Food for trips (nothing left)   2,000
Rent on equipment used by kayakers on trips   3,000
Travel expenses   4,000
A new kayak and paddles (At the beginning of the summer,
   Diane bought a new kayak and paddles. Up to this time,
   she had always borrowed her father's. Diane expects to
   use the equipment for about five years. At that time, she
   expects it to have no value.)   3,500

A trial balance based on this information follows. As you will note, Diane's trial balance is not consistent with some of the concepts discussed in this chapter.

Diane Kiefner's Wilderness Kayaking Tours
Work Sheet
For Summer Ended 20 - -

	ACCOUNT TITLE	TRIAL BALANCE DEBIT	TRIAL BALANCE CREDIT		
1	Cash	11 5 0 0 00			1
2	Diane Kiefner, Capital		15 0 0 0 00		2
3	Tour Revenue		10 0 0 0 00		3
4	Advertising Supplies Expense	1 0 0 0 00			4
5	Food Expense	2 0 0 0 00			5
6	Equipment Rental Expense	3 0 0 0 00			6
7	Travel Expense	4 0 0 0 00			7
8	Kayak Expense	3 5 0 0 00			8
9		25 0 0 0 00	25 0 0 0 00		9

(Columns: ADJUSTMENTS, ADJUSTED TRIAL BALANCE, INCOME STATEMENT, BALANCE SHEET — all blank)

REQUIRED

1. Complete Diane's work sheet by making appropriate adjustments and extensions. *Note*: (a) You may need to add new accounts. (b) Some of the adjustments you need to make are actually "corrections of errors" Diane has made in classifying certain items.
2. What is your best measure of Diane's net income for the summer of 20--?

Answers to Self-Study Test Questions

True/False

1. F (match revenues and expenses)
2. F (to bring accounts up to date)
3. T
4. F (depreciable cost = cost − salvage value)
5. F (to match cost of asset against revenues it will help generate)

Multiple Choice

1. a   **2.** c   **3.** d   **4.** c   **5.** a

Checkpoint Exercises

1. Supplies should be reduced (credited) for $30.

2. Adjusting.

3. A. Account Title

B. Trial Balance

C. Adjustments

D. Adjusted Trial Balance

E. Income Statement

F. Balance Sheet

4. Errors are highlighted in yellow.

		ACCOUNT TITLE	TRIAL BALANCE		ADJUSTMENTS		ADJUSTED TRIAL BALANCE		INCOME STATEMENT		BALANCE SHEET		
			DEBIT	CREDIT	DEBIT	CREDIT	DEBIT	CREDIT	DEBIT	CREDIT	DEBIT	CREDIT	
1	Cash		3 7 0 00				3 7 0 00				3 7 0 00		1
2	Accounts Receivable		6 5 0 00				6 5 0 00				6 5 0 00		2
3	Supplies		8 0 00			(a) 6 0 00	1 4 0 00				1 4 0 00		3
4	Prepaid Insurance		2 0 0 00			(b) 2 5 00	1 7 5 00				1 7 5 00		4
5	Delivery Equipment		3 6 0 0 00				3 6 0 0 00				3 6 0 0 00		5
6	Accum. Depr.—Delivery Equipment					(d) 1 0 0 00		1 0 0 00				1 0 0 00	6
7	Accounts Payable			1 8 0 0 00				1 8 0 0 00				1 8 0 0 00	7
8	Wages Payable					(c) 5 0 00		5 0 00				5 0 00	8
9	Rohan Macsen, Capital			2 0 0 0 00				2 0 0 0 00				2 0 0 0 00	9
10	Rohan Macsen, Drawing		1 5 0 00				1 5 0 00				1 5 0 00		10
11	Delivery Fees			2 1 5 0 00				2 1 5 0 00		2 1 5 0 00			11
12	Wages Expense		6 5 0 00		(c) 5 0 00		7 0 0 00		7 0 0 00				12
13	Rent Expense		2 0 0 00				2 0 0 00		2 0 0 00				13
14	Supplies Expense				(a) 6 0 00		6 0 00		6 0 00				14
15	Phone Expense		5 0 00				5 0 00		5 0 00				15
16	Insurance Expense				(b) 2 5 00		2 5 00		2 5 00				16
17	Depr. Expense—Delivery Equipment				(d) 1 0 0 00		1 0 0 00		1 0 0 00				17
18			5 9 5 0 00	5 9 5 0 00	2 3 5 00	2 3 5 00	6 2 2 0 00	6 1 0 0 00	1 1 3 5 00	2 1 5 0 00	5 0 8 5 00	3 9 5 0 00	18
19	Net Income								1 0 1 5 00			1 1 3 5 00	19
20									2 1 5 0 00	2 1 5 0 00	5 0 8 5 00	5 0 8 5 00	20
21													21

5.

		Adjusting Entry		
Dec. 31	Insurance Expense	50.00	
	Prepaid Insurance		50.00

6.

Transaction	Cash Basis	Accrual Basis	Modified Cash Basis
Services on account	$ —	$500	$ —
Payment for legal research assistance	(50)	(50)	(50)
Office supplies used		(10)	(10)
Net Income (Net Loss)	$(50)	$440	$(60)

Chapter 5 Appendix
Depreciation Methods

LEARNING OBJECTIVES

In Chapter 5, we introduced the straight-line method of depreciation. Here, we will review this method and illustrate three others: sum-of-the-years'-digits; double-declining-balance; and, for tax purposes, the Modified Accelerated Cost Recovery System. For all illustrations, we will assume that a delivery van was purchased for $40,000. It has a five-year useful life and salvage value of $4,000.

Careful study of this appendix should enable you to:

LO1 Prepare a depreciation schedule using the straight-line method.

LO2 Prepare a depreciation schedule using the sum-of-the-years'-digits method.

LO3 Prepare a depreciation schedule using the double-declining-balance method.

LO4 Prepare a depreciation schedule for tax purposes using the Modified Accelerated Cost Recovery System.

STRAIGHT-LINE METHOD

LO1 Prepare a depreciation schedule using the straight-line method.

Under the straight-line depreciation method, an equal amount of depreciation will be taken each period. First, compute the depreciable cost by subtracting the salvage value from the cost of the asset. This is done because we expect to sell the asset for $4,000 at the end of its useful life. Thus, the total cost to be recognized as an expense over the five years is $36,000, not $40,000.

Cost	–	Salvage Value	=	Depreciable Cost
$40,000	–	$4,000	=	$36,000

Next, we divide the depreciable cost by the expected life of the asset, five years.

Depreciation Expense per Year	=	Depreciable Cost / Years of Life
$7,200 per year	=	$36,000 / 5 years

When preparing a depreciation schedule, it is often convenient to use a depreciation rate per year. In this case, it would be 20% (100% ÷ 5 years of life). Figure 5A-1 shows the depreciation expense, accumulated depreciation, and book value for each of the five years.

FIGURE 5A-1 Depreciation Schedule Using Straight-Line Method

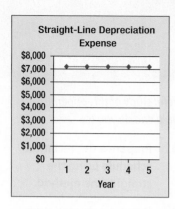

Straight-Line Depreciation Expense

		STRAIGHT-LINE DEPRECIATION				
Year	Depreciable Cost	×	Rate	=	Depreciation Expense	Accumulated Depreciation (End of Year)	Book Value (End of Year)
1	$36,000		20%		$7,200	$ 7,200	$32,800
2	36,000		20%		7,200	14,400	25,600
3	36,000		20%		7,200	21,600	18,400
4	36,000		20%		7,200	28,800	11,200
5	36,000		20%		7,200	36,000	4,000

Cost	$40,000
− Salvage Value	4,000
Depreciable Cost	$36,000

$\dfrac{100\%}{5 \text{ Years}} = 20\%$

Same amount each year

Accum. Depr. increases by the same amount each year, $7,200.

Cost	
− Accum. Depr.	
Book Value	

SUM-OF-THE-YEARS'-DIGITS

LO2 Prepare a depreciation schedule using the sum-of-the-years'-digits method.

Under the **sum-of-the-years'-digits depreciation method,** depreciation is determined by multiplying the depreciable cost by a schedule of fractions. The numerator of the fraction for a specific year is the number of years of remaining useful life for the asset, measured from the beginning of the year. The denominator for all fractions is determined by adding the digits that represent the years of the estimated life of the asset. The calculation of the **sum-of-the-years'-digits** for our delivery van with a five-year useful life is shown below.

Sum-of-the-Years'-Digits = 5 + 4 + 3 + 2 + 1 = 15

A depreciation schedule using these fractions is shown in Figure 5A-2.

FIGURE 5A-2 Depreciation Schedule Using Sum-of-the-Years'-Digits Method

Sum-of-the-Years'-Digits Depreciation Expense

		SUM-OF-THE-YEARS'-DIGITS				
Year	Depreciable Cost	×	Rate	=	Depreciation Expense	Accumulated Depreciation (End of Year)	Book Value (End of Year)
1	$36,000		5/15		$12,000	$12,000	$28,000
2	36,000		4/15		9,600	21,600	18,400
3	36,000		3/15		7,200	28,800	11,200
4	36,000		2/15		4,800	33,600	6,400
5	36,000		1/15		2,400	36,000	4,000

Cost	$40,000
− Salvage Value	4,000
Depreciable Cost	$36,000

$\dfrac{\text{Remaining life from beginning of period}}{\text{SYD}}$

Expense gets smaller each year

Accum. Depr. increases by amount of current year's depreciation expense.

Cost	
− Accum. Depr.	
Book Value	

DOUBLE-DECLINING-BALANCE METHOD

LO3 Prepare a depreciation schedule using the double-declining-balance method.

Under the double-declining-balance depreciation method, the book value is multiplied by a fixed rate, often double the straight-line rate. The van has a five-year life, so the straight-line rate is 1 ÷ 5, or 20%. Double the straight-line rate is 2 × 20%, or 40%. The double-declining-balance depreciation schedule is shown in Figure 5A-3. Note that the rate is applied to the book value of the asset. Once the book value is reduced to the expected salvage value, $4,000, no more depreciation may be recognized.

FIGURE 5A-3   Depreciation Schedule Using Double-Declining-Balance Method

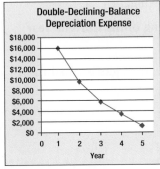

	DOUBLE-DECLINING-BALANCE METHOD					
Year	Book Value (Beginning of Year)	× Rate =		Depreciation Expense	Accumulated Depreciation (End of Year)	Book Value (End of Year)
1	$40,000	40%		$16,000	$16,000	$24,000
2	24,000	40%		9,600	25,600	14,400
3	14,400	40%		5,760	31,360	8,640
4	8,640	40%		3,456	34,816	5,184
5	5,184			1,184	36,000	4,000

Cost − Accum. Depr. = Book Value

Double the Straight Line Rate 1/5 x 2 = 2/5 = 40%

LEARNING KEY
Double means double the straight-line rate. Declining-balance means that the rate is multiplied by the book value (not depreciable cost) at the beginning of each year. This amount is declining each year.

MODIFIED ACCELERATED COST RECOVERY SYSTEM

LO4 Prepare a depreciation schedule for tax purposes using the Modified Accelerated Cost Recovery System.

For assets purchased since 1986, many firms use the Modified Accelerated Cost Recovery System (MACRS) for tax purposes. Under this method, the Internal Revenue Service (IRS) classifies various assets according to useful life and sets depreciation rates for each year of the asset's life. These rates are then multiplied by the cost of the asset. Even though the van is expected to have a useful life of five years, and a salvage value of $4,000, the IRS schedule, shown in Figure 5A-4, spreads the depreciation over a six-year period and assumes no salvage value.

FIGURE 5A-4   Depreciation Schedule Using Modified Accelerated Cost Recovery System

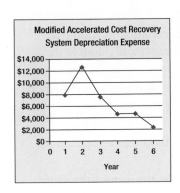

	MODIFIED ACCELERATED COST RECOVERY SYSTEM					
Year	Cost	× Rate =		Depreciation Expense	Accumulated Depreciation (End of Year)	Book Value (End of Year)
1	$40,000	20.00%		$ 8,000	$ 8,000	$32,000
2	40,000	32.00%		12,800	20,800	19,200
3	40,000	19.20%		7,680	28,480	11,520
4	40,000	11.52%		4,608	33,088	6,912
5	40,000	11.52%		4,608	37,696	2,304
6	40,000	5.76%		2,304	40,000	0

Rate set by IRS

Cost − Accum. Depr. = Book Value

LEARNING OBJECTIVES	Key Points to Remember
LO1 Prepare a depreciation schedule using the straight-line method.	Under straight-line depreciation, an equal amount of depreciation is taken each period. Depreciation expense for each year is computed as follows: Cost – Salvage Value = Depreciable Cost/Expected Years of Life = Depreciation Expense per Year
LO2 Prepare a depreciation schedule using the sum-of-the-years'-digits method.	Under the sum-of-the-years'-digits method, the depreciable cost is multiplied by a fraction. The fraction consists of the following: $$\frac{\text{Remaining Years of Life Measured from the Beginning of the Current Year}}{\text{Sum-of-the-Years'-Digits}}$$ If an asset has a life of three years, the sum-of-the-years'-digits is equal to: $$3 + 2 + 1 = 6$$ Depreciation would be computed as follows: Year 1: 3/6 × Depreciable Cost Year 2: 2/6 × Depreciable Cost Year 3: 1/6 × Depreciable Cost
LO3 Prepare a depreciation schedule using the double-declining-balance method.	Under this method, the book value (the declining balance) is multiplied by a fixed rate, often double the straight-line rate.
LO4 Prepare a depreciation schedule for tax purposes using the Modified Accelerated Cost Recovery System.	Under this method, the IRS provides the depreciation rates to be applied to the cost of the asset. Simply multiply the rate provided by the IRS by the cost of the asset.

KEY TERMS

double-declining-balance depreciation method (181)   A depreciation method that recognizes depreciation each year by multiplying a rate (typically double the straight-line rate) by the book value of the asset.

Modified Accelerated Cost Recovery System (MACRS) (181)   A depreciation method in which rates determined by the IRS are multiplied by the cost of the asset to determine depreciation expense for the year.

straight-line depreciation method (179)   A depreciation method that recognizes an equal amount of depreciation each year.

sum-of-the-years'-digits (180)   If an asset has a five-year life, the sum-of-the-years'-digits is computed as follows: 5 + 4 + 3 + 2 + 1 = 15.

sum-of-the-years'-digits depreciation method (180)   A depreciation method that recognizes depreciation each year by multiplying a fraction by the depreciable cost. The numerator of the fraction is the remaining life of the asset, measured from the beginning of the year. The denominator is the sum-of-the-years'-digits.

REVIEW QUESTIONS

1. List three depreciation methods used for financial reporting.
2. Which depreciation method is used for tax purposes?

SERIES A EXERCISES

E 5Apx-1A   (LO1)
✓ Accum. depr. end of Yr. 2: $10,000

STRAIGHT-LINE DEPRECIATION A small delivery truck was purchased on January 1 at a cost of $25,000. It has an estimated useful life of four years and an estimated salvage value of $5,000. Prepare a depreciation schedule showing the depreciation expense, accumulated depreciation, and book value for each year under the straight-line method.

E 5Apx-2A   (LO2)
✓ Accum. depr. end of Yr. 2: $14,000

SUM-OF-THE-YEARS'-DIGITS DEPRECIATION Using the information given in Exercise 5Apx-1A, prepare a depreciation schedule showing the depreciation expense, accumulated depreciation, and book value for each year under the sum-of-the-years'-digits method.

E 5Apx-3A   (LO3)
✓ Accum. depr. end of Yr. 2: $18,750

DOUBLE-DECLINING-BALANCE DEPRECIATION Using the information given in Exercise 5Apx-1A, prepare a depreciation schedule showing the depreciation expense, accumulated depreciation, and book value for each year under the double-declining-balance method.

E 5Apx-4A   (LO4)
✓ Accum. depr. end of Yr. 2: $13,000

MODIFIED ACCELERATED COST RECOVERY SYSTEM Using the information given in Exercise 5Apx-1A and the rates shown in Figure 5A-4, prepare a depreciation schedule showing the depreciation expense, accumulated depreciation, and book value for each year under the Modified Accelerated Cost Recovery System. For tax purposes, assume that the truck has a useful life of five years. (The IRS schedule will spread depreciation over six years.)

SERIES B EXERCISES

E 5Apx-1B   (LO1)
✓ Accum. depr. end of Yr. 2: $1,800

STRAIGHT-LINE DEPRECIATION A computer was purchased on January 1 at a cost of $5,000. It has an estimated useful life of five years and an estimated salvage value of $500. Prepare a depreciation schedule showing the depreciation expense, accumulated depreciation, and book value for each year under the straight-line method.

E 5Apx-2B   (LO2)
✓ Accum. depr. end of Yr. 2: $2,700

SUM-OF-THE-YEARS'-DIGITS DEPRECIATION Using the information given in Exercise 5Apx-1B, prepare a depreciation schedule showing the depreciation expense, accumulated depreciation, and book value for each year under the sum-of-the-years'-digits method.

E 5Apx-3B   (LO3)
✓ Accum. depr. end of Yr. 2: $3,200

DOUBLE-DECLINING-BALANCE DEPRECIATION Using the information given in Exercise 5Apx-1B, prepare a depreciation schedule showing the depreciation expense, accumulated depreciation, and book value for each year under the double-declining-balance method.

E 5Apx-4B   (LO4)
✓ Accum. depr. end of Yr. 2: $2,600

MODIFIED ACCELERATED COST RECOVERY SYSTEM Using the information given in Exercise 5Apx-1B and the rates shown in Figure 5A-4, prepare a depreciation schedule showing the depreciation expense, accumulated depreciation, and book value for each year under the Modified Accelerated Cost Recovery System. For tax purposes, assume that the computer has a useful life of five years. (The IRS schedule will spread depreciation over six years.)

RICH MILLER

Chapter 6

Financial Statements and the Closing Process

Indy Express Band is central Indiana's premier variety band. It offers a popular mix of musical styles from Top 40 to Big Band. The eight-piece band is led by Greg Imboden, fronted by Cozette Myers, driven by a three-piece horn section, and backed by a tight rhythm section. The **Indy Express Band** is perfect for a wedding reception, corporate function, conference event, dinner dance, or charity ball. Members of **Indy Express Band** have provided music for entertainers such as Jay Leno, Rod Stewart, Natalie Cole, Dionne Warwick, and Al Jarreau.

In addition to playing at weddings and other events, the band generally performs on New Year's Eve, the same day many businesses prepare closing entries. In this chapter, we complete the accounting cycle by demonstrating how to make closing entries and prepare the post-closing trial balance.

The work sheet, introduced in Chapter 5, is used for three major end-of-period activities:

1. journalizing adjusting entries,

2. preparing financial statements, and

3. journalizing closing entries.

This chapter illustrates the use of the work sheet for preparing financial statements and closing entries. In addition, the post-closing trial balance is explained and illustrated. All of these activities take place at the end of the firm's fiscal year. However, to continue our illustration of Rohan's Campus Delivery, we demonstrate these activities at the end of the first month of operations.

THE FINANCIAL STATEMENTS

LO1 Prepare financial statements with the aid of a work sheet.

The work sheet prepared in Chapter 5 supplies most of the information needed to prepare an income statement, a statement of owner's equity, and a balance sheet. The statements and work sheet columns from which they are derived for Rohan's Campus Delivery are shown in Figures 6-1 and 6-2.

As you refer to the financial statements in Figures 6-1 and 6-2, notice the placement of dollar signs, single rulings, and double rulings. Dollar signs are placed at the top of each column and beneath rulings. Single rulings indicate addition or subtraction, and double rulings are placed under totals. Notice that each statement heading contains three lines: (1) company name, (2) statement title, and (3) period ended or date.

The Income Statement

Figure 6-1 shows how the Income Statement columns of the work sheet provide the information needed to prepare an income statement. Revenue is shown first, followed by an itemized and totaled list of expenses. Then, net income is calculated to double check the accuracy of the work sheet. It is presented with a double ruling as the last item in the statement.

The expenses could be listed in the same order that they appear in the chart of accounts or in descending order by dollar amount. The second approach helps the reader identify the most important expenses.

The Statement of Owner's Equity

The Balance Sheet columns of the work sheet provide most of the information needed to prepare a statement of owner's equity. Figure 6-2 shows that Rohan's capital account balance and the drawing account balance are in the Balance Sheet columns. Be careful, however, when using the capital account balance reported on the work sheet. This account balance is the beginning balance *plus any investments made during the period*. Recall that Rohan's beginning capital balance was zero. During June, he made an investment of $2,000. Thus, as reported previously, the beginning balance on the statement of owner's equity must be zero with the $2,000 reported as an investment

> Multiple columns are used on the financial statements to make them easier to read. There are no debit or credit columns on the financial statements.

> **LEARNING KEY**
> The owner's capital account in the general ledger must be reviewed to determine if additional investments were made during the accounting period.

FIGURE 6-1 Linkages Between the Work Sheet and Income Statement

	Rohan's Campus Delivery Work Sheet (Partial) For Month Ended June 30, 20 - -				
	ACCOUNT TITLE	INCOME STATEMENT			
		DEBIT		CREDIT	
1	Cash				
2	Accounts Receivable				
3	Supplies				
4	Prepaid Insurance				
5	Delivery Equipment				
6	Accum. Depr.—Delivery Equipment				
7	Accounts Payable				
8	Wages Payable				
9	Rohan Macsen, Capital				
10	Rohan Macsen, Drawing				
11	Delivery Fees			2 1 5 0 00	
12	Wages Expense	7 0 0 00			
13	Rent Expense	2 0 0 00			
14	Supplies Expense	6 0 00			
15	Phone Expense	5 0 00			
16	Insurance Expense	2 5 00			
17	Depr. Expense—Delivery Equipment	1 0 0 00			
18		1 1 3 5 00		2 1 5 0 00	
19	Net Income	1 0 1 5 00			
20		2 1 5 0 00		2 1 5 0 00	
21					
22					
23					

Formatting Reminders:
Statement Heading
 Name of company
 Title of statement
 Accounting period ended
Revenues listed first
Expenses listed second by amount (largest to smallest), or in chart of accounts order. Amounts are itemized in left column, subtotaled in right column.

Prepare Income Statement First

Rohan's Campus Delivery
Income Statement
For Month Ended June 30, 20 --

Revenue:		
Delivery fees		$2,150
Expenses:		
Wages expense	$700	
Rent expense	200	
Supplies expense	60	
Phone expense	50	
Insurance expense	25	
Depr. expense—delivery equip.	100	
Total expenses		1,135
Net income		$1,015

Dollar signs used at top of columns and under rulings.
Single rulings indicate addition or subtraction.
Double rulings indicate totals.

during June. The net income for the month can be found either on the work sheet at the bottom of the Income Statement (see Figure 6-1) and Balance Sheet columns or on the income statement itself. With these items of information, the statement of owner's equity can be prepared.

The Balance Sheet

As shown in Figure 6-2, the work sheet and the statement of owner's equity are used to prepare Rohan's balance sheet. The asset and liability amounts can be found in the Balance Sheet columns of the work sheet. The ending balance in Rohan Macsen Capital has been computed on the statement of owner's equity. This amount should be copied from the statement of owner's equity to the balance sheet.

Two important features of the balance sheet in Figure 6-2 should be noted. First, it is a **report form of balance sheet**, which means that the liabilities and owner's equity sections are shown below the assets section. It differs from an **account form of balance sheet** in which the assets are on the left and the liabilities and owner's equity sections are on the right. (See Rohan's balance sheet illustrated in Figure 2-2 on page 33 in Chapter 2.)

Second, it is a **classified balance sheet**, which means that similar items are grouped together on the balance sheet. Assets are classified as current assets and property, plant, and equipment. Similarly, liabilities are broken down into current and long-term sections. The following major balance sheet classifications are generally used.

FIGURE 6-2   Linkages Between the Work Sheet, Statement of Owner's Equity, and Balance Sheet

Statement Heading
  Name of company
  Title of statement
  Date for BS and accounting period ended for SOE
Current assets: cash and items that will be converted to cash or consumed within a year.
Property, plant, and equipment: durable assets that will help produce revenues for several years.
Current liabilities: amounts owed that will be paid within a year (will require the use of current assets).

Note: The statement of owner's equity is prepared before the balance sheet. The S.O.E. is shown below the B.S. to enhance the illustration of the linkages between the work sheet and financial statements.

Rohan's Campus Delivery
Work Sheet (Partial)
For Month Ended June 30, 20 - -

	ACCOUNT TITLE	BALANCE SHEET	
		DEBIT	CREDIT
1	Cash	3 7 0 00	
2	Accounts Receivable	6 5 0 00	
3	Supplies	2 0 00	
4	Prepaid Insurance	1 7 5 00	
5	Delivery Equipment	3 6 0 0 00	
6	Accum. Depr.—Delivery Equip.		1 0 0 00
7	Accounts Payable		1 8 0 0 00
8	Wages Payable		5 0 00
9	Rohan Macsen, Capital		2 0 0 0 00
10	Rohan Macsen, Drawing	1 5 0 00	
11	Delivery Fees		
12	Wages Expense		
13	Rent Expense		
14	Supplies Expense		
15	Phone Expense		
16	Insurance Expense		
17	Depr. Expense—Delivery Equip.		
18		4 9 6 5 00	3 9 5 0 00
19	Net Income		1 0 1 5 00
20		4 9 6 5 00	4 9 6 5 00
21			

Prepare BS Third →
Rohan's Campus Delivery
Balance Sheet
June 30, 20 --

Assets		
Current assets:		
Cash	$ 370	
Accounts receivable	650	
Supplies	20	
Prepaid insurance	175	
Total current assets		$1,215
Property, plant, and equipment:		
Delivery equipment	$3,600	
Less accumulated depreciation	100	3,500
Total assets		$4,715
Liabilities		
Current liabilities:		
Accounts payable	$1,800	
Wages payable	50	
Total current liabilities		$1,850
Owner's Equity		
Rohan Macsen, capital		2,865
Total liabilities and owner's equity		$4,715

Prepare SOE Second →
Rohan's Campus Delivery
Statement of Owner's Equity
For Month Ended June 30, 20 --

Rohan Macsen, capital, June 1, 20--		$ —
Investments during June		2,000
Total investment		$2,000
Net income for June	$1,015	
Less: withdrawals for June	150	
Increase in capital		865
Rohan Macsen, capital, June 30, 20--		$2,865

Ending capital is not taken from the work sheet. It is computed on the statement of owner's equity.
Dollar signs used at top of columns and under rulings.
Single rulings indicate addition or subtraction.
Double rulings indicate totals.

Current Assets

Current assets include cash and assets that will be converted into cash or consumed within either one year or the normal operating cycle of the business, whichever is longer. Examples include cash, accounts receivable, supplies, and prepaid insurance. As shown in Figure 6-3, an operating cycle is the period of time required to purchase supplies and services and convert them back into cash.

FIGURE 6-3   Operating Cycle

Operating Cycle for a Service Business

Property, Plant, and Equipment

Property, plant, and equipment, also called plant assets or long-term assets, represent assets that are expected to serve the business for many years. Examples include land, buildings, and equipment.

Current Liabilities

Current liabilities are due within either one year or the normal operating cycle of the business, whichever is longer. They will be paid out of current assets. Accounts payable and wages payable are classified as current liabilities.

Long-Term Liabilities

Long-term liabilities, or long-term debt, are obligations that are not expected to be paid within a year and do not require the use of current assets. A mortgage on an office building is an example of a long-term liability. Rohan has no long-term debts. If he did, they would be listed on the balance sheet in the long-term liabilities section immediately following the current liabilities.

Additional Investments by the Owner (Revisited)

If the owner of a business made additional investments during the accounting period, the owner's capital reported in the Balance Sheet columns of the work sheet represents the beginning balance plus any additional investments made during the accounting period. Thus, it may not represent the beginning balance of the capital account and should not be used to prepare the statements. If this amount were used as the beginning balance on the statement of owner's equity, it would not equal the ending balance from last period and would create confusion for those comparing the two statements. In addition, the statement would not reflect all of the activities affecting the owner's capital account during the period.

Therefore, we must also review the owner's capital account in the general ledger to get the information needed to prepare the statement of owner's equity. Figure 6-4 illustrates this situation for another business, Ramon's Shopping Service. The $5,000 balance of July 1, 20--, in Ramon Balboa's general ledger capital account is used as the beginning balance on the statement of owner's equity. Note that this is also the ending balance on June 30, 20--. The additional investment of $3,000 made on July 5 and posted to Balboa's general ledger capital account is reported by writing "Investments during period" on the line immediately after the beginning balance. The beginning balance plus investments during the period equals the total investment by the owner in the business and is the amount reported in the Balance Sheet columns of the work sheet. From this point, the preparation of the statement is the same as for businesses without additional investments.

FIGURE 6-4 Statement of Owner's Equity with Additional Investment

GENERAL LEDGER

ACCOUNT: Ramon Balboa, Capital   ACCOUNT NO. 311

DATE		ITEM	POST. REF.	DEBIT	CREDIT	BALANCE DEBIT	BALANCE CREDIT
20-- July	1	Balance	J5		5 0 0 0 00		5 0 0 0 00
	5		J5		3 0 0 0 00		8 0 0 0 00

Additional investment   Amount reported on work sheet

Ramon's Shopping Service
Statement of Owner's Equity
For Months Ended June 30 and July 31, 20 - -

	June	July
Ramon Balboa, beginning capital	$4,000	$5,000
Investments during period		3,000
Total investment		$8,000
Net income for the month	$1,500	$2,100
Less withdrawals for the month	500	250
Increase in capital	1,000	1,850
Ramon Balboa, ending capital	$5,000	$9,850

From general ledger

From work sheet

Checkpoint ✓

Complete Checkpoint-1 on page 202 to test your basic understanding of LO1.

THE CLOSING PROCESS

LO2 Journalize and post closing entries.

Assets, liabilities, and the owner's capital account accumulate information across accounting periods. For example, the cash balance at the end of one accounting period must be the same as the cash balance at the beginning of the next period. Thus, the balance reported for Cash is a result of all cash transactions since the business first opened. This is true for all accounts reported on the balance sheet. For this reason, they are called **permanent accounts**.

Revenue, expense, and drawing accounts accumulate information *for only a specific accounting period*. When preparing the financial statements, only revenues, expenses, and withdrawals for *this year* should be reported. Revenues, expenses, and withdrawals from prior years should not be included in *this year's* financial statements. Similarly, *this year's* revenues, expenses, and withdrawals should not be included in next year's financial statements. Thus, at the end of the fiscal year, these accounts must be *closed*. The **closing process** gives these accounts zero balances so they are prepared to accumulate new information for the next accounting period. Since these accounts are closed at the end of each period, they are called **temporary accounts**.

The accounting records are closed "as of" December 31, or another fiscal year-end chosen by the business. The actual adjusting entries, closing entries, and financial statements are generally prepared several weeks after the official closing date. However, it is important to include all transactions occurring prior to year-end in the *current* year's financial statements. Similarly, transactions taking place after year-end must be included in the *next* year's financial statements. Improper timing of the recognition of transactions taking place around the end of the year can have major effects on the reported profits. For example, some businesses have been found to "leave the books open" for a few days to include a major sale, or other profitable transactions, that actually took place after the end of the fiscal year. Thus, proper treatment of transactions taking place around the end of the year is carefully monitored by auditors.

The closing process is most clearly demonstrated by returning to the accounting equation and T accounts. As shown in Figure 6-5, revenue, expense, and drawing

LEARNING KEY

Permanent accounts contain the results of all transactions since the business started. Their balances are carried forward to each new accounting period.

LEARNING KEY

Temporary accounts contain information for one accounting period. These accounts are closed at the end of each accounting period.

FIGURE 6-5 The Closing Process

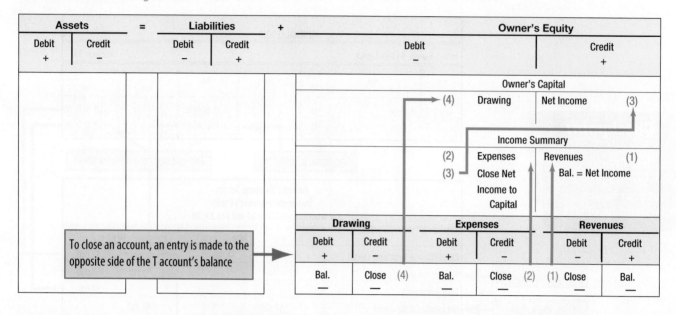

accounts impact owner's equity and should be considered "under the umbrella" of the capital account. The effect of these accounts on owner's equity is formalized at the end of the accounting period when the balances of the temporary accounts are transferred to the owner's capital account (a permanent account) during the closing process.

The four basic steps in the closing process are illustrated in Figure 6-5. As you can see, a new account, **Income Summary**, is used in the closing process. This account may also be called *Expense and Revenue Summary*. This temporary account is used to close the revenue and expense accounts. After closing the revenues and expenses to Income Summary, the balance of this account is equal to the net income. This is why it is called Income Summary. Income Summary is opened during the closing process. Then it is closed to the owner's capital account. It does not appear on any financial statement. The four steps in the closing process are explained below.

STEPS IN THE CLOSING PROCESS

STEP 1 Close Revenue Accounts to Income Summary. Revenues have credit balances and increase owner's equity. Therefore, the revenue account is debited to create a zero balance. Income Summary is credited for the same amount.

STEP 2 Close Expense Accounts to Income Summary. Expenses have debit balances and reduce owner's equity. Therefore, the expense accounts are credited to create a zero balance. Income Summary must be debited for the total of the expenses.

STEP 3 Close Income Summary to the Owner's Capital Account. The balance in Income Summary represents the net income (credit balance) or net loss (debit balance). If net income has been earned, Income Summary is debited to create a zero balance, and the owner's capital account is credited. If a net loss has been incurred, the owner's capital account is debited and Income Summary is credited to create a zero balance. Figure 6-6 shows examples for closing net income and net loss.

STEP 4 Close Drawing to the Owner's Capital Account. Drawing has a debit balance and reduces owner's equity. Therefore, it is credited to create a zero balance. The owner's capital account is debited.

LEARNING KEY

The owner can make withdrawals from the business at any time, as long as the assets are available. These withdrawals have nothing to do with measuring the profitability of the firm. Thus, they are closed directly to the owner's capital account.

Upon completion of these four steps, all temporary accounts have zero balances. The earnings and withdrawals for the period have been transferred to the owner's capital account. Closing entries for Rohan's Campus Delivery, in T account form, are illustrated in Figure 6-7.

FIGURE 6-6   Step 3: Closing Net Income and Closing Net Loss

NET INCOME				NET LOSS			
Capital				**Capital**			
	1,000	STEP 3		STEP 3	2,000		
		(Net Income)		(Net Loss)			
Income Summary				**Income Summary**			
(Expenses)	4,000	5,000	(Revenues)	(Expenses)	6,000	4,000	(Revenues)
STEP 3 to close	1,000	1,000	(Bal. before closing)	(Bal. before closing)	2,000	2,000	STEP 3 to close
	—	—			—	—	

Dashes (—) in the T Accounts indicate zero balances

FIGURE 6-7   Closing Entries in T Account Form

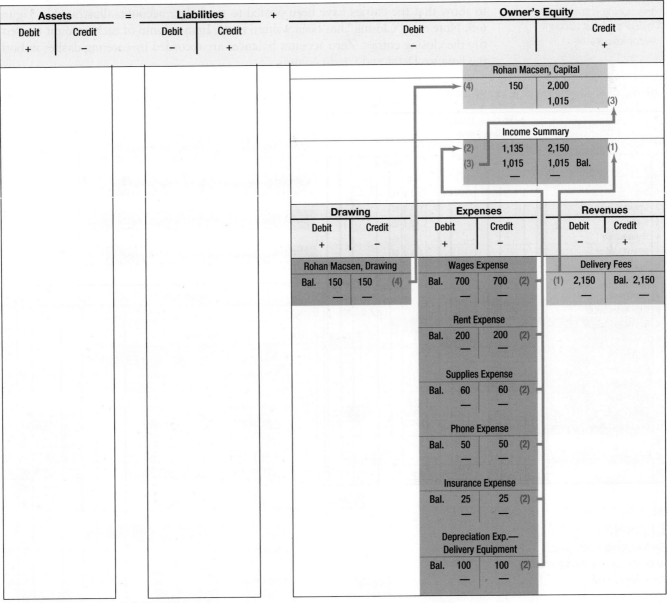

Dashes (—) in the T Accounts indicate zero balances

Journalize Closing Entries

Of course, to actually change the ledger accounts, the closing entries must be journalized and posted to the general ledger. As shown in Figure 6-8, the balances of the accounts to be closed are readily available from the Income Statement and Balance Sheet columns of the work sheet. These balances are used to illustrate the closing entries for Rohan's Campus Delivery, in general journal form. Remember: Closing entries are made at the end of the *fiscal year*. Closing entries made at the end of June are illustrated here so you can see the completion of the accounting cycle for Rohan's Campus Delivery. Like adjusting entries, the closing entries are made on the last day of the accounting period. "Closing Entries" is written in the Description column before the first entry and no explanations are required. Note that it is best to make one compound entry to close the expense accounts.

Post the Closing Entries

Computer programs post the closing entries to the owner's capital account automatically.

The account numbers have been entered in the Posting Reference column of the journal to show that the entries have been posted to the ledger accounts illustrated in Figure 6-9. Note that "Closing" has been written in the Item column of each account to identify the closing entries. Zero account balances are recorded by entering dashes in both the Balance Debit and Credit columns.

FIGURE 6-8   Closing Entries in Journal Form

Rohan's Campus Delivery — Work Sheet (Partial) — For Month Ended June 30, 20 - -

	ACCOUNT TITLE	INCOME STATEMENT DEBIT	INCOME STATEMENT CREDIT	BALANCE SHEET DEBIT	BALANCE SHEET CREDIT
1	Cash			3 7 0 00	
2	Accounts Receivable			6 5 0 00	
3	Supplies			2 0 00	
4	Prepaid Insurance			1 7 5 00	
5	Delivery Equipment			3 6 0 0 00	
6	Accum. Depr.—Delivery Equipment				1 0 0 00
7	Accounts Payable				1 8 0 0 00
8	Wages Payable				5 0 00
9	Rohan Macsen, Capital				2 0 0 0 00
10	Rohan Macsen, Drawing			1 5 0 00	
11	Delivery Fees		2 1 5 0 00		
12	Wages Expense	7 0 0 00			
13	Rent Expense	2 0 0 00			
14	Supplies Expense	6 0 00			
15	Phone Expense	5 0 00			
16	Insurance Expense	2 5 00			
17	Depr. Expense—Delivery Equipment	1 0 0 00			
18		1 1 3 5 00	2 1 5 0 00	4 9 6 5 00	3 9 5 0 00
19	Net Income	1 0 1 5 00			1 0 1 5 00
20		2 1 5 0 00	2 1 5 0 00	4 9 6 5 00	4 9 6 5 00

STEP 1: Close revenue accounts to Income Summary.

STEP 2: Close expense accounts to Income Summary.

STEP 3: Close Income Summary to the owner's capital account.

STEP 4: Close Drawing to the owner's capital account.

GENERAL JOURNAL — PAGE 4

	DATE	DESCRIPTION	POST. REF.	DEBIT	CREDIT	
		Closing Entries				1
20-- June	30	Delivery Fees	401	2 1 5 0 00		2
		Income Summary	313		2 1 5 0 00	3
						4
	30	Income Summary	313	1 1 3 5 00		5
		Wages Expense	511		7 0 0 00	6
		Rent Expense	521		2 0 0 00	7
		Supplies Expense	523		6 0 00	8
		Phone Expense	525		5 0 00	9
		Insurance Expense	535		2 5 00	10
		Depr. Expense—Delivery Equipment	541		1 0 0 00	11
						12
	30	Income Summary	313	1 0 1 5 00		13
		Rohan Macsen, Capital	311		1 0 1 5 00	14
						15
	30	Rohan Macsen, Capital	311	1 5 0 00		16
		Rohan Macsen, Drawing	312		1 5 0 00	17
						18

LEARNING KEY

Each individual revenue, expense, and drawing account must be closed.

Your Perspective

BOOKKEEPER AT AN ACCOUNTING FIRM

As a bookkeeper for an accounting firm such as Robins, Eskew, Smith, & Jordan, located in Atlanta, Georgia, your duties would include assisting the Certified Public Accountants (CPA's) with maintaining the clients' books during the fiscal year. You would also perform other tasks such as bank account reconciliations, paying bills for clients, and entering data for tax return preparation. Did you know that helping to maintain the books also involves the year-end closing process and preparing financial statements, just what you are learning about in this chapter?

The closing process not only gives temporary accounts zero balances so they are prepared to accumulate new information for the next accounting period, but this process updates the owner's equity account as well. Financial statements *must be* prepared accurately and timely because the information is necessary to make critical business decisions, which makes the bookkeeper's job extremely important. Since this accounting firm is providing a service to earn a profit, this is an example of a service business.

FIGURE 6-9   Closing Entries Posted to the General Ledger

GENERAL LEDGER

ACCOUNT: Rohan Macsen, Capital   ACCOUNT NO. 311

DATE		ITEM	POST. REF.	DEBIT	CREDIT	BALANCE DEBIT	BALANCE CREDIT
20-- June	1		J1		2 0 0 0 00		2 0 0 0 00
	30	Closing	J4		1 0 1 5 00		3 0 1 5 00
	30	Closing	J4	1 5 0 00			2 8 6 5 00

ACCOUNT: Rohan Macsen, Drawing   ACCOUNT NO. 312

DATE		ITEM	POST. REF.	DEBIT	CREDIT	BALANCE DEBIT	BALANCE CREDIT
20-- June	30		J2	1 5 0 00		1 5 0 00	
	30	Closing	J4		1 5 0 00		

ACCOUNT: Income Summary   ACCOUNT NO. 313

DATE		ITEM	POST. REF.	DEBIT	CREDIT	BALANCE DEBIT	BALANCE CREDIT
20-- June	30	Closing	J4		2 1 5 0 00		2 1 5 0 00
	30	Closing	J4	1 1 3 5 00			1 0 1 5 00
	30	Closing	J4	1 0 1 5 00			

ACCOUNT: Delivery Fees   ACCOUNT NO. 401

DATE		ITEM	POST. REF.	DEBIT	CREDIT	BALANCE DEBIT	BALANCE CREDIT
20-- June	6		J1		5 0 0 00		5 0 0 00
	15		J1		6 0 0 00		1 1 0 0 00
	30		J2		1 0 5 0 00		2 1 5 0 00
	30	Closing	J4	2 1 5 0 00			

(continued)

FIGURE 6-9 Closing Entries Posted to the General Ledger *(concluded)*

ACCOUNT: Wages Expense   ACCOUNT NO. 511

DATE		ITEM	POST. REF.	DEBIT	CREDIT	BALANCE DEBIT	BALANCE CREDIT
20-- June	27		J2	6 5 0 00		6 5 0 00	
	30	Adjusting	J3	5 0 00		7 0 0 00	
	30	Closing	J4		7 0 0 00		

ACCOUNT: Rent Expense   ACCOUNT NO. 521

DATE		ITEM	POST REF.	DEBIT	CREDIT	BALANCE DEBIT	BALANCE CREDIT
20-- June	7		J1	2 0 0 00		2 0 0 00	
	30	Closing	J4		2 0 0 00		

ACCOUNT: Supplies Expense   ACCOUNT NO. 523

DATE		ITEM	POST. REF.	DEBIT	CREDIT	BALANCE DEBIT	BALANCE CREDIT
20-- June	30	Adjusting	J3	6 0 00		6 0 00	
	30	Closing	J4		6 0 00		

ACCOUNT: Phone Expense   ACCOUNT NO. 525

DATE		ITEM	POST. REF.	DEBIT	CREDIT	BALANCE DEBIT	BALANCE CREDIT
20-- June	15		J1	5 0 00		5 0 00	
	30	Closing	J4		5 0 00		

ACCOUNT: Insurance Expense   ACCOUNT NO. 535

DATE		ITEM	POST. REF.	DEBIT	CREDIT	BALANCE DEBIT	BALANCE CREDIT
20-- June	30	Adjusting	J3	2 5 00		2 5 00	
	30	Closing	J4		2 5 00		

ACCOUNT: Depreciation Expense—Delivery Equipment   ACCOUNT NO. 541

DATE		ITEM	POST. REF.	DEBIT	CREDIT	BALANCE DEBIT	BALANCE CREDIT
20-- June	30	Adjusting	J3	1 0 0 00		1 0 0 00	
	30	Closing	J4		1 0 0 00		

Checkpoint ✓

Complete Checkpoint-2 on page 202 to test your basic understanding of LO2.

LO3 Prepare a post-closing trial balance.

LEARNING KEY

Once the closing entries are posted, the general ledger capital account balance will agree with the amount reported on the balance sheet.

POST-CLOSING TRIAL BALANCE

After posting the closing entries, a **post-closing trial balance** should be prepared to prove the equality of the debit and credit balances in the general ledger accounts. The ending balance of each general ledger account that remains open at the end of the year is listed. Remember: Only the permanent accounts remain open after the closing process is completed. Figure 6-10 shows the post-closing trial balance for Rohan's ledger.

Note that all amounts reflected on the post-closing trial balance are the same as reported in the Balance Sheet columns of the work sheet except Drawing and Owner's Capital. Drawing was closed. Owner's Capital was updated to reflect revenues, expenses, and drawing for the accounting period.

FIGURE 6-10 Post-Closing Trial Balance

ACCOUNT TITLE	ACCOUNT NO.	DEBIT BALANCE	CREDIT BALANCE
Rohan's Campus Delivery Post-Closing Trial Balance June 30, 20 - -			
Cash	101	3 7 0 00	
Accounts Receivable	122	6 5 0 00	
Supplies	141	2 0 00	
Prepaid Insurance	145	1 7 5 00	
Delivery Equipment	185	3 6 0 0 00	
Accumulated Depreciation—Delivery Equipment	185.1		1 0 0 00
Accounts Payable	202		1 8 0 0 00
Wages Payable	219		5 0 00
Rohan Macsen, Capital	311		2 8 6 5 00
		4 8 1 5 00	4 8 1 5 00

Checkpoint ✓

Complete Checkpoint-3 on page 202 to test your basic understanding of LO3.

A Broader View

Importance of Earnings to the Stock Market

Investors in the stock market pay close attention to earnings reported on the income statement. If earnings are different from what investors are expecting, the price of the stock may go up or down. For example, AT&T's share prices dipped simply because they missed expected earnings by a penny per share.

THE ACCOUNTING CYCLE

LO4 List and describe the steps in the accounting cycle.

The steps involved in accounting for all of the business activities during an accounting period are called the accounting cycle. The cycle begins with the analysis of source documents and ends with a post-closing trial balance. A brief summary of the steps in the cycle follows.

STEPS IN THE ACCOUNTING CYCLE

During Accounting Period

STEP 1 Analyze source documents.

STEP 2 Journalize the transactions.

STEP 3 Post to the general ledger accounts.

End of Accounting Period

STEP 4 Prepare a trial balance.

STEP 5 Determine and prepare the needed adjustments on the work sheet.

LEARNING KEY
Properly analyzing and journalizing transactions is very important. A mistake made in step 1 is carried through the entire accounting cycle.

STEP 6   Complete an end-of-period work sheet.

STEP 7   Journalize and post the adjusting entries.

STEP 8   Prepare an income statement, a statement of owner's equity, and a balance sheet.

STEP 9   Journalize and post the closing entries.

STEP 10   Prepare a post-closing trial balance.

Steps 4 through 10 in the preceding list are performed *as of* the last day of the accounting period. This does not mean that they are actually done on the last day. The accountant may not be able to do any of these things until the first few days (sometimes weeks) of the next period. Nevertheless, the work sheet, statements, and entries are prepared as of the closing date.

Self-Study

LEARNING OBJECTIVES	Key Points to Remember
LO1 Prepare financial statements with the aid of a work sheet.	The work sheet is used as an aid in preparing: 1. adjusting entries, 2. financial statements, and 3. closing entries. The following classifications are used for accounts reported on the balance sheet. • *Current assets* include cash and assets that will be converted into cash or consumed within either one year or the normal operating cycle of the business, whichever is longer. An *operating cycle* is the time required to purchase supplies and services and convert them back into cash. • *Property, plant, and equipment*, also called *plant assets* or *long-term assets*, represent assets that are expected to serve the business for many years. • *Current liabilities* are liabilities that are due within either one year or the normal operating cycle of the business, whichever is longer, and that are to be paid out of current assets. • *Long-term liabilities*, or *long-term debt*, are obligations that are not expected to be paid within a year and do not require the use of current assets.
LO2 Journalize and post closing entries.	Steps in the closing process are: 1. Close revenue accounts to Income Summary. 2. Close expense accounts to Income Summary. 3. Close Income Summary to the owner's capital account. 4. Close Drawing to the owner's capital account.

(continued)

LEARNING OBJECTIVES   Key Points to Remember

Assets		=	Liabilities		+	Owner's Equity	
Debit +	Credit −		Debit −	Credit +		Debit −	Credit +

Owner's Capital

(4)	Drawing	Net Income (3)

Income Summary

(2)	Expenses	Revenues (1)
(3)	Close Net Income to Capital	Bal. = Net Income

Drawing		Expenses		Revenues	
Debit +	Credit −	Debit +	Credit −	Debit −	Credit +
Bal. —	Close (4) —	Bal. —	Close (2) —	(1) Close —	Bal. —

LO3	**Prepare a post-closing trial balance.**	After posting the closing entries, a post-closing trial balance should be prepared to prove the equality of the debit and credit balances in the general ledger accounts. The accounts shown in the post-closing trial balance are the permanent accounts.

LO4	**List and describe the steps in the accounting cycle.**	Steps in the accounting cycle are:

During Accounting Period

1. Analyze source documents.
2. Journalize the transactions.
3. Post to the general ledger accounts.

End of Accounting Period

4. Prepare a trial balance.
5. Determine and prepare the needed adjustments on the work sheet.
6. Complete an end-of-period work sheet.
7. Journalize and post the adjusting entries.
8. Prepare an income statement, a statement of owner's equity, and a balance sheet.
9. Journalize and post the closing entries.
10. Prepare a post-closing trial balance.

DEMONSTRATION PROBLEM

Timothy Chang owns and operates Hard Copy Printers. A work sheet for the year ended December 31, 20--, is provided on the next page. Chang made no additional investments during the year.

REQUIRED

1. Prepare financial statements.
2. Prepare closing entries.

Hard Copy Printers
Work Sheet
For Year Ended December 31, 20--

	ACCOUNT TITLE	TRIAL BALANCE DEBIT	TRIAL BALANCE CREDIT	ADJUSTMENTS DEBIT	ADJUSTMENTS CREDIT	ADJUSTED TRIAL BALANCE DEBIT	ADJUSTED TRIAL BALANCE CREDIT	INCOME STATEMENT DEBIT	INCOME STATEMENT CREDIT	BALANCE SHEET DEBIT	BALANCE SHEET CREDIT	
1	Cash	1 1 8 0 00				1 1 8 0 00				1 1 8 0 00		1
2	Paper Supplies	3 6 0 0 00			(a) 3 5 5 0 00	5 0 00				5 0 00		2
3	Prepaid Insurance	1 0 0 0 00			(b) 5 0 5 00	4 9 5 00				4 9 5 00		3
4	Printing Equipment	5 8 0 0 00				5 8 0 0 00				5 8 0 0 00		4
5	Accum. Depr.—Printing Equipment				(d) 1 2 0 0 00		1 2 0 0 00				1 2 0 0 00	5
6	Accounts Payable		5 0 0 00				5 0 0 00				5 0 0 00	6
7	Wages Payable				(c) 3 0 00		3 0 00				3 0 00	7
8	Timothy Chang, Capital		10 0 0 0 00				10 0 0 0 00				10 0 0 0 00	8
9	Timothy Chang, Drawing	13 0 0 0 00				13 0 0 0 00				13 0 0 0 00		9
10	Printing Fees		35 1 0 0 00				35 1 0 0 00		35 1 0 0 00			10
11	Wages Expense	11 9 7 0 00		(c) 3 0 00		12 0 0 0 00		12 0 0 0 00				11
12	Rent Expense	7 5 0 0 00				7 5 0 0 00		7 5 0 0 00				12
13	Paper Supplies Expense			(a) 3 5 5 0 00		3 5 5 0 00		3 5 5 0 00				13
14	Phone Expense	5 5 0 00				5 5 0 00		5 5 0 00				14
15	Utilities Expense	1 0 0 0 00				1 0 0 0 00		1 0 0 0 00				15
16	Insurance Expense			(b) 5 0 5 00		5 0 5 00		5 0 5 00				16
17	Depr. Expense—Printing Equipment			(d) 1 2 0 0 00		1 2 0 0 00		1 2 0 0 00				17
18		45 6 0 0 00	45 6 0 0 00	5 2 8 5 00	5 2 8 5 00	46 8 3 0 00	46 8 3 0 00	26 3 0 5 00	35 1 0 0 00	20 5 2 5 00	11 7 3 0 00	18
19	Net Income							8 7 9 5 00			8 7 9 5 00	19
20								35 1 0 0 00	35 1 0 0 00	20 5 2 5 00	20 5 2 5 00	20
21												21
22												22
23												23
24												24
25												25
26												26
27												27
28												28
29												29
30												30

Solution 1.

Hard Copy Printers Income Statement For Year Ended December 31, 20 --		
Revenue:		
Printing fees		$35,100
Expenses:		
Wages expense	$12,000	
Rent expense	7,500	
Paper supplies expense	3,550	
Phone expense	550	
Utilities expense	1,000	
Insurance expense	505	
Depreciation expense—printing equipment	1,200	
Total expenses		26,305
Net income		$ 8,795

Hard Copy Printers Statement of Owner's Equity For Year Ended December 31, 20 --		
Timothy Chang, capital, January 1, 20 - -		$10,000
Net income for 20 - -	$ 8,795	
Less withdrawals for 20 - -	13,000	
Decrease in capital		(4,205)
Timothy Chang, capital, December 31, 20 - -		$ 5,795

Hard Copy Printers Balance Sheet December 31, 20 - -		
Assets		
Current assets:		
Cash	$ 1,180	
Paper supplies	50	
Prepaid insurance	495	
Total current assets		$ 1,725
Property, plant, and equipment:		
Printing equipment	$ 5,800	
Less accumulated depreciation	1,200	4,600
Total assets		$ 6,325
Liabilities		
Current liabilities:		
Accounts payable	$ 500	
Wages payable	30	
Total current liabilities		$ 530
Owner's Equity		
Timothy Chang, capital		5,795
Total liabilities and owner's equity		$ 6,325

2.

	DATE		DESCRIPTION	POST. REF.	DEBIT					CREDIT					
1			Closing Entries												1
2	20-- Dec.	31	Printing Fees		35	1	0	0	00						2
3			Income Summary							35	1	0	0	00	3
4															4
5		31	Income Summary		26	3	0	5	00						5
6			Wages Expense							12	0	0	0	00	6
7			Rent Expense							7	5	0	0	00	7
8			Paper Supplies Expense							3	5	5	0	00	8
9			Phone Expense								5	5	0	00	9
10			Utilities Expense							1	0	0	0	00	10
11			Insurance Expense								5	0	5	00	11
12			Depr. Expense—Printing Equipment							1	2	0	0	00	12
13															13
14		31	Income Summary		8	7	9	5	00						14
15			Timothy Chang, Capital							8	7	9	5	00	15
16															16
17		31	Timothy Chang, Capital		13	0	0	0	00						17
18			Timothy Chang, Drawing							13	0	0	0	00	18
19															19

GENERAL JOURNAL — PAGE 4

KEY TERMS

account form of balance sheet (186) A balance sheet in which the assets are on the left and the liabilities and the owner's equity sections are on the right.

accounting cycle (195) The steps involved in accounting for all of the business activities during an accounting period.

classified balance sheet (186) A balance sheet with separate categories for current assets; property, plant, and equipment; current liabilities; and long-term liabilities.

closing process (189) The process of giving zero balances to the temporary accounts so that they can accumulate information for the next accounting period.

current assets (188) Cash and assets that will be converted into cash or consumed within either one year or the normal operating cycle of the business, whichever is longer.

current liabilities (188) Liabilities that are due within either one year or the normal operating cycle of the business, whichever is longer, and that are to be paid out of current assets.

Income Summary (190) A temporary account used in the closing process to summarize the effects of all revenue and expense accounts.

long-term assets (188) See property, plant, and equipment.

long-term debt (188) See long-term liabilities.

long-term liabilities (188) Obligations that are not expected to be paid within a year and do not require the use of current assets. Also called long-term debt.

operating cycle (188) The period of time required to purchase supplies and services and convert them back into cash.

permanent accounts (189)   Accounts that accumulate information across accounting periods; all accounts reported on the balance sheet.

plant assets (188)   See property, plant, and equipment.

post-closing trial balance (194)   Prepared after posting the closing entries to prove the equality of the debit and credit balances in the general ledger accounts.

property, plant, and equipment (188)   Assets that are expected to serve the business for many years. Also called plant assets or long-term assets.

report form of balance sheet (186)   A balance sheet in which the liabilities and the owner's equity sections are shown below the assets section.

temporary accounts (189)   Accounts that do not accumulate information across accounting periods but are closed, such as the drawing account and all income statement accounts.

SELF-STUDY TEST QUESTIONS

True/False

1. LO1   Expenses are listed on the income statement as they appear in the chart of accounts or in descending order (by dollar amount).

2. LO1   Additional investments of capital during the month are not reported on the statement of owner's equity.

3. LO1   The income statement cannot be prepared using the work sheet alone.

4. LO1   A classified balance sheet groups similar items, such as current assets together.

5. LO2   Temporary accounts are closed at the end of each accounting period.

Multiple Choice

1. LO2   Which of these types of accounts is considered a "permanent" account?

    (a) Revenue   (c) Drawing
    (b) Asset   (d) Expense

2. LO2   Which of these accounts is considered a "temporary" account?

    (a) Cash   (c) J. Jones, Capital
    (b) Accounts Payable   (d) J. Jones, Drawing

3. LO2   Which of these is the first step in the closing process?

    (a) Close revenue account(s).   (c) Close the Income Summary account.
    (b) Close expense accounts.   (d) Close the drawing account.

4. LO3   The _____ is prepared after closing entries are posted to prove the equality of debit and credit balances.

    (a) balance sheet   (c) post-closing trial balance
    (b) income statement   (d) statement of owner's equity

5. LO4   Steps that begin with analyzing source documents and conclude with the post-closing trial balance are called the

    (a) closing process.   (c) adjusting entries.
    (b) accounting cycle.   (d) posting process.

Checkpoint Exercises

1. **LO1**   Joe Fisher operates Fisher Consulting. A partial work sheet for August 20-- is provided below. Fisher made no additional investments during the month. Prepare an income statement, statement of owner's equity, and balance sheet.

Fisher Consulting
Work Sheet (Partial)
For Month Ended August 31, 20 - -

	ACCOUNT TITLE	INCOME STATEMENT		BALANCE SHEET		
		DEBIT	CREDIT	DEBIT	CREDIT	
1	Cash			2 5 0 0 00		1
2	Accounts Receivable			8 0 0 00		2
3	Equipment			3 8 0 0 00		3
4	Accum. Depr.— Equipment				2 0 0 00	4
5	Accounts Payable				1 0 0 0 00	5
6	Joe Fisher, Capital				3 0 0 0 00	6
7	Joe Fisher, Drawing			3 0 0 00		7
8	Professional Fees		5 0 0 0 00			8
9	Wages Expense	1 0 0 0 00				9
10	Rent Expense	7 0 0 00				10
11	Depreciation Expense	1 0 0 00				11
12		1 8 0 0 00	5 0 0 0 00	7 4 0 0 00	4 2 0 0 00	12
13	Net Income	3 2 0 0 00			3 2 0 0 00	13
14		5 0 0 0 00	5 0 0 0 00	7 4 0 0 00	7 4 0 0 00	14
15						15
16						16

2. **LO2**   Using the work sheet provided in Checkpoint Exercise 1, prepare closing entries in general journal form.

3. **LO3**   Using the work sheet provided in Checkpoint Exercise 1 and financial statements prepared for that exercise, prepare a post-closing trial balance.

The answers to the Self-Study Test Questions are at the end of the chapter (pages 215–217).

Applying Your Knowledge

REVIEW QUESTIONS

LO1   1. Identify the source of the information needed to prepare the income statement.

LO1   2. Describe two approaches to listing the expenses in the income statement.

LO1   3. Identify the sources of the information needed to prepare the statement of owner's equity.

LO1   4. If additional investments were made during the year, what information in addition to the work sheet would be needed to prepare the statement of owner's equity?

LO1   5. Identify the sources of the information needed to prepare the balance sheet.

LO2   6. What is a permanent account? On which financial statement are permanent accounts reported?

LO2   7. Name three types of temporary accounts.

LO2   8. List the four steps for closing the temporary accounts.

LO2   9. Describe the net effect of the four closing entries on the balance of the owner's capital account. Where else is this same amount calculated?

LO3   10. What is the purpose of the post-closing trial balance?

LO4   11. List the 10 steps in the accounting cycle.

SERIES A EXERCISES

E 6-1A   (LO1)
✓ Net income: $2,220

SHOW
ME HOW

INCOME STATEMENT From the partial work sheet for Major Advising below, prepare an income statement.

E 6-2A   (LO1)
✓ Capital 1/31: $5,420

SHOW
ME HOW

STATEMENT OF OWNER'S EQUITY From the partial work sheet below, prepare a statement of owner's equity, assuming no additional investment was made by the owner.

E 6-3A   (LO1)
✓ Total assets: $6,720

SHOW
ME HOW

BALANCE SHEET From the partial work sheet below, prepare a balance sheet.

(FOR EXERCISES 6-1A, 6-2A, 6-3A, AND 6-4A)

Major Advising
Work Sheet (Partial)
For Month Ended January 31, 20 - -

	ACCOUNT TITLE	INCOME STATEMENT DEBIT	INCOME STATEMENT CREDIT	BALANCE SHEET DEBIT	BALANCE SHEET CREDIT	
1	Cash			1 3 3 9 00		1
2	Accounts Receivable			9 3 5 00		2
3	Supplies			3 4 6 00		3
4	Prepaid Insurance			8 0 0 00		4
5	Office Equipment			3 5 0 0 00		5
6	Accum. Depr.—Office Equipment				2 0 0 00	6
7	Accounts Payable				1 0 0 0 00	7
8	Wages Payable				3 0 0 00	8
9	Ed Major, Capital				4 1 0 0 00	9
10	Ed Major, Drawing			9 0 0 00		10
11	Advising Fees		4 1 4 0 00			11
12	Wages Expense	7 0 0 00				12
13	Advertising Expense	9 0 00				13
14	Rent Expense	5 0 0 00				14
15	Supplies Expense	1 5 0 00				15
16	Phone Expense	6 7 00				16
17	Electricity Expense	4 8 00				17
18	Insurance Expense	8 9 00				18
19	Gas and Oil Expense	5 3 00				19
20	Depr. Expense—Office Equipment	2 0 0 00				20
21	Miscellaneous Expense	2 3 00				21
22		1 9 2 0 00	4 1 4 0 00	7 8 2 0 00	5 6 0 0 00	22
23	Net Income	2 2 2 0 00			2 2 2 0 00	23
24		4 1 4 0 00	4 1 4 0 00	7 8 2 0 00	7 8 2 0 00	24

E 6-4A (LO2)

✓ Capital 1/31: $5,420

CLOSING ENTRIES (NET INCOME) Set up T accounts for Major Advising based on the work sheet in Exercise 6-1A and the chart of accounts provided below. Enter the existing balance for each account. Prepare closing entries in general journal form. Then post the closing entries to the T accounts.

Chart of Accounts

Assets		Revenues	
101	Cash	401	Advising Fees
122	Accounts Receivable		
141	Supplies	**Expenses**	
145	Prepaid Insurance	511	Wages Expense
181	Office Equipment	512	Advertising Expense
181.1	Accum. Depr.—Office Equip.	521	Rent Expense
		524	Supplies Expense
Liabilities		525	Phone Expense
202	Accounts Payable	533	Electricity Expense
219	Wages Payable	535	Insurance Expense
		538	Gas and Oil Expense
		541	Depr. Exp.—Office Equip.
Owner's Equity		549	Miscellaneous Expense
311	Ed Major Capital		
312	Ed Major Drawing		
313	Income Summary		

E 6-5A (LO2)

SHOW ME HOW

CLOSING ENTRIES (NET INCOME) Using the following partial listing of T accounts, prepare closing entries in general journal form dated April 30, 20--. Then post the closing entries to the T accounts.

Cash 101		Income Summary 313		Supplies Expense 524	
Bal. 500				Bal. 500	

Accounts Receivable 122		Golf Instruction Fees 401		Insurance Expense 535	
Bal. 1,500			Bal. 4,000	Bal 100	

Wages Payable 219		Wages Expense 511		Postage Expense 536	
	Bal. 400	Bal. 800		Bal. 50	

Chris Williams, Capital 311		Advertising Expense 512		Gas and Oil Expense 538	
	Bal. 9,000	Bal. 200		Bal. 150	

Chris Williams, Drawing 312		Travel Expense 515		Miscellaneous Expense 549	
Bal. 1,000		Bal. 600		Bal. 80	

E 6-6A   (LO2)

✓ Capital 1/31: $2,597

SHOW
ME HOW

CLOSING ENTRIES (NET LOSS) Using the following partial listing of T accounts, prepare closing entries in general journal form dated January 31, 20--. Then post the closing entries to the T accounts.

Accum. Depr.— Del. Equip.	185.1
	Bal. 100

Wages Expense	511
Bal. 1,800	

Electricity Expense	533
Bal. 44	

Wages Payable	219
	Bal. 200

Advertising Expense	512
Bal. 80	

Insurance Expense	535
Bal 30	

Saburo Goto, Capital	311
	Bal. 4,000

Rent Expense	521
Bal. 500	

Gas and Oil Expense	538
Bal. 38	

Saburo Goto, Drawing	312
Bal. 800	

Supplies Expense	523
Bal. 120	

Depr. Exp.— Del. Equip.	541
Bal. 100	

Income Summary	313

Phone Expense	525
Bal. 58	

Miscellaneous Expense	549
Bal. 33	

Delivery Fees	401
	Bal. 2,200

SERIES A PROBLEMS

P 6-7A   (LO1)

✓ Net income: $838
✓ Capital 1/31: $7,738
✓ Total assets 1/31: $9,338

FINANCIAL STATEMENTS Page 206 shows a work sheet for Megaffin's Repairs. No additional investments were made by the owner during the month.

REQUIRED

1. Prepare an income statement.

2. Prepare a statement of owner's equity.

3. Prepare a balance sheet.

PROBLEM 6-7A

Megaffin's Repairs
Work Sheet
For Month Ended January 31, 20--

	ACCOUNT TITLE	TRIAL BALANCE DEBIT	TRIAL BALANCE CREDIT	ADJUSTMENTS DEBIT	ADJUSTMENTS CREDIT	ADJUSTED TRIAL BALANCE DEBIT	ADJUSTED TRIAL BALANCE CREDIT	INCOME STATEMENT DEBIT	INCOME STATEMENT CREDIT	BALANCE SHEET DEBIT	BALANCE SHEET CREDIT	
1	Cash	3 6 7 3 00				3 6 7 3 00				3 6 7 3 00		1
2	Accounts Receivable	1 4 5 0 00				1 4 5 0 00				1 4 5 0 00		2
3	Supplies	7 0 0 00			3 0 0 00	4 0 0 00				4 0 0 00		3
4	Prepaid Insurance	9 0 0 00			2 3 0 00	6 7 0 00				6 7 0 00		4
5	Delivery Equipment	3 2 0 0 00				3 2 0 0 00				3 2 0 0 00		5
6	Accum. Depr. - Delivery Equipment				5 5 00		5 5 00				5 5 00	6
7	Accounts Payable		1 2 0 0 00				1 2 0 0 00				1 2 0 0 00	7
8	Wages Payable				4 0 0 00		4 0 0 00				4 0 0 00	8
9	Don Megaffin, Capital		8 0 0 0 00				8 0 0 0 00				8 0 0 0 00	9
10	Don Megaffin, Drawing	1 1 0 0 00				1 1 0 0 00				1 1 0 0 00		10
11	Repair Fees		4 7 0 0 00				4 7 0 0 00		4 7 0 0 00			11
12	Wages Expense	1 7 5 0 00		4 0 0 00		2 1 5 0 00		2 1 5 0 00				12
13	Advertising Expense	2 0 0 00				2 0 0 00		2 0 0 00				13
14	Rent Expense	6 4 0 00				6 4 0 00		6 4 0 00				14
15	Supplies Expense			3 0 0 00		3 0 0 00		3 0 0 00				15
16	Phone Expense	5 0 00				5 0 00		5 0 00				16
17	Insurance Expense			2 3 0 00		2 3 0 00		2 3 0 00				17
18	Gas and Oil Expense	2 0 0 00				2 0 0 00		2 0 0 00				18
19	Depr. Expense - Delivery Equipment			5 5 00		5 5 00		5 5 00				19
20	Miscellaneous Expense	3 7 00				3 7 00		3 7 00				20
21		13 9 0 0 00	13 9 0 0 00	9 8 5 00	9 8 5 00	14 3 5 5 00	14 3 5 5 00	3 8 6 2 00	4 7 0 0 00	10 4 9 3 00	9 6 5 5 00	21
22	Net Income							8 3 8 00			8 3 8 00	22
23								4 7 0 0 00	4 7 0 0 00	10 4 9 3 00	10 4 9 3 00	23
24												24
25												25
26												26
27												27
28												28
29												29
30												30

P 6-8A   (LO2/3)

✓ Capital 1/31: $7,738

✓ Post-closing trial balance total debits: $9,393

CLOSING ENTRIES AND POST-CLOSING TRIAL BALANCE Refer to the work sheet in Problem 6-7A for Megaffin's Repairs. The trial balance amounts (before adjustments) have been entered in the ledger accounts provided in the working papers. If you are not using the working papers that accompany this book, set up ledger accounts and enter these balances as of January 31, 20--. A chart of accounts is provided below.

Megaffin's Repairs
Chart of Accounts

Assets			Revenues	
101	Cash		401	Repair Fees
122	Accounts Receivable			
141	Supplies		Expenses	
145	Prepaid Insurance		511	Wages Expense
185	Delivery Equipment		512	Advertising Expense
185.1	Accum. Depr.—Delivery Equip.		521	Rent Expense
			523	Supplies Expense
Liabilities			525	Phone Expense
202	Accounts Payable		535	Insurance Expense
219	Wages Payable		538	Gas and Oil Expense
			541	Depr. Exp.—Delivery Equip.
Owner's Equity			549	Miscellaneous Expense
311	Don Megaffin, Capital			
312	Don Megaffin, Drawing			
313	Income Summary			

REQUIRED

1. Journalize (page 10) and post the adjusting entries.

2. Journalize (page 11) and post the closing entries.

3. Prepare a post-closing trial balance.

P 6-9A   (LO1)

✓ Capital 1/31: $6,820

SHOW
ME HOW

STATEMENT OF OWNER'S EQUITY The capital account for Autumn Chou, including an additional investment, and a partial work sheet are shown below and on page 208.

REQUIRED

Prepare a statement of owner's equity.

GENERAL LEDGER							
ACCOUNT: Autumn Chou, Capital						ACCOUNT NO. 311	
DATE	ITEM	POST. REF.	DEBIT	CREDIT	BALANCE		
					DEBIT	CREDIT	
20-- Jan. 1	Balance	✔				4 8 0 0 00	
18		J 1		1 2 0 0 00		6 0 0 0 00	

		Autumn's Home Designs Work Sheet (Partial) For Month Ended January 31, 20 --															
		INCOME STATEMENT						BALANCE SHEET									
	ACCOUNT TITLE	DEBIT				CREDIT		DEBIT				CREDIT					
1	Cash							3	2	0	0	00					1
2	Accounts Receivable							1	6	0	0	00					2
3	Supplies								8	0	0	00					3
4	Prepaid Insurance								9	0	0	00					4
5	Office Equipment							2	5	0	0	00					5
6	Accum. Depr.—Office Equipment													5	0	00	6
7	Accounts Payable												1	9	5	0	00	7
8	Wages Payable													1	8	0	00	8
9	Autumn Chou, Capital												6	0	0	0	00	9
10	Autumn Chou, Drawing							1	0	0	0	00					10
11	Design Fees					4	8	6	6	00							11
12	Wages Expense	1	9	0	0	00											12
13	Advertising Expense		2	1	0	00											13
14	Rent Expense		6	0	0	00											14
15	Supplies Expense		2	0	0	00											15
16	Phone Expense			8	5	00											16
17	Electricity Expense			4	8	00											17
18	Insurance Expense			6	0	00											18
19	Gas and Oil Expense			3	2	00											19
20	Depr. Expense—Office Equipment			5	0	00											20
21	Miscellaneous Expense			5	0	00											21
22		3	0	4	6	00	4	8	6	6	00	10	0	0	0	00	8	1	8	0	00	22
23	Net Income	1	8	2	0	00								1	8	2	0	00	23
24		4	8	6	6	00	4	8	6	6	00	10	0	0	0	00	10	0	0	0	00	24

SERIES B EXERCISES

E 6-1B (LO1)
✓ Net income: $1,826

SHOW ME HOW

INCOME STATEMENT From the partial work sheet for Adams' Shoe Shine on the next page, prepare an income statement.

E 6-2B (LO1)
✓ Capital 6/30: $5,826

SHOW ME HOW

STATEMENT OF OWNER'S EQUITY From the partial work sheet on the next page, prepare a statement of owner's equity, assuming no additional investment was made by the owner.

E 6-3B (LO1)
✓ Total assets: $7,936

SHOW ME HOW

BALANCE SHEET From the partial work sheet on the next page, prepare a balance sheet for Adams' Shoe Shine.

(FOR EXERCISES 6-1B, 6-2B, 6-3B, AND 6-4B)

Adams' Shoe Shine
Work Sheet (Partial)
For Month Ended June 30, 20 - -

	ACCOUNT TITLE	INCOME STATEMENT		BALANCE SHEET		
		DEBIT	CREDIT	DEBIT	CREDIT	
1	Cash			3 2 6 2 00		1
2	Accounts Receivable			1 2 4 4 00		2
3	Supplies			8 0 0 00		3
4	Prepaid Insurance			6 4 0 00		4
5	Office Equipment			2 1 0 0 00		5
6	Accum. Depr.—Office Equipment				1 1 0 00	6
7	Accounts Payable				1 8 5 0 00	7
8	Wages Payable				2 6 0 00	8
9	Mary Adams, Capital				6 0 0 0 00	9
10	Mary Adams, Drawing			2 0 0 0 00		10
11	Service Fees		4 8 1 3 00			11
12	Wages Expense	1 0 8 0 00				12
13	Advertising Expense	3 4 00				13
14	Rent Expense	9 0 0 00				14
15	Supplies Expense	3 2 2 00				15
16	Phone Expense	1 3 3 00				16
17	Utilities Expense	1 0 2 00				17
18	Insurance Expense	1 2 0 00				18
19	Gas and Oil Expense	8 8 00				19
20	Depr. Expense—Office Equipment	1 1 0 00				20
21	Miscellaneous Expense	9 8 00				21
22		2 9 8 7 00	4 8 1 3 00	10 0 4 6 00	8 2 2 0 00	22
23	Net Income	1 8 2 6 00			1 8 2 6 00	23
24		4 8 1 3 00	4 8 1 3 00	10 0 4 6 00	10 0 4 6 00	24

E 6-4B   (LO2)

✓ Capital 6/30: $5,826

CLOSING ENTRIES (NET INCOME) Set up T accounts for Adams' Shoe Shine based on the work sheet above and the chart of accounts provided below. Enter the existing balance for each account. Prepare closing entries in general journal form. Then post the closing entries to the T accounts.

Chart of Accounts

Assets
101   Cash
122   Accounts Receivable
141   Supplies
145   Prepaid Insurance
181   Office Equipment
181.1   Accum. Depr.—Office Equip.

Liabilities
202   Accounts Payable
219   Wages Payable

Owner's Equity
311   Mary Adams, Capital
312   Mary Adams, Drawing
313   Income Summary

Revenues
401   Service Fees

Expenses
511   Wages Expense
512   Advertising Expense
521   Rent Expense
523   Supplies Expense
525   Phone Expense
533   Utilities Expense
535   Insurance Expense
538   Gas and Oil Expense
542   Depr. Exp.—Office Equip.
549   Miscellaneous Expense

E 6-5B   (LO2)

SHOW
ME HOW

CLOSING ENTRIES (NET INCOME) Using the following partial listing of T accounts, prepare closing entries in general journal form dated May 31, 20--. Then post the closing entries to the T accounts.

	Cash	101
Bal.	600	

	Income Summary	313

	Supplies Expense	524
Bal.	900	

	Accounts Receivable	122
Bal.	1,800	

	Lawn Service Fees	401
	Bal.	5,000

	Insurance Expense	535
Bal.	300	

	Wages Payable	219
	Bal.	500

	Wages Expense	511
Bal.	400	

	Postage Expense	536
Bal.	40	

	Mark Thrasher, Capital	311
	Bal.	8,000

	Advertising Expense	512
Bal.	600	

	Gas and Oil Expense	538
Bal.	700	

	Mark Thrasher, Drawing	312
Bal.	800	

	Travel Expense	515
Bal.	100	

	Miscellaneous Expense	549
Bal.	200	

E 6-6B   (LO2)

✓ Capital 6/30: $3,826

SHOW
ME HOW

CLOSING ENTRIES (NET LOSS) Using the following partial listing of T accounts, prepare closing entries in general journal form dated June 30, 20--. Then post the closing entries to the T accounts.

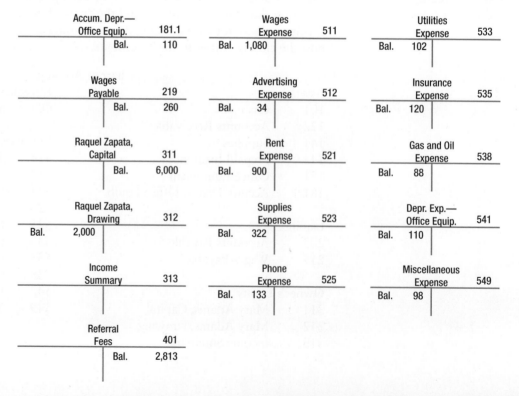

	Accum. Depr.— Office Equip.	181.1
	Bal.	110

	Wages Expense	511
Bal.	1,080	

	Utilities Expense	533
Bal.	102	

	Wages Payable	219
	Bal.	260

	Advertising Expense	512
Bal.	34	

	Insurance Expense	535
Bal.	120	

	Raquel Zapata, Capital	311
	Bal.	6,000

	Rent Expense	521
Bal.	900	

	Gas and Oil Expense	538
Bal.	88	

	Raquel Zapata, Drawing	312
Bal.	2,000	

	Supplies Expense	523
Bal.	322	

	Depr. Exp.— Office Equip.	541
Bal.	110	

	Income Summary	313

	Phone Expense	525
Bal.	133	

	Miscellaneous Expense	549
Bal.	98	

	Referral Fees	401
	Bal.	2,813

SERIES B PROBLEMS

P 6-7B   (LO1)
✓ Net income: $1,450
✓ Capital 6/30: $7,650
✓ Total assets: $9,350

FINANCIAL STATEMENTS A work sheet for Juanita's Consulting is shown on the following page. There were no additional investments made by the owner during the month.

REQUIRED

    1. Prepare an income statement.

    2. Prepare a statement of owner's equity.

    3. Prepare a balance sheet.

P 6-8B   (LO2/3)
✓ Capital 6/30: $7,650
✓ Post-closing trial bal.
   total debits: $9,460

CLOSING ENTRIES AND POST-CLOSING TRIAL BALANCE Refer to the work sheet for Juanita's Consulting in Problem 6-7B. The trial balance amounts (before adjustments) have been entered in the ledger accounts provided in the working papers. If you are not using the working papers that accompany this book, set up ledger accounts and enter these balances as of June 30, 20--. A chart of accounts is provided below.

Juanita's Consulting
Chart of Accounts

Assets			Revenues	
101	Cash		401	Consulting Fees
122	Accounts Receivable			
141	Supplies		Expenses	
145	Prepaid Insurance		511	Wages Expense
181	Office Equipment		512	Advertising Expense
181.1	Accum. Depr.—Office Equip.		521	Rent Expense
			523	Supplies Expense
Liabilities			525	Phone Expense
202	Accounts Payable		533	Electricity Expense
219	Wages Payable		535	Insurance Expense
			538	Gas and Oil Expense
Owner's Equity			541	Depr. Exp.—Office Equip.
311	Juanita Alvarez, Capital		549	Miscellaneous Expense
312	Juanita Alvarez, Drawing			
313	Income Summary			

REQUIRED

    1. Journalize (page 10) and post the adjusting entries.

    2. Journalize (page 11) and post the closing entries.

    3. Prepare a post-closing trial balance.

PROBLEM 6-7B

Juanita's Consulting
Work Sheet
For Month Ended June 30, 20--

#	ACCOUNT TITLE	TRIAL BALANCE DEBIT	TRIAL BALANCE CREDIT	ADJUSTMENTS DEBIT	ADJUSTMENTS CREDIT	ADJUSTED TRIAL BALANCE DEBIT	ADJUSTED TRIAL BALANCE CREDIT	INCOME STATEMENT DEBIT	INCOME STATEMENT CREDIT	BALANCE SHEET DEBIT	BALANCE SHEET CREDIT
1	Cash	5 2 8 5 00				5 2 8 5 00				5 2 8 5 00	
2	Accounts Receivable	1 0 7 5 00				1 0 7 5 00				1 0 7 5 00	
3	Supplies	7 5 0 00			(a) 2 5 0 00	5 0 0 00				5 0 0 00	
4	Prepaid Insurance	5 0 0 00			(b) 1 0 0 00	4 0 0 00				4 0 0 00	
5	Office Equipment	2 2 0 0 00				2 2 0 0 00				2 2 0 0 00	
6	Accum. Depr.—Office Equipment				(d) 1 1 0 00		1 1 0 00				1 1 0 00
7	Accounts Payable		1 5 0 0 00				1 5 0 0 00				1 5 0 0 00
8	Wages Payable				(c) 2 0 0 00		2 0 0 00				2 0 0 00
9	Juanita Alvarez, Capital		7 0 0 0 00				7 0 0 0 00				7 0 0 0 00
10	Juanita Alvarez, Drawing	8 0 0 00				8 0 0 00				8 0 0 00	
11	Consulting Fees		4 2 0 4 00				4 2 0 4 00		4 2 0 4 00		
12	Wages Expense	1 4 0 0 00		(c) 2 0 0 00		1 6 0 0 00		1 6 0 0 00			
13	Advertising Expense	6 0 0 00				6 0 0 00		6 0 0 00			
14	Rent Expense	5 0 0 00				5 0 0 00		5 0 0 00			
15	Supplies Expense			(a) 2 5 0 00		2 5 0 00		2 5 0 00			
16	Phone Expense	4 6 00				4 6 00		4 6 00			
17	Electricity Expense	3 9 00				3 9 00		3 9 00			
18	Insurance Expense			(b) 1 0 0 00		1 0 0 00		1 0 0 00			
19	Gas and Oil Expense	2 8 00				2 8 00		2 8 00			
20	Depr. Expense—Office Equipment			(d) 1 1 0 00		1 1 0 00		1 1 0 00			
21	Miscellaneous Expense	2 1 00				2 1 00		2 1 00			
22		12 7 0 4 00	12 7 0 4 00	6 6 0 00	6 6 0 00	13 0 1 4 00	13 0 1 4 00	2 7 5 4 00	4 2 0 4 00	10 2 6 0 00	8 8 1 0 00
23	Net Income							1 4 5 0 00			1 4 5 0 00
24								4 2 0 4 00	4 2 0 4 00	10 2 6 0 00	10 2 6 0 00
25											
26											
27											
28											
29											
30											

P 6-9B (LO1)

✓ Capital 1/31: $9,975

SHOW
ME HOW

STATEMENT OF OWNER'S EQUITY The capital account for Minta's Editorial Services, including an additional investment, and a partial work sheet are shown below.

GENERAL LEDGER							
ACCOUNT: Minta Berry, Capital						ACCOUNT NO. 311	

DATE	ITEM	POST. REF.	DEBIT	CREDIT	BALANCE DEBIT	BALANCE CREDIT
20-- Jan. 1	Balance	✔				3 6 0 0 00
22		J1		2 9 0 0 00		6 5 0 0 00

Minta's Editorial Services
Work Sheet (Partial)
For Month Ended January 31, 20 --

	ACCOUNT TITLE	INCOME STATEMENT DEBIT	INCOME STATEMENT CREDIT	BALANCE SHEET DEBIT	BALANCE SHEET CREDIT	
1	Cash			3 8 0 0 00		1
2	Accounts Receivable			2 2 0 0 00		2
3	Supplies			1 0 0 0 00		3
4	Prepaid Insurance			9 5 0 00		4
5	Computer Equipment			4 5 0 0 00		5
6	Accum. Depr.—Computer Equipment				2 2 5 00	6
7	Accounts Payable				2 1 0 0 00	7
8	Wages Payable				1 5 0 00	8
9	Minta Berry, Capital				6 5 0 0 00	9
10	Minta Berry, Drawing			1 7 0 0 00		10
11	Editing Fees		7 0 1 2 00			11
12	Wages Expense	6 0 0 00				12
13	Advertising Expense	4 9 00				13
14	Rent Expense	4 5 0 00				14
15	Supplies Expense	2 8 8 00				15
16	Phone Expense	4 4 00				16
17	Utilities Expense	3 8 00				17
18	Insurance Expense	1 2 5 00				18
19	Depr. Expense—Computer Equipment	2 2 5 00				19
20	Miscellaneous Expense	1 8 00				20
21		1 8 3 7 00	7 0 1 2 00	14 1 5 0 00	8 9 7 5 00	21
22	Net Income	5 1 7 5 00			5 1 7 5 00	22
23		7 0 1 2 00	7 0 1 2 00	14 1 5 0 00	14 1 5 0 00	23

REQUIRED

Prepare a statement of owner's equity.

MANAGING YOUR WRITING

At lunch, two bookkeepers got into a heated discussion about whether closing entries should be made before or after preparing the financial statements. They have come to you to resolve this issue and have agreed to accept your position. Write a memo explaining the purpose of closing entries and whether they should be made before or after preparing the financial statements.

MASTERY PROBLEM

Elizabeth Soltis owns and operates Aunt Ibby's Styling Salon. A year-end work sheet is provided on the following page. Using this information, prepare adjusting entries, financial statements, and closing entries. Soltis made no additional investments during the year.

☑ Check List
☐ Managing
☐ Planning
☐ Drafting
☐ Break
☐ Revising
☐ Managing

✓ Total assets: $4,740
✓ E. Soltis, capital, Dec. 31: $4,475

 CLGL

MASTERY PROBLEM

Aunt Ibby's Styling Salon
Work Sheet
For Year Ended December 31, 20--

#	ACCOUNT TITLE	TRIAL BALANCE DEBIT	TRIAL BALANCE CREDIT	ADJUSTMENTS DEBIT	ADJUSTMENTS CREDIT	ADJUSTED TRIAL BALANCE DEBIT	ADJUSTED TRIAL BALANCE CREDIT	INCOME STATEMENT DEBIT	INCOME STATEMENT CREDIT	BALANCE SHEET DEBIT	BALANCE SHEET CREDIT
1	Cash	9 4 0 00				9 4 0 00				9 4 0 00	
2	Styling Supplies	1 5 0 0 00			(a) 1 4 5 0 00	5 0 00				5 0 00	
3	Prepaid Insurance	8 0 0 00			(b) 6 5 0 00	1 5 0 00				1 5 0 00	
4	Salon Equipment	4 5 0 0 00				4 5 0 0 00				4 5 0 0 00	
5	Accum. Depr.—Salon Equipment				(d) 9 0 0 00		9 0 0 00				9 0 0 00
6	Accounts Payable		2 2 5 00				2 2 5 00				2 2 5 00
7	Wages Payable				(c) 4 0 00		4 0 00				4 0 00
8	Elizabeth Soltis, Capital		2 7 6 5 00				2 7 6 5 00				2 7 6 5 00
9	Elizabeth Soltis, Drawing	12 0 0 0 00				12 0 0 0 00				12 0 0 0 00	
10	Styling Fees		32 0 0 0 00				32 0 0 0 00		32 0 0 0 00		
11	Wages Expense	8 0 0 0 00		(c) 4 0 00		8 0 4 0 00		8 0 4 0 00			
12	Rent Expense	6 0 0 0 00				6 0 0 0 00		6 0 0 0 00			
13	Styling Supplies Expense			(a) 1 4 5 0 00		1 4 5 0 00		1 4 5 0 00			
14	Phone Expense	4 5 0 00				4 5 0 00		4 5 0 00			
15	Utilities Expense	8 0 0 00				8 0 0 00		8 0 0 00			
16	Insurance Expense			(b) 6 5 0 00		6 5 0 00		6 5 0 00			
17	Depr. Expense—Salon Equipment			(d) 9 0 0 00		9 0 0 00		9 0 0 00			
18		34 9 9 0 00	34 9 9 0 00	3 0 4 0 00	3 0 4 0 00	35 9 3 0 00	35 9 3 0 00	18 2 9 0 00	32 0 0 0 00	17 6 4 0 00	3 9 3 0 00
19	Net Income							13 7 1 0 00			13 7 1 0 00
20								32 0 0 0 00	32 0 0 0 00	17 6 4 0 00	17 6 4 0 00

CHALLENGE PROBLEM

Provided below is a partial work sheet for Ardery Advising.

This problem challenges you to apply your cumulative accounting knowledge to move a step beyond the material in the chapter.

✓ **Net loss: $2,100**
✓ **Capital, 1/31/20--: ($700)**

Ardery Advising
Work Sheet (Partial)
For Month Ended January 31, 20 - -

	ACCOUNT TITLE	INCOME STATEMENT DEBIT	INCOME STATEMENT CREDIT	BALANCE SHEET DEBIT	BALANCE SHEET CREDIT	
1	Cash			2 4 1 2 00		1
2	Accounts Receivable			8 9 6 00		2
3	Supplies			4 8 2 00		3
4	Prepaid Insurance			9 0 0 00		4
5	Office Equipment			3 0 0 0 00		5
6	Accum. Depr.—Office Equipment				2 0 0 0 00	6
7	Accounts Payable				2 1 9 0 00	7
8	Wages Payable				1 2 0 0 00	8
9	Notes Payable				3 0 0 0 00	9
10	Sam Ardery, Capital				2 2 0 0 00	10
11	Sam Ardery, Drawing			8 0 0 00		11
12	Advising Fees		3 8 0 2 00			12
13	Wages Expense	1 8 0 0 00				13
14	Advertising Expense	4 0 0 00				14
15	Rent Expense	1 5 0 0 00				15
16	Supplies Expense	1 2 0 00				16
17	Phone Expense	3 0 0 00				17
18	Electricity Expense	4 4 00				18
19	Insurance Expense	2 0 0 00				19
20	Gas and Oil Expense	3 8 00				20
21	Depr. Expense—Office Equipment	1 0 0 0 00				21
22	Miscellaneous Expense	5 0 0 00				22
23		5 9 0 2 00	3 8 0 2 00	8 4 9 0 00	10 5 9 0 00	23
24	Net Loss		2 1 0 0 00	2 1 0 0 00		24
25		5 9 0 2 00	5 9 0 2 00	10 5 9 0 00	10 5 9 0 00	25

REQUIRED

During January, Ardery made an additional investment of $1,200. Prepare an income statement, statement of owner's equity, and balance sheet for Ardery Advising.

Answers to Self-Study Test Questions

Checkpoint Exercises

1.

Fisher Consulting		
Income Statement		
For Month Ended August 31, 20 --		
Revenue:		
Professional fees		$5,000
Expenses:		
Wages expense	$1,000	
Rent expense	700	
Depreciation expense	100	
Total expenses		1,800
Net income		$3,200

Fisher Consulting		
Statement of Owner's Equity		
For Month Ended August 31, 20 --		
Joe Fisher, capital, August 1, 20 - -		$3,000
Net income for August	$3,200	
Less withdrawals for August	300	
Increase in capital		2,900
Joe Fisher, capital, August 31, 20 - -		$5,900

Fisher Consulting		
Balance Sheet		
August 31, 20 --		
Assets		
Current assets:		
Cash	$2,500	
Accounts receivable	800	
Total current assets		$3,300
Property, plant, and equipment:		
Equipment	$3,800	
Less accumulated depreciation	200	3,600
Total assets		$6,900
Liabilities		
Current liabilities:		
Accounts payable		$1,000
Owner's Equity		
Joe Fisher, capital, August 31, 20--		5,900
Total liabilities and owner's equity		$6,900

2.

DATE		DESCRIPTION	POST. REF.	DEBIT					CREDIT				
		Closing Entries											
20-- Aug.	31	Professional Fees		5	0	0	0	00					
		Income Summary							5	0	0	0	00
	31	Income Summary		1	8	0	0	00					
		Wages Expense							1	0	0	0	00
		Rent Expense								7	0	0	00
		Depreciation Expense								1	0	0	00
	31	Income Summary		3	2	0	0	00					
		Joe Fisher, capital							3	2	0	0	00
	31	Joe Fisher, Capital			3	0	0	00					
		Joe Fisher, Drawing								3	0	0	00

3.

Joe Fisher, Consulting Post-Closing Trial Balance August 31, 20 - -									
ACCOUNT TITLE	ACCOUNT NO	DEBIT BALANCE				CREDIT BALANCE			
Cash		2	5	0	0	00			
Accounts Receivable			8	0	0	00			
Equipment		3	8	0	0	00			
Accumulated Depr.—Equipment							2	0	0	00
Accounts Payable							1	0	0	0	00
Joe Fisher, Capital							5	9	0	0	00
		7	1	0	0	00	7	1	0	0	00

Chapter 6 Appendix
Statement of Cash Flows

LEARNING OBJECTIVES

Careful study of this appendix should enable you to:

LO1 Classify business transactions as operating, investing, or financing.

LO2 Prepare a statement of cash flows by analyzing and categorizing a series of business transactions.

LO1 Classify business transactions as operating, investing, or financing.

LEARNING KEY
There are three types of business activities: operating, investing, and financing.

LEARNING KEY
Lending money to another entity is an outflow of cash from investing activities. The collection of the principal when the loan is due is an inflow of cash from investing activities. Borrowing cash is an inflow from financing activities. Repayment of the loan principal is an outflow from financing activities.

Thus far, we have discussed three financial statements: the income statement, the statement of owner's equity, and the balance sheet. A fourth statement, the statement of cash flows, is also very important. It explains what the business did to generate cash and how the cash was used. This is done by categorizing all cash transactions into three types of activities: operating, investing, and financing.

TYPES OF BUSINESS ACTIVITIES

Cash flows from operating activities are related to the revenues and expenses reported on the income statement. Examples include cash received for services performed and the payment of cash for expenses.

Investing activities are those transactions involving the purchase and sale of long-term assets, lending money, and collecting the principal on the related loans.

Financing activities are those transactions dealing with the exchange of cash between the business and its owners and creditors. Examples include cash received from the owner to finance the operations and cash paid to the owner as withdrawals. Financing activities also include borrowing cash and repaying the loan principal.

Figure 6A-1 provides a review of the transactions for Rohan's Campus Delivery for the month of June. The transactions are classified as operating, investing, or financing, and an explanation for the classification is provided.

FIGURE 6A-1 Summary of Transactions for Rohan's Campus Delivery

SUMMARY OF TRANSACTIONS FOR ROHAN'S CAMPUS DELIVERY	TYPE OF TRANSACTION	EXPLANATION
(a) Rohan Macsen invested cash in his business, $2,000.	Financing	Cash received from the owner is an inflow from financing activities. Don't be fooled by the word "invested." From the company's point of view, this is a way to *finance* the business.
(b) Purchased delivery equipment for cash, $1,200.	Investing	Purchases of long-term assets are investments.
(c) Purchased delivery equipment on account from Big Red Scooters, $900. (*Note*: Big Red has loaned Rohan $900.)	No cash involved	This transaction will not affect the main sections of the statement of cash flows. (This is a noncash investing and financing activity.)
(d) Paid first installment to Big Red Scooters, $300. [See transaction (c).]	Financing	Repayments of loans are financing activities.
(e) Received cash for delivery services rendered, $500.	Operating	Cash received as a result of providing services is classified as an operating activity.
(f) Paid cash for June office rent, $200.	Operating	Cash payments for expenses are classified as operating activities.
(g) Paid phone bill, $50.	Operating	Cash payments for expenses are classified as operating activities.
(h) Made deliveries on account for a total of $600: $400 for the Accounting Department and $200 for the School of Music.	No cash involved	This transaction will not affect the statement of cash flows.
(i) Purchased supplies for cash, $80.	Operating	Cash payments for expenses are classified as operating activities. Most of these supplies were used up. Those that remain will be used in the near future. These are not long-term assets and, thus, do not qualify as investments.
(j) Paid cash for an eight-month liability insurance policy, $200. Coverage began on June 1.	Operating	Cash payments for expenses are classified as operating activities. Prepaid Insurance is not considered a long-term asset and, thus, does not qualify as an investment.
(k) Received $570 in cash for services performed in transaction (h): $400 from the Accounting Department and $170 from the School of Music.	Operating	Cash received as a result of providing services is classified as an operating activity.
(l) Purchased a third scooter from Big Red Scooters, $1,500. A down payment of $300 was made with the remaining payments expected over the next four months.	Investing	Purchases of long-term assets are investments. Only the $300 cash paid will be reported on the statement of cash flows.
(m) Paid wages of part-time employees, $650.	Operating	Cash payments for expenses are classified as operating activities.
(n) Earned delivery fees for the remainder of the month amounting to $1,050: $430 in cash and $620 on account. Deliveries on account: $250 for the Accounting Department and $370 for the Athletic Ticket Office.	Operating	Cash received ($430) as a result of providing services is classified as an operating activity.
(o) Rohan withdrew cash for personal use, $150.	Financing	Cash payments to owners are classified as a financing activity.

LO2 Prepare a statement of cash flows by analyzing and categorizing a series of business transactions.

PREPARING THE STATEMENT OF CASH FLOWS

The classifications of the cash transactions for Rohan's Campus Delivery are summarized in the expanded cash T account shown in Figure 6A-2. Using this information, we can prepare a statement of cash flows. As shown in Figure 6A-3, the heading is similar to that used for the income statement. Since the statement of cash flows reports on the flow of cash for a period of time, the statement is dated for the month ended June 30, 20--.

The main body of the statement is arranged in three sections: operating, investing, and financing activities. First, cash received from customers is listed under operating activities. Then, cash payments for operating activities are listed and totaled. The net amount is reported as net cash provided by operating activities. Since this is the main

FIGURE 6A-2 Cash T Account for Rohan's Campus Delivery with Classifications of Cash Transactions

CASH						
Event	Classification	Amount	Amount	Classification	Event	
(a) Investment by Rohan.	Financing	2,000	1,200	Investing	Purchased delivery equipment.	(b)
(e) Cash received for services.	Operating	500	300	Financing	Made payment on loan.	(d)
(k) Cash received for services.	Operating	570	200	Operating	Paid office rent.	(f)
(n) Cash received for services.	Operating	430	50	Operating	Paid phone bill.	(g)
		3,500	80	Operating	Purchased supplies.	(i)
			200	Operating	Paid for insurance.	(j)
			300	Investing	Purchased delivery equipment.	(l)
			650	Operating	Paid wages.	(m)
			150	Financing	Withdrawal by owner.	(o)
			3,130			
	Bal.	370				

FIGURE 6A-3 Statement of Cash Flows for Rohan's Campus Delivery

Rohan's Campus Delivery Statement of Cash Flows For Month Ended June 30, 20 - -		
Cash flows from operating activities:		
Cash received from customers for delivery services		$1,500
Cash paid for wages	$ (650)	
Cash paid for rent	(200)	
Cash paid for supplies	(80)	
Cash paid for phone	(50)	
Cash paid for insurance	(200)	
Total cash paid for operations		(1,180)
Net cash provided by operating activities		$ 320
Cash flows from investing activities:		
Cash paid for delivery equipment	$(1,500)	
Net cash used for investing activities		(1,500)
Cash flows from financing activities:		
Cash investment by owner	$ 2,000	
Cash withdrawal by owner	(150)	
Payment made on loan	(300)	
Net cash provided by financing activities		1,550
Net increase in cash		$ 370

purpose of the business, it is important to be able to generate positive cash flows from operating activities.

The next two sections list the inflows and outflows from investing and financing activities. Debits to the cash account are inflows and credits are outflows. Note that there was an outflow, or net use of cash, from investing activities resulting from the purchase of the motor scooters. In addition, cash was provided from financing activities because Rohan's initial investment more than covered his withdrawal and the payment on the loan. These investing and financing activities are typical for a new business.

The sum of the inflows and outflows from operating, investing, and financing activities equals the net increase (or decrease) in the cash account during the period. Since this is a new business, the cash account had a beginning balance of zero. The ending balance is $370. This agrees with the net increase in cash of $370 reported on the statement of cash flows.

LEARNING KEY

To prove the accuracy of the statement of cash flows, compare the net increase or decrease reported on the statement with the change in the balance of the cash account.

This appendix introduces you to the purpose and format of the statement of cash flows. Here, we classified entries made to the cash account as operating, investing, or financing. These classifications were then used to prepare the statement. Businesses have thousands of entries to the cash account. Thus, this approach to preparing the statement is not really practical. Other approaches to preparing the statement will be discussed in Chapter 23. However, the purpose and format of the statements are the same.

LEARNING OBJECTIVES   Key Points to Remember

LO1 Classify business transactions as operating, investing, or financing.	The purpose of the statement of cash flows is to report what the firm did to generate cash and how the cash was used. Business transactions are classified as operating, investing, and financing activities. *Operating activities* are those transactions related to the revenues and expenses reported on the income statement. *Investing activities* are those transactions involving the purchase and sale of long-term assets, lending money, and collecting the principal on the related loans. *Financing activities* are those transactions dealing with the exchange of cash between the business and its owners and creditors.
LO2 Prepare a statement of cash flows by analyzing and categorizing a series of business transactions.	The main body of the statement of cash flows consists of three sections: operating, investing, and financing activities.

Name of Business
Statement of Cash Flows
For Period Ended Date

Cash flows from operating activities:		
Cash received from customers		$ x,xxx
List cash paid for various expenses	$ (xxx)	
Total cash paid for operations		(x,xxx)
Net cash provided by (used for) operating activities		$ xxx
Cash flows from investing activities:		
List cash received from the sale of long-term assets and other		
investing activities	$ x,xxx	
List cash paid for the purchase of long-term assets and other		
investing activities	(x,xxx)	
Net cash provided by (used for) investing activities		x,xxx
Cash flows from financing activities:		
List cash received from owners and creditors	$ x,xxx	
List cash paid to owners and creditors	(xxx)	
Net cash provided by (used for) financing activities		x,xxx
Net increase (decrease) in cash		$ xxx

KEY TERMS

financing activities (218)   Those transactions dealing with the exchange of cash between the business and its owners and creditors.

investing activities (218)   Those transactions involving the purchase and sale of long-term assets, lending money, and collecting the principal on the related loans.

operating activities (218)   Those transactions related to the revenues and expenses reported on the income statement.

REVIEW QUESTIONS

LO1   1. Explain the purpose of the statement of cash flows.

LO1   2. Define and provide examples of the three types of business activities.

SERIES A EXERCISE

E 6Apx-1A   (LO1)

CLASSIFYING BUSINESS TRANSACTIONS Dolores Lopez opened a new consulting business. The following transactions occurred during January of the current year. Classify each transaction as an operating, an investing, or a financing activity.

(a) Invested cash in the business, $10,000.

(b) Paid office rent, $500.

(c) Purchased office equipment. Paid $1,500 cash and agreed to pay the balance of $2,000 in four monthly installments.

(d) Received cash for services rendered, $900.

(e) Paid phone bill, $65.

(f) Made payment on loan in transaction (c), $500.

(g) Paid wages to part-time employee, $500.

(h) Received cash for services rendered, $800.

(i) Paid electricity bill, $85.

(j) Withdrew cash for personal use, $100.

(k) Paid wages to part-time employee, $500.

SERIES A PROBLEM

P 6Apx-2A   (LO2)
✓ Operating activities: $50
✓ Investing activities: ($1,500)
✓ Financing activities: $9,400

PREPARING A STATEMENT OF CASH FLOWS Prepare a statement of cash flows based on the transactions reported in Exercise 6Apx-1A.

SERIES B EXERCISE

E 6Apx-1B   (LO1)

CLASSIFYING BUSINESS TRANSACTIONS Bob Jacobs opened an advertising agency. The following transactions occurred during January of the current year. Classify each transaction as an operating, an investing, or a financing activity.

(a) Invested cash in the business, $5,000.

(b) Purchased office equipment. Paid $2,500 cash and agreed to pay the balance of $2,000 in four monthly installments.

(c) Paid office rent, $400.

(d) Received cash for services rendered, $700.

(e) Paid phone bill, $95.

(f) Received cash for services rendered, $600.

(g) Made payment on loan in transaction (b), $500.

(h) Paid wages to part-time employee, $800.

(i) Paid electricity bill, $100.

(j) Withdrew cash for personal use, $500.

(k) Paid wages to part-time employee, $600.

SERIES B PROBLEM

P 6Apx-2B   (LO2)
✓ Operating activities: ($695)
✓ Investing activities: ($2,500)
✓ Financing activities: $4,000

PREPARING A STATEMENT OF CASH FLOWS Prepare a statement of cash flows based on the transactions reported in Exercise 6Apx-1B.

Comprehensive Problem 1:
The Accounting Cycle

This comprehensive problem is intended to serve as a mini-practice set without the source documents. As such, students should plan on about three to four hours to complete this problem.

Bob Night opened "The General's Favorite Fishing Hole." The fishing camp is open from April through September and attracts many famous college basketball coaches during the off-season. Guests typically register for one week, arriving on Sunday afternoon and returning home the following Saturday afternoon. The registration fee includes room and board, the use of fishing boats, and professional instruction in fishing techniques. The chart of accounts for the camping operations is provided below.

The General's Favorite Fishing Hole
Chart of Accounts

Assets		Revenues	
101	Cash	401	Registration Fees
142	Office Supplies		
144	Food Supplies	Expenses	
145	Prepaid Insurance	511	Wages Expense
181	Fishing Boats	521	Rent Expense
181.1	Accum. Depr.—Fishing Boats	523	Office Supplies Expense
		524	Food Supplies Expense
Liabilities		525	Phone Expense
202	Accounts Payable	533	Utilities Expense
219	Wages Payable	535	Insurance Expense
		536	Postage Expense
Owner's Equity		542	Depr. Exp.—Fishing Boats
311	Bob Night, Capital		
312	Bob Night, Drawing		
313	Income Summary		

The following transactions took place during April 20--.

Apr. 1 Night invested cash in business, $90,000.

1 Paid insurance premium for six-month camping season, $9,000.

2 Paid rent for lodge and campgrounds for the month of April, $40,000.

2 Deposited registration fees, $35,000.

2 Purchased 10 fishing boats on account for $60,000. The boats have estimated useful lives of five years, at which time they will be donated to a local day camp. Arrangements were made to pay for the boats in July.

3 Purchased food supplies from Acme Super Market on account, $7,000.

5 Purchased office supplies from Gordon Office Supplies on account, $500.

7 Deposited registration fees, $38,600.

10 Purchased food supplies from Acme Super Market on account, $8,200.

10 Paid wages to fishing guides, $10,000.

14 Deposited registration fees, $30,500.

(continued)

Apr. 16   Purchased food supplies from Acme Super Market on account, $9,000.

17   Paid wages to fishing guides, $10,000.

18   Paid postage, $150.

21   Deposited registration fees, $35,600.

24   Purchased food supplies from Acme Super Market on account, $8,500.

24   Paid wages to fishing guides, $10,000.

28   Deposited registration fees, $32,000.

29   Paid wages to fishing guides, $10,000.

30   Purchased food supplies from Acme Super Market on account, $6,000.

30   Paid Acme Super Market on account, $32,700.

30   Paid utilities bill, $2,000.

30   Paid phone bill, $1,200.

30   Bob Night withdrew cash for personal use, $6,000.

Adjustment information for the end of April is provided below.

(a) Office supplies remaining on hand, $100.

(b) Food supplies remaining on hand, $8,000.

(c) Insurance expired during the month of April, $1,500.

(d) Depreciation on the fishing boats for the month of April, $1,000.

(e) Wages earned, but not yet paid, at the end of April, $500.

REQUIRED

1. Enter the transactions in a general journal. Enter transactions from April 1–5 on page 1, April 7–18 on page 2, April 21–29 and the first two entries for April 30 on page 3, and the remaining entries for April 30 on page 4.

2. Post the entries to the general ledger. (If you are not using the working papers that accompany this text, you will need to enter the account titles and account numbers in the general ledger accounts.)

3. Prepare a trial balance on a work sheet.

4. Complete the work sheet.

5. Journalize the adjusting entries (page 5).

6. Post the adjusting entries to the general ledger.

7. Prepare the income statement.

8. Prepare the statement of owner's equity.

9. Prepare the balance sheet.

10. Journalize the closing entries (pages 5 and 6).

11. Post the closing entries to the general ledger.

12. Prepare a post-closing trial balance.

Comprehensive Problem 1, Period 2: The Accounting Cycle

During the month of May 20--, The General's Favorite Fishing Hole engaged in the following transactions. These transactions required an expansion of the chart of accounts as shown below.

This comprehensive problem is intended to serve as a mini-practice set without the source documents. As such, students should plan on about three to four hours to complete this problem.

Assets

101	Cash
122	Accounts Receivable
142	Office Supplies
144	Food Supplies
145	Prepaid Insurance
146	Prepaid Subscriptions
161	Land
171	Buildings
171.1	Accum. Depr.—Buildings
181	Fishing Boats
181.1	Accum. Depr.—Fishing Boats
182	Surround Sound System
182.1	Accum. Depr.—Surround Sound Sys.
183	Big Screen TV
183.1	Accum. Depr.—Big Screen TV

Liabilities

202	Accounts Payable
219	Wages Payable

Owner's Equity

311	Bob Night, Capital
312	Bob Night, Drawing
313	Income Summary

Revenues

401	Registration Fees
404	Vending Commission Revenue

Expenses

511	Wages Expense
512	Advertising Expense
521	Rent Expense
523	Office Supplies Expense
524	Food Supplies Expense
525	Phone Expense
533	Utilities Expense
535	Insurance Expense
536	Postage Expense
537	Repair Expense
540	Depr. Exp.—Buildings
541	Depr. Exp.—Surround Sound Sys.
542	Depr. Exp.—Fishing Boats
543	Depr. Exp.—Big Screen TV
546	Satellite Programming Exp.
548	Subscriptions Expense

May 1	In order to provide snacks for guests on a 24-hour basis, Night signed a contract with Snack Attack. Snack Attack will install vending machines with food and drinks and pay a 10% commission on all sales. Estimated payments are made at the beginning of each month. Night received a check for $200, the estimated commission on sales for May.
2	Night purchased a surround sound system and big screen TV with a digital satellite system for the guest lounge. The surround sound system cost $3,600 and has an estimated useful life of five years and no salvage value. The TV cost $8,000, has an estimated useful life of eight years, and has a salvage value of $800. Night paid cash for both items.
2	Paid for May's programming on the new digital satellite system, $125.
3	Night's office manager returned $100 worth of office supplies to Gordon Office Supply. Night received a $100 reduction on the account.
3	Deposited registration fees, $52,700.

(continued)

May 3   Paid rent for lodge and campgrounds for the month of May, $40,000.

3   In preparation for the purchase of a nearby campground, Night invested an additional $600,000.

4   Paid Gordon Office Supply on account, $400.

4   Purchased the assets of a competing business and paid cash for the following: land, $100,000; lodge, $530,000; and fishing boats, $9,000. The lodge has a remaining useful life of 50 years and a $50,000 salvage value. The boats have remaining lives of five years and no salvage value.

5   Paid May's insurance premium for the new camp, $1,000. (See above transaction.)

5   Purchased food supplies from Acme Super Market on account, $22,950.

5   Purchased office supplies from Gordon Office Supplies on account, $1,200.

7   Night paid $40 each for one-year subscriptions to *Fishing Illustrated, Fishing Unlimited*, and *Fish Master*. The magazines are published monthly.

10   Deposited registration fees, $62,750.

13   Paid wages to fishing guides, $30,000. (Don't forget wages payable.)

14   A guest became ill and was unable to stay for the entire week. A refund was issued in the amount of $1,000.

17   Deposited registration fees, $63,000.

19   Purchased food supplies from Acme Super Market on account, $18,400.

21   Deposited registration fees, $63,400.

23   Paid $2,500 for advertising spots on National Sports Talk Radio.

25   Paid repair fee for damaged boat, $850.

27   Paid wages to fishing guides, $30,000.

28   Paid $1,800 for advertising spots on billboards.

29   Purchased food supplies from Acme Super Market on account, $14,325.

30   Paid utilities bill, $3,300.

30   Paid phone bill, $1,800.

30   Paid Acme Super Market on account, $47,350.

31   Bob Night withdrew cash for personal use, $7,500.

Adjustment information at the end of May is provided below.

(a) Total vending machine sales were $2,300 for the month of May. A 10% commission is earned on these sales.

(b) Straight-line depreciation is used for the 10 boats purchased on April 2 for $60,000. The useful life for these assets is five years and there is no salvage value. A full month's depreciation was taken in April on these boats. Straight-line depreciation is also used for the two boats purchased in May. Make one adjusting entry for all depreciation on the boats.

(c) Straight-line depreciation is used to depreciate the surround sound system.

(d) Straight-line depreciation is used to depreciate the big screen TV.

(e) Straight-line depreciation is used for the building purchased in May.

(f) On April 2, Night paid $9,000 for insurance during the six-month camping season. May's portion of this premium was used up during this month.

(g) Night received his May issues of *Fishing Illustrated*, *Fishing Unlimited*, and *Fish Master*.

(h) Office supplies remaining on hand, $150.

(i) Food supplies remaining on hand, $5,925.

(j) Wages earned, but not yet paid, at the end of May, $6,000.

REQUIRED

1. Enter the transactions in a general journal. Enter transactions from May 1–4 on page 5, May 5–28 on page 6, and the remaining entries on page 7. To save time and space, don't enter descriptions for the journal entries.

2. Post the entries to the general ledger. (If you are not using the working papers that accompany this text, you will need to enter the account titles, account numbers, and balances from April 30 in the general ledger accounts.)

3. Prepare a trial balance on a work sheet.

4. Complete the work sheet.

5. Journalize the adjusting entries on page 8 of the general journal.

6. Post the adjusting entries to the general ledger.

7. Prepare the income statement.

8. Prepare the statement of owner's equity.

9. Prepare the balance sheet.

10. Journalize the closing entries on page 9 of the general journal.

11. Post the closing entries to the general ledger.

12. Prepare a post-closing trial balance.

Accounting for Cash and Payroll

PART

2

Add Some Color to Your Learning!

Throughout the text, you will be introduced to many important terms and types of accounts. To help you learn the different terms and types of accounts, we have coded many of them using the following color key in Part 2:

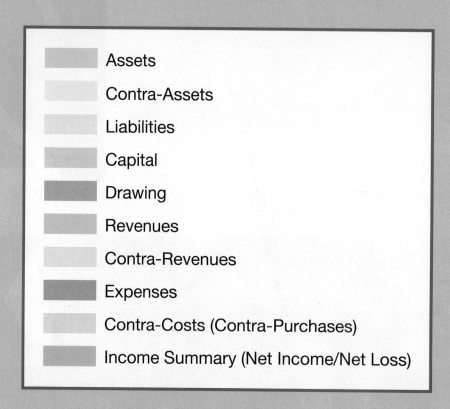

Assets

Contra-Assets

Liabilities

Capital

Drawing

Revenues

Contra-Revenues

Expenses

Contra-Costs (Contra-Purchases)

Income Summary (Net Income/Net Loss)

Accounting for Cash

H2O Audio was founded in 2003 with its home office in San Diego, California. Its key products were waterproof head-phones, armbands and cases, and headsets designed to enable swimmers, surfers, and divers to use their iPods underwater. H20 Audio has now grown to become X-1 Audio. Its products include water-proof, weatherproof, and sweatproof audio equipment for athletes across virtually all sports. X-1 sells its merchandise online, in major electronics stores, in sports shops, and in other retailers throughout the United States and in more than 30 other countries. The company started quite small, but it has grown rapidly. In a recent four-year period, its revenues increased more than 800%.

Two of the challenges for a company growing as fast as X-1 Audio are managing and protecting its cash. X-1 has multiple checking accounts, receives cash receipts from multiple sources, and makes cash payments for many different bills. The company must have clear procedures and complete and accurate records in order to properly control cash and to plan for future needs. In this chapter, you will learn some of the ways to manage this critical business asset.

LEARNING OBJECTIVES

Careful study of this chapter should enable you to:

LO1 Describe how to open and use a checking account.

LO2 Prepare a bank reconciliation and related journal entries.

LO3 Establish and use a petty cash fund.

LO4 Establish a change fund and use the cash short and over account.

C ash is an asset that is quite familiar and important to all of us. We generally think of **cash** as the currency and coins in our pockets and the money we have in our checking accounts. To a business, cash also includes checks received from customers, money orders, and bank cashier's checks.

Because it plays such a central role in operating a business, cash must be carefully managed and controlled. A business should have a system of **internal control**—a set of policies and procedures designed to ensure proper accounting for transactions. For good internal control of cash transactions, all cash received should be deposited daily in a bank. All disbursements, except for payments from petty cash, should be made by check.

CHECKING ACCOUNT

LO1 Describe how to open and use a checking account.

The key documents and forms required in opening and using a checking account are the signature card, deposit tickets, checks, and bank statements.

Opening a Checking Account

The USA PATRIOT Act was passed in 2001. The primary purpose of the act was to help detect and prevent terrorism. As a result of the act, all banks must have a CIP that provides clear identification of every account holder of the bank.

Every bank is required to maintain a **Customer Identification Program (CIP)** that provides clear identification of every account holder. The specific documents required from the customer vary depending on the bank's program and services provided to the customer. For example, for a checking account, each person authorized to sign checks must complete and sign a **signature card** (Figure 7-1 on page 233). The bank can use this card to verify the depositor's signature on banking transactions. The taxpayer identification number (TIN) is the depositor's Social Security number or employer identification number (EIN). This number is shown on the card to identify the depositor for income tax purposes. An EIN can be obtained from the Internal Revenue Service.

Making Deposits

Because of the high volume of transactions that they process, banks normally review signatures only on checks for large amounts and a sample of others. This makes it important for you to review your monthly bank statement.

A **deposit ticket** (Figure 7-2 on page 234) is a form showing a detailed listing of items being deposited. Currency, coins, and checks are listed separately. Each check can be identified by its **ABA (American Bankers Association) Number**. This number is the small fraction printed in the upper right-hand corner of each check (see Figure 7-4 on page 236). Part of this number also appears in **magnetic ink character recognition (MICR)** code on the lower left side of the front of each check. The code is used to sort and route checks throughout the U.S. banking system. Normally, only the numerator of the fraction is used in identifying checks on the deposit ticket. Alternatively, the individual checks can be identified by the name of the writer of the check.

The depositor delivers or mails the deposit ticket and all items being deposited to the bank. The bank then gives or mails a receipt to the depositor. The deposit also can be made after business hours by using the night depository provided by most banks. The deposit is put in a locked bag, which is placed in a secure drawer or chute at the bank, for processing the following morning.

Endorsements

When checks are deposited, there commonly is a delay before the funds are available for withdrawal. The delay can vary from one to eleven days, depending on the newness of the account, size and source of the checks, and many other factors.

Each check being deposited (or cashed) must be endorsed by the payee, the party to whom the check is payable. The endorsement consists of stamping or writing the

FIGURE 7-1　Signature Card

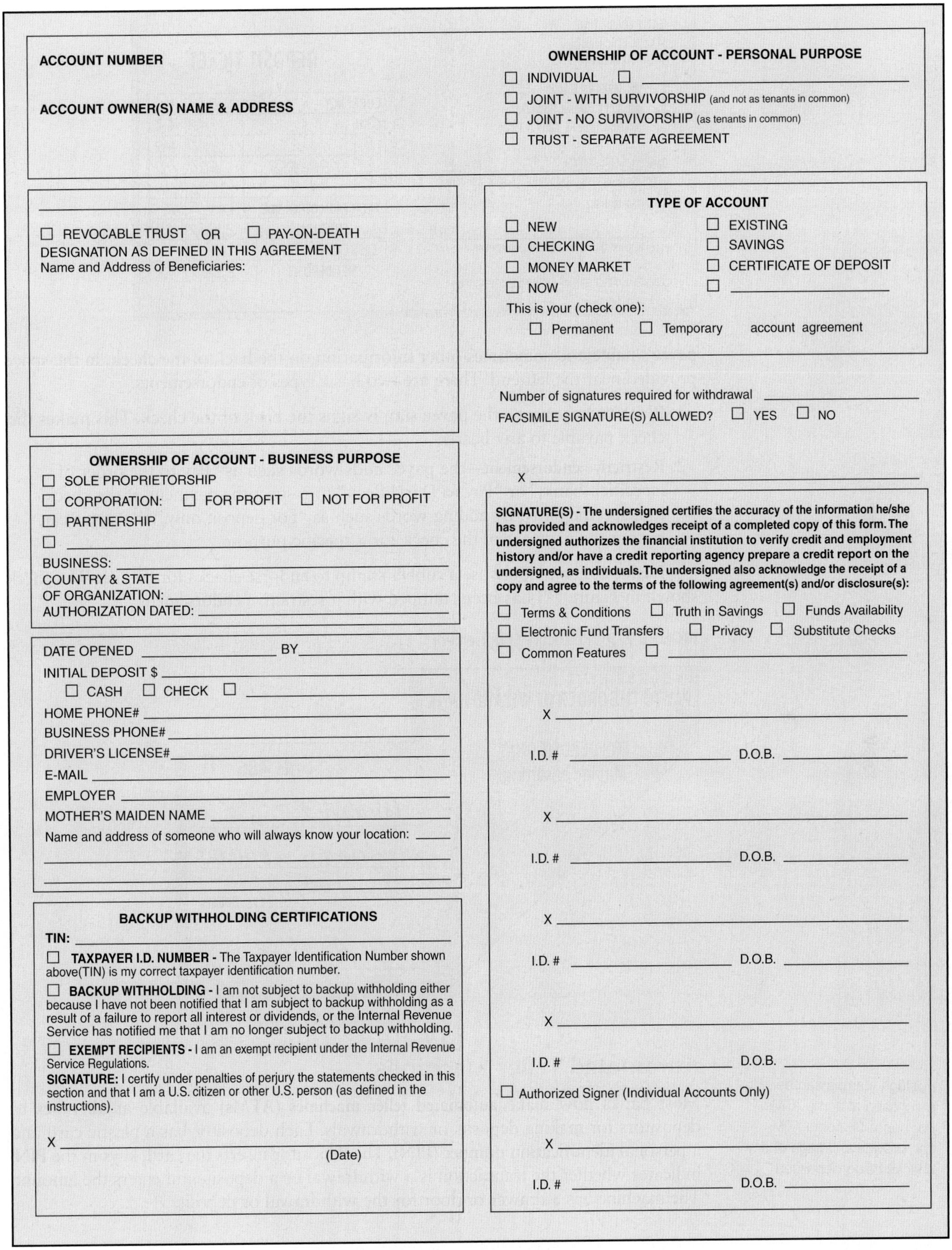

ACCOUNT NUMBER

ACCOUNT OWNER(S) NAME & ADDRESS

OWNERSHIP OF ACCOUNT - PERSONAL PURPOSE
- ☐ INDIVIDUAL ☐ _____
- ☐ JOINT - WITH SURVIVORSHIP (and not as tenants in common)
- ☐ JOINT - NO SURVIVORSHIP (as tenants in common)
- ☐ TRUST - SEPARATE AGREEMENT

☐ REVOCABLE TRUST OR ☐ PAY-ON-DEATH
DESIGNATION AS DEFINED IN THIS AGREEMENT
Name and Address of Beneficiaries:

TYPE OF ACCOUNT
- ☐ NEW ☐ EXISTING
- ☐ CHECKING ☐ SAVINGS
- ☐ MONEY MARKET ☐ CERTIFICATE OF DEPOSIT
- ☐ NOW ☐ _____
This is your (check one):
☐ Permanent ☐ Temporary account agreement

Number of signatures required for withdrawal _____
FACSIMILE SIGNATURE(S) ALLOWED? ☐ YES ☐ NO

X _____

OWNERSHIP OF ACCOUNT - BUSINESS PURPOSE
- ☐ SOLE PROPRIETORSHIP
- ☐ CORPORATION: ☐ FOR PROFIT ☐ NOT FOR PROFIT
- ☐ PARTNERSHIP
- ☐ _____
BUSINESS: _____
COUNTRY & STATE
OF ORGANIZATION: _____
AUTHORIZATION DATED: _____

SIGNATURE(S) - The undersigned certifies the accuracy of the information he/she has provided and acknowledges receipt of a completed copy of this form. The undersigned authorizes the financial institution to verify credit and employment history and/or have a credit reporting agency prepare a credit report on the undersigned, as individuals. The undersigned also acknowledge the receipt of a copy and agree to the terms of the following agreement(s) and/or disclosure(s):

- ☐ Terms & Conditions ☐ Truth in Savings ☐ Funds Availability
- ☐ Electronic Fund Transfers ☐ Privacy ☐ Substitute Checks
- ☐ Common Features ☐ _____

DATE OPENED _____ BY _____
INITIAL DEPOSIT $ _____
☐ CASH ☐ CHECK ☐ _____
HOME PHONE# _____
BUSINESS PHONE# _____
DRIVER'S LICENSE# _____
E-MAIL _____
EMPLOYER _____
MOTHER'S MAIDEN NAME _____
Name and address of someone who will always know your location: _____

X _____
I.D. # _____ D.O.B. _____

X _____
I.D. # _____ D.O.B. _____

X _____
I.D. # _____ D.O.B. _____

BACKUP WITHHOLDING CERTIFICATIONS
TIN: _____
☐ **TAXPAYER I.D. NUMBER -** The Taxpayer Identification Number shown above(TIN) is my correct taxpayer identification number.
☐ **BACKUP WITHHOLDING -** I am not subject to backup withholding either because I have not been notified that I am subject to backup withholding as a result of a failure to report all interest or dividends, or the Internal Revenue Service has notified me that I am no longer subject to backup withholding.
☐ **EXEMPT RECIPIENTS -** I am an exempt recipient under the Internal Revenue Service Regulations.
SIGNATURE: I certify under penalties of perjury the statements checked in this section and that I am a U.S. citizen or other U.S. person (as defined in the instructions).

X _____
(Date)

X _____
I.D. # _____ D.O.B. _____

☐ Authorized Signer (Individual Accounts Only)

X _____
I.D. # _____ D.O.B. _____

FIGURE 7-2 Deposit Ticket

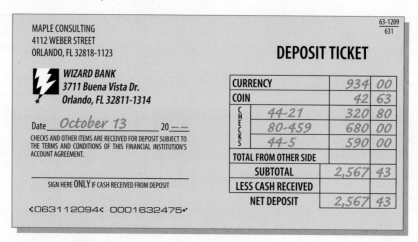

payee's name and sometimes other information on the back of the check, in the space provided near the left end. There are two basic types of endorsements.

1. **Blank endorsement**—the payee simply signs the back of the check. This makes the check payable to any bearer.

2. **Restrictive endorsement**—the payee adds words such as "Pay to the order of (specific) bank," or "Pay to Daryl Beck" to restrict the payment of the check to a specific party. By adding words such as "For deposit only," the payee can restrict the payment of the check for a specific purpose.

Businesses commonly use a rubber stamp to endorse checks for deposit. The check shown in Figure 7-3 has been stamped with a restrictive endorsement.

FIGURE 7-3 Restrictive Endorsement

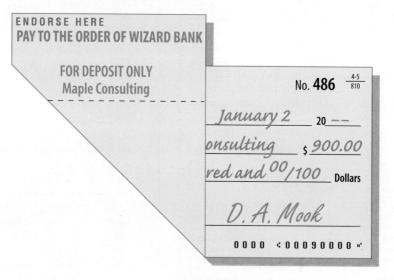

Automated Teller Machines

Postage stamps can be purchased at some ATMs. For deposits, some ATMs can provide an image of any checks being deposited.

Most banks now make **automated teller machines (ATMs)** available at all times to depositors for making deposits or withdrawals. Each depositor has a plastic card and a personal identification number (PIN). The depositor inserts the card, keys in the PIN, indicates whether the transaction is a withdrawal or a deposit, and enters the amount. The machine has a drawer or door for the withdrawal or deposit.

Most ATMs are now on a system such as Cirrus that allows noncustomers to use other ATMs in both the United States and foreign countries. There are also "cash machines" that supply only cash and do not take deposits. These are often found at airports and convenience stores.

It is important for the depositor to keep an accounting record of ATM withdrawals and deposits. This is done on the check stub or register described in the following section, and with an appropriate journal entry.

Writing Checks

A **check** is a document ordering a bank to pay cash from a depositor's account. There are three parties to every check.

1. **Drawer**—the depositor who orders the bank to pay the cash.
2. **Drawee**—the bank on which the check is drawn.
3. **Payee**—the party to whom the check is payable.

Checks used by businesses are usually bound in the form of a book. In some checkbooks, each check is attached to a **check stub** (Figure 7-4) that contains space to record all relevant information about the check. Other checkbooks are accompanied by a small register book in which the relevant information is noted. If a financial computer software package is used, both the check and the register can be prepared electronically.

Note that the check stubs in Figure 7-4 contain space to record amounts deposited. It generally is a good idea also to indicate the date of the deposit, as shown on check stub No. 108.

Use the following three steps in preparing a check:

STEP 1   Complete the check stub or register.

STEP 2   Enter the date, payee name, and amount on the check.

STEP 3   Sign the check.

The check stub is completed first so that the drawer retains a record of each check issued. This information is needed to determine the proper journal entry for the transaction.

The payee name is entered on the first long line on the check, followed by the amount in figures. The amount in words is then entered on the second long line. If the amount in figures does not agree with the amount in words, the bank usually contacts the drawer for the correct amount or returns the check unpaid.

The most critical point in preparing a check is signing it, and this should be done last. The signature authorizes the bank to pay cash from the drawer's account. The check signer should make sure that all other aspects of the check are correct before signing it.

Bank Statement

A statement of account issued by a bank to each depositor once a month is called a **bank statement**. Figure 7-5 is a bank statement for a checking account. The statement shows the following:

1. The balance at the beginning of the period.
2. Deposits and other amounts added during the period.
3. Checks and other amounts subtracted during the period.
4. The balance at the end of the period.

When a check needs to be voided, follow these procedures: 1. tear off or completely cross out (deface) the signature, 2. write "Void" by the check number on the check stub or check register, and 3. file the voided check numerically with the other records of canceled checks.

LEARNING KEY
The check should not be signed until the check signer has verified that all aspects of the check are correct.

FIGURE 7-4   Checks and Check Stubs

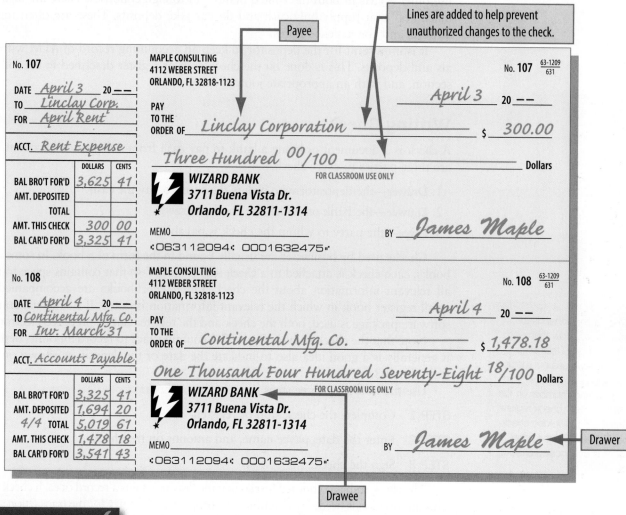

With the bank statement, the bank normally sends the following to the depositor:

1. Listing of canceled checks—a list of the depositor's checks paid by the bank during the period. The bank may send "imaged" sheets showing only the faces of the checks or the checks themselves, although this is increasingly uncommon today.

2. Any other forms representing items added to or subtracted from the account.

RECONCILING THE BANK STATEMENT

LO2 Prepare a bank reconciliation and related journal entries.

On any given day, the balance in the cash account on the depositor's books (the book balance) is unlikely to be the same as that on the bank's books (the bank balance). This difference can be due to errors, but it usually is caused by timing. Transactions generally are recorded by the business at a time that is different from when the bank records them.

Deposits

Suppose there are cash receipts of $600 on April 30. These cash receipts would be recorded on the depositor's books on April 30, and a deposit of $600 would be sent to the bank. The deposit would not reach the bank, however, until at least the following

FIGURE 7-5   Bank Statement

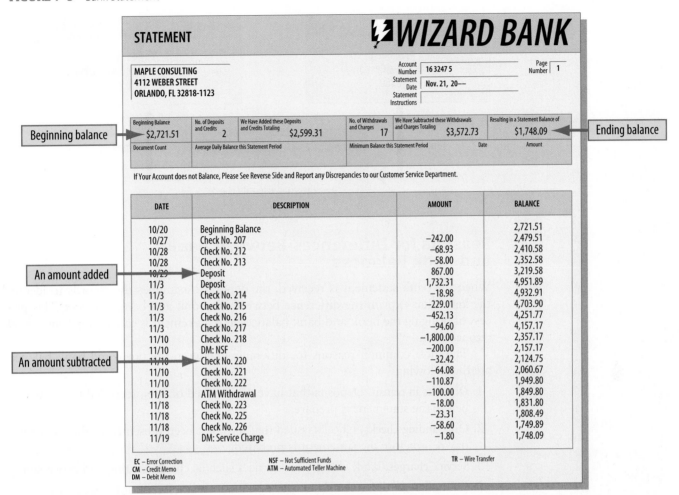

day, May 1. This timing difference in recording the $600 of cash receipts is illustrated in Figure 7-6. Notice that on April 30, the balances in the depositor's books and in the bank's books would be different. The depositor's book balance would be $600 more than the bank's book balance.

FIGURE 7-6   Depositor and Bank Records—Deposits

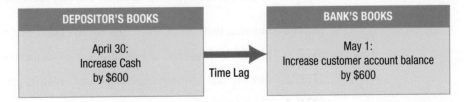

Cash Payments

Similar timing differences occur with cash payments. Suppose a check for $350 is written on April 30. This cash payment would be recorded on the depositor's books on April 30 and the check mailed to the payee. The check probably would not be received by the payee until May 3. If the payee deposited the check promptly, it still would not clear the bank until May 4. This timing difference in recording the $350 cash payment is illustrated in Figure 7-7. Notice once again that on April 30, the balances in the depositor's books and in the bank's books would be different. The depositor's book balance would be $350 less than the bank's book balance.

FIGURE 7-7   Depositor and Bank Records—Cash Payments

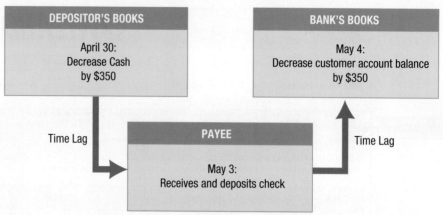

Reasons for Differences Between Bank and Book Balances

When the bank statement is received, the depositor examines the records to identify the items that explain the difference between the book and bank balances. This process of bringing the book and bank balances into agreement is called preparing a **bank reconciliation**.

The most common reasons for differences between the book and bank balances are the following:

1. **Deposits in transit.** Deposits that have not reached or been recorded by the bank before the statement is prepared.
2. **Outstanding checks.** Checks issued that have not been presented to the bank for payment before the statement is prepared.
3. **Service charges.** Bank charges for services such as check printing and processing.
4. **Collections.** Collections of promissory notes or charge accounts made by the bank on behalf of the depositor.
5. **Not sufficient funds (NSF) checks.** Checks deposited by the depositor that are not paid because the drawer did not have sufficient funds.
6. **Errors.** Errors made by the bank or the depositor in recording cash transactions.

Steps in Preparing the Bank Reconciliation

Use the following three steps in preparing the bank reconciliation:

STEP 1   Identify deposits in transit and any related errors.

STEP 2   Identify outstanding checks and any related errors.

STEP 3   Identify additional reconciling items.

Deposits in Transit and Related Errors

Follow these steps:

STEP 1   Compare deposits listed on the bank statement with deposits in transit on last month's bank reconciliation. All of last month's deposits in transit should appear on the current month's bank statement.

STEP 2   Compare the remaining deposits on the bank statement with deposits listed in the accounting records. Any deposits listed in the accounting records but not on the bank statement are deposits in transit on the current bank reconciliation.

STEP 3   Compare the individual deposit amounts on the bank statement and in the accounting records. If they differ, the error needs to be corrected.

Outstanding Checks and Related Errors

Follow these steps:

STEP 1   Compare canceled checks with the bank statement and the accounting records. If the amounts differ, the error needs to be corrected.

STEP 2   As each canceled check is compared with the accounting records, place a check mark on the check stub or other accounting record to indicate that the check has cleared.

STEP 3   Any checks written that have not been checked off represent outstanding checks on the bank reconciliation. This includes outstanding checks from last month's bank reconciliation that have not yet cleared.

Additional Reconciling Items

Some banks pay interest on checking account balances. This reconciling item would be handled in the same manner as a bank credit memo.

Compare any additions and deductions on the bank statement that are not deposits or checks with the accounting records. Items that the bank adds to the account are called **credit memos**. Items that the bank deducts from the account are called **debit memos**. Remember that a depositor's account is a liability to the bank. Thus, a credit memo increases this liability; a debit memo reduces the liability. Any of these items not appearing in the accounting records represent additional items on the bank reconciliation.

Illustration of a Bank Reconciliation

A general format for the bank reconciliation is shown in Figure 7-8. Not every item shown in this illustration would be in every bank reconciliation, but this format is helpful in determining where to put items. A bank reconciliation form also can be found on the back of most bank statements. Figure 7-9 is an example of such a form with instructions. Some banks also include a reconciliation form on their website.

To illustrate the preparation of a bank reconciliation, we will use the Maple Consulting bank statement shown in Figure 7-5. That statement shows a balance of $1,748.09 as of November 21. The balance in Maple's check stubs and general ledger

FIGURE 7-8   Bank Reconciliation Format

BANK RECONCILIATION		
Bank statement balance		$xxxx
Add: Deposits in transit	$xxxx	
Bank errors (that understate balance)	xxxx	xxxx
		$xxxx
Deduct: Outstanding checks	$xxxx	
Bank errors (that overstate balance)	xxxx	xxxx
Adjusted bank balance		$xxxx
Book balance		$xxxx
Add: Bank credit memos	$xxxx	
Book errors (that understate balance)	xxxx	xxxx
		$xxxx
Deduct: Bank debit memos	$xxxx	
Book errors (that overstate balance)	xxxx	xxxx
Adjusted book balance		$xxxx

FIGURE 7-9 Reconciliation Form From Bank Statement

Outstanding Deposits

Date	Amount
Total	$

Outstanding Withdrawals

Date	Amount
Total	$

1. List any deposits that do not appear on your statement in the Outstanding Deposits section at the left. Record the total.

2. Check off in your checkbook register all checks, withdrawals (including Check Card and ATM) and automatic payments that appear on your statement. Withdrawals that are NOT checked off should be recorded in the Outstanding Withdrawals section at the left. Record the total.

3. Enter the ending balance shown on this statement. $_____

4. Enter the total deposits recorded in the Outstanding Deposits section. $_____

5. Total lines 3 and 4. $_____

6. Enter the total withdrawals recorded in the Outstanding Withdrawals section. $_____

7. Subtract line 6 from line 5. This is your balance. $_____

8. Enter in your register and subtract from your register balance any checks, withdrawals or other debits (including fees, if any) that appear on your statement but have not been recorded in your register.

9. Enter in your register and add to your register balance any deposits or other credits (including interest, if any) that appear in your statement but have not been recorded in your register.

10. The balance in your register should be the same as the balance shown in #7. If it does not match, review and check all figures used, and check the addition and subtraction in your register. If necessary, review and balance your statement from the previous month.

FIGURE 7-10 Bank Reconciliation

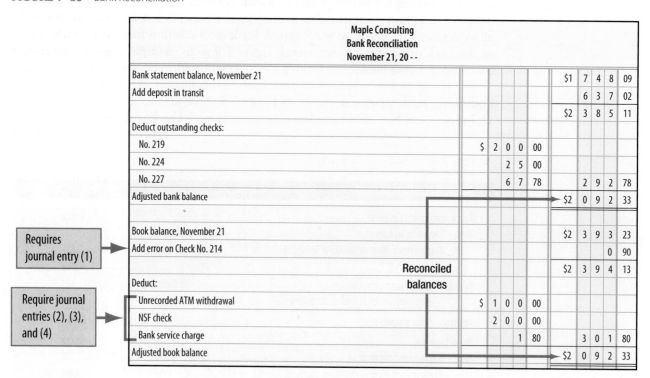

cash account is $2,393.23. The three steps described on page 238 were used to identify the following items, and the reconciliation in Figure 7-10 was prepared.

1. A deposit of $637.02 recorded on November 21 had not been received by the bank. Maple has received the funds but the amount has not yet been counted by the bank. This deposit in transit is added to the bank statement balance.

2. Check numbers 219, 224, and 227 are outstanding. The funds have been disbursed by Maple but have not yet been paid out by the bank. The amount of these outstanding checks is subtracted from the bank statement balance.

3. Check number 214 was written for $18.98 but was entered on the check stub and on the books as $19.88. This $0.90 error is added to the book balance because $0.90 too much had been deducted from the book balance.

4. Maple made an ATM withdrawal of $100 on November 13 for personal use but did not record the withdrawal on the books. The bank has reduced Maple's balance by this amount. Thus, this amount is deducted from the book balance.

5. The bank returned an NSF check of $200. This was a check received by Maple from a customer. The bank has reduced Maple's balance by $200, but Maple has not yet recorded it. This amount is deducted from the book balance.

6. The bank service charge was $1.80. The bank has reduced Maple's balance by this amount, but Maple has not yet recorded it. This amount is deducted from the book balance.

Journal Entries

LEARNING KEY
Journal entries are needed to correct errors in the books and to record bank additions and deductions that are not in the books.

Only two kinds of items appearing on a bank reconciliation require journal entries.

1. Errors in the depositor's books.

2. Bank additions and deductions that do not already appear in the books.

Note the four items in the lower portion of the bank reconciliation in Figure 7-10. A journal entry always is required for each item in this book balance portion of the bank reconciliation. The four journal entries for Maple Consulting are shown below, using entry numbers matching those noted in Figure 7-10.

The $0.90 item is an error in the accounting records that occurred when the check amount was incorrectly entered. Assume the $18.98 was in payment of an account payable which had been incorrectly debited for $19.88. The entry to correct this error is as follows:

4	(1)	Cash			0	90					4
5		Accounts Payable						0	90	5
6		Error in recording check								6

The $100 ATM withdrawal has been deducted from Maple's account by the bank. Maple has not yet recorded the withdrawal. Maple withdrew the funds for personal use, so the following journal entry is required:

8	(2)	James Maple, Drawing		1	0	0	00						8
9		Cash						1	0	0	00	9
10		Unrecorded ATM withdrawal										10

The $200 NSF check is a deduction by the bank for a check deposited by Maple that proved to be worthless. This amount must be deducted from the book balance. Assuming the $200 was received from a customer on account, the following journal entry is required:

12	(3)	Accounts Receivable		2	0	0	00						12
13		Cash						2	0	0	00	13
14		Unrecorded NSF check										14

The $1.80 bank service charge is a fee for bank services received by Maple. The bank has deducted this amount from Maple's account. Bank service charges are usually small and are charged to Miscellaneous Expense.

16		(4) Miscellaneous Expense			1	80				16
17		Cash						1	80	17
18		Bank service charge								18

Figure 7-11 contains a detailed list of items that require journal entries.

FIGURE 7-11 Bank Reconciliation Items that Require Journal Entries

ADDITIONS TO CASH BALANCE	DEDUCTIONS FROM CASH BALANCE

* Unrecorded deposits (including ATM)
* Note collected by bank
* Interest earned
* Errors:
  1. Added too little as a deposit
  2. Deducted too much as a check
	* Unrecorded ATM withdrawals
	* NSF checks
	* Bank service charges
	* Deposits recorded twice
	* Unrecorded checks
	* Loan payments
	* Interest payments
	* Errors:
	  1. Added too much as a deposit
	  2. Deducted too little as a check

Electronic Banking

Thus far in the chapter, we have explained and illustrated mainly a world of paper deposits, payments, and bank statements. Such a world still exists. But while many businesses and individuals still write and receive checks, the paper world of banking is shrinking rapidly. In fact, virtually every aspect of banking processes can be handled electronically.

Electronic Funds Transfer

Both deposits and payments can be made with **electronic funds transfer (EFT)**, using a computer rather than paper checks. Your net pay can be sent electronically by your employer to your bank, and you can review the summary of your compensation and various deductions on your computer. You can transfer funds between savings and checking accounts electronically. You can buy lunch or groceries, or withdraw money from a bank machine using your debit card. Payments on your credit card account or for utility bills can be made electronically. And your bank statement probably is sent to you electronically by your bank.

Businesses also are making increasing use of EFT in handling cash transactions. For example, as noted above, employee wages can be paid using EFT. Bills from suppliers also can be paid by EFT. Payments from customers frequently are in electronic form. And funds can be transferred electronically among multiple accounts at different banks.

Bank Reconciliations

Even the idea of the monthly bank reconciliation requires adjustment in an electronic banking world. In a paper world, you deposit paper checks, write paper checks, and keep paper records of your financial activities. Once a month, the bank sends you a bank statement and you "reconcile" your transactions and balance with the bank's records. In the electronic banking world, you can use your smartphone to regularly (daily?) view the effects of your transactions on your balance. There is no waiting until month-end to compare your records with the bank's. With fully electronic banking, the monthly reconciliation can be replaced by a regular "monitoring" of the account. If the bank's processing of a transaction is different from yours, you can see it immediately and correct your records or contact the bank. There should be very little news in a monthly bank statement in an electronic banking world.

Checkpoint ✓

Complete Checkpoint-2 on page 254 to test your basic understanding of LO2.

Heavy use of EFT will present record keeping challenges. Many of the documents handled in a purely manual environment disappear when EFT is used. Bank accounts are just one of many areas where computers require accountants to think in new ways. Regardless of what system is used, the key point to remember is that the accounting records must be correctly updated.

A Broader View

Fraud—A Real Threat to Small Business

Every two years, the Association of Certified Fraud Examiners (ACFE) surveys its members on the occupational fraud they have investigated during the preceding two years. The most recent survey showed that more than 29% of the frauds occurred in small businesses. In addition, the median loss suffered by small businesses was $154,000. The most commonly cited factor that allowed the fraud to occur was a lack of adequate internal control. And the majority of the asset misappropriation cases involved theft or misuse of cash.

These survey findings show the importance of the kinds of internal controls over cash described in this chapter and the appendix.

DON FARRALL/PHOTODISC/GETTY IMAGES

THE PETTY CASH FUND

LO3 Establish and use a petty cash fund.

For good control over cash, payments generally should be made by check. Unfortunately, payments of very small amounts by check can be both inconvenient and inefficient. For example, the time and cost required to write a check for $0.70 to mail a letter might be greater than the cost of the postage. Therefore, businesses customarily establish a **petty cash fund** to pay for small items with cash. "Petty" means small, and both the amount of the fund and the maximum amount of any bill that can be paid from the fund are small.

Establishing a Petty Cash Fund

To establish a petty cash fund, a check is written to the petty cash custodian for the amount to be set aside in the fund. The amount may be $50, $100, $200, or any amount considered necessary. The journal entry to establish a petty cash fund of $100 would be as follows:

4		Petty Cash		1	0	0	00						4
5		Cash							1	0	0	00	5
6		Establish petty cash fund											6

Petty Cash is an asset that is listed immediately below Cash on the balance sheet.

The custodian cashes the check and places the money in a petty cash box. For good control, the custodian should be the only person authorized to make payments from the fund. The custodian should be able to account for the full amount of the fund at any time.

Making Payments from a Petty Cash Fund

A receipt called a **petty cash voucher** (Figure 7-12) should be prepared for every payment from the fund. The voucher shows the name of the payee, the purpose of the payment, and the account to be charged for the payment. Each voucher should be signed by the custodian and by the person receiving the cash. The vouchers should be numbered consecutively so that all vouchers can be accounted for. At any time, the sum of the current vouchers and the unused cash should equal the original amount of the fund.

FIGURE 7-12 Petty Cash Voucher

PETTY CASH VOUCHER		
	NO. _2_	
	DATE _December 8,_ 20 _– –_	
PAID TO _James Maple_	**$**	**¢**
FOR _Client Luncheon_		
CHARGE TO _Travel & Entertainment Expense_	25	75
REMITTANCE RECEIVED _James Maple_	APPROVED BY _Tina Blank_	

Petty Cash Payments Record

When a petty cash fund is maintained, a formal record is often kept of all payments from the fund. The **petty cash payments record** (Figure 7-13) is a special multi-column record that supplements the regular accounting records. It is not a journal. The headings of the Distribution of Payments columns may vary, depending upon the types of expenditures.

The petty cash payments record of Maple Consulting is shown in Figure 7-13. A narrative of the petty cash transactions shown in Figure 7-13 is as follows:

Dec. 1   Maple issued a check for $200 payable to Tina Blank, Petty Cash Custodian. Blank cashed the check and placed the money in a secure cash box.

A notation of the amount received is made in the Description column of the petty cash payments record. In addition, this transaction is entered in the journal as follows:

8	Dec. 1	Petty Cash		2 0 0 00			8
9		Cash			2 0 0 00		9
10		Establish petty cash fund					10

During the month of December, the following payments were made from the petty cash fund:

Dec. 5   Paid $32.80 to Jerry's Auto for servicing the company automobile. Voucher No. 1.

8   Reimbursed Maple $25.75 for the amount spent for lunch with a client. Voucher No. 2.

9   Gave Maple $30 for personal use. Voucher No. 3.

There is no special Distribution column for entering amounts withdrawn by the owner for personal use. Therefore, this payment is entered by writing the account name in the Account column and $30 in the Amount column at the extreme right of the petty cash payments record.

FIGURE 7-13   Maple Consulting's Petty Cash Payments Record

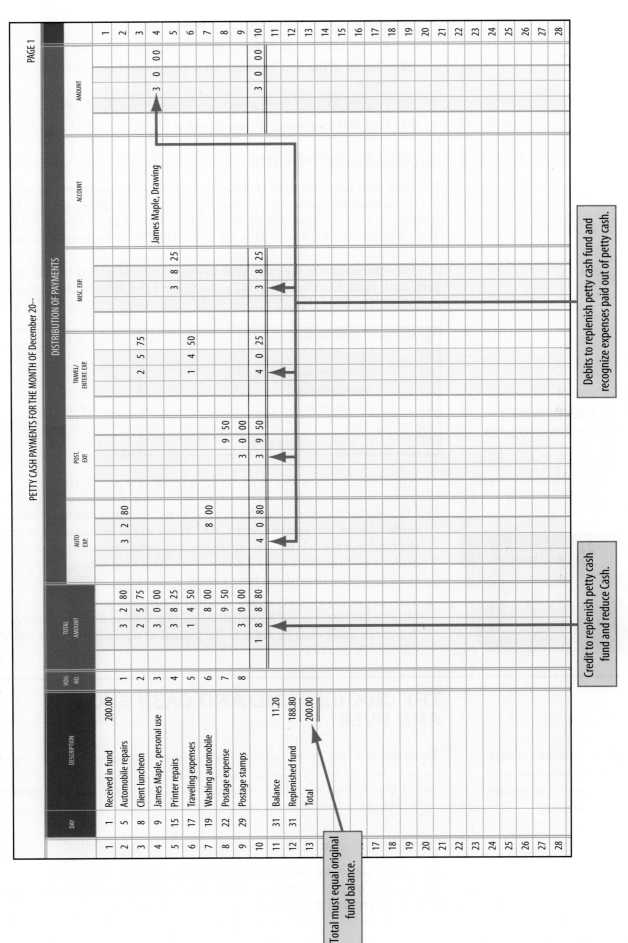

PAGE 1

PETTY CASH PAYMENTS FOR THE MONTH OF December 20--

DAY		DESCRIPTION		VOU. NO.	TOTAL AMOUNT			DISTRIBUTION OF PAYMENTS							
								AUTO EXP.	POST. EXP.	TRAVEL/ ENTERT. EXP.	MISC. EXP.		ACCOUNT	AMOUNT	
1	1	Received in fund	200.00												1
2	5	Automobile repairs		1	3 2 80			3 2 80							2
3	8	Client luncheon		2	2 5 75					2 5 75					3
4	9	James Maple, personal use		3	3 0 00							James Maple, Drawing	3 0 00	4
5	15	Printer repairs		4	3 8 25						3 8 25				5
6	17	Traveling expenses		5	1 4 50					1 4 50					6
7	19	Washing automobile		6	8 00			8 00							7
8	22	Postage expense		7	9 50				9 50						8
9	29	Postage stamps		8	3 0 00				3 0 00						9
10					1 8 8 80			4 0 80	3 9 50	4 0 25	3 8 25		3 0 00		10
11	31	Balance	11.20												11
12	31	Replenished fund	188.80												12
13		Total	200.00												13
14															14
15															15
16															16
17															17
18															18
19															19
20															20
21															21
22															22
23															23
24															24
25															25
26															26
27															27
28															28

Debits to replenish petty cash fund and recognize expenses paid out of petty cash.

Credit to replenish petty cash fund and reduce Cash.

Total must equal original fund balance.

15 Paid $38.25 for printer repairs. Voucher No. 4.

17 Reimbursed Maple $14.50 for travel expenses. Voucher No. 5.

19 Paid $8 to Big Red Car Care for washing the company automobile. Voucher No. 6.

22 Paid $9.50 for mailing a package. Voucher No. 7.

29 Paid $30 for postage stamps. Voucher No. 8.

Replenishing the Petty Cash Fund

The petty cash fund should be replenished whenever the fund runs low and at the end of each accounting period, so that the accounts are brought up to date. The amount columns of the petty cash payments record are totaled to verify that the total of the Total Amount column equals the total of the Distribution columns. The amount columns are then ruled as shown in Figure 7-13.

The information in the petty cash payments record is then used to replenish the petty cash fund. On December 31, a check for $188.80 is issued to the petty cash custodian. The journal entry to record the replenishment of the fund is as follows:

18	Dec.	31	Automobile Expense				4	0	80								18
19			Postage Expense				3	9	50								19
20			Travel and Entertainment Expense				4	0	25								20
21			Miscellaneous Expense				3	8	25								21
22			James Maple, Drawing				3	0	00								22
23			Cash										1	8	8	80	23
24			Replenishment of petty cash fund														24

LEARNING KEY
Once the petty cash fund is established, an entry is made to Petty Cash only if the amount of the fund is being changed.

Checkpoint ✓

Complete Checkpoint-3 on page 254 to test your basic understanding of LO3.

Note two important aspects of the functioning of a petty cash fund.

1. Once the fund is established by debiting Petty Cash and crediting Cash, no further entries are made to Petty Cash. Notice in the journal entry to replenish the fund that the debits are to appropriate expense and drawing accounts and the credit is to Cash. Only if the amount of the fund itself is being changed would there be a debit or credit to Petty Cash.

2. The petty cash payments record is strictly a supplement to the regular accounting records. Because it is not a journal, no posting is done from this record. A separate entry must be made in the journal to replenish the fund and update the expense accounts.

THE CHANGE FUND AND CASH SHORT AND OVER

LO4 Establish a change fund and use the cash short and over account.

Businesses generally must be able to make change when customers use cash to pay for goods or services received. To do so, generally it is a good idea to establish a change fund. A change fund is a supply of currency and coins kept in a cash register or cash drawer for use in handling cash sales.

Establishing and Operating the Change Fund

The journal entries for establishing and maintaining a change fund are very similar to the ones just used for petty cash. To establish a change fund of $200 on June 1, the following entry would be made:

8	June 1	Change Fund			2	0	0	00						8
9		Cash								2	0	0	00	9
10		Establish change fund												10

At the end of the day, cash received during the day is deposited, but the change fund is held back for use the following business day. For example, if cash of $1,250 was received on June 3 for services provided, the cash drawer would contain $1,450, as follows:

Change fund	$ 200
Cash sales	1,250
Total cash on hand	$1,450

The $1,250 would be deposited in the bank, and the following journal entry would be made:

12	June 3	Cash		1	2	5	0	00						12
13		Service Fees								1	2	5	0	00	13
14		Cash received for services												14

Notice the additional similarity between the change fund and the petty cash fund. Once the change fund is established by a debit to Change Fund and a credit to Cash, no further entries are made to the change fund. Only if the amount of the change fund itself is being changed would there be a debit or credit to Change Fund.

Cash Short and Over

An unavoidable part of the change-making process is that errors can occur. It is important to know whether such errors have occurred and how to account for them.

Businesses commonly use cash registers with tapes that accumulate a record of the day's receipts. The amount of cash according to the tapes plus the amount of the change fund can be compared with the amount of cash in the register to determine any error. For example, assume a cash shortage is identified for June 19.

Change fund	$ 200
Receipts per register tapes	963
Total	$1,163
Cash count	1,161
Cash shortage	$ 2

Similarly, assume a cash overage is identified for June 20.

Change fund	$ 200
Receipts per register tapes	814
Total	$1,014
Cash count	1,015
Cash overage	$ 1

We account for such errors by using an account called Cash Short and Over. In T account form, Cash Short and Over appears as follows:

Cash Short and Over	
Shortage (Expense)	Overage (Revenue)

The register tapes on June 19 showed receipts of $963 and the change fund was $200, but only $1,161 in cash was counted. The journal entry on June 19 to record the revenues and cash shortage (remember that we hold back the change fund) would be as follows:

18	June	19	Cash		9	6	1	00					18
19			Cash Short and Over				2	00					19
20			Service Fees							9	6	3	00	20
21			Record service fees and cash shortage										21

The entry on June 20 to record the revenues and cash overage (holding back the change fund) would be as follows:

23	June	20	Cash		8	1	5	00					23
24			Service Fees							8	1	4	00	24
25			Cash Short and Over									1	00	25
26			Record service fees and cash overage										26

The cash short and over account is used to accumulate cash shortages and overages throughout the accounting period. At the end of the period, a debit balance in the account (a net shortage) is treated as an expense. A credit balance in the account (a net overage) is treated as revenue.

Checkpoint ✓

Complete Checkpoint-4 on page 254 to test your basic understanding of LO4.

Your Perspective CASHIER

If you've ever worked in a fast food restaurant, such as Burger King, or any restaurant where you've been a cashier, you know that cash is a precious asset. At the beginning of each shift, you begin by counting the change fund in the assigned register. This is part of how the business maintains control over cash. As explained in this chapter, the change fund is a supply of currency and coins kept in a cash register or drawer used in handling cash sales.

At the end of your shift, you recount the cash and compare it to the register tape to determine any shortages or overages. This is extremely important, because the business needs to know if any errors have occurred, and how to account for them.

Self-Study

LEARNING OBJECTIVES	Key Points to Remember
LO1 Describe how to open and use a checking account.	Three steps to follow in preparing a check are as follows: 1. Complete the check stub or register. 2. Enter the date, payee name, and amount on the check. 3. Sign the check.

LEARNING OBJECTIVES	Key Points to Remember

LO2 Prepare a bank reconciliation and related journal entries.	The most common reasons for differences between the book and bank cash balances are as follows:
	1. Deposits in transit
	2. Outstanding checks
	3. Bank service charges
	4. Bank collections for the depositor
	5. NSF checks
	6. Errors by the bank or the depositor
	Three steps to follow in preparing a bank reconciliation are as follows:
	1. Identify deposits in transit and any related errors.
	2. Identify outstanding checks and any related errors.
	3. Identify additional reconciling items.
	Only two kinds of items on a bank reconciliation require journal entries.
	1. Errors in the depositor's books.
	2. Bank additions and deductions that do not already appear in the books.
LO3 Establish and use a petty cash fund.	Two important aspects of the functioning of a petty cash fund are as follows:
	1. Once the fund is established, subsequent entries do not affect the petty cash account balance, unless the size of the fund itself is being changed.
	2. The petty cash payments record is supplemental to the regular accounting records. No posting is done from this record.
LO4 Establish a change fund and use the cash short and over account.	A change fund is established by debiting Change Fund and crediting Cash. Cash shortages and overages are accounted for using the cash short and over account. A debit balance in this account represents expense; a credit balance represents revenue.

DEMONSTRATION PROBLEM

Jason Kuhn's check stubs indicated a balance of $4,565.12 for Kuhn's Wilderness Outfitters on March 31. This included a record of a deposit of $926.10 mailed to the bank on March 30, but not credited to Kuhn's account until April 1. In addition, the following checks were outstanding on March 31:

No. 462	$524.26
No. 465	$213.41
No. 473	$543.58
No. 476	$351.38
No. 477	$197.45

The bank statement showed a balance of $5,419 as of March 31. The bank statement included a service charge of $4.10 with the date of March 29. In matching the canceled checks and record of deposits with the stubs, it was discovered that Check No. 456, a payment on account to Office Suppliers, Inc., for $39 was erroneously recorded on the stub as $93. This caused the bank balance on that stub and those following to be $54 too small. It was also discovered that an ATM withdrawal of $100 for personal use was not recorded on the books.

Kuhn maintains a $200 petty cash fund. His petty cash payments record showed the following totals at the end of March of the current year:

Automobile expense	$ 32.40
Postage expense	27.50
Charitable contributions expense	35.00
Phone expense	6.20
Travel and entertainment expense	38.60
Miscellaneous expense	17.75
Jason Kuhn, drawing	40.00
Total	$197.45

This left a balance of $2.55 in the petty cash fund, and the fund was replenished.

REQUIRED

1. Prepare a bank reconciliation for Jason Kuhn as of March 31, 20--.

2. Journalize the entries that should be made by Kuhn on his books as of March 31, 20--, (a) as a result of the bank reconciliation and (b) to replenish the petty cash fund.

3. Show proof that, after these entries, the total of the cash and petty cash account balances equals $4,715.02.

Solution

1.

Kuhn's Wilderness Outfitters Bank Reconciliation March 31, 20 --															
Bank statement balance, March 31											$5	4	1	9	00
Add deposit in transit												9	2	6	10
											$6	3	4	5	10
Deduct outstanding checks:															
No. 462	$	5	2	4	26										
No. 465		2	1	3	41										
No. 473		5	4	3	58										
No. 476		3	5	1	38										
No. 477		1	9	7	45		1	8	3	0	08				
Adjusted bank balance											$4	5	1	5	02
Book balance, March 31											$4	5	6	5	12
Add error on Check No. 456													5	4	00
											$4	6	1	9	12
Deduct: Bank service charge	$			4	10										
Unrecorded ATM withdrawal		1	0	0	00			1	0	4	10				
Adjusted book balance											$4	5	1	5	02

2a.

3															3
4	Mar.	31	Miscellaneous Expense				4	10							4
5			Cash									4	10	5
6			Bank service charge												6
7															7
8			Cash			5	4	00							8
9			Accounts Payable—Office Suppliers, Inc.								5	4	00	9
10			Error on Check No. 456												10
11															11
12			Jason Kuhn, Drawing		1	0	0	00							12
13			Cash							1	0	0	00	13
14			Unrecorded ATM withdrawal												14
15															15
16		31	Automobile Expense			3	2	40							16
17			Postage Expense			2	7	50							17
18			Charitable Contributions Expense			3	5	00							18
19			Phone Expense				6	20							19
20			Travel and Entertainment Expense			3	8	60							20
21			Miscellaneous Expense			1	7	75							21
22			Jason Kuhn, Drawing			4	0	00							22
23			Cash							1	9	7	45	23
24			Replenishment of petty cash fund												24
25															25

b. (rows 16–24)

3. Cash in bank:

Check stub balance, March 31	$4,565.12	
Plus error on Ck. No. 456	54.00	
Less bank charges	(104.10)	
Adjusted cash in bank		$4,515.02

Cash on hand:

Petty cash fund	$ 2.55	
Add replenishment	197.45	
Adjusted cash on hand		200.00
Total cash in bank and petty cash on hand		$4,715.02

KEY TERMS

ABA (American Bankers Association) Number (232)   The small fraction printed in the upper right-hand corner of each check.

automated teller machine (ATM) (234)   A machine used by depositors to make withdrawals or deposits at any time.

bank reconciliation (238)   A report used to bring the book and bank balances into agreement.

bank statement (235)   A statement of account issued by a bank to each depositor once a month.

blank endorsement (234)   An endorsement where the payee simply signs the back of the check, making the check payable to any bearer.

canceled check (236)   A depositor's check paid by the bank during the bank statement period.

cash (232)   To a business, cash includes currency, coins, checks received from customers, money orders, and bank cashier's checks.

change fund (246)   A supply of currency and coins kept in a cash register or cash drawer for use in handling cash sales.

check (235)   A document ordering a bank to pay cash from a depositor's account.

check stub (235)   In some checkbooks, a document attached to a check that contains space for relevant information about the check.

collections (238)   Collections of promissory notes or charge accounts made by the bank on behalf of the depositor.

credit memo (239)   An item that the bank adds to the account.

Customer Identification Program (CIP) (232)   A program every bank is required to maintain that provides clear identification of every account holder.

debit memo (239)   An item that the bank deducts from the account.

deposit ticket (232)   A form showing a detailed listing of items being deposited.

deposits in transit (238)   Deposits that have not reached or been recorded by the bank before the bank statement is prepared.

drawee (235)   The bank on which the check is drawn.

drawer (235)   The depositor who orders the bank to pay the cash.

electronic funds transfer (EFT) (242)   A process using a computer rather than paper checks to complete transactions with the bank.

endorsement (232)   Stamping or writing the payee's name and sometimes other information on the back of the check.

errors (238)   Errors made by the bank or the depositor in recording cash transactions.

internal control (232)   A set of procedures designed to ensure proper accounting for transactions.

magnetic ink character recognition (MICR) code (232)   The character code used to print identifying information on the lower left front side of each check.

not sufficient funds (NSF) check (238)   A check deposited by the depositor that is not paid because the drawer did not have sufficient funds.

outstanding check (238)   A check issued that has not been presented to the bank for payment before the statement is prepared.

payee (235)   The person being paid the cash.

petty cash fund (243)   A fund established to pay for small items with cash.

petty cash payments record (244)   A special multi-column record that supplements the regular accounting records.

petty cash voucher (244)   A receipt that is prepared for every payment from the petty cash fund.

restrictive endorsement (234)   An endorsement where the payee adds words such as "Pay to the order of (specific) bank" or "For deposit only" to restrict the payment of the check.

service charge (238)   A bank charge for services such as check printing and processing.

signature card (232)   A card that is completed and signed by each person authorized to sign checks.

SELF-STUDY TEST QUESTIONS

True/False

1. LO2   The primary purpose of a bank reconciliation is to detect and correct errors made by the bank in its records.

2. LO2   NSF checks are subtracted from the bank's ending balance on the bank reconciliation.

3. LO2   The bank service charge requires a journal entry to record its effects on the cash account.

4. LO2   Unrecorded ATM withdrawals are added to the checkbook balance on the bank reconciliation.

5. LO3   The petty cash record is a journal of original entry (entries are posted from it to the general ledger accounts).

Multiple Choice

1. LO2   Which of these could be *added* to the ending checkbook balance?

   (a) service charges   (c) checkbook errors
   (b) NSF check   (d) outstanding checks

2 LO2   Which of these is *subtracted* from the ending checkbook balance?

   (a) deposits in transit   (c) note collection
   (b) service charges   (d) bank errors

3. LO2   Which of these is *added* to the ending bank statement balance?

   (a) outstanding checks   (c) checkbook errors
   (b) service charges   (d) deposits in transit

4. LO3   To establish a petty cash fund, which account is debited?

   (a) Cash   (c) Miscellaneous Expense
   (b) Petty Cash   (d) Revenue

5. LO4   When the cash short and over account has a debit balance at the end of the month, it is considered

   (a) an expense.   (c) revenue.
   (b) an asset.   (d) a liability.

Checkpoint Exercises

1. LO1   Match the following words with their definitions by entering the correct number in the spaces below.

   1. deposit ticket
   2. ATM
   3. check
   4. bank statement
   5. blank endorsement

   _____ a. A document ordering a bank to pay cash from a depositor's account.

   _____ b. An endorsement where the payee simply signs the back of the check, making the check payable to any bearer.

____ c. Automated teller machine—a machine used by depositors to make withdrawals or deposits at any time.

____ d. A statement of account issued by a bank to each depositor once a month.

____ e. A form showing a detailed listing of items being deposited.

2. LO2   Indicate how each of the following items should be treated in a bank reconciliation by entering the correct letter in the spaces provided.

a.   Add to bank statement balance

b.   Subtract from bank statement balance

c.   Add to book balance

d.   Subtract from book balance

____ 1. Interest earned on checking account balance

____ 2. Error in checkbook whereby a check for $82 was entered in the checkbook as $28

____ 3. Deposit in transit

____ 4. Outstanding checks

3. LO3   A petty cash fund established for $200 had the following cash payments during the month:

Phone expense $23.50
Automobile expense   49.10
H. Appy, drawing   50.00

Prepare the journal entry to replenish the petty cash fund at the end of the month.

4. LO4   The cash register tape for June 30 showed cash receipts of $876, and the cash in the register drawer was $1,070. A change fund of $200 is maintained.

Prepare the journal entry for service fees and cash short and over at June 30.
The answers to the Self-Study Test Questions are at the end of the chapter (page 266).

Applying Your Knowledge

REVIEW QUESTIONS

LO1   1. Why must a signature card be filled out and signed to open a checking account?

LO1   2. Explain the difference between a blank endorsement and a restrictive endorsement.

LO1   3. Who are the three parties to every check?

LO1   4. What are the three steps to follow in preparing a check?

LO2   5. What are the most common reasons for differences between the book and bank cash balances?

LO2   6. What are the three steps to follow in preparing a bank reconciliation?

LO2   7. What two kinds of items on a bank reconciliation require journal entries?

LO2   8. Name five common uses of electronic funds transfer.

LO3   9. What is the purpose of a petty cash fund?

LO3   10. What should be prepared every time a petty cash payment is made?

LO3   11. At what two times should the petty cash fund be replenished?

LO3   12. From what source is the information obtained for issuing a check to replenish the petty cash fund?

LO4   13. At what two times would an entry be made affecting the change fund?

LO4   14. What does a debit balance in the cash short and over account represent? What does a credit balance in this account represent?

SERIES A EXERCISES

E 7-1A   (LO1)

CHECKING ACCOUNT TERMS Match the following words with their definitions:

1. An endorsement where the payee simply signs on the back of the check
2. An endorsement that contains words like "For Deposit Only" together with the signature
3. A card filled out and signed by each person authorized to sign checks on an account
4. The depositor who orders the bank to pay cash from the depositor's account
5. The bank on which the check is drawn
6. The person being paid the cash
7. A check that has been paid by the bank and is being returned to the depositor

a. signature card
b. canceled check
c. blank endorsement
d. drawer
e. restrictive endorsement
f. drawee
g. payee

E 7-2A   (LO1)
✓ Net deposit: $962.20

PREPARE DEPOSIT TICKET Based on the following information, prepare a deposit ticket:

Date:		January 15, 20--
Currency:		$396.00
Coin:		23.20
Checks:	No. 4-12	372.00
	No. 80-318	127.00
	No. 3-8	44.00

E 7-3A   (LO1)

PREPARE CHECK AND STUB Based on the following information, prepare a check and stub:

Date:	January 15, 20--
Balance brought forward:	$2,841.50
Deposit:	(from Exercise 7-2A)
Check to:	J. M. Suppliers
Amount:	$150.00
For:	Office Supplies
Signature:	Sign your name

E 7-4A   (LO2)

BANK RECONCILIATION PROCEDURES In a format similar to the following, indicate whether the action at the left will result in an addition to (+) or subtraction from (−) the ending bank balance or the ending checkbook balance.

	Ending Bank Balance	Ending Checkbook Balance
1. Deposits in transit to the bank	_____	_____
2. Error in checkbook: check recorded as $32 but was actually for $23	_____	_____
3. Service fee charged by bank	_____	_____
4. Outstanding checks	_____	_____
5. NSF check deposited earlier	_____	_____
6. Error in checkbook: check recorded as $22 but was actually for $220	_____	_____
7. Bank credit memo advising a note was collected for us	_____	_____

E 7-5A   (LO2)

✓ NSF check: Dr. Accounts Receivable, $468

SHOW
ME HOW

PREPARE JOURNAL ENTRIES FOR BANK RECONCILIATION Based on the following bank reconciliation, prepare the journal entries:

Carmen Lui Associates Bank Reconciliation July 31, 20 - -			
Bank statement balance, July 31			$3 3 1 6 80
Add deposits in transit	$ 3 0 0 00		
	1 1 8 00	4 1 8 00	
		$3 7 3 4 80	
Deduct outstanding checks:			
No. 296	$ 4 2 4 20		
No. 299	2 2 60		
No. 301	3 9 90	4 8 6 70	
Adjusted bank balance		$3 2 4 8 10	
Book balance, July 31		$3 7 0 0 50	
Add error on Check No. 291*		2 7 60	
		$3 7 2 8 10	
Deduct: NSF check	$ 4 6 8 00		
Bank service charge	1 2 00	4 8 0 00	
Adjusted book balance		$3 2 4 8 10	
*Accounts Payable was debited in original entry.			

E 7-6A   (LO3)

✓ Replenishment: Cr. Cash, $228.10

SHOW
ME HOW

PETTY CASH JOURNAL ENTRIES Based on the following petty cash information, prepare (a) the journal entry to establish a petty cash fund, and (b) the journal entry to replenish the petty cash fund.

On January 1, 20--, a check was written in the amount of $300 to establish a petty cash fund. During January, the following vouchers were written for cash removed from the petty cash drawer:

Voucher No.	Account Debited	Amount
1	Phone Expense	$21.20
2	Automobile Expense	39.60
3	James Lucas, Drawing	85.00
4	Postage Expense	15.30
5	Charitable Contributions Expense	20.00
6	Miscellaneous Expense	47.00

E 7-7A   (LO4)

✓ Apr. 16: Cr. Cash Short and Over, $1.75

SHOW
ME HOW

CASH SHORT AND OVER ENTRIES Based on the following information, prepare the weekly entries for cash receipts from service fees and cash short and over. A change fund of $100 is maintained.

Date	Change Fund	Cash Register Receipt Amount	Actual Cash Counted
Apr. 2	$100	$268.50	$366.50
9	100	237.75	333.50
16	100	309.25	411.00
23	100	226.50	324.00
30	100	318.00	422.00

SERIES A PROBLEMS

P 7-8A   (LO2)

✓ Adjusted book balance: $5,023

SHOW
ME HOW

BANK RECONCILIATION AND RELATED JOURNAL ENTRIES The book balance in the checking account of Johnson Enterprises as of October 31 is $5,718. The bank statement shows an ending balance of $5,217. The following information is discovered by (1) comparing last month's deposits in transit and outstanding checks with this month's bank statement, (2) comparing deposits and checks written per books and per bank in the current month, and (3) noting service charges and other debit and credit memos shown on the bank statement.

Deposits in transit:	10/29	$210.00
	10/30	406.00
Outstanding checks:	No. 1635	56.40
	No. 1639	175.00
	No. 1641	135.50
	No. 1653	443.10
Unrecorded ATM withdrawal:*		200.00
Bank service charge:		37.00
NSF check:		476.00

Error on Check No. 1624   Checkbook shows it was for $75, but it was actually written for $57. Accounts Payable was debited.

*Funds were withdrawn by Enoch Johnson for personal use.

(continued)

1. Prepare a bank reconciliation as of October 31, 20--.

2. Prepare the required journal entries.

P 7-9A   (LO2)

✓ Adjusted bank balance: $3,069.95

BANK RECONCILIATION AND RELATED JOURNAL ENTRIES The book balance in the checking account of Lyle's Salon as of November 30 is $3,282.95. The bank statement shows an ending balance of $2,127. By examining last month's bank reconciliation, comparing the deposits and checks written per books and per bank in November, and noting the service charges and other debit and credit memos shown on the bank statement, the following were found:

(a) An ATM withdrawal of $150 on November 18 by Lyle for personal use was not recorded on the books.

(b) A bank debit memo issued for an NSF check from a customer of $19.50.

(c) A bank credit memo issued for interest of $19 earned during the month.

(d) On November 30, a deposit of $1,177 was made, which is not shown on the bank statement.

(e) A bank debit memo issued for $17.50 for bank service charges.

(f) Checks No. 549, 561, and 562 for the amounts of $185, $21, and $9.40, respectively, were written during November but have not yet been received by the bank.

(g) The reconciliation from the previous month showed outstanding checks totaling $271.95. One of those checks, No. 471 for $18.65, has not yet been received by the bank.

(h) Check No. 523 written to a creditor in the amount of $372.90 was recorded in the books as $327.90.

REQUIRED

1. Prepare a bank reconciliation as of November 30.

2. Prepare the required journal entries.

P 7-10A   (LO3)

✓ Replenishment: Cr. Cash, $149

PETTY CASH RECORD AND JOURNAL ENTRIES On May 1, a petty cash fund was established for $150. The following vouchers were issued during May:

Date	Voucher No.	Purpose	Amount
May 1	1	postage due	$ 3.50
3	2	office supplies	11.00
5	3	auto repair (miscellaneous)	43.00
7	4	drawing (Joy Adams)	25.00
11	5	donation (Red Cross)	10.00
15	6	travel expenses	28.00
22	7	postage stamps	3.50
26	8	phone call	5.00
30	9	donation (Boy Scouts)	20.00

REQUIRED

1. Prepare the journal entry to establish the petty cash fund.

2. Record the vouchers in the petty cash record. Total and rule the petty cash record.

3. Prepare the journal entry to replenish the petty cash fund. Make the appropriate entry in the petty cash record.

P 7-11A   (LO4)

✓ July 23: Dr. Cash Short and Over, $2.50

CASH SHORT AND OVER ENTRIES Listed below are the weekly cash register tape amounts for service fees and the related cash counts during the month of July. A change fund of $100 is maintained.

Date	Change Fund	Cash Register Receipt Amount	Actual Cash Counted
July 2	$100	$289.50	$387.00
9	100	311.50	411.50
16	100	306.00	408.50
23	100	317.50	415.00
30	100	296.00	399.50

REQUIRED

1. Prepare the journal entries to record the cash service fees and cash short and over for each of the five weeks.
2. Post to the cash short and over account (use Account No. 516).
3. Determine the ending balance of the cash short and over account. Does it represent an expense or revenue?

SERIES B EXERCISES

E 7-1B   (LO1)

CHECKING ACCOUNT TERMS Match the following words with their definitions:

1. Banking number used to identify checks for deposit tickets
2. A card filled out to open a checking account
3. A machine from which withdrawals can be taken or deposits made to accounts
4. A place where relevant information is recorded about a check
5. A set of procedures designed to ensure proper accounting for transactions
6. A statement of account issued to each depositor once a month
7. A detailed listing of items being deposited to an account

a. bank statement
b. deposit ticket
c. signature card
d. internal control
e. check stub
f. ATM
g. ABA number

E 7-2B   (LO1)

✓ Total deposit: $645

PREPARE DEPOSIT TICKET Based on the following information, prepare a deposit ticket:

Date:		November 15, 20--	
Currency:			$283
Coin:			19
Checks:	No. 3-22		201
	No. 19-366		114
	No. 3-2		28

(continued)

E 7-3B   (LO1)

PREPARE CHECK AND STUB Based on the following information, prepare a check and stub:

Date:	November 15, 20--
Balance brought forward:	$3,181
Deposit:	(from Exercise 7-2B)
Check to:	R. J. Smith Co.
Amount:	$120
For:	Payment on account
Signature:	Sign your name

E 7-4B   (LO2)

BANK RECONCILIATION PROCEDURES In a format similar to the following, indicate whether the action at the left will result in an addition to (+) or subtraction from (−) the ending bank balance or the ending checkbook balance.

	Ending Bank Balance	Ending Checkbook Balance
1. Service fee of $12 charged by bank	_____	_____
2. Outstanding checks	_____	_____
3. Error in checkbook: check recorded as $36 was actually for $28	_____	_____
4. NSF check deposited earlier	_____	_____
5. Bank credit memo advising a note was collected for us	_____	_____
6. Deposits in transit to the bank	_____	_____
7. Error in checkbook: check recorded as $182 was actually for $218	_____	_____

E 7-5B   (LO2)

✓ NSF check: Dr. Accounts Receivable, $66

SHOW
ME HOW

PREPARE JOURNAL ENTRIES FOR BANK RECONCILIATION Based on the following bank reconciliation, prepare the journal entries:

Ruggero Celini Associates Bank Reconciliation July 31, 20 --									
Bank statement balance, July 31							$1	7 8 4	00
Add deposits in transit	$ 4	1 8	50						
	1	0 0	50		5	1 9	00		
					$2	3 0 3	00		
Deduct outstanding checks:									
No. 185	$ 2	0 6	50						
No. 203	3	1 7	40						
No. 210		5 6	10		5	8 0	00		
Adjusted bank balance					$1	7 2 3	00		
Book balance, July 31					$1	7 9 2	00		
Add: Error on Check No. 191*		1 0	00						
Interest earned		2	00			1 2	00		
					$1	8 0 4	00		
Deduct: NSF check	$	6 6	00						
Bank service charge		1 5	00			8 1	00		
Adjusted book balance					$1	7 2 3	00		
*Accounts Payable was debited in original entry.									

E 7-6B   (LO3)

✓ Replenishment: Cr. Cash, $190

SHOW
ME HOW

PETTY CASH JOURNAL ENTRIES Based on the following petty cash information, prepare (a) the journal entry to establish a petty cash fund, and (b) the journal entry to replenish the petty cash fund.

On October 1, 20--, a check was written in the amount of $200 to establish a petty cash fund. During October, the following vouchers were written for cash taken from the petty cash drawer:

Voucher No.	Account Debited	Amount
1	Postage Expense	$13
2	Miscellaneous Expense	17
3	John Flanagan, Drawing	45
4	Phone Expense	36
5	Charitable Contributions Expense	50
6	Automobile Expense	29

E 7-7B   (LO4)

✓ June 15: Dr. Cash Short and Over, $2

SHOW
ME HOW

CASH SHORT AND OVER ENTRIES Based on the following information, prepare the weekly entries for cash receipts from service fees and cash short and over. A change fund of $100 is maintained.

Date	Change Fund	Cash Register Receipt Amount	Actual Cash Counted
June 1	$100	$330.00	$433.00
8	100	297.00	400.00
15	100	233.00	331.00
22	100	302.00	396.50
29	100	316.00	412.00

SERIES B PROBLEMS

P 7-8B   (LO2)

✓ Adjusted book balance: $2,674

SHOW
ME HOW

BANK RECONCILIATION AND RELATED JOURNAL ENTRIES The book balance in the checking account of Kyri Enterprises as of November 30 is $2,964. The bank statement shows an ending balance of $2,525. The following information is discovered by (1) comparing last month's deposits in transit and outstanding checks with this month's bank statement, (2) comparing deposits and checks written per books and per bank in the current month, and (3) noting service charges and other debit and credit memos shown on the bank statement.

Deposits in transit:	11/29	$125
	11/30	200
Outstanding checks:	No. 322	17
	No. 324	105
	No. 327	54
Unrecorded ATM withdrawal:*		100
Bank service charge:		25
NSF check:		185

Error on Check No. 321   Checkbook shows it was for $64, but it was actually written for $44. Accounts Payable was debited.

*Funds were withdrawn by Susan Kyri for personal use.

(continued)

P 7-9B   (LO2)

✓ Adjusted bank balance: $4,518.70

BANK RECONCILIATION AND RELATED JOURNAL ENTRIES The book balance in the checking account of Tori's Health Center as of April 30 is $4,690.30. The bank statement shows an ending balance of $3,275.60. By examining last month's bank reconciliation, comparing the deposits and checks written per books and per bank in April, and noting the service charges and other debit and credit memos shown on the bank statement, the following were found:

(a) An ATM withdrawal of $200 on April 20 by Tori for personal use was not recorded on the books.

(b) A bank debit memo issued for an NSF check from a customer of $29.10.

(c) A bank credit memo issued for interest of $28 earned during the month.

(d) On April 30, a deposit of $1,592 was made, which is not shown on the bank statement.

(e) A bank debit memo issued for $24.50 for bank service charges.

(f) Checks No. 481, 493, and 494 for the amounts of $215, $71, and $24.30, respectively, were written during April but have not yet been received by the bank.

(g) The reconciliation from the previous month showed outstanding checks totaling $418.25. One of these checks, No. 397 for $38.60, has not yet been received by the bank.

(h) Check No. 422 written to a creditor in the amount of $217.90 was recorded in the books as $271.90.

REQUIRED

1. Prepare a bank reconciliation as of April 30.

2. Prepare the required journal entries.

P 7-10B   (LO3)

✓ Replenishment: Cr. Cash, $87

PETTY CASH RECORD AND JOURNAL ENTRIES On July 1, a petty cash fund was established for $100. The following vouchers were issued during July:

Date	Voucher No.	Purpose	Amount
July 1	1	office supplies	$ 3.00
3	2	donation (Goodwill)	15.00
5	3	travel expenses	5.00
7	4	postage due	2.00
8	5	office supplies	4.00
11	6	postage due	3.50
15	7	phone call	5.00
21	8	travel expenses	11.00
25	9	withdrawal by owner (L. Ortiz)	20.00
26	10	copier repair (miscellaneous)	18.50

REQUIRED

1. Prepare the journal entry to establish the petty cash fund.

2. Record the vouchers in the petty cash record. Total and rule the petty cash record.

3. Prepare the journal entry to replenish the petty cash fund. Make the appropriate entry in the petty cash record.

P 7-11B   (LO4)

✓ Aug. 8: Dr. Cash Short and Over, $3.50

CASH SHORT AND OVER ENTRIES Listed below are the weekly cash register tape amounts for service fees and the related cash counts during the month of July. A change fund of $200 is maintained.

Date	Change Fund	Cash Register Receipt Amount	Actual Cash Counted
Aug. 1	$200	$292.50	$495.00
8	200	305.00	501.50
15	200	286.00	486.00
22	200	330.25	532.75
29	200	299.20	495.00

REQUIRED

1. Prepare the journal entries to record the cash service fees and cash short and over for each of the five weeks.

2. Post to the cash short and over account (use Account No. 516).

3. Determine the ending balance of the cash short and over account. Does it represent an expense or revenue?

Check List
- ✓ Check List
- ☐ Managing
- ☐ Planning
- ☐ Drafting
- ☐ Break
- ☐ Revising
- ☐ Managing

MANAGING YOUR WRITING

The current month's bank statement for your account arrives in the mail. In reviewing the statement, you notice a deposit listed for $400 that you did not make. It has been credited in error to your account.

Discuss whether you have an ethical or legal obligation to inform the bank of the error. What action should you take?

ETHICS CASE

Ben Thomas works as a teller for First National Bank. When he arrived at work on Friday, the branch manager, Frank Mills, asked him to get his cash drawer out early because the head teller, Naomi Ray, was conducting a surprise cash count for all the tellers. Surprise cash counts are usually done four or five times a year by the branch manager or the head teller and once or twice a year by internal auditors. Ben's drawer was $100 short and his reconciliation tape showed that he was in balance on Thursday night. Naomi asked Ben for an explanation, and Ben immediately took $100 out of his pocket and handed it to her. He went on to explain he needed the cash to buy prescriptions for his son and pay for groceries and intended to put the $100 back in his cash drawer on Monday, which was pay day. He also told Naomi that this was the first time he had ever "borrowed" money from his cash drawer and that he would never do it again.

1. What are the ethical considerations in this case from both Ben's and Naomi's perspectives?

2. What options does Naomi have to address this problem?

3. Assume Naomi chooses to inform the branch manager. Write a short incident report describing the findings.

4. In small groups, come up with as many ideas as possible on how to safeguard cash on hand in a bank (petty cash, teller drawer cash, and vault cash) from employee theft and mismanagement.

MASTERY PROBLEM

✓ Adjusted bank balance: $4,324.05

Turner Excavation maintains a checking account and has decided to open a petty cash fund. The following petty cash fund transactions occurred during July:

July 2   Established a petty cash fund by issuing Check No. 301 for $100.

   5   Paid $25 from the petty cash fund for postage. Voucher No. 1.

   7   Paid $30 from the petty cash fund for delivery of flowers (Miscellaneous Expense). Voucher No. 2.

   8   Paid $20 from the petty cash fund to repair a tire on the company truck. Voucher No. 3.

   12   Paid $22 from the petty cash fund for a newspaper advertisement. Voucher No. 4.

   13   Issued Check No. 303 to replenish the petty cash fund. (Total and rule the petty cash payments record. Record the balance and the amount needed to replenish the fund in the Description column of the petty cash payments record.)

   20   Paid $26 from the petty cash fund to reimburse an employee for expenses incurred to repair the company truck. Voucher No. 5.

   24   Paid $12.50 from the petty cash fund for phone calls made from a phone booth. Voucher No. 6.

   28   Paid $25 from the petty cash fund as a contribution to the YMCA. Voucher No. 7.

   31   Issued Check No. 308 to replenish the petty cash fund. (Total and rule the petty cash payments record. Record the balance and the amount needed to replenish the fund in the Description column of the petty cash payments record.)

The following additional transactions occurred during July:

July 5   Issued Check No. 302 to pay office rent, $650.

   15   Issued Check No. 304 for office equipment, $525.

   17   Issued Check No. 305 for the purchase of supplies, $133.

   18   Issued Check No. 306 to pay attorney fees, $1,000.

   30   Issued Check No. 307 to pay newspaper for an advertisement, $200.20.

REQUIRED

1. Record the petty cash transactions in a petty cash payments record.

2. Make all required general journal entries for the cash transactions. (*Note:* The petty cash fund was established and replenished twice during July.)

3. The bank statement on page 265 was received in the mail. Deposits were made on July 6 for $3,500 and on July 29 for $2,350. The checkbook balance on July 31 is $4,331.55. Notice the discrepancy in Check No. 302 that cleared the bank for $655. This check was written on July 5 for rent expense, but was incorrectly entered on the check stub and in the journal as $650. Prepare a bank reconciliation and make any necessary journal entries as of July 31.

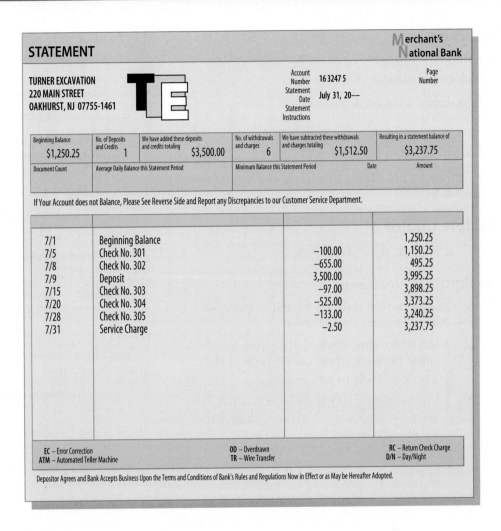

STATEMENT						Merchant's National Bank

TURNER EXCAVATION
220 MAIN STREET
OAKHURST, NJ 07755-1461

		Account Number	16 3247 5		Page Number

Statement Date   July 31, 20—-

Statement Instructions

Beginning Balance	No. of Deposits and Credits	We have added these deposits and credits totaling	No. of withdrawals and charges	We have subtracted these withdrawals and charges totaling	Resulting in a statement balance of
$1,250.25	1	$3,500.00	6	$1,512.50	$3,237.75

Document Count	Average Daily Balance this Statement Period	Minimum Balance this Statement Period	Date	Amount

If Your Account does not Balance, Please See Reverse Side and Report any Discrepancies to our Customer Service Department.

7/1	Beginning Balance		1,250.25
7/5	Check No. 301	−100.00	1,150.25
7/8	Check No. 302	−655.00	495.25
7/9	Deposit	3,500.00	3,995.25
7/15	Check No. 303	−97.00	3,898.25
7/20	Check No. 304	−525.00	3,373.25
7/28	Check No. 305	−133.00	3,240.25
7/31	Service Charge	−2.50	3,237.75

EC – Error Correction
ATM – Automated Teller Machine

OD – Overdrawn
TR – Wire Transfer

RC – Return Check Charge
D/N – Day/Night

Depositor Agrees and Bank Accepts Business Upon the Terms and Conditions of Bank's Rules and Regulations Now in Effect or as May be Hereafter Adopted.

CHALLENGE PROBLEM

This problem challenges you to apply your cumulative accounting knowledge to move a step beyond the material in the chapter.

✓ 2. Item 4: Dr. Depositor Accounts, $350

Susan Panera is preparing the June 30 bank reconciliation for Panera Bakery. She discovers the following items that explain the difference between the cash balance on her books and the balance as reported by Lawrence Bank:

1. An ATM withdrawal of $200 for personal use was not recorded by Susan.

2. A deposit of $850 was recorded by Susan but has not been received by Lawrence Bank as of June 30.

3. A check written in payment on account to Jayhawk Supply for $340 was recorded by Susan as $430 and by Lawrence Bank as $530.

4. An ATM deposit of $350 was recorded twice by Lawrence Bank.

5. An electronic funds transfer of $260 to Sunflower Mills as a payment on account was not recorded by Susan.

6. Checks No. 103 for $235 and No. 110 for $127 had not cleared Lawrence Bank as of June 30.

REQUIRED

1. Prepare the journal entries required to correct Panera Bakery's books as of June 30.

2. Prepare the journal entries required to correct Lawrence Bank's books as of June 30.

Answers to Self-Study Test Questions

True/False

1. F (primary purpose is to reconcile book balance with bank balance)
2. F (deducted from book balance)
3. T
4. F (deducted from book balance)
5. F (entries are not posted from petty cash record to general ledger)

Multiple Choice

1. c   2. b   3. d   4. b   5. a

Checkpoint Exercises

1. __3__ a. A document ordering a bank to pay cash from a depositor's account.

   __5__ b. An endorsement where the payee simply signs the back of the check, making the check payable to any bearer.

   __2__ c. Automated teller machine—a machine used by depositors to make withdrawals or deposits at any time.

   __4__ d. A statement of account issued by a bank to each depositor once a month.

   __1__ e. A form showing a detailed listing of items being deposited.

2. __c__ 1. Interest earned on checking account balance

   __d__ 2. Error in checkbook whereby a check for $82 was entered in the checkbook as $28

   __a__ 3. Deposit in transit

   __b__ 4. Outstanding checks

3. Phone Expense   23.50
   Automobile Expense   49.10
   H. Appy, Drawing   50.00
      Cash   122.60
      Replenished petty cash fund

4. Cash   870.00
   Cash Short and Over   6.00
      Service Fees   876.00
      Recorded service fees and cash shortage

Chapter 7 Appendix
Internal Controls

LEARNING OBJECTIVES

In Chapter 7, we introduced the concept of internal control and provided some examples of good internal control over cash transactions. Here, we examine internal control in greater depth.

We do the following:

1. Explain why internal control has achieved greater importance today.
2. Identify the key components of internal control.
3. Give examples of internal control over cash receipts.
4. Describe internal control of cash payments using a voucher system.

Careful study of this appendix should enable you to:

LO1 Explain the importance of internal control.

LO2 Define internal control and describe its key components.

LO3 Describe selected internal controls over cash receipts.

LO4 Describe selected internal controls over cash payments and the use of a voucher system.

IMPORTANCE OF INTERNAL CONTROL

LO1 Explain the importance of internal control.

To be successful, management must have adequate control of the operations of the business. For example, the records of business activities must be reliable and timely, so that management has the information it needs to take necessary actions. The assets of the business must be known and protected. Employees must follow the rules and procedures defined by management. Accurate information must be available to report to owners, lenders, and regulatory bodies, such as the IRS. Without good internal control, it simply would not be possible to effectively and efficiently run a business.

The importance of strong internal control for managing a business has been known for years. But in 2002, the importance of internal control was raised to a whole new level. In July 2002, Congress passed the Sarbanes-Oxley Act (SOX). SOX applies to all **publicly held companies**—companies whose stock is traded on the major stock exchanges. Section 404 of SOX requires these companies to report annually on the effectiveness of internal control over financial reporting. For decades, these corporations have been required to provide audited financial statements. Now, they must also report on the quality of their internal control system. Figure 7A-1 provides an example of management's Section 404 report for Microsoft.

One of the interesting effects of SOX is how widely its rules are being felt. Officially, SOX applies to all publicly held companies and their external auditors. But SOX is causing many other companies and managements to look closely at the quality of their internal controls. The logic is simple: if internal controls are so important for publicly held companies, they probably deserve attention in other companies as well. Clearly, internal controls are a hot topic today.

FIGURE 7A-1 Section 404 Internal Control Report

REPORT OF MANAGEMENT ON INTERNAL CONTROL OVER FINANCIAL REPORTING

Our management [of Microsoft] is responsible for establishing and maintaining adequate internal control over financial reporting for the company. Internal control over financial reporting is a process to provide reasonable assurance regarding the reliability of our financial reporting for external purposes in accordance with accounting principles generally accepted in the United States of America. Internal control over financial reporting includes maintaining records that in reasonable detail accurately and fairly reflect our transactions; providing reasonable assurance that transactions are recorded as necessary for preparation of our financial statements; providing reasonable assurance that receipts and expenditures of company assets are made in accordance with management authorization; and providing reasonable assurance that unauthorized acquisition, use, or disposition of company assets that could have a material effect on our financial statements would be prevented or detected on a timely basis. Because of its inherent limitations, internal control over financial reporting is not intended to provide absolute assurance that a misstatement of our financial statements would be prevented or detected.

Management conducted an evaluation of the effectiveness of our internal control over financial reporting based on the framework in Internal Control—Integrated Framework issued by the Committee of Sponsoring Organizations (2013) of the Treadway Commission. Our assessment of, and conclusion on, the effectiveness of internal control over financial reporting did not include the internal controls of Nokia Corporation's Devices and Services business, acquired on April 25, 2014, which is included in our 2014 consolidated financial statements and represented approximately 9% of our total assets as of June 30, 2014, and 2% of our total revenues for the year ended June 30, 2014. Based on this evaluation, management concluded that the company's internal control over financial reporting was effective as of June 30, 2014. There were no changes in our internal control over financial reporting during the quarter ended June 30, 2014 that have materially affected, or are reasonably likely to materially affect, our internal control over financial reporting. Deloitte & Touche LLP has audited our internal control over financial reporting as of June 30, 2014; their report follows.

KEY COMPONENTS OF INTERNAL CONTROL

LO2 Define internal control and describe its key components.

Internal control is really important. So what exactly do we mean by internal control? Both the concept and attempts to define it have existed for many years. For our purposes, the following is a good definition:

> Internal control is a system developed by a company to provide reasonable assurance of achieving (1) effective and efficient operations, (2) reliable financial reporting, and (3) compliance with laws and regulations.

Several internal control frameworks have been developed that are consistent with this definition. The most widely accepted framework in the United States contains the following five components:

- Control environment
- Risk assessment
- Control activities
- Information and communication system
- Monitoring processes

Control Environment

The control environment is the policies, procedures, and attitudes of the top management and owners of the business. It is often referred to as the "tone at the top." It includes the organization structure, management's philosophy and operating style, integrity and ethical values, and commitment to competent, trustworthy employees. The control environment provides the foundation for all other components of internal control.

Risk Assessment

Risk assessment is management's process for identifying, analyzing, and responding to its business risks. All businesses face various and changing risks from both external and internal sources. These risks include error and fraud. As part of the risk assessment component of internal control, management must deal with these risks. For example, if a business sells products like computers that are affected by rapid technology changes, its marketing and inventory plans should carefully guard against obsolete inventory. If a business has high employee turnover, its employee screening and training programs should be very thorough and up to date. If a business is growing rapidly, it should regularly review its internal controls to see that they fit the size and activities of the business.

Control Activities

Control activities are the policies and procedures established to help management meet its control objectives. Control activities can be classified in various ways. Four types of control activities are particularly important for our purposes.

1. Segregation of duties
2. Authorization procedures and related responsibilities
3. Adequate documents and records
4. Protection of assets and records

   Segregation of duties means that:

   1. Different employees should be responsible for different parts of a transaction; and
   2. Employees who account for transactions should not also have custody of the assets.

For example, one employee should be responsible for ordering goods and another employee should be responsible for issuing the check to pay for them. One employee should be responsible for recording the purchase of goods and another employee should be responsible for receiving and placing the goods in inventory. This segregation of duties provides a built-in check by one employee on another. One employee cannot obtain goods for personal use without being caught by another employee.

In computerized systems, programs and data files often combine the duties of several employees. For example, programs can order goods automatically at a preset level from approved vendors, and payments then can be made based on an electronic billing. This requires a different segregation of duties. Three functions must be segregated: (1) system design and programming, (2) system operations, and (3) data file and program storage.

Authorization procedures and related responsibilities means that every business activity should be properly authorized. In addition, it should be possible to identify who is responsible for every activity that has occurred. For example, to acquire new equipment, a signed document should authorize the purchase. After the purchase is made, this signed document shows who is responsible for the action.

In computerized systems, as noted above, the combination of processing programs and data files can initiate transactions. Therefore, special authorization procedures are needed. Once a program is operating, no changes should be allowed in that program without authorization. Similarly, no changes should be allowed in a data file without authorization. It is essential to protect both the programs and data files from unauthorized access.

Adequate documents and records means that accounting documents and records should be used so that all business transactions are recorded. For example, every purchase that occurs should be supported by a document. These documents should be:

- prenumbered,
- used in sequence, and
- subsequently accounted for.

In this way, the business can be sure that it has made a record of each transaction.

One of the benefits of a computerized system is that the programs can automatically account for the sequence of transactions or documents. Numbers and sequences of sales, purchases, employees for payroll, and payments can be accounted for. If there is any break in the proper numbering sequence, an error message is created.

A computerized system also requires additional documentation. For example, complete documentation is needed of all code, development, and testing of programs before they are put in operation.

Protection of assets and records means that assets and records should be physically and logically protected. For assets, this generally means physical protection. Some examples are vaults for cash, securities, and precious gems, or secure storage rooms for inventory. For records, this can mean storing journals, ledgers, and key documents in physically secure locations. In computerized systems, both physical and logical protection are needed. For example, an online retailer needs assurance that transactions are valid and accurate, customer credit card information is protected, and its website is secure. Passwords are a common form of logical protection of data files and processing programs.

Information and Communication System

The information and communication system is the set of procedures, processes, and records used to initiate, process, record, and report the business's transactions. In addition, the system accounts for the related assets and liabilities. Typically, the system has several subcomponents for different business processes, such as:

- sales,
- cash receipts,
- purchases, and
- cash payments.

The journals and ledgers we learned to use in the previous chapters would be part of an information and communication system.

A computerized system provides great opportunities in this area of internal control. Because of the power of the computer, data files can be compared across departments or other business units to identify problem areas. Data can be screened to ensure their quality, and input from customers and suppliers can be gathered and analyzed.

Monitoring Processes

Monitoring processes are the methods used by management to determine that controls are operating properly, and that the controls are modified in response to changes in assessed risks. Figure 7A-2 provides some examples of such processes. Monitoring can be part of the ongoing activities of the business or a separate process. One ongoing activity could be comparisons of financial reports with expectations. If financial reports differ from expectations, it could indicate internal control failures. Follow-up on customer complaints regarding account balances might also uncover internal control weaknesses. The most common form of separate process is the work of the internal audit department. Internal auditors evaluate the design of the internal control system in light of the business risks. They also perform specific tests to determine whether internal controls are operating properly. If a business is not large enough to have an internal audit department, these responsibilities must be assumed by top management.

Computers also can help with the monitoring process. Large volumes of data can be analyzed at very low cost. For example, an entire data file of payment transactions can be examined to identify large amounts, duplicates, and unknown suppliers.

FIGURE 7A-2   Sample Monitoring Processes

- Comparison of results with expectations
- Review of customer correspondence
- Internal audit

INTERNAL CONTROLS OVER CASH RECEIPTS

LO3 **Describe selected internal controls over cash receipts.**

The main purposes of internal controls over cash receipts are to make sure that

- all cash received by the business is recorded in the accounts, and
- the cash is promptly deposited in the business bank account.

The exact form of some of these controls will vary depending on whether the cash is received directly from customers for sales, or is received by mail as a collection on account. Some of the key internal controls are shown in Figure 7A-3 and described in the following paragraphs.

FIGURE 7A-3   Sample Controls over Cash Receipts

Do these three amounts agree?

Cash receipts per register record	=	Cash receipts per register drawer	=	Cash receipts per bank deposit

Do these two amounts agree?

Cash receipts per remittance list	=	Cash receipts per bank deposit

Do transactions and balances per books and bank agree?

Monthly bank reconciliation

If cash is received directly from customers, the use of a cash register or terminal with a printed receipt is essential. Only authorized employees should be allowed to operate the register. The register should generate an internal record of all transactions entered, including a total of cash receipts. This amount should be reconciled with the actual cash (and checks) in the register drawer. Any differences greater than a small amount to allow for errors in making change should be investigated. All cash receipts should be deposited daily in the business bank account. The total deposited and the total cash receipts according to the register should be reconciled and any differences investigated.

If cash is received as collections on account, the mail room should be supervised and employees who handle the cash (checks) should have no access to the accounting records. One reason for separating the handling of cash from the accounting records is to prevent lapping. **Lapping** means stealing cash received on account from one customer and hiding the theft by applying the cash received on account from another customer to the first customer's account. For example, assume customer A sends a check for $500 as a payment on account and that the employee keeps the $500 for him/herself. This causes customer A's account to be in error by $500. So when customer B makes a $500 payment on account, the employee applies this cash receipt to customer A's account. The dishonest employee must continue lapping the accounts receivable in this manner to continue to conceal the theft.

When the mail is opened, a remittance list should be prepared showing all amounts received and from whom they are received. Checks should be immediately endorsed "For deposit" to the business bank account.

The remittance list is sent to the accounting department for use in recording the collections in the journal and ledgers. The cash is sent to the cash receipts department to deposit in the business bank account. The total of the remittance list and the amount of the bank deposit should be independently verified and any differences investigated.

An additional internal control common to both systems described above is the independent monthly preparation of a bank reconciliation. Procedures for preparing the bank reconciliation are described in Chapter 7. The cash receipts, cash payments, and beginning and ending balances per bank and per books must be reconciled. The reconciliation should be prepared by employees who have no access to cash. Any differences should be investigated.

Many businesses have multiple bank accounts and transfer cash among them. When there are multiple bank accounts, it is possible to overstate the cash balance by engaging in kiting. **Kiting** consists of recording a transfer of cash *into* one bank account in the current period, but not recording the transfer *out of* another bank account until the following period. For example, assume a $1,000 check is written on bank account A on June 30, but not recorded as a cash payment until July 1. This check is deposited in bank account B and recorded as a cash receipt on June 30. By recording the transaction in this manner, the cash balance in both bank accounts includes the $1,000 at June 30. The total cash balance is thus overstated by $1,000 on June 30.

One of the reasons internal controls over cash are so important is that they help businesses manage their cash resources. Naturally, it is important to plan to have sufficient cash to meet current obligations. But it is also important not to allow too much cash to lie idle. Management should carefully monitor and plan for its cash needs. Strong internal controls help with this process.

INTERNAL CONTROLS OVER CASH PAYMENTS

LO4 Describe selected internal controls over cash payments and the use of a voucher system.

The main purpose of internal controls over cash payments is to make sure cash is paid only for goods and services received by the business, consistent with its best interests. To achieve this objective, controls are needed from the beginning of the process of acquiring goods and services through the payment of cash for those goods and services. An effective way to do so is with a voucher system.

Voucher System

Three of the four control activities described above can be combined to control cash payments by using a **voucher system**. A voucher system is a control technique that requires every acquisition and subsequent payment to be supported by an approved voucher. A **voucher** is a document which shows that an acquisition is proper and that payment is authorized.

The Purchasing Process

Figure 7A-4 is a simplified illustration of how the purchasing portion of a voucher system operates. An authorized person or department prepares a purchase requisition to indicate the need for goods. The purchasing department reviews and approves the purchase requisition and prepares a purchase order to send to the supplier. When the goods are received, a receiving report is prepared. A copy of each of these documents is sent to the vouchers payable section in the accounting department.

When the purchase invoice arrives, it is compared with the purchase requisition, purchase order, and receiving report. If the purchase invoice is

- for the goods ordered (purchase requisition and purchase order),
- at the correct price (purchase order),
- and for the correct quantity (receiving report),

then a voucher like the one in Figure 7A-5 on page 274 is prepared. This is the first key control provided by the voucher system. If any aspect of the purchase is improper, it will be caught when the voucher is prepared.

FIGURE 7A-4   Voucher System—Purchasing Process

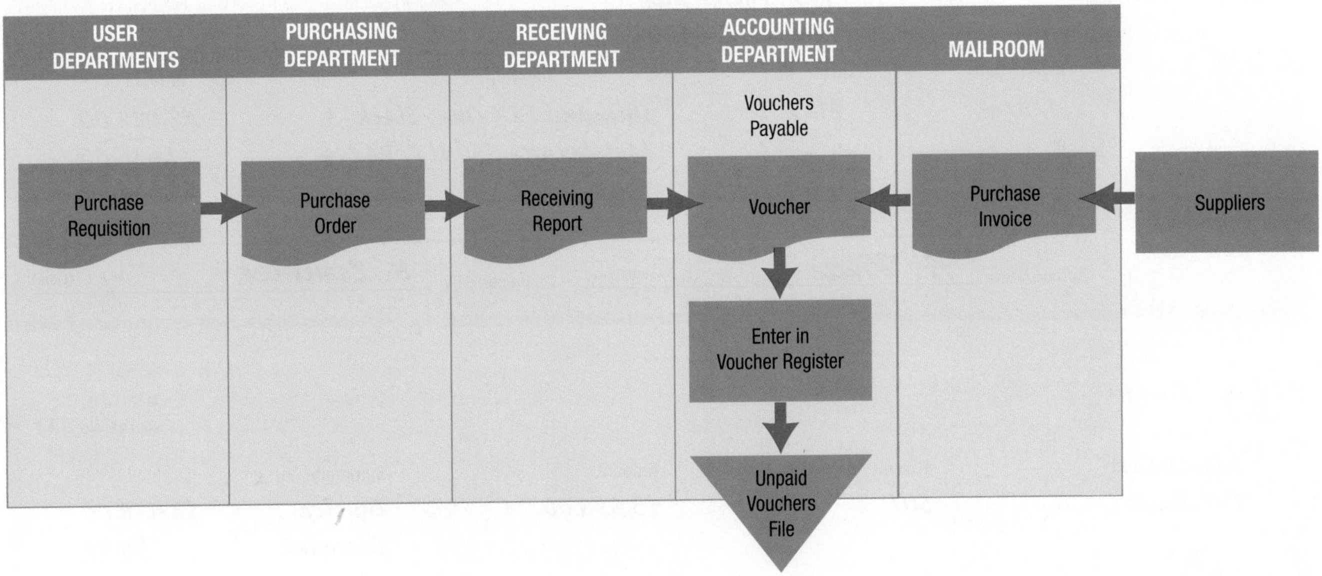

The front of the voucher usually shows the voucher number, date, supplier, and what was purchased. The back indicates the accounts to be debited and the payment date, check number, and amount.

After the voucher is prepared and approved, it is entered in a special journal called a **voucher register**. A voucher register is used to record purchases of all types of assets and services.

After the voucher is entered in the voucher register, the voucher and supporting documents (purchase requisition, purchase order, receiving report, and purchase invoice) are stapled together. This "voucher packet" is then filed in an **unpaid vouchers file**, normally by due date. Alternatively, vouchers can be filed by supplier name. Filing by due date is preferred because this helps management plan for cash needs. It also helps ensure that vouchers are paid on the due date and cash discounts are taken.

The completed voucher provides the basis for paying the supplier's invoice on the due date. This is the second key control provided by the voucher system. No payment may be made without an approved voucher.

Notice how three of the four control activities that are part of an internal control system can be seen in this system.

- *Duties are segregated* because different employees order, receive, and record the purchases.
- *Authorization* is required to order the goods and to prepare the voucher.
- The *documents and records* include purchase requisitions, purchase orders, receiving reports, and vouchers that are prenumbered and accounted for. This means that every recorded purchase is supported by the following five documents:
  1. Voucher
  2. Purchase invoice

FIGURE 7A-5 Voucher

		Voucher No. **111**

Sunflower **CYCLE**
804 Massachusetts St., Lawrence, KS 66044

Date 4/11/-- Terms: 1/15/, n/30 Due: 4/24/--
To: King Creek Corp.
1545 Power Rd.
Mesa, AZ 85206

Invoice Date	Invoice No.	Description	Amount
4/9/--	4123	Shimano FSX One, Black-3	$2,022.00
		Motobecane 550 HT, Red-4	1,636.00
			$3,658.00

Authorization **A. White** (Supervisor) Prepared By **B. Zimmer** (Clerk)

Voucher No. **111**

Account Debited	Account No.	Amount	Summary	
Purchases	501	$3,658.00	Invoice	$3,658.00
			Discount	36.58
			Net	$3,621.42

Payment Date 4/24/-- Check No. 331 Amount $3,621.42

Approved Distribution **J. G.** Payment

Back

3. Receiving report
4. Purchase order
5. Purchase requisition

This provides management with strong assurance that purchasing activities are properly controlled.

The Payment Process

Figure 7A-6 is a simplified illustration of the payment process when a voucher system is used. On the due date, the voucher is pulled from the unpaid vouchers file. The voucher is given to the person responsible for preparing and signing checks (the cashier in this illustration). The cashier reviews each voucher and supporting documents to see that the expenditure is proper. The cashier then prepares and signs the check and sends it to the supplier. It is important for internal control that no check be prepared without a supporting voucher and that the check be mailed as soon as it is signed.

Ordinary checks may be used to make payments, but under the voucher system, voucher checks often are used. A voucher check is a check with space for entering data about the voucher being paid. Figure 7A-7 on page 276 shows a voucher check used to pay Voucher No. 111 (Figure 7A-5).

The voucher check has two parts:

1. The check itself, which is similar to an ordinary check, and
2. An attached statement, which indicates the invoice being paid and any deductions.

In addition, the voucher check stub identifies the voucher number being paid.

LEARNING KEY
For good internal control of cash payments, it is important for the check to be mailed as soon as it is signed.

FIGURE 7A-6   Voucher System—Payment Process

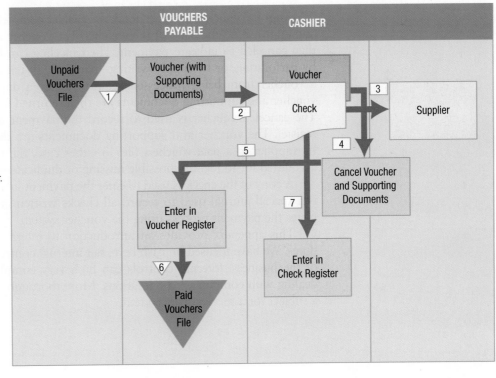

FIGURE 7A-7 Voucher Check

NO. 437

Date April 24, 20--

To King Creek Corp.

Voucher No. 111

Amount of Voucher $ 3,658.00

Discount $ 36.58

Amount of Check $ 3,621.42

Remarks

Sunflower CYCLE

804 Massachusetts St., Lawrence, KS 66044

3-4/740

NO. 437

Date April 24, 20--

Pay to the Order of King Creek Corp. $ 3,621.42

Three thousand six hundred twenty one 42/100 Dollars

Commerce Bank

Kansas City, Kansas

Dan Hughes

⑆074000009⑆ 926418⑈

Detach this Statement Before Depositing Check

Date April 24, 20--

Attached Voucher Check is Full Settlement of the Following:

INVOICE		DESCRIPTION	INVOICE AMOUNT		DEDUCTIONS			NET AMOUNT	
Date	No.				For	Amount			
Apr. 9	4123	3 Shimano 4 Motobecane	3,658	00	Discount	$36	58	3,621	42

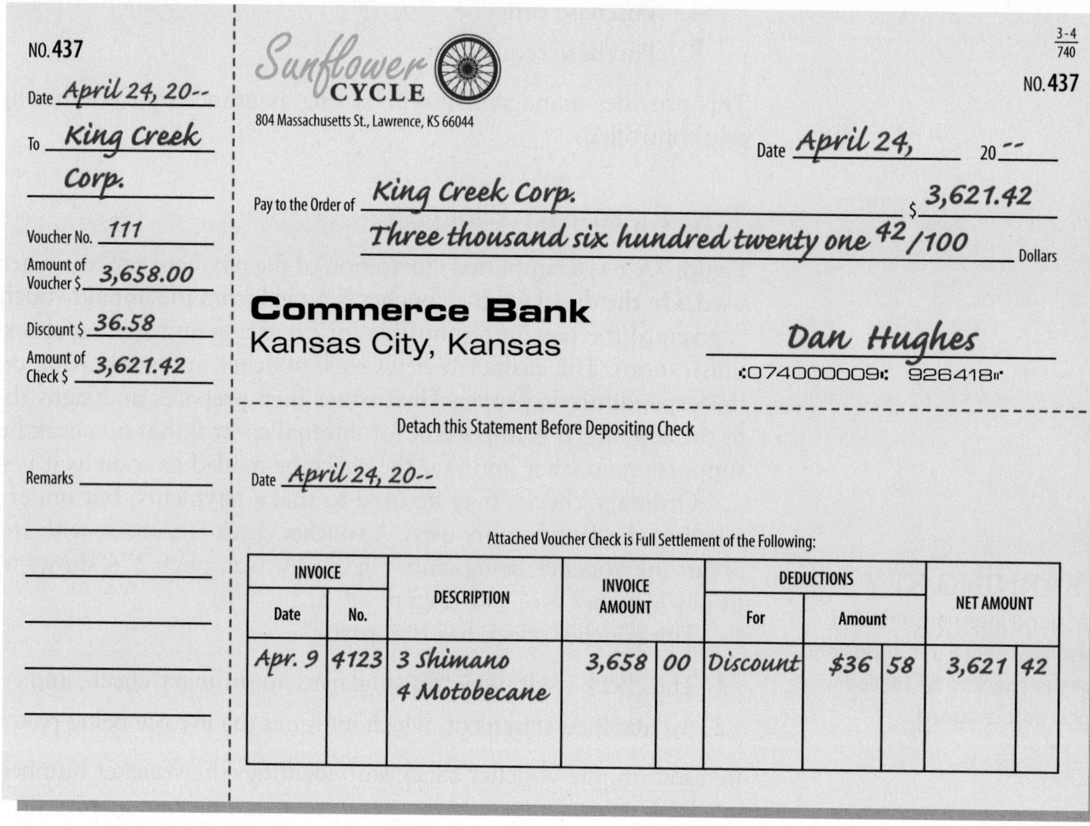

After the voucher has been paid, the cashier completes the "Payment" information and approval on the back of the voucher. The voucher and supporting documents are then canceled to indicate payment. The canceling can be done with a rubber stamp, by perforating, or by simply writing "paid" on all relevant documents. This prevents a voucher from being processed again to create a duplicate payment. The canceled voucher and supporting documents are then returned to the vouchers payable section. The canceled voucher is used to record the payment of the voucher in the voucher register. The voucher and supporting documents are then filed either numerically or by supplier in a **paid vouchers file**. In either case, the numerical sequence should be accounted for to identify possible missing or duplicate vouchers.

A copy of the check is used to enter the payment in a check register. A **check register** is a special journal used to record all checks written in a voucher system. This completes the payment process using the voucher system.

This appendix provides an introduction to internal control concepts and procedures. We have focused on cash here, but internal controls are important in every area of the business. Internal controls can be a very complicated subject, particularly in dealing with computerized operations. More thorough analysis of internal controls is a subject for a more advanced text.

LEARNING OBJECTIVES   Key Points to Remember

LO1	Explain the importance of internal control.	Internal controls help assure management that it has reliable records to run the business and prepare needed reports. In addition, SOX requires publicly held companies to report annually on the quality of their internal control system.
LO2	Define internal control and describe its key components.	Internal control is a system developed by a company to provide reasonable assurance of achieving (1) effective and efficient operations, (2) reliable financial reporting, and (3) compliance with laws and regulations. The key components are as follows: • Control environment • Risk assessment • Control activities • Information and communication system • Monitoring processes
LO3	Describe selected internal controls over cash receipts.	If cash is received directly from customers, a cash register should be used. The record of cash receipts per the register should be reconciled with the actual cash in the drawer. If cash is received by mail, a remittance list should be prepared and sent to accounting. The checks should be endorsed immediately "For deposit" and sent to the cash receipts department for deposit in the bank. The remittance list and bank deposit should be independently reconciled.
LO4	Describe selected internal controls over cash payments and the use of a voucher system.	Every acquisition and subsequent payment should be supported by an approved voucher. The voucher should be supported by a purchase requisition, purchase order, receiving report, and purchase invoice. On the due date, checks are written only for approved vouchers, and vouchers and supporting documents are canceled to prevent reuse.

KEY TERMS

check register (276)   A special journal used to record all checks written in a voucher system.

kiting (272)   Recording a transfer of cash *into* one bank account in the current period, but not recording the transfer *out of* another bank account until the following period.

lapping (272)   Stealing cash received on account from one customer and hiding the theft by applying the cash received on account from another customer to the first customer's account.

paid vouchers file (276)   A file in which paid vouchers and supporting documents are placed, organized either numerically or by supplier.

publicly held companies (267)   Companies whose stock is traded on the major stock exchanges.

unpaid vouchers file (274)   A file in which unpaid voucher packets are placed, normally organized by due date.

voucher (273)   A document that shows that an acquisition is proper and that payment is authorized.

voucher check (275)   A check with space for entering data about the voucher being paid.

voucher register (273) A special journal used to record purchases of all types of assets and services.

voucher system (273) A control technique that requires that every acquisition and subsequent payment be supported by an approved voucher.

REVIEW QUESTIONS

LO1   1. What does Section 404 of the Sarbanes-Oxley Act require?

LO2   2. What is the meaning of internal control?

LO2   3. What are the five components of internal control?

LO2   4. What are the four types of control activities?

LO3   5. What are the main purposes of internal controls over cash receipts?

LO4   6. What is the main purpose of internal controls over cash payments?

LO4   7. What is a voucher system?

LO4   8. In a voucher system, each recorded purchase is supported by what five documents?

LO4   9. What is the purpose of canceling the voucher and supporting documents when a payment is made?

SERIES A EXERCISES

E 7Apx-1A   (LO2)

INTERNAL CONTROL COMPONENTS The most widely accepted internal control framework in the United States contains the following five components. Describe each of them.

1. Control environment
2. Risk assessment
3. Control activities
4. Information and communication system
5. Monitoring processes

E 7Apx-2A   (LO2)

INTERNAL CONTROL PROCEDURES AND PROCESSES In the left column below, five different internal control procedures and processes are described. In the right column, the five components of internal control are listed. Match the procedures and processes with the components by placing the letter of the appropriate component on the blank provided.

1. ____ A company publishes and uses a code of ethical conduct.

2. ____ The accounting system automatically generates monthly sales reports for each product line.

3. ____ A company has established an internal audit department.

4. ____ All purchases above $5,000 must be approved in writing by the head of the purchasing department.

5. ____ A company invests heavily in employee training programs because of the technical nature of its products.

a. Control environment
b. Risk assessment
c. Control activities
d. Information and communication system
e. Monitoring processes

E 7Apx-3A   (LO4)   **PURCHASING PROCESS USING A VOUCHER SYSTEM** In the following flow-chart, identify the documents, records, and procedures that illustrate the purchasing process in a voucher system.

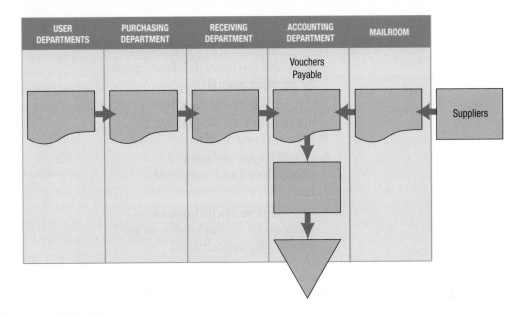

SERIES A PROBLEM

P 7Apx-4A   (LO2/3/4)   **USING INTERNAL CONTROLS TO PREVENT ERRORS** The following misstatements occurred in the records of ICW Company. For each misstatement, suggest a control to prevent it from happening.

1. A bill from a supplier was paid even though the shipment was not received.
2. A supplier's bill was paid twice for the same purchase.
3. A plant employee increased his pay rate by entering the computer system using a plant terminal and altering the payroll records.
4. The cash receipts clerk kept a portion of the regular bank deposits for personal use and concealed the theft by manipulating the monthly bank reconciliation she prepared.

SERIES B EXERCISES

E 7Apx-1B   (LO2)   **INTERNAL CONTROL COMPONENTS** Four types of internal control activities are listed below. Describe each of them.

1. Segregation of duties
2. Authorization procedures and related responsibilities
3. Adequate documents and records
4. Protection of assets and records

E 7Apx-2B   (LO2)

INTERNAL CONTROL PROCEDURES AND PROCESSES In the left column below, four different internal control procedures are described. In the right column, the four basic types of internal control activities are listed. Match the procedures with the activities by placing the letter of the appropriate activity on the blank provided.

a. Segregation of duties
b. Authorization procedures and related responsibilities
c. Adequate documents and records
d. Protection of assets and records

1. ____ All passwords for access to sales and inventory databases must be changed monthly.

2. ____ All new hires must be approved by the department of human resources.

3. ____ All sales invoices are prenumbered and accounted for.

4. ____ Bank reconciliations are prepared by an employee with no other cash responsibilities.

E 7Apx-3B   (LO4)

PAYMENT PROCESS USING A VOUCHER SYSTEM In the following flowchart, identify the documents, records, and procedures that illustrate the payment process using a voucher system.

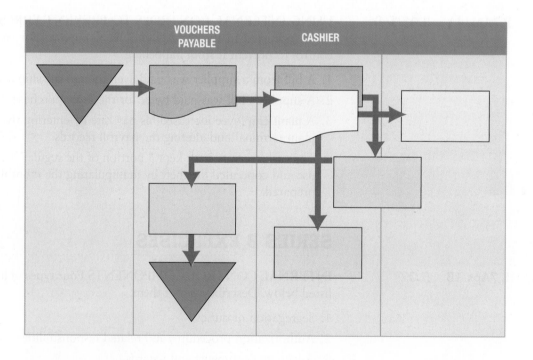

SERIES B PROBLEM

P 7Apx-4B   (LO2/3/4)   **USING INTERNAL CONTROLS TO PREVENT ERRORS** The following misstatements occurred in the records of MW Company. For each misstatement, suggest a control to prevent it from happening.

1. A bill from a supplier was paid for goods that had not been ordered.

2. A supplier's bill for 50 boxes of materials was paid even though only 40 boxes were received.

3. Expensive product components were stolen by an employee from a loading dock area after hours.

4. No bill was sent to a customer for a shipment because the shipping document was lost after the shipment was made.

Chapter 8

Payroll Accounting: Employee Earnings and Deductions

When a company upgrades its computers and needs to dump its old ones, it might be time to call Intechra Group. Intechra Group provides computer hardware, software, and database disposal and recycling services nationwide. Founded in 1987, the company grew rapidly in response to environmental and privacy concerns about the use of IT assets. Intechra now is one of the largest electronics life cycle management companies in the United States. The company currently processes more than 1,000,000 pounds of electronics annually. With more than 500 employees, it offers both on-site services and secure transport of assets to its locations. Consistent with environmental concerns, the entire recycling operation is performed under a zero-landfill policy for e-waste.

A company such as Intechra requires a variety of employees—from highly technical to basic materials handling staff—with very different rates of pay. For legal and operating efficiency reasons, a company must accurately track and control its payroll costs. It needs to know not only what to pay its people, but also what taxes to withhold from their wages. In this chapter, you will learn how to identify and account for payroll expenses for multiple employees.

The only contact most of us have with payroll is receiving a paycheck. Few of us have seen the large amount of record keeping needed to produce that paycheck. Employers maintain complete payroll accounting records for two reasons. First, payroll costs are major expenditures for most companies. Payroll accounting records provide data useful in analyzing and controlling these expenditures. Second, federal, state, and local laws require employers to keep payroll records. Companies must accumulate payroll data both for the business as a whole and for each employee.

There are two major types of payroll taxes: those paid by the employee and those paid by the employer. In this chapter, we discuss employee taxes. In Chapter 9, we address payroll taxes paid by the employer.

EMPLOYEES AND INDEPENDENT CONTRACTORS

LO1 Distinguish between employees and independent contractors.

Not every person who performs services for a business is considered an employee. An employee works under the control and direction of an employer. Examples include secretaries, maintenance workers, salesclerks, and plant supervisors. In contrast, an independent contractor performs a service for a fee and does not work under the control and direction of the company paying for the service. Examples of independent contractors include public accountants, real estate agents, and lawyers.

The distinction between an employee and an independent contractor is important for payroll purposes. Government laws and regulations regarding payroll are much more complex for employees than for independent contractors. Employers must deduct certain taxes, maintain payroll records, and file numerous reports for all employees. Only one form (Form 1099) must be filed for independent contractors. The payroll accounting procedures described in this chapter apply only to employer/employee relationships.

EMPLOYEE EARNINGS AND DEDUCTIONS

LO2 Calculate employee earnings and deductions.

Three steps are required to determine how much to pay an employee for a pay period:

1. Calculate total earnings.
2. Determine the amounts of deductions.
3. Subtract deductions from total earnings to compute net pay.

Salaries and Wages

Compensation for managerial or administrative services usually is called **salary**. A salary normally is expressed in biweekly (every two weeks), monthly, or annual terms. Compensation for skilled or unskilled labor usually is referred to as **wages**. Wages ordinarily are expressed in terms of hours, weeks, or units produced. The terms "salaries" and "wages" often are used interchangeably in practice.

The **Fair Labor Standards Act (FLSA)**, often called the Federal Wage and Hour Law, requires employers to pay overtime at 1½ times the regular rate to any hourly employee who works over 40 hours in a week. Some companies pay a higher rate for hours worked on Saturday or Sunday, but this is not required by the FLSA. Some salaried employees are exempt from the FLSA rules and are not paid overtime.

Computing Total Earnings

Compensation usually is based on the time worked during the payroll period. Sometimes it is based on sales or units of output during the period. When compensation is based on time, a record must be kept of the time worked by each employee. Time cards (Figure 8-1) are helpful for this purpose. In large businesses with computer-based timekeeping systems, plastic cards or badges with special magnetic strips or bar codes (Figure 8-2) can be used. Employees use the cards to clock in and out at terminals with card readers. For increased security, these terminals also are available with fingerprint readers.

FIGURE 8-1 Time Card

Westly, Inc.
Time Card — Hourly Payroll

Emp. Name **Kuzmik, Helen**   Base Dept.: **Sales**

Emp. ID: **359-47-1138**   Pay Per. End: **12/19/20--**

					HOURS			
Date	Time In	Time Out	Time In	Time Out	Reg	OT	DT	Total
12/13	8:00	12:30	13:00	17:30	8	1		9
12/14	8:00	12:30	13:00	17:30	8	1		9
12/15	8:00	12:30	13:00	17:30	8	1		9
12/16	8:00	12:30	13:00	17:30	8	1		9
12/17	8:00	12:30	13:00	17:30	8	1		9
12/18	10:00	16:00				6		6
12/19	13:00	17:00					4	4
TOTAL					40	11	4	55

Remarks_____

_____

Approval_____TM_____

Dept. Head

To illustrate the computation of total earnings, look at the time card of Helen Kuzmik in Figure 8-1. The card shows that Kuzmik worked 55 hours for the week.

Regular hours	40 hours
Overtime	11
Double time	4
Total hours worked	55 hours

Kuzmik's regular rate of pay is $12 per hour. She is paid 1½ times the regular rate for hours in excess of 8 on Monday through Friday and any hours worked on

FIGURE 8-2 Time Cards and Clock Terminal

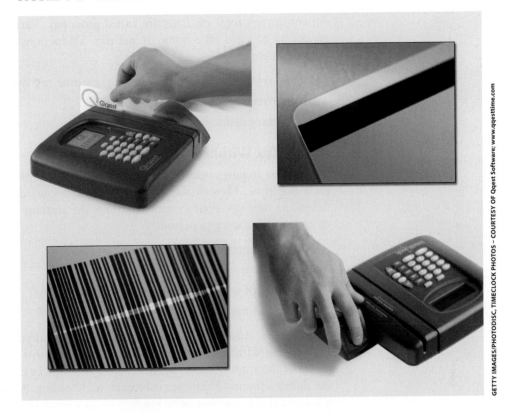

Saturday, and twice the regular rate for hours on Sunday. Kuzmik's total earnings for the week ended December 19 are computed as follows:

40 hours × $12	$480
11 hours × $18 (1½ × $12 = $18)	198
4 hours (on Sunday) × $24 (2 × $12 = $24)	96
Total earnings for the week	$774

Salaried employees who are not exempt from the FSLA rules may also be entitled to premium pay for overtime. If this is the case, it is necessary to compute the regular hourly rate of pay before computing the overtime rate. To illustrate, assume that Linda Swaney has a salary of $2,288 a month plus 1½ times the regular hourly rate for hours in excess of 40 per week. Swaney's overtime rate of pay is computed as follows:

$2,288 × 12 months	$27,456 annual pay
$27,456 ÷ 52 weeks	$528.00 pay per week
$528.00 ÷ 40 hours	$13.20 pay per regular hour
$13.20 × 1½	$19.80 overtime pay per hour

There are 52 weeks in each year but not 4 weeks in each month. That is why monthly salaries must be annualized in order to determine the hourly rate.

If Swaney worked 50 hours during the week ended December 19, her total earnings for the week would be computed as follows:

40 hours × $13.20	$528.00
10 hours × $19.80	198.00
Total earnings for the week	$726.00

GETTY IMAGES/PHOTODISC, TIMECLOCK PHOTOS – COURTESY OF Qqest Software; www.qqesttime.com

Deductions from Total Earnings

An employee's total earnings are called **gross pay**. Various deductions are made from gross pay to yield take-home or **net pay**. Deductions from gross pay fall into three major categories:

1. Federal (and possibly state and city) income tax withholding
2. Employee FICA tax withholding
3. Voluntary deductions

Income Tax Withholding

Federal law requires employers to withhold certain amounts from the total earnings of each employee. These withholdings are applied toward the payment of the employee's federal income tax. Four factors determine the amount to be withheld from an employee's gross pay each pay period:

1. Total earnings
2. Marital status
3. Number of withholding allowances claimed
4. Length of the pay period

Withholding Allowances. Each employee is required to furnish the employer an Employee's Withholding Allowance Certificate, Form W-4 (Figure 8-3). The marital status of the employee and the number of allowances claimed on Form W-4 determine the dollar amount of earnings subject to withholding. A **withholding allowance** exempts a specific dollar amount of an employee's gross pay from federal income tax withholding. In general, each employee is permitted one personal withholding allowance, one for a spouse who does not also claim an allowance, and one for each dependent.

FIGURE 8-3 Employee's Withholding Allowance Certificate (Form W-4)

Form **W-4**
Department of the Treasury
Internal Revenue Service

Employee's Withholding Allowance Certificate

▶ **Whether you are entitled to claim a certain number of allowances or exemption from withholding is subject to review by the IRS. Your employer may be required to send a copy of this form to the IRS.**

OMB No. 1545-0074
20--

1 Your first name and middle initial: Ken M. | Last name: Istone | 2 Your social security number: 393 58 8194

Home address (number and street or rural route): 1546 Swallow Drive

3 ☐ Single ☒ Married ☐ Married, but withhold at higher Single rate.
Note. *If married, but legally separated, or spouse is a nonresident alien, check the "Single" box.*

City or town, state, and ZIP code: St. Louis, MO 63144-4752

4 **If your last name differs from that shown on your social security card, check here. You must call 1-800-772-1213 for a replacement card.** ▶ ☐

5 Total number of allowances you are claiming (from line **H** above **or** from the applicable worksheet on page 2) . . . 5 | 4

6 Additional amount, if any, you want withheld from each paycheck . . . 6 | $

7 I claim exemption from withholding for 20--, and I certify that I meet **both** of the following conditions for exemption.
- Last year I had a right to a refund of **all** federal income tax withheld because I had **no** tax liability **and**
- This year I expect a refund of **all** federal income tax withheld because I expect to have **no** tax liability.

If you meet both conditions, write "Exempt" here . . . ▶ 7

Under penalties of perjury, I declare that I have examined this certificate and to the best of my knowledge and belief, it is true, correct, and complete.

Employee's signature
(Form is not valid unless you sign it.) ▶ *Ken M. Istone* Date ▶ *January 3, 20--*

8 Employer's name and address (Employer: Complete lines 8 and 10 only if sending to the IRS.) | 9 Office code (optional) | 10 Employer identification number (EIN)

For Privacy Act and Paperwork Reduction Act Notice, see page 2. Cat. No. 10220Q Form **W-4** (20--)

A withholding certificate completed by Ken Istone is shown in Figure 8-3. Istone is married, has a spouse who does not claim an allowance, and has two dependent children. On line 5 of the W-4 form, Istone claims four allowances, calculated as follows:

Personal allowance	1
Spouse allowance	1
Allowances for dependents	2
Total withholding allowances	4

Wage-Bracket Method. Employers generally use the **wage-bracket method** or the **percentage method** to determine the amount of tax to be withheld from an employee's pay. We will illustrate the wage-bracket method here. The employee's gross pay for a specific time period is traced into the appropriate wage-bracket table provided by the Internal Revenue Service (IRS). These tables cover various time periods, and there are separate tables for single and married taxpayers. Copies are provided in *Circular E—Employer's Tax Guide*, also known as Publication 15, which may be obtained from any local IRS office or at the IRS Internet site.

Portions of weekly income tax wage-bracket withholding tables for single and married persons are illustrated in Figure 8-4. Assume that Ken Istone (who claims 4 allowances) had gross earnings of $545 for the week ending December 19, 20--. The amount to withhold for Istone is determined by using the following steps, as shown in Figure 8-4 for married persons (on page 289):

1. Find the row for wages of "at least $540, but less than $550."

2. Find the column headed "4 withholding allowances."

3. Where the row and column cross, $7 is given as the amount to be withheld.

For state or city income taxes, withholding generally is handled in one of two ways: (1) forms and tables similar to those provided by the IRS are used or (2) an amount equal to a percentage of the federal withholding amount is withheld.

Employee FICA Tax Withholding

The Federal Insurance Contributions Act requires employers to withhold **FICA taxes** from employees' earnings. FICA taxes include amounts for both Social Security and Medicare programs. Social Security provides pensions and disability benefits. Medicare provides health insurance.

Congress has frequently changed the tax rates and the maximum amounts of earnings subject to FICA taxes. For this text, we assume the Social Security rate is 6.2% on maximum earnings of $118,500. The Medicare rate is 1.45% on all earnings; there is no maximum.

To illustrate the calculation of FICA taxes, assume the following earnings for Sarah Cadrain:

	Earnings	
Pay Period	Week	Year-to-Date
Dec. 6–12	$2,000	$117,640
Dec. 13–19	$1,860	$119,500

For the week of December 6–12, FICA taxes on Cadrain's earnings would be:

Gross Pay	×	Tax Rate		=	Tax
$2,000		Social Security	6.2%		$124.00
		Medicare	1.45%		29.00
					$153.00

A large number of IRS publications and forms can be found at the IRS Web site: www.irs.gov

LEARNING KEY

To determine the amount to withhold:

1. Find the row for wages.

2. Find the column for withholding allowances.

3. Find the amount where they cross.

An additional Medicare tax of 0.9% is imposed on employee earnings of more than $200,000 for single filers, and more than $250,000 for joint filers.

FIGURE 8-4   Federal Withholding Tax Table: Single Persons

SINGLE Persons—WEEKLY Payroll Period
(For Wages Paid through December 31, 2015)

And the wages are—		And the number of withholding allowances claimed is—										
At least	But less than	0	1	2	3	4	5	6	7	8	9	10
		The amount of income tax to be withheld is—										
$300	$310	$30	$19	$11	$3	$0	$0	$0	$0	$0	$0	$0
310	320	32	20	12	4	0	0	0	0	0	0	0
320	330	33	22	13	5	0	0	0	0	0	0	0
330	340	35	23	14	6	0	0	0	0	0	0	0
340	350	36	25	15	7	0	0	0	0	0	0	0
350	360	38	26	16	8	0	0	0	0	0	0	0
360	370	39	28	17	9	1	0	0	0	0	0	0
370	380	41	29	18	10	2	0	0	0	0	0	0
380	390	42	31	19	11	3	0	0	0	0	0	0
390	400	44	32	21	12	4	0	0	0	0	0	0
400	410	45	34	22	13	5	0	0	0	0	0	0
410	420	47	35	24	14	6	0	0	0	0	0	0
420	430	48	37	25	15	7	0	0	0	0	0	0
430	440	50	38	27	16	8	1	0	0	0	0	0
440	450	51	40	28	17	9	2	0	0	0	0	0
450	460	53	41	30	18	10	3	0	0	0	0	0
460	470	54	43	31	20	11	4	0	0	0	0	0
470	480	56	44	33	21	12	5	0	0	0	0	0
480	490	57	46	34	23	13	6	0	0	0	0	0
490	500	59	47	36	24	14	7	0	0	0	0	0
500	510	60	49	37	26	15	8	0	0	0	0	0
510	520	62	50	39	27	16	9	1	0	0	0	0
520	530	63	52	40	29	17	10	2	0	0	0	0
530	540	65	53	42	30	19	11	3	0	0	0	0
540	550	66	55	43	32	20	12	4	0	0	0	0
550	560	68	56	45	33	22	13	5	0	0	0	0
560	570	69	58	46	35	23	14	6	0	0	0	0
570	580	71	59	48	36	25	15	7	0	0	0	0
580	590	72	61	49	38	26	16	8	0	0	0	0
590	600	74	62	51	39	28	17	9	1	0	0	0
600	610	75	64	52	41	29	18	10	2	0	0	0
610	620	77	65	54	42	31	19	11	3	0	0	0
620	630	78	67	55	44	32	21	12	4	0	0	0
630	640	80	68	57	45	34	22	13	5	0	0	0
640	650	81	70	58	47	35	24	14	6	0	0	0
650	660	83	71	60	48	37	25	15	7	0	0	0
660	670	84	73	61	50	38	27	16	8	1	0	0
670	680	86	74	63	51	40	28	17	9	2	0	0
680	690	87	76	64	53	41	30	18	10	3	0	0
690	700	89	77	66	54	43	31	20	11	4	0	0
700	710	90	79	67	56	44	33	21	12	5	0	0
710	720	92	80	69	57	46	34	23	13	6	0	0
720	730	93	82	70	59	47	36	24	14	7	0	0
730	740	95	83	72	60	49	37	26	15	8	0	0
740	750	96	85	73	62	50	39	27	16	9	1	0
750	760	98	86	75	63	52	40	29	17	10	2	0
760	770	99	88	76	65	53	42	30	18	11	3	0
770	780	102	89	78	66	55	43	32	20	12	4	0
780	790	104	91	79	68	56	45	33	21	13	5	0
790	800	107	92	81	69	58	46	35	23	14	6	0

FIGURE 8-4 Federal Withholding Tax Table: (*concluded*) Married Persons

MARRIED Persons—WEEKLY Payroll Period
(For Wages Paid through December 31, 2015)

And the wages are—		And the number of withholding allowances claimed is—										
At least	But less than	0	1	2	3	(2) 4	5	6	7	8	9	10
		The amount of income tax to be withheld is—										
$300	$310	$14	$6	$0	$0	$0	$0	$0	$0	$0	$0	$0
310	320	15	7	0	0	0	0	0	0	0	0	0
320	330	16	8	1	0	0	0	0	0	0	0	0
330	340	17	9	2	0	0	0	0	0	0	0	0
340	350	18	10	3	0	0	0	0	0	0	0	0
350	360	19	11	4	0	0	0	0	0	0	0	0
360	370	20	12	5	0	0	0	0	0	0	0	0
370	380	21	13	6	0	0	0	0	0	0	0	0
380	390	22	14	7	0	0	0	0	0	0	0	0
390	400	23	15	8	0	0	0	0	0	0	0	0
400	410	24	16	9	1	0	0	0	0	0	0	0
410	420	25	17	10	2	0	0	0	0	0	0	0
420	430	26	18	11	3	0	0	0	0	0	0	0
430	440	27	19	12	4	0	0	0	0	0	0	0
440	450	28	20	13	5	0	0	0	0	0	0	0
450	460	29	21	14	6	0	0	0	0	0	0	0
460	470	30	22	15	7	0	0	0	0	0	0	0
470	480	31	23	16	8	0	0	0	0	0	0	0
480	490	32	24	17	9	1	0	0	0	0	0	0
490	500	33	25	18	10	2	0	0	0	0	0	0
500	510	34	26	19	11	3	0	0	0	0	0	0
510	520	35	27	20	12	4	0	0	0	0	0	0
520	530	36	28	21	13	5	0	0	0	0	0	0
530	540	38	29	22	14	6	0	0	0	0	0	0
(1) 540	550	39	30	23	15	(3) 7	0	0	0	0	0	0
550	560	41	31	24	16	8	1	0	0	0	0	0
560	570	42	32	25	17	9	2	0	0	0	0	0
570	580	44	33	26	18	10	3	0	0	0	0	0
580	590	45	34	27	19	11	4	0	0	0	0	0
590	600	47	35	28	20	12	5	0	0	0	0	0
600	610	48	37	29	21	13	6	0	0	0	0	0
610	620	50	38	30	22	14	7	0	0	0	0	0
620	630	51	40	31	23	15	8	0	0	0	0	0
630	640	53	41	32	24	16	9	1	0	0	0	0
640	650	54	43	33	25	17	10	2	0	0	0	0
650	660	56	44	34	26	18	11	3	0	0	0	0
660	670	57	46	35	27	19	12	4	0	0	0	0
670	680	59	47	36	28	20	13	5	0	0	0	0
680	690	60	49	37	29	21	14	6	0	0	0	0
690	700	62	50	39	30	22	15	7	0	0	0	0
700	710	63	52	40	31	23	16	8	0	0	0	0
710	720	65	53	42	32	24	17	9	1	0	0	0
720	730	66	55	43	33	25	18	10	2	0	0	0
730	740	68	56	45	34	26	19	11	3	0	0	0
740	750	69	58	46	35	27	20	12	4	0	0	0
750	760	71	59	48	36	28	21	13	5	0	0	0
760	770	72	61	49	38	29	22	14	6	0	0	0
770	780	74	62	51	39	30	23	15	7	0	0	0
780	790	75	64	52	41	31	24	16	8	0	0	0
790	800	77	65	54	42	32	25	17	9	1	0	0
800	810	78	67	55	44	33	26	18	10	2	0	0
1,300	1,310	153	142	130	119	107	96	84	72	61	49	38
1,310	1,320	155	143	132	120	109	97	85	74	62	51	39
1,320	1,330	156	145	133	122	110	99	87	75	64	52	41
1,330	1,340	158	146	135	123	112	100	88	77	65	54	42
1,340	1,350	159	148	136	125	113	102	90	78	67	55	44
1,350	1,360	161	149	138	126	115	103	91	80	68	57	45
1,360	1,370	162	151	139	128	116	105	93	81	70	58	47
1,370	1,380	164	152	141	129	118	106	94	83	71	60	48
1,380	1,390	165	154	142	131	119	108	96	84	73	61	50
1,390	1,400	167	155	144	132	121	109	97	86	74	63	51

When the Social Security program was established in 1937, the tax was 1% on earnings up to $3,000 per year!

During the week of December 13–19, Cadrain's earnings for the calendar year went over the $118,500 Social Security maximum by $1,000 ($119,500 – $118,500). Therefore, $1,000 of her $1,860 earnings for the week would not be subject to the Social Security tax.

Year-to-date earnings	$119,500
Social Security maximum	118,500
Amount not subject to Social Security tax	$ 1,000

The Social Security tax on Cadrain's December 13–19 earnings would be:

Gross pay	$1,860.00
Amount not subject to Social Security tax	1,000.00
Amount subject to Social Security tax	$ 860.00
Tax rate	6.2%
Social Security tax	$ 53.32

Since there is no Medicare maximum, all of Cadrain's December 13–19 earnings would be subject to the Medicare tax.

Gross pay	$1,860.00
Tax rate	1.45%
Medicare tax	$ 26.97

The total FICA tax would be:

Social Security tax	$53.32
Medicare tax	26.97
Total FICA tax	$80.29

For the rest of the calendar year through December 31, Cadrain's earnings would be subject only to Medicare taxes.

Voluntary Deductions

In addition to the mandatory deductions from employee earnings for income and FICA taxes, many other deductions are possible. These deductions are usually voluntary and depend on specific agreements between the employee and employer. Examples of voluntary deductions are:

1. U.S. savings bond purchases
2. Health insurance premiums
3. Credit union deposits
4. Pension plan payments
5. Charitable contributions

Computing Net Pay

To compute an employee's net pay for the period, subtract all tax withholdings and voluntary deductions from the gross pay. Ken Istone's net pay for the week ended December 19 would be calculated as follows:

Gross pay		$545.00
Deductions:		
Federal income tax withholding	$ 7.00	
Social Security tax withholding	33.79	
Medicare tax withholding	7.90	
Health insurance premiums	10.00	
Total deductions		58.69
Net pay		$486.31

If you use Microsoft® Excel to create a payroll register, a column or row *may* be off by a few cents. This usually occurs in the Social Security and Medicare tax calculations because of rounding. To get an accurate number, use the "ROUND" function in any cell with more than two non-zero decimal places.

Checkpoint ✓

Complete Checkpoint-1 on page 305 to test your basic understanding of LO2.

PAYROLL RECORDS

LO3 Describe and prepare payroll records.

Payroll records should provide the following information for each employee:

1. Name, address, occupation, Social Security number, marital status, and number of withholding allowances
2. Gross amount of earnings, date of payment, and period covered by each payroll
3. Gross amount of earnings accumulated for the year
4. Amounts of taxes and other items withheld

Three types of payroll records are used to accumulate this information:

1. The payroll register
2. The payroll check (or record of direct deposit) with earnings statement attached
3. The employee earnings record

These records can be prepared by either manual or automated methods. The illustrations in this chapter are based on a manual system. The forms and procedures illustrated are equally applicable to both manual and automated systems.

Payroll Register

A good example of a deduction column that could be added is State Income Tax. In the payroll register in Figure 8-5, the column could be inserted immediately after Federal Income Tax.

A **payroll register** is a form used to assemble the data required at the end of each payroll period. Figure 8-5 on pages 292 and 293 illustrates Westly, Inc.'s payroll register for the payroll period ended December 19, 20--. Detailed information on earnings, taxable earnings, deductions, and net pay is provided for each employee. Column headings for deductions may vary, depending on which deductions are commonly used by a particular business. The sources of key information in the register are indicated in Figure 8-5.

Note four important things about Westly's payroll register:

1. The first $118,500 of earnings of each employee is subject to Social Security tax. The Cumulative Total column, under the Earnings category, shows that Sarah Cadrain has exceeded this limit during the period. Thus, only $860 of her earnings for this pay period is subject to Social Security tax, as shown in the Taxable Earnings columns.
2. There are two Taxable Earnings columns: Unemployment Compensation and Social Security. Only one of these columns (Social Security) is needed to determine employee taxes. Both columns are shown here because they are a standard part of a payroll register. The Unemployment Compensation column is needed to determine this payroll tax on employers. The Social Security column is needed to determine both employee and employer Social Security taxes. The two employer taxes (Unemployment Compensation and Social Security) are discussed in Chapter 9.
3. Regular deductions are made from employee earnings for federal income tax and Social Security and Medicare taxes.
4. Voluntary deductions are made for health insurance and United Way contributions, based on agreements with individual employees.

FIGURE 8-5 Payroll Register (left side)

	NAME	ALLOWANCES	MARITAL STATUS	EARNINGS — REGULAR	EARNINGS — OVERTIME	EARNINGS — TOTAL	CUMULATIVE TOTAL	TAXABLE EARNINGS — UNEMPLOYMENT COMPENSATION	TAXABLE EARNINGS — SOCIAL SECURITY
1	Cadrain, Sarah	4	M	1 8 0 0 00	6 0 00	1 8 6 0 00	119 5 0 0 00	0 00	8 6 0 00
2	Gruder, James	1	S	7 6 0 00	1 4 0 00	9 0 0 00	43 4 0 0 00	0 00	9 0 0 00
3	Istone, Ken	4	M	5 4 5 00		5 4 5 00	27 0 2 5 00	0 00	5 4 5 00
4	Kuzmik, Helen	2	M	4 8 0 00	2 9 4 00	7 7 4 00	31 0 0 0 00	0 00	7 7 4 00
5	Lee, Hoseoup	3	M	4 4 0 00		4 4 0 00	22 3 4 0 00	0 00	4 4 0 00
6	Swaney, Linda	2	S	5 2 8 00	1 9 8 00	7 2 6 00	27 5 0 0 00	0 00	7 2 6 00
7	Tucci, Paul	3	M	4 9 0 00		4 9 0 00	25 0 5 0 00	0 00	4 9 0 00
8	Wiles, Harry	1	S	3 0 0 00		3 0 0 00	6 3 0 0 00	3 0 0 00	3 0 0 00
9				5 3 4 3 00	6 9 2 00	6 0 3 5 00	302 1 1 5 00	3 0 0 00	5 0 3 5 00
10									

PAYROLL REGISTER

Time cards, pay rates

Prior period total + current period earnings

Current below $7,000 cumul. total

Current below $118,500 cumul. total

Discussed in Chapter 9

After the data for each employee have been entered, the amount columns in the payroll register should be totaled and the totals verified as follows:

Regular earnings		$5,343.00
Overtime earnings		692.00
Gross earnings		$6,035.00
Deductions:		
Federal income tax	$467.00	
Social Security tax	312.17	
Medicare tax	87.51	
Health insurance premiums	46.00	
United Way	40.00	952.68
Net amount of payroll		$5,082.32

In a computerized accounting system, the payroll software performs this proof. An error in the payroll register could cause the payment of an incorrect amount to an employee. It also could result in sending an incorrect amount to the government or other agencies for whom funds are withheld.

Paying Employees

Employees should be paid by check or by direct deposit. Data needed to prepare a paycheck for each employee are contained in the payroll register. In a computer-based system, the paychecks and payroll register normally are prepared at the same time. The employer furnishes an earnings statement to each employee along with each paycheck. Paychecks with detachable earnings statements, like the one for Ken Istone illustrated in Figure 8-6, are widely used for this purpose. Before the check is deposited or cashed, the employee should detach the stub and keep it for his records.

FIGURE 8-5 Payroll Register (right side)

—WEEK ENDED 12/19/--

FEDERAL INCOME TAX	SOCIAL SECURITY TAX	MEDICARE TAX	HEALTH INSURANCE	UNITED WAY	OTHER	TOTAL	NET PAY	CHECK NO.	
1 9 0 00	5 3 32	2 6 97				2 7 0 29	1 5 8 9 71	409	1
1 1 5 00	5 5 80	1 3 05		2 0 00		2 0 3 85	6 9 6 15	410	2
7 00	3 3 79	7 90	1 0 00			5 8 69	4 8 6 31	411	3
5 1 00	4 7 99	1 1 22	1 3 00	2 0 00		1 4 3 21	6 3 0 79	412	4
5 00	2 7 28	6 38	1 3 00			5 1 66	3 8 8 34	413	5
7 0 00	4 5 01	1 0 53				1 2 5 54	6 0 0 46	414	6
1 0 00	3 0 38	7 11	1 0 00			5 7 49	4 3 2 51	415	7
1 9 00	1 8 60	4 35				4 1 95	2 5 8 05	416	8
									9
4 6 7 00	3 1 2 17	8 7 51	4 6 00	4 0 00	0 0 00	9 5 2 68	5 0 8 2 32		10

DEDUCTIONS

Withholding Tax Table

6.2% × Social Security taxable earnings

1.45% × total earnings

Specific employer–employee agreements

Total earnings – total deductions

FIGURE 8-6 Paycheck and Earnings Statement

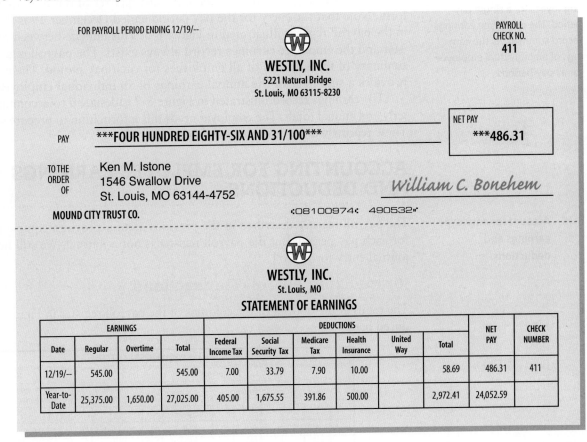

FOR PAYROLL PERIOD ENDING 12/19/--

PAYROLL CHECK NO. 411

WESTLY, INC.
5221 Natural Bridge
St. Louis, MO 63115-8230

PAY   ***FOUR HUNDRED EIGHTY-SIX AND 31/100***

NET PAY
***486.31

TO THE ORDER OF
Ken M. Istone
1546 Swallow Drive
St. Louis, MO 63144-4752

William C. Bonehem

MOUND CITY TRUST CO.   ⑈08100974⑈ 490532⑈

WESTLY, INC.
St. Louis, MO
STATEMENT OF EARNINGS

	EARNINGS			DEDUCTIONS						NET PAY	CHECK NUMBER
Date	Regular	Overtime	Total	Federal Income Tax	Social Security Tax	Medicare Tax	Health Insurance	United Way	Total		
12/19/--	545.00		545.00	7.00	33.79	7.90	10.00		58.69	486.31	411
Year-to-Date	25,375.00	1,650.00	27,025.00	405.00	1,675.55	391.86	500.00		2,972.41	24,052.59	

FIGURE 8-7 Employee Earnings Record (left side)

	EARNINGS				TAXABLE EARNINGS		EMPLOYEE EARNINGS RECORD
PERIOD ENDED	REGULAR	OVERTIME	TOTAL	CUMULATIVE TOTAL	UNEMPLOYMENT COMPENSATION	SOCIAL SECURITY	
11/28	5 4 5 00	7 5 00	6 2 0 00	25 2 4 0 00		6 2 0 00	
12/5	5 4 5 00	7 5 00	6 2 0 00	25 8 6 0 00		6 2 0 00	
12/12	5 4 5 00	7 5 00	6 2 0 00	26 4 8 0 00		6 2 0 00	
12/19	5 4 5 00		5 4 5 00	27 0 2 5 00		5 4 5 00	

GENDER	DEPARTMENT	OCCUPATION	SOCIAL SECURITY NUMBER	MARITAL STATUS	ALLOWANCES
M ✔ F	Maintenance	Service	393-58-8194	M	4

When direct deposit is used, the employee does not even handle the paycheck. Rather, payment is deposited directly by the employer into the employee's bank account using an electronic funds transfer (EFT). The employee receives only the earnings statement from the check indicating the deposit has been made. Payment by check or direct deposit provides better internal accounting control than payment by cash.

Employee Earnings Record

A separate record of each employee's earnings is called an **employee earnings record**. An employee earnings record for Ken M. Istone for a portion of the last quarter of the calendar year is illustrated in Figure 8-7 above.

The information in this record is obtained from the payroll register. In a computer-based system, the employee earnings record can be updated at the same time the payroll register is prepared.

Istone's earnings for four weeks of the last quarter of the year are shown on this form. Note that the entry for the pay period ended December 19 is the same as that in the payroll register illustrated in Figure 8-5. This linkage between the payroll register and the employee earnings record always exists. The payroll register provides a summary of the earnings of all employees for each pay period. The earnings record provides a summary of the annual earnings of an individual employee.

The earnings record illustrated in Figure 8-7 is designed to accumulate both quarterly and annual totals. The employer needs this information to prepare several reports. These reports will be discussed in Chapter 9.

ACCOUNTING FOR EMPLOYEE EARNINGS AND DEDUCTIONS

LO4 Account for employee earnings and deductions.

The payroll register described in the previous section provides complete payroll data for each pay period. But the payroll register is not a journal. We still need to make a journal entry for payroll.

Journalizing Payroll Transactions

The totals at the bottom of the columns of the payroll register in Figure 8-5 are reproduced here.

PAYROLL REGISTER (LEFT SIDE)						
EARNINGS				TAXABLE EARNINGS		
REGULAR	OVERTIME	TOTAL	CUMULATIVE TOTAL	UNEMPLOYMENT COMPENSATION	SOCIAL SECURITY	
5 3 4 3 00	6 9 2 00	6 0 3 5 00	302 1 1 5 00	3 0 0 00	5 0 3 5 00	

FIGURE 8-7 Employee Earnings Record (right side)

FOR PERIOD ENDED						20--			
				DEDUCTIONS					
FEDERAL INCOME TAX	SOCIAL SECURITY TAX	MEDICARE TAX	HEALTH INSURANCE	UNITED WAY	OTHER	TOTAL	CHECK NO.	AMOUNT	
15 00	38 44	8 99	10 00			72 43	387	547 57	
15 00	38 44	8 99	10 00			72 43	395	547 57	
15 00	38 44	8 99	10 00			72 43	403	547 57	
7 00	33 79	7 90	10 00			58 69	411	486 31	

PAY RATE	DATE OF BIRTH	DATE HIRED	NAME/ADDRESS	EMPLOYEE NUMBER
$545/wk	8/17/64	1/3/87	Ken M. Istone 1546 Swallow Drive St. Louis, MO 63144-4752	3

A Broader View

Payroll Fraud—Paying for Ghosts

A supervisor at Haas Transfer Warehouse embezzled $12,000 from the company by collecting paychecks for former employees. When an employee left the company, the supervisor continued to submit a department time report for the employee. This caused a paycheck to be generated for the "ghost" employee. The supervisor then simply kept this paycheck when others were distributed to actual employees.

This fraud shows the importance of two procedures that appear in this chapter: (1) a time card, plastic card, or badge should be used for each employee to keep an accurate record of time worked and (2) payment by direct deposit or electronic funds transfer to the employee's bank is a good internal control.

The numbered amounts in the payroll register column totals thus provide the basis for recording the payroll. If the employee paychecks are written from the regular bank account, the following journal entry is made:

PAYROLL REGISTER (RIGHT SIDE)						20--		
				DEDUCTIONS				NET PAY
FEDERAL INCOME TAX	SOCIAL SECURITY TAX	MEDICARE TAX	HEALTH INSURANCE	UNITED WAY	OTHER	TOTAL		
467 00	312 17	87 51	46 00	40 00	0 00	0 00	952 68	5082 32
(2)	(3)	(4)	(5)	(6)				(7)

	DATE		DESCRIPTION	POST REF.	DEBIT					CREDIT					
(1) 5	Dec.	19	Wages and Salaries Expense		6	0	3	5	00						5
(2) 6			Employee Federal Income Tax Payable								4	6	7	00	6
(3) 7			Social Security Tax Payable								3	1	2	17	7
(4) 8			Medicare Tax Payable									8	7	51	8
(5) 9			Health Insurance Premiums Payable									4	6	00	9
(6) 10			United Way Contributions Payable									4	0	00	10
(7) 11			Cash							5	0	8	2	32	11
12			Payroll for week ended Dec. 19												12

Employee paychecks also can be written from a special payroll bank account. Large businesses with many employees commonly use a payroll bank account. If Westly used a payroll bank account, it first would have made the following entry on December 19 to transfer funds from the regular bank account to the payroll bank account:

	DATE		DESCRIPTION	POST REF.	DEBIT					CREDIT					
1	Dec.	19	Payroll Cash		5	0	8	2	32						1
2			Cash							5	0	8	2	32	2
3			Cash for Dec. 19 payroll												3

Then, the payroll entry shown above would be made, except that the credit of $5,082.32 would be to Payroll Cash rather than Cash.

If a payroll bank account is used, individual checks totaling $5,082.32 are written to the employees from that account. Otherwise, individual checks totaling that amount are written to the employees from the regular bank account.

Notice two important facts about the payroll entry. First, Wages and Salaries Expense is debited for the gross pay of the employees. The expense to the employer is the gross pay, not the employees' net pay after deductions. Second, a separate account is kept for each deduction.

The accounts needed in entering deductions depend upon the deductions involved. To understand the accounting for these deductions, consider what the employer is doing. By deducting amounts from employees' earnings, the employer is simply serving as an agent for the government and other groups. Amounts that are deducted from an employee's gross earnings must be paid by the employer to these groups. Therefore, a separate account should be kept for the liability for each type of deduction.

To help us understand the journal entry for payroll, let's use the accounting equation to examine the accounts involved. The seven accounts affected by the payroll entry above are shown in the accounting equation in Figure 8-8.

LEARNING KEY
Wages and Salaries Expense is debited for the gross pay. A separate account is kept for each earnings deduction. Cash is credited for the net pay.

FIGURE 8-8 Accounting for Payroll

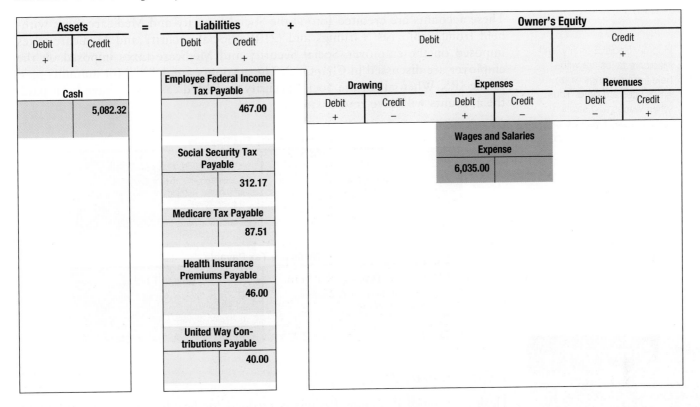

Wages and Salaries Expense

This account is debited for the gross pay of all employees for each pay period. Sometimes separate expense accounts are kept for the employees of different departments. Thus, separate accounts may be kept for Office Salaries Expense, Sales Salaries Expense, and Factory Wages Expense.

Wages and Salaries Expense

Debit	Credit
gross pay of employees for each pay period	

Employee Federal Income Tax Payable

This account is credited for the total federal income tax withheld from employees' earnings. The account is debited for amounts paid to the IRS. When all of the income taxes withheld have been paid, the account will have a zero balance. A state or city income tax payable account is used in a similar manner.

Employee Federal Income Tax Payable

Debit	Credit
payment of federal income tax previously withheld	federal income tax withheld from employees' earnings

Social Security and Medicare Taxes Payable

These accounts are credited for (1) the Social Security and Medicare taxes withheld from employees' earnings and (2) the Social Security and Medicare taxes imposed on the employer. Social Security and Medicare taxes imposed on the employer are discussed in Chapter 9. The accounts are debited for amounts paid to the IRS. When all of the Social Security and Medicare taxes have been paid, the accounts will have zero balances.

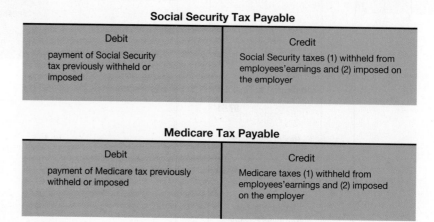

Social Security Tax Payable

Debit	Credit
payment of Social Security tax previously withheld or imposed	Social Security taxes (1) withheld from employees' earnings and (2) imposed on the employer

Medicare Tax Payable

Debit	Credit
payment of Medicare tax previously withheld or imposed	Medicare taxes (1) withheld from employees' earnings and (2) imposed on the employer

Other Deductions

Health Insurance Premiums Payable is credited for health insurance contributions deducted from an employee's pay. The account is debited for the subsequent payment of these amounts to the health insurer. United Way Contributions Payable is handled in a similar manner.

PAYROLL RECORD-KEEPING METHODS

LO5 Describe various payroll record-keeping methods.

You probably noticed that the same information appears in several places in the payroll records—in the payroll register, paycheck and stub, and employee earnings records. If all records are prepared by hand (a **manual system**), the same information would be recorded several times. Unless an employer has only a few employees, this can be very inefficient. Various approaches are available to make payroll accounting more efficient and accurate.

Both medium- and large-size businesses commonly use two approaches for payroll record keeping: payroll processing centers and electronic systems. A **payroll processing center** is a business that sells payroll record-keeping services. The employer provides the center with all basic employee data and each period's report of hours worked. The processing center maintains all payroll records and prepares each period's payroll checks. Payroll processing center fees tend to be much less than the cost to an employer of handling payroll internally.

An **electronic system** is a computer system based on a software package that performs all payroll record keeping and prepares payroll checks or EFT records. In this system, only the employee number and hours worked need to be entered into a computer each pay period, as shown in Figure 8-9. All other payroll data needed to prepare the payroll records can be stored in the computer. The computer uses the employee number and hours worked to determine the gross pay, deductions, and net pay. The payroll register, checks (or EFTs), and employee earnings records are provided as outputs.

FIGURE 8-9   Electronic Payroll System

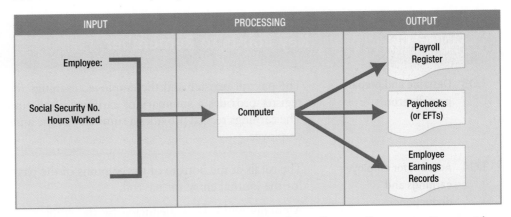

The same inputs and outputs are required in all payroll systems. Even with a computer, the data required for payroll processing have to be entered into the system at some point. The outputs—the payroll register, paychecks, and employee earnings records—are basically the same under each system.

Self-Study

LEARNING OBJECTIVES	Key Points to Remember
LO1 Distinguish between employees and independent contractors.	Employees work under the control and direction of an employer. Independent contractors perform a service for a fee and do not work under the control and direction of the company paying for the service. Payroll accounting procedures apply only to employees, not to independent contractors.
LO2 Calculate employee earnings and deductions.	Three steps are required to determine how much to pay an employee for a pay period: 1. Calculate total earnings. 2. Determine the amounts of deductions. 3. Subtract deductions from total earnings to compute net pay. Deductions from gross pay fall into three categories: 1. Income tax withholding 2. Employee Social Security and Medicare taxes withholding 3. Voluntary deductions Four factors determine the amount to be withheld from an employee's gross pay each pay period: 1. Total earnings 2. Marital status 3. Number of withholding allowances claimed 4. Length of the pay period

(continued)

LEARNING OBJECTIVES	Key Points to Remember
LO3 Describe and prepare payroll records.	The payroll register and the employee earnings record are linked. The payroll register provides a summary of earnings of all employees for each pay period. The earnings record provides a summary of the annual earnings of an individual employee.
LO4 Account for employee earnings and deductions.	The totals at the bottom of the columns of the payroll register provide the basis for the journal entry for payroll. Amounts withheld or deducted by the employer from employee earnings are credited to liability accounts. The employer must pay these amounts to the proper government groups and other appropriate groups.
LO5 Describe various payroll record-keeping methods.	In a manual payroll system, the same information needs to be recorded several times. An electronic payroll system is much more efficient.

DEMONSTRATION PROBLEM

Carole Vohsen operates a pet grooming salon called Canine Coiffures. She has five employees, all of whom are paid on a weekly basis. Canine Coiffures uses a payroll register, individual employee earnings records, a journal, and a general ledger.

The payroll data for each employee for the week ended January 21, 20--, are given below. Employees are paid 1½ times the regular rate for work over 40 hours a week.

Name	Employee No.	No. of Allowances	Marital Status	Total Hours Worked Jan. 15–21	Rate	Total Earnings Jan. 1–14
DeNourie, Katie	1	2	S	44	$11.50	$1,058.00
Garriott, Pete	2	1	M	40	12.00	1,032.00
Martinez, Sheila	3	3	M	39	12.50	987.50
Parker, Nancy	4	2	M	42	11.00	957.00
Shapiro, John	5	2	S	40	11.50	931.50

Sheila Martinez is the manager of the Shampooing Department. Her Social Security number is 500-88-4189, and she was born April 12, 1969. She lives at 46 Darling Crossing, Norwich, CT, 06360. Martinez was hired September 1 of last year.

Canine Coiffures uses a federal income tax withholding table. A portion of this weekly table is provided in Figure 8-4 on pages 288 and 289. Social Security tax is withheld at the rate of 6.2% of the first $118,500 earned. Medicare tax is withheld at the rate of 1.45%, and city earnings tax at the rate of 1%, both applied to gross pay. Garriott and Parker each have $14 and DeNourie and Martinez each have $4 withheld for health insurance. DeNourie, Martinez, and Shapiro each have $15 withheld to be invested in the groomers' credit union. Garriott and Shapiro each have $18.75 withheld under a savings bond purchase plan.

Canine Coiffures' payroll is met by drawing checks on its regular bank account. This week, the checks were issued in sequence, beginning with No. 811.

REQUIRED

1. Prepare a payroll register for Canine Coiffures for the week ended January 21, 20--. (In the Taxable Earnings/Unemployment Compensation column, enter the same amounts as in the Social Security column.) Total the amount columns, verify the totals, and rule with single and double lines.

2. Prepare an employee earnings record for Sheila Martinez for the week ended January 21, 20--.

3. Assuming that the wages for the week ended January 21 were paid on January 23, prepare the journal entry for the payment of this payroll.

4. Post the entry in requirement (3) to the affected accounts in the ledger of Canine Coiffures. Do not enter any amounts in the Balance columns. Use account numbers as follows: Cash—101; Employee Federal Income Tax Payable—211; Social Security Tax Payable—212; Medicare Tax Payable—213; City Earnings Tax Payable—215; Health Insurance Premiums Payable—216; Credit Union Payable—217; Savings Bond Deductions Payable—218; Wages and Salaries Expense—511.

Solution 1.

PAYROLL REGISTER

	NAME	EMPLOYEE NO.	ALLOWANCES	MARITAL STATUS	EARNINGS REGULAR	EARNINGS OVERTIME	EARNINGS TOTAL	CUMULATIVE TOTAL	TAXABLE EARNINGS UNEMPLOYMENT COMPENSATION	TAXABLE EARNINGS SOCIAL SECURITY
1	DeNourie, Katie	1	2	S	4 6 0 00	6 9 00	5 2 9 00	1 5 8 7 00	5 2 9 00	5 2 9 00
2	Garriott, Pete	2	1	M	4 8 0 00		4 8 0 00	1 5 1 2 00	4 8 0 00	4 8 0 00
3	Martinez, Sheila	3	3	M	4 8 7 50		4 8 7 50	1 4 7 5 00	4 8 7 50	4 8 7 50
4	Parker, Nancy	4	2	M	4 4 0 00	3 3 00	4 7 3 00	1 4 3 0 00	4 7 3 00	4 7 3 00
5	Shapiro, John	5	2	S	4 6 0 00		4 6 0 00	1 3 9 1 50	4 6 0 00	4 6 0 00
6					2 3 2 7 50	1 0 2 00	2 4 2 9 50	7 3 9 5 50	2 4 2 9 50	2 4 2 9 50
7										
8										
9										
10										

—WEEK ENDED 12/19/--

	DEDUCTIONS FEDERAL INCOME TAX	DEDUCTIONS SOCIAL SECURITY TAX	DEDUCTIONS MEDICARE TAX	DEDUCTIONS CITY TAX	DEDUCTIONS HEALTH INSURANCE	DEDUCTIONS CREDIT UNION	DEDUCTIONS OTHER	DEDUCTIONS TOTAL	NET PAY	CHECK NO.	
	4 0 00	3 2 80	7 67	5 29	4 00	1 5 00		1 0 4 76	4 2 4 24	811	1
	2 4 00	2 9 76	6 96	4 80	1 4 00		1 8 75	9 8 27	3 8 1 73	812	2
	9 00	3 0 23	7 07	4 88	4 00	1 5 00		7 0 18	4 1 7 32	813	3
	1 6 00	2 9 33	6 86	4 73	1 4 00			7 0 92	4 0 2 08	814	4
	3 1 00	2 8 52	6 67	4 60		1 5 00	1 8 75	1 0 4 54	3 5 5 46	815	5
	1 2 0 00	1 5 0 64	3 5 23	2 4 30	3 6 00	4 5 00	3 7 50	4 4 8 67	1 9 8 0 83		6
											7
											8
											9
											10

2.

		EARNINGS											TAXABLE EARNINGS				
20-- PERIOD ENDED		REGULAR		OVERTIME		TOTAL		CUMULATIVE TOTAL			UNEMPLOYMENT COMPENSATION			SOCIAL SECURITY			
1/7																	
1/14																	
1/21		4 8 7 50				4 8 7 50		1 4 7 5 00			4 8 7 50			4 8 7 50			
1/28																	

EMPLOYEE EARNINGS RECORD

GENDER		DEPARTMENT	OCCUPATION	SOCIAL SECURITY NUMBER	MARITAL STATUS	ALLOWANCES
M	F ✔	Shampooing	Manager	500-88-4189	M	3

FOR PERIOD ENDED 20--

	DEDUCTIONS																
FEDERAL INCOME TAX		SOCIAL SECURITY TAX		MEDICARE TAX		CITY TAX		HEALTH INSURANCE		CREDIT UNION		OTHER		TOTAL		CHECK NO.	AMOUNT
9 00		3 0 23		7 07		4 88		4 00		1 5 00				7 0 18		813	4 1 7 32

PAY RATE	DATE OF BIRTH	DATE HIRED	NAME/ADDRESS	EMPLOYEE NUMBER
$12.50	4/12/69	9/1/--	Sheila Martinez 46 Darling Crossing Norwich, CT 06360	3

3.

	DATE		DESCRIPTION	POST. REF.	DEBIT					CREDIT					
	20--														
1	Jan.	23	Wages and Salaries Expense	511	2	4	2 9	50							1
2			Employee Federal Income Tax Payable	211						1	2	0	00		2
3			Social Security Tax Payable	212						1	5	0	64		3
4			Medicare Tax Payable	213							3	5	23		4
5			City Earnings Tax Payable	215							2	4	30		5
6			Health Insurance Premiums Payable	216							3	6	00		6
7			Credit Union Payable	217							4	5	00		7
8			Savings Bond Deductions Payable	218							3	7	50		8
9			Cash	101						1	9	8 0	83		9
10			Payroll for week ended Jan. 21												10

GENERAL JOURNAL PAGE 1

4.

GENERAL LEDGER

ACCOUNT: Cash   **ACCOUNT NO.** 101

DATE	ITEM	POST. REF.	DEBIT	CREDIT	BALANCE DEBIT	BALANCE CREDIT
20-- Jan. 23		J1		1 9 8 0 83		

ACCOUNT: Employee Federal Income Tax Payable   **ACCOUNT NO.** 211

DATE	ITEM	POST. REF.	DEBIT	CREDIT	BALANCE DEBIT	BALANCE CREDIT
20-- Jan. 23		J1		1 2 0 00		

ACCOUNT: Social Security Tax Payable   **ACCOUNT NO.** 212

DATE	ITEM	POST. REF.	DEBIT	CREDIT	BALANCE DEBIT	BALANCE CREDIT
20-- Jan. 23		J1		1 5 0 64		

ACCOUNT: Medicare Tax Payable   **ACCOUNT NO.** 213

DATE	ITEM	POST. REF.	DEBIT	CREDIT	BALANCE DEBIT	BALANCE CREDIT
20-- Jan. 23		J1		3 5 23		

ACCOUNT: City Earnings Tax Payable   **ACCOUNT NO.** 215

DATE	ITEM	POST. REF.	DEBIT	CREDIT	BALANCE DEBIT	BALANCE CREDIT
20-- Jan. 23		J1		2 4 30		

ACCOUNT: Health Insurance Premiums Payable   **ACCOUNT NO.** 216

DATE	ITEM	POST. REF.	DEBIT	CREDIT	BALANCE DEBIT	BALANCE CREDIT
20-- Jan. 23		J1		3 6 00		

ACCOUNT: Credit Union Payable   **ACCOUNT NO.** 217

DATE	ITEM	POST. REF.	DEBIT	CREDIT	BALANCE DEBIT	BALANCE CREDIT
20-- Jan. 23		J1		4 5 00		

ACCOUNT: Savings Bond Deductions Payable   **ACCOUNT NO.** 218

DATE	ITEM	POST. REF.	DEBIT	CREDIT	BALANCE DEBIT	BALANCE CREDIT
20-- Jan. 23		J1		3 7 50		

ACCOUNT: Wages and Salaries Expense   **ACCOUNT NO.** 511

DATE	ITEM	POST. REF.	DEBIT	CREDIT	BALANCE DEBIT	BALANCE CREDIT
20-- Jan. 23		J1	2 4 2 9 50			

KEY TERMS

direct deposit (294)   A payroll method in which the employee does not handle the paycheck; payment is made by the employer directly to the employee's bank using EFT.

electronic system (298)   A computer system based on a software package that performs all payroll record keeping and prepares payroll checks.

employee (283)   Someone who works under the control and direction of an employer.

employee earnings record (294)   A separate record of each employee's earnings.

Fair Labor Standards Act (FLSA) (283)   A law that requires employers to pay overtime at 1½ times the regular rate to any hourly employee who works over 40 hours in a week.

FICA taxes (287)   Payroll taxes withheld to provide Social Security and Medicare benefits.

gross pay (286)   An employee's total earnings.

independent contractor (283)   Someone who performs a service for a fee and does not work under the control and direction of the company paying for the service.

manual system (298)   Payroll system in which all records are prepared by hand.

net pay (286)   Gross pay less mandatory and voluntary deductions.

payroll processing center (298)   A business that sells payroll record-keeping services.

payroll register (291)   A form used to assemble the data required at the end of each payroll period.

percentage method (287)   A method of determining the amount to withhold from an employee's gross pay for a specific period.

salary (283)   Compensation for managerial or administrative services.

wage-bracket method (287)   A method of determining the amount to withhold from an employee's gross pay for a specific time period. Wage-bracket tables are provided by the Internal Revenue Service.

wages (283)   Compensation for skilled or unskilled labor.

withholding allowance (286)   A specific dollar amount of an employee's gross pay that is exempt from federal income tax withholding.

SELF-STUDY TEST QUESTIONS

True/False

1. **LO1**   An independent contractor is one who works under the control and direction of an employer.

2. **LO1**   Government laws and regulations regarding payroll are more complex for employees than for independent contractors.

3. **LO2**   Compensation for skilled or unskilled labor expressed in terms of hours, weeks, or units is called salary.

4. **LO2**   An employee's total earnings is called gross pay.

5. **LO3**   A payroll register is a multi-column form used to assemble the data required at the end of each payroll period.

Multiple Choice

1. **LO2**   Jack Smith is married, has a spouse who is not employed and has five dependent children. How many withholding allowances is Smith entitled to?

   (a) 5   (c) 7
   (b) 6   (d) 8

2. **LO2**   Nancy Summers worked 44 hours during the past week. She is entitled to 1½ times her regular pay for all hours worked in excess of 40 during the week. Her regular rate of pay is $12.00. Social Security tax is withheld at the rate of 6.2% and Medicare tax is withheld at the rate of 1.45%; federal income tax withheld is $68; and $5 of union dues are withheld. Her net pay for the week is

   (a) $440.89.   (c) $552.
   (b) $472.   (d) $436.78.

3. **LO2**   Which of the following is *not* a factor that determines the amount of federal income tax to be withheld from an employee's gross pay?

   (a) marital status   (c) total earnings
   (b) number of withholding allowances claimed   (d) age of employee

4. **LO3**   A separate record of each employee's earnings is called a(n)

   (a) payroll register.   (c) W-4.
   (b) employee earnings record.   (d) earnings statement.

5. **LO4**   Social Security Tax Payable and Medicare Tax Payable are classified as

   (a) liabilities.   (c) owner's equity.
   (b) assets.   (d) expenses.

Checkpoint Exercises

1. **LO2**   Qian Wang is paid a regular rate of $14 per hour and 1½ times the regular rate for hours worked over 40 in a week. During the past week, Qian worked 45 hours.

   (a) Compute Qian's gross pay for the week.
   (b) Assume Qian is married and claims two withholding allowances. Compute the amount of federal income tax her employer should withhold for the week.

2. **LO4**   The column totals from the payroll register of Jawhawk Supplies for the week ended February 9 were as follows:

Total earnings	$4,600.00
Federal income tax	417.00
Social Security tax	285.20
Medicare tax	66.70
State income tax	46.00
Health insurance	181.00

   Prepare the journal entry to record the payroll, crediting Cash for the net pay.

The answers to the Self-Study Test Questions are at the end of the chapter (page 316).

Applying Your Knowledge

LO1 1. Why is it important for payroll accounting purposes to distinguish between an employee and an independent contractor?

LO2 2. Name three major categories of deductions from an employee's gross pay.

LO2 3. Identify the four factors that determine the amount of federal income tax that is withheld from an employee's pay each pay period.

LO2 4. In general, an employee is entitled to withholding allowances for what purposes?

LO3 5. Identify the three payroll records usually needed by an employer.

LO3 6. Describe the information contained in the payroll register.

LO3 7. Why is it important to total and verify the totals of the payroll register after the data for each employee have been entered?

LO3 8. Distinguish between the payroll register and the employee earnings record.

LO4 9. Explain what an employer does with the amounts withheld from an employee's pay.

LO5 10. Explain why payroll processing centers and electronic systems are commonly used in payroll accounting.

SERIES A EXERCISES

E 8-1A (LO2)
✓ Gross pay: $795

COMPUTING WEEKLY GROSS PAY Ryan Lawrence's regular hourly rate is $15. He receives 1½ times the regular rate for any hours worked over 40 a week and double the rate for work on Sunday. During the past week, Lawrence worked 8 hours each day Monday through Thursday, 10 hours on Friday, and 5 hours on Sunday. Compute Lawrence's gross pay for the past week.

E 8-2A (LO2)
✓ b: $712.50

COMPUTING OVERTIME RATE OF PAY AND GROSS WEEKLY PAY Rebecca Huang receives a regular salary of $2,600 a month and is paid 1½ times the regular hourly rate for hours worked in excess of 40 per week.

(a) Calculate Huang's overtime rate of pay.

(b) Calculate Huang's total gross weekly pay if she works 45 hours during the week.

E 8-3A (LO2)
✓ e: $15

COMPUTING FEDERAL INCOME TAX Using the table in Figure 8-4 on pages 288 and 289, determine the amount of federal income tax an employer should withhold weekly for employees with the following marital status, earnings, and withholding allowances:

	Marital Status	Total Weekly Earnings	Number of Allowances	Amount of Withholding
(a)	S	$347.60	2	_____
(b)	S	451.50	1	_____
(c)	M	481.15	3	_____
(d)	S	490.52	0	_____
(e)	M	691.89	5	_____

E 8-4A   (LO2)

✓ 3d row, Soc. Sec. tax: $161.20

CALCULATING SOCIAL SECURITY AND MEDICARE TAXES Assume a Social Security tax rate of 6.2% is applied to maximum earnings of $118,500 and a Medicare tax rate of 1.45% is applied to all earnings. Calculate the Social Security and Medicare taxes for the following situations:

Cumul. Pay Before Current Weekly Payroll	Current Gross Pay	Year-to-Date Earnings	Soc. Sec. Maximum	Amount Over Max. Soc. Sec.	Amount Subject to Soc. Sec.	Soc. Sec. Tax Withheld	Medicare Tax Withheld
$ 22,000	$1,700	_____	$118,500	_____	_____	_____	_____
54,000	4,200	_____	118,500	_____	_____	_____	_____
115,900	3,925	_____	118,500	_____	_____	_____	_____
117,900	4,600	_____	118,500	_____	_____	_____	_____

E 8-5A   (LO2)

✓ Net pay: $450.51

SHOW
ME HOW

COMPUTING NET PAY Mary Sue Guild works for a company that pays its employees 1½ times the regular rate for all hours worked in excess of 40 per week. Guild's pay rate is $10 per hour. Her wages are subject to deductions for federal income tax, Social Security tax, and Medicare tax. She is married and claims four withholding allowances. Guild has a ½-hour lunch break during an 8½-hour day. Her time card is shown below.

Name	Mary Sue Guild					
Week Ending	March 30, 20--					
Day	In	Out	In	Out	Regular	Overtime
M	7:57	12:05	12:35	4:33	8	
T	7:52	12:09	12:39	5:05	8	½
W	7:59	12:15	12:45	5:30	8	1
T	8:00	12:01	12:30	6:31	8	2
F	7:56	12:05	12:34	4:30	8	
S	8:00	10:31				2½

(*continued*)

Complete the following for the week:

(a) _____ regular hours × $10 per hour $_____

(b) _____ overtime hours × $15 per hour $_____

(c) Total gross wages $_____

(d) Federal income tax withholding (from tax tables in
Figure 8-4, pages 288 and 289) $_____

(e) Social Security withholding at 6.2% $_____

(f) Medicare withholding at 1.45% $_____

(g) Total withholding $_____

(h) Net pay $_____

E 8-6A   (LO4)

✓ Med. tax: $126.15

SHOW
ME HOW

JOURNALIZING PAYROLL TRANSACTIONS On December 31, the payroll register
of Hamstreet Associates indicated the following information:

Wages and Salaries Expense	$8,700.00
Employee Federal Income Tax Payable	920.00
United Way Contributions Payable	200.00
Earnings subject to Social Security tax	8,000.00

Determine the amount of Social Security and Medicare taxes to be withheld and
record the journal entry for the payroll, crediting Cash for the net pay.

E 8-7A   (LO4)

✓ Cr. Cash: $4,932.37

SHOW
ME HOW

PAYROLL JOURNAL ENTRY Journalize the following data taken from the payroll
register of CopyMasters as of April 15, 20—:

Regular earnings	$5,715.00
Overtime earnings	790.00
Deductions:	
Federal income tax	625.00
Social Security tax	403.31
Medicare tax	94.32
Pension plan	80.00
Health insurance premiums	270.00
United Way contributions	100.00

SERIES A PROBLEMS

P 8-8A   (LO2/4)

✓ Net pay: $183.19

GROSS PAY, DEDUCTIONS, AND NET PAY Donald Chin works for Northwest
Supplies. His rate of pay is $8.50 per hour, and he is paid 1½ times the regular rate
for all hours worked in excess of 40 per week. During the last week of January of the
current year, he worked 48 hours. Chin is married and claims three withholding allowances on his W-4 form. His weekly wages are subject to the following deductions:

(a) Employee federal income tax (use Figure 8-4 on pages 288 and 289)

(b) Social Security tax at 6.2%

(c) Medicare tax at 1.45%

(d) Health insurance premium, $85

(e) Credit union, $125

(f) United Way contribution, $10

REQUIRED

1. Compute Chin's regular pay, overtime pay, gross pay, and net pay.

2. Journalize the payment of his wages for the week ended January 31, crediting Cash for the net amount.

P 8-9A   (LO2/3/4)

✓ Cr. Cash: $1,900.31

PAYROLL REGISTER AND PAYROLL JOURNAL ENTRY Mary Losch operates a travel agency called Mary's Luxury Travel. She has five employees, all of whom are paid on a weekly basis. The travel agency uses a payroll register, individual employee earnings records, and a general journal.

Mary's Luxury Travel uses a weekly federal income tax withholding table like the one in Figure 8-4 on pages 288 and 289. The payroll data for each employee for the week ended March 22, 20—, are given below. Employees are paid 1½ times the regular rate for working over 40 hours a week.

Name	No. of Allowances	Marital Status	Total Hours Worked Mar. 16–22	Rate	Total Earnings Jan. 1–Mar. 15
Bacon, Andrea	4	M	45	$12.00	$5,480.00
Cole, Andrew	1	S	40	12.00	5,760.00
Hicks, Melvin	3	M	44	10.50	4,960.00
Leung, Cara	1	S	36	11.00	5,125.50
Melling, Melissa	2	M	40	10.50	4,720.50

Social Security tax is withheld from the first $118,500 of earnings at the rate of 6.2%. Medicare tax is withheld at the rate of 1.45%, and city earnings tax at the rate of 1%, both applied to gross pay. Bacon and Leung have $15 withheld and Cole and Hicks have $5 withheld for health insurance. Bacon and Leung have $20 withheld to be invested in the travel agency's credit union. Cole has $38.75 withheld and Hicks has $18.75 withheld under a savings bond purchase plan.

Mary's Luxury Travel's payroll is met by drawing checks on its regular bank account. The checks were issued in sequence, beginning with Check No. 423.

REQUIRED

1. Prepare a payroll register for Mary's Luxury Travel for the week ended March 22, 20--. (In the Taxable Earnings/Unemployment Compensation column, enter the same amounts as in the Social Security column.) Total the amount columns, verify the totals, and rule with single and double lines.

2. Assuming that the wages for the week ended March 22 were paid on March 24, prepare the journal entry for the payment of the payroll.

P 8-10A   (LO3)

✓ Soc. Sec. tax: $29.76

EMPLOYEE EARNINGS RECORD Mary's Luxury Travel in Problem 8-9A keeps employee earnings records. Andrew Cole, employee number 62, is employed as a manager in the ticket sales department. He was born on May 8, 1986, and was hired on June 1 of last year. His Social Security number is 544-67-1283. He lives at 28 Quarry Drive, Vernon, CT, 06066.

REQUIRED

For the week ended March 22, complete an employee earnings record for Andrew Cole. (Insert earnings data only for the week of March 22.)

SERIES B EXERCISES

E 8-1B (LO2)
✓ Gross pay: $678

COMPUTING WEEKLY GROSS PAY Manuel Soto's regular hourly rate is $12. He receives 1½ times the regular rate for hours worked in excess of 40 a week and double the rate for work on Sunday. During the past week, Soto worked 8 hours each day Monday through Thursday, 11 hours on Friday, and 6 hours on Sunday. Compute Soto's gross pay for the past week.

E 8-2B (LO2)
✓ b: $918.75

COMPUTING OVERTIME RATE OF PAY AND GROSS WEEKLY PAY Mike Fritz receives a regular salary of $3,250 a month and is paid 1½ times the regular hourly rate for hours worked in excess of 40 per week.

(a) Calculate Fritz's overtime rate of pay. (Compute to the nearest half cent.)

(b) Calculate Fritz's total gross weekly pay if he works 46 hours during the week.

E 8-3B (LO2)
✓ e: $77

COMPUTING FEDERAL INCOME TAX Using the table in Figure 8-4 on pages 288 and 289, determine the amount of federal income tax an employer should withhold weekly for employees with the following marital status, earnings, and withholding allowances:

	Marital Status	Total Weekly Earnings	Number of Allowances	Amount of Withholding
(a)	M	$546.00	4	_____
(b)	M	390.00	1	_____
(c)	S	461.39	2	_____
(d)	M	522.88	2	_____
(e)	S	612.00	0	_____

E 8-4B (LO2)
✓ 3rd row, Soc. Sec. tax: $179.80

CALCULATING SOCIAL SECURITY AND MEDICARE TAXES Assume a Social Security tax rate of 6.2% is applied to maximum earnings of $118,500 and a Medicare tax rate of 1.45% is applied to all earnings. Calculate the Social Security and Medicare taxes for the following situations:

Cumul. Pay Before Current Weekly Payroll	Current Gross Pay	Year-to-Date Earnings	Soc. Sec. Maximum	Amount Over Max. Soc. Sec.	Amount Subject to Soc. Sec.	Soc. Sec. Tax Withheld	Medicare Tax Withheld
$ 31,000	$1,500	_____	$118,500	_____	_____	_____	_____
53,000	2,860	_____	118,500	_____	_____	_____	_____
115,600	3,140	_____	118,500	_____	_____	_____	_____
117,900	2,920	_____	118,500	_____	_____	_____	_____

E 8-5B (LO2)
✓ Net pay: $531.70

SHOW ME HOW

COMPUTING NET PAY Tom Hallinan works for a company that pays its employees 1½ times the regular rate for all hours worked in excess of 40 per week. Hallinan's pay rate is $12 per hour. His wages are subject to deductions for federal income tax, Social Security tax, and Medicare tax. He is married and claims five withholding allowances. Hallinan has a ½-hour lunch break during an 8½-hour day. His time card is on next page.

Name	Tom Hallinan					
Week Ending	March 30, 20--					
Day	In	Out	In	Out	Hours Worked	
					Regular	Overtime
M	7:55	12:02	12:32	5:33	8	1
T	7:59	12:04	12:34	6:05	8	1½
W	7:59	12:05	12:35	4:30	8	
T	8:00	12:01	12:30	5:01	8	½
F	7:58	12:02	12:31	5:33	8	1
S	7:59	9:33				1½

Complete the following for the week:

(a) _____ regular hours × $12 per hour $_____

(b) _____ overtime hours × $18 per hour $_____

(c) Total gross wages $_____

(d) Federal income tax withholding (from tax tables in Figure 8-4, pages 289 and 288) $_____

(e) Social Security withholding at 6.2% $_____

(f) Medicare withholding at 1.45% $_____

(g) Total withholding $_____

(h) Net pay $_____

E 8-6B   (LO4)

✓ Med. tax: $136.30

SHOW
ME HOW

JOURNALIZING PAYROLL TRANSACTIONS On November 30, the payroll register of Webster & Smith indicated the following information:

Wages and Salaries Expense	$9,400.00
Employee Federal Income Tax Payable	985.00
United Way Contributions Payable	200.00
Earnings subject to Social Security tax	9,400.00

Determine the amount of Social Security and Medicare taxes to be withheld and record the journal entry for the payroll, crediting Cash for the net pay.

E 8-7B   (LO4)

✓ Cr. Cash: $5,696.54

SHOW
ME HOW

PAYROLL JOURNAL ENTRY Journalize the following data taken from the payroll register of Himes Bakery as of June 12, 20--:

Regular earnings	$6,520.00
Overtime earnings	950.00
Deductions:	
Federal income tax	782.00
Social Security tax	463.14
Medicare tax	108.32
Pension plan	80.00
Health insurance premiums	190.00
United Way contributions	150.00

SERIES B PROBLEMS

P 8-8B   (LO2/4)

✓ Net pay: $187.27

GROSS PAY, DEDUCTIONS, AND NET PAY Elyse Lin works for Columbia Industries. Her rate of pay is $9 per hour, and she is paid 1½ times the regular rate for all hours worked in excess of 40 per week. During the last week of January of the current year, she worked 46 hours. Lin is married and claims two withholding allowances on her W-4 form. Her weekly wages are subject to the following deductions:

(a) Employee federal income tax (use Figure 8-4 on pages 288 and 289)

(b) Social Security tax at 6.2%

(c) Medicare tax at 1.45%

(d) Health insurance premium, $92

(e) Credit union, $110

(f) United Way contribution, $5

REQUIRED

1. Compute Lin's regular pay, overtime pay, gross pay, and net pay.

2. Journalize the payment of her wages for the week ended January 31, crediting Cash for the net amount.

P 8-9B   (LO2/3/4)

✓ Cr. Cash: $1,774.40

PAYROLL REGISTER AND PAYROLL JOURNAL ENTRY Karen Jolly operates a bakery called Karen's Cupcakes. She has five employees, all of whom are paid on a weekly basis. Karen's Cupcakes uses a payroll register, individual employee earnings records, and a general journal.

Karen's Cupcakes uses a weekly federal income tax withholding table like the one in Figure 8-4 on pages 288 and 289. The payroll data for each employee for the week ended February 15, 20--, are given below. Employees are paid 1½ times the regular rate for working over 40 hours a week.

Name	No. of Allowances	Marital Status	Total Hours Worked Feb. 9–15	Rate	Total Earnings Jan. 1–Feb. 8
Barone, William	1	S	40	$10.00	$2,400.00
Hastings, Gene	4	M	45	12.00	3,360.00
Nitobe, Isako	3	M	46	8.75	2,935.00
Smith, Judy	2	M	42	11.00	2,745.00
Tarshis, Dolores	1	S	39	10.50	2,650.75

Social Security tax is withheld from the first $118,500 of earnings at the rate of 6.2%. Medicare tax is withheld at the rate of 1.45%, and city earnings tax at the rate of 1%, both applied to gross pay. Hastings and Smith have $35 withheld and Nitobe and Tarshis have $15 withheld for health insurance. Nitobe and Tarshis have $25 withheld to be invested in the bakers' credit union. Hastings has $18.75 withheld and Smith has $43.75 withheld under a savings bond purchase plan.

Karen's Cupcakes' payroll is met by drawing checks on its regular bank account. The checks were issued in sequence, beginning with No. 365.

REQUIRED

1. Prepare a payroll register for Karen's Cupcakes for the week ended February 15, 20--. (In the Taxable Earnings/Unemployment Compensation column, enter the same amounts as in the Social Security column.) Total the amount columns, verify the totals, and rule with single and double lines.

2. Assuming that the wages for the week ended February 15 were paid on February 17, prepare the journal entry for the payment of this payroll.

P 8-10B   (LO3)

✓ Soc. Sec. tax: $24.80

EMPLOYEE EARNINGS RECORD Karen's Cupcakes in Problem 8-9B keeps employee earnings records. William Barone, employee number 19, is employed as a baker in the desserts department. He was born on August 26, 1979, and was hired on October 1 of last year. His Social Security number is 342-73-4681. He lives at 30 Timber Lane, Willington, CT, 06279.

REQUIRED

For the week ended February 15, complete an employee earnings record for William Barone. (Insert earnings data only for the week of February 15.)

MANAGING YOUR WRITING

The minimum wage originally was only 25 cents an hour. Today it is $7.25 an hour. Assume that Congress is considering raising the minimum wage again and your U.S. representative is asking for public opinion on this issue. Write a letter to your representative with arguments for and against a higher minimum wage.

Check List
- ✔ Check List
- ☐ Managing
- ☐ Planning
- ☐ Drafting
- ☐ Break
- ☐ Revising
- ☐ Managing

ETHICS

ETHICS CASE

Maura Lowe is a payroll accountant for N & L Company. She prepares and processes the company's payroll on a weekly basis and has been at N & L for only three months. All employees are paid on Friday. On Wednesday afternoon, Simon Lentz, one of the company's top sales associates, asks Maura to not take out any payroll deductions from his pay this week. He explains that he is short of cash and needs the full amount of his gross salary just to put food on the table and make his past-due car payment. He promises Maura that she can catch up on the deductions over the next month. The deductions include employee income tax, Social Security tax, Medicare tax, and health insurance premiums.

1. Is Simon's request of Maura ethical? Why or why not?

2. If this were the first pay period of the year and Maura agreed not to take out deductions from Simon's pay, what effect would this have on the liabilities section of the balance sheet?

3. Write a short paragraph from Maura to Simon explaining how omitting deductions from a pay period will cause errors in the company's financial statements.

4. In small groups, discuss what action Maura should take regarding Simon's request.

MASTERY PROBLEM

✓ Cr. Cash: $4,323.83

Abigail Trenkamp owns and operates the Trenkamp Collection Agency. Listed below are the name, number of allowances claimed, marital status, information from time cards on hours worked each day, and the hourly rate of each employee. All hours worked in excess of 40 hours for Monday through Friday are paid at 1½ times the regular rate. All weekend hours are paid at double the regular rate.

Trenkamp uses a weekly federal income tax withholding table (see Figure 8-4 on pages 288 and 289). Social Security tax is withheld at the rate of 6.2% for the first $118,500 earned. Medicare tax is withheld at 1.45% and state income tax at 3.5%. Each employee has $5 withheld for health insurance. All employees use payroll deduction to the credit union for varying amounts as listed.

Trenkamp Collection Agency
Payroll Information for the Week Ended November 18, 20--

Name	Employee No.	No of Allow.	Marital Status	Regular Hours Worked S S M T W T F							Hourly Rate	Credit Union Deposit	Total Earnings 1/1–11/11
Berling, James	1	3	M	2	2	9	8	8	9	10	$12	$149.60	$ 24,525
Merz, Linda	2	4	M	0	0	8	8	8	8	10	15	117.00	30,480
Goetz, Ken	3	2	M	0	0	6	7	8	9	10	11	91.30	21,500
Menick, Judd	4	2	S	8	8	0	0	8	8	9	11	126.50	22,625
Morales, Eva	5	3	M	0	0	8	8	8	6	8	13	117.05	24,730
Heimbrock, Jacob	6	5	M	0	0	8	8	8	8	8	34	154.25	117,540
Townsley, Sarah	7	2	M	4	0	6	6	6	6	4	9	83.05	21,425
Salzman, Beth	8	2	M	6	2	8	8	6	6	6	11	130.00	6,635
Layton, Esther	9	3	M	0	0	8	8	8	8	8	11	88.00	5,635
Thompson, David	10	5	M	0	2	10	9	7	7	10	11	128.90	21,635
Vadillo, Carmen	11	2	S	8	0	4	8	8	8	9	13	139.11	24,115

The Trenkamp Collection Agency follows the practice of drawing a single check for the net amount of the payroll and depositing the check in a special payroll account at the bank. Individual checks issued were numbered consecutively, beginning with No. 331.

REQUIRED

1. Prepare a payroll register for Trenkamp Collection Agency for the week ended November 18, 20--. (In the Taxable Earnings/Unemployment Compensation column, enter $365 for Salzman and $440 for Layton. Leave this column blank for all other employees.) Total the amount columns, verify the totals, and rule with single and double lines.

2. Assuming that the wages for the week ended November 18 were paid on November 21, prepare the journal entry for the payment of this payroll.

3. The current employee earnings record for Beth Salzman is provided in the working papers. Update Salzman's earnings record to reflect the November 18 payroll. Although this information should have been entered earlier, complete the required information on the earnings record. The necessary information is as follows:

Name	Beth F. Salzman
Address	12 Windmill Lane
	Trumbull, CT 06611
Employee No.	8
Gender	Female
Department	Administration
Occupation	Office Assistant
Social Security No.	446-46-6321
Marital Status	Married
Allowances	2
Pay Rate	$11.00 per hour
Date of Birth	4/5/84
Date Hired	7/22/--

CHALLENGE PROBLEM

This problem challenges you to apply your cumulative accounting knowledge to move a step beyond the material in the chapter.

✓ Dr. Wages and Salaries Expense: $1,596

Irina Company pays its employees weekly. The last pay period for 20-1 was on December 28. From December 28 through December 31, the employees earned $1,754, so the following adjusting entry was made:

	20-1																
5	Dec	31	Wages and Salaries Expense				1	7	5	4	00						5
6			Wages and Salaries Payable									1	7	5	4	00	6
7			To record accrued wages and salaries														7

The first pay period in 20-2 was on January 4. The totals line from Irina Company's payroll register for the week ended January 4, 20-2, was as follows:

PAYROLL REGISTER

					EARNINGS					TAXABLE EARNINGS		
				REGULAR	OVERTIME	TOTAL	CUMULATIVE TOTAL		UNEMPLOYMENT COMPENSATION		SOCIAL SECURITY	
1	Totals			3 3 5 0 00		3 3 5 0 00	3 3 5 0 00		3 3 5 0 00		3 3 5 0 00	

—WEEK ENDED January 4, 20-2

			DEDUCTIONS						NET PAY	
FEDERAL INCOME TAX	SOCIAL SECURITY TAX	MEDICARE TAX	HEALTH INSURANCE	UNITED WAY	OTHER		TOTAL			
3 4 2 00	2 0 7 70	4 8 58	5 0 00	8 0 00			7 2 8 28	2 6 2 1 72	1

REQUIRED

1. Prepare the journal entry for the payment of the payroll on January 4, 20-2.
2. Prepare T accounts for Wages and Salaries Expense and Wages and Salaries Payable showing the beginning balance, January 4, 20-2, entry, and ending balance as of January 4, 20-2.

Answers to Self-Study Test Questions

True/False

1. F (does *not* work under control and direction)

2. T

3. F (is called wages)

4. T

5. T

Multiple Choice

1. c   **2.** d   **3.** d   **4.** b   **5.** a

Checkpoint Exercises

1.
   (a) $40 \times \$14 =$ $\$560$
          $5 \times \$14 \times 1.5 =$ $\underline{105}$
               Gross pay $\underline{\$665}$

   (b) $35

2. Wages and Salaries Expense	4,600.00	
Employee Federal Income Tax Payable		417.00
Social Security Tax Payable		285.20
Medicare Tax Payable		66.70
State Income Tax Payable		46.00
Health Insurance Premiums Payable		181.00
Cash		3,604.10

LISEGAGNE/ISTOCKPHOTO.COM

Chapter 9

Payroll Accounting:
Employer Taxes and Reports

As competition has become more global, many challenges to businesses have developed. Learning how to function in many different languages and cultures is one of these challenges. LinguaLinx is a full-service translation company that offers help with language issues. Founded in 2002, LinguaLinx has offices in the United States, the United Kingdom, and China. It hires qualified professional linguists with skills tailored to provide services in more than 100 languages. Some examples of its capabilities include simple text translation, simultaneous interpretation, sign language, copywriting, and even Braille production. It can also provide on-site language instruction classes.

LinguaLinx faces the same kinds of payroll issues as Intechra, the company described in the introduction to Chapter 8. But LinguaLinx would face the added challenge of employees in multiple countries, so it would need to know the regulations in each location. In addition, you will learn in this chapter that employers must account for not just *employee* wages and taxes but also *employer* taxes. The complexity of payroll accounting is a major reason why many businesses hire an outside company to manage their payroll. You will also learn about two of these payroll service companies in this chapter's "A Broader View."

LEARNING OBJECTIVES

Careful study of this chapter should enable you to:

LO1 Describe and calculate employer payroll taxes.

LO2 Account for employer payroll taxes expense.

LO3 Describe employer reporting and payment responsibilities.

LO4 Describe and account for workers' compensation insurance.

The taxes we discussed in Chapter 8 had one thing in common—they all were levied on the employee. The employer withheld them from employees' earnings and paid them to the government. They did not add anything to the employer's payroll expenses.

In this chapter, we will examine several taxes that are imposed directly on the employer. All of these taxes represent additional payroll expenses. You will see that the total cost of employees includes not only wages but also payroll taxes and benefits such as vacation and sick pay.

EMPLOYER PAYROLL TAXES

LO1 Describe and calculate employer payroll taxes.

Most employers must pay FICA, FUTA (Federal Unemployment Tax Act), and SUTA (state unemployment tax) taxes.

Employer FICA Taxes

Employer FICA taxes are levied on employers at the same rates and on the same earnings bases as the employee FICA taxes. As explained in Chapter 8, we are assuming the Social Security component is 6.2% on maximum earnings of $118,500 for each employee. Since there is no maximum on the Medicare component, this tax is 1.45% on all earnings.

The payroll register we saw in Chapter 8 is a key source of information for computing employer payroll taxes. That payroll register is reproduced in Figure 9-1. The Taxable Earnings Social Security column shows that $5,035 of employee earnings were subject to Social Security tax for the pay period. The employer's Social Security tax on these earnings is computed as follows:

FIGURE 9-1   Payroll Register (left side)

PAYROLL REGISTER

	NAME	ALLOWANCES	MARITAL STATUS	EARNINGS				TAXABLE EARNINGS	
				REGULAR	OVERTIME	TOTAL	CUMULATIVE TOTAL	UNEMPLOYMENT COMPENSATION	SOCIAL SECURITY
1	Cadrain, Sarah	4	M	1 8 0 0 00	6 0 00	1 8 6 0 00	119 5 0 0 00	0 00	8 6 0 00
2	Gruder, James	1	S	7 6 0 00	1 4 0 00	9 0 0 00	43 4 0 0 00	0 00	9 0 0 00
3	Istone, Ken	4	M	5 4 5 00		5 4 5 00	27 0 2 5 00	0 00	5 4 5 00
4	Kuzmik, Helen	2	M	4 8 0 00	2 9 4 00	7 7 4 00	31 0 0 0 00	0 00	7 7 4 00
5	Lee, Hoseoup	3	M	4 4 0 00		4 4 0 00	22 3 4 0 00	0 00	4 4 0 00
6	Swaney, Linda	2	S	5 2 8 00	1 9 8 00	7 2 6 00	27 5 0 0 00	0 00	7 2 6 00
7	Tucci, Paul	3	M	4 9 0 00		4 9 0 00	25 0 5 0 00	0 00	4 9 0 00
8	Wiles, Harry	1	S	3 0 0 00		3 0 0 00	6 3 0 0 00	3 0 0 00	3 0 0 00
9				5 3 4 3 00	6 9 2 00	6 0 3 5 00	302 1 1 5 00	3 0 0 00	5 0 3 5 00
10									

Time cards, pay rates

Prior period total + current period earnings

Current below $7,000 cumul. total

Current below $118,500 cumul. total

Social Security Taxable Earnings	×	Tax Rate	=	Tax
$5,035		0.062		$312.17

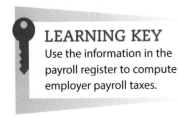

The Medicare tax applies to the total earnings of $6,035. The employer's Medicare tax on these earnings is computed as follows:

Total Earnings	×	Tax Rate	=	Tax
$6,035		0.0145		$87.51

These amounts plus the employees' Social Security and Medicare taxes withheld must be paid by the employer to the Internal Revenue Service (IRS).

Self-Employment Tax

Individuals who own and run their own business are considered self-employed. These individuals can be viewed as both employer and employee. They do not receive salary or wages from the business, but they do have earnings in the form of the business net income. **Self-employment income** is the net income of a trade or business run by an individual. The **Self-Employment Contributions Act (SECA)** requires self-employed individuals earning net self-employment income of $400 or more to pay a **self-employment tax**. Self-employment tax is a contribution to the FICA program. The tax rates are double the Social Security and Medicare rates (12.4% + 2.9% = 15.3% total). They are applied to the same income bases as those used for the Social Security and Medicare taxes. *Publication 334, Tax Guide for Small Business*, contains helpful information for self-employed persons.

> The self-employment tax rate is double the employee and employer Social Security and Medicare rates because the self-employed person is considered both the employer and employee.

Employer FUTA Tax

The **FUTA (Federal Unemployment Tax Act) tax** is levied only on employers. It is not deducted from employees' earnings. The purpose of this tax is to raise funds to

FIGURE 9-1   Payroll Register (right side)

—WEEK ENDED 12/19/--															
					DEDUCTIONS								NET PAY	CHECK NO.	
FEDERAL INCOME TAX		SOCIAL SECURITY TAX		MEDICARE TAX		HEALTH INSURANCE		UNITED WAY		OTHER		TOTAL			
1 9 0	00	5 3	32	2 6	97							2 7 0	29	1 5 8 9 71	409	1
1 1 5	00	5 5	80	1 3	05			2 0	00			2 0 3	85	6 9 6 15	410	2
7	00	3 3	79	7	90	1 0	00					5 8	69	4 8 6 31	411	3
5 1	00	4 7	99	1 1	22	1 3	00	2 0	00			1 4 3	21	6 3 0 79	412	4
5	00	2 7	28	6	38	1 3	00					5 1	66	3 8 8 34	413	5
7 0	00	4 5	01	1 0	53							1 2 5	54	6 0 0 46	414	6
1 0	00	3 0	38	7	11	1 0	00					5 7	49	4 3 2 51	415	7
1 9	00	1 8	60	4	35							4 1	95	2 5 8 05	416	8
4 6 7	00	3 1 2	17	8 7	51	4 6	00	4 0	00	0 0	00	9 5 2	68	5 0 8 2 32		9
															10

Withholding Tax Table → (Federal Income Tax)

6.2% × Social Security taxable earnings → (Social Security Tax)

1.45% × total earnings → (Medicare Tax)

Specific employer–employee agreements → (Health Insurance / United Way)

Total earnings – total deductions → (Net Pay)

administer the combined federal/state unemployment compensation program. The maximum amount of earnings subject to the FUTA tax and the tax rate can be changed by Congress. The current rate is 6.0% applied to maximum earnings of $7,000 for each employee, but employers are allowed a credit of up to 5.4% for participation in state unemployment programs. Thus, the effective federal rate is commonly 0.6%.

Gross FUTA rate	6.0%
Credit for state unemployment taxes	5.4%
Net FUTA rate	0.6%

To illustrate the computation of the FUTA tax, refer to Figure 9-1. The Taxable Earnings Unemployment Compensation column shows that only $300 of employee earnings were subject to the FUTA tax. This amount is low because the payroll period is late in the calendar year (December 19, 20--). It is common for most employees to exceed the $7,000 earnings limit by this time. The FUTA tax is computed as shown in Figure 9-2.

FIGURE 9-2 Computation of FUTA Tax

FUTA Taxable Earnings	×	Tax Rate	=	Tax
$300		0.006		$1.80

SUTA Tax

The **SUTA (state unemployment tax) tax** is also levied only on employers in most states. The purpose of this tax is to raise funds to pay unemployment benefits. Tax rates and unemployment benefits vary among the states. In this text, we will use a rate of 5.4% applied to maximum earnings of $7,000 for each employee. Most states have an **experience-rating system** to encourage employers to provide regular employment to workers. If an employer has very few former employees receiving unemployment compensation, the employer qualifies for a lower state unemployment tax rate. If an employer qualifies for a lower state rate, the full credit of 5.4% would still be allowed in computing the federal unemployment tax due.

Refer to the payroll register in Figure 9-1. As we saw with the FUTA tax, only $300 of employee earnings for this pay period are subject to the state unemployment tax. The tax is computed as shown in Figure 9-3.

State unemployment tax rates and maximum earnings amounts vary greatly. Current rates range from 5.4% to 13.1%. Maximum earnings amounts are $7,000 to $41,300.

FIGURE 9-3 Computation of SUTA Tax

State Unemployment Taxable Earnings	×	Tax Rate	=	Tax
$300		0.054		$16.20

Checkpoint ✓

Complete Checkpoint-1 on page 340 to test your basic understanding of LO1.

ACCOUNTING FOR EMPLOYER PAYROLL TAXES

LO2 Account for employer payroll taxes expense.

Now that we have computed the employer payroll taxes, we need to journalize them. It is common to debit all employer payroll taxes to a single account—Payroll Taxes Expense. However, we usually credit separate liability accounts for Social Security, Medicare, FUTA, and SUTA taxes payable.

Journalizing Employer Payroll Taxes

The employer payroll taxes computed in the previous section can be summarized as follows:

Employer's Social Security tax	$312.17
Employer's Medicare tax	87.51
FUTA tax	1.80
SUTA tax	16.20
Total employer payroll taxes	$417.68

These amounts provide the basis for the following journal entry:

5	Dec.	19	Payroll Taxes Expense			4	1	7	68				5
6			Social Security Tax Payable							3	1	2	17	6
7			Medicare Tax Payable								8	7	51	7
8			FUTA Tax Payable									1	80	8
9			SUTA Tax Payable								1	6	20	9
10			Employer payroll taxes for week ended Dec. 19											10

The steps needed to prepare this journal entry for employer payroll taxes are:

STEP 1 Obtain the total earnings and taxable earnings amounts from the Earnings— Total and Taxable Earnings columns of the payroll register. In this case, total earnings were $6,035; Social Security taxable earnings were $5,035; and Unemployment Compensation taxable earnings were $300.

STEP 2 Compute the amount of employer Social Security tax by multiplying the Social Security taxable earnings by 6.2%.

STEP 3 Compute the amount of employer Medicare tax by multiplying total earnings by 1.45%.

STEP 4 Compute the amount of FUTA tax by multiplying the Unemployment Taxable earnings by 0.6%.

STEP 5 Compute the amount of SUTA tax by multiplying the Unemployment Taxable earnings by 5.4%.

STEP 6 Prepare the appropriate journal entry using the amounts computed in steps 2–5.

To understand the journal entry for employer payroll taxes, let's use the accounting equation to examine the accounts involved. The five accounts affected by the payroll taxes entry above are shown in the accounting equation in Figure 9-4.

FIGURE 9-4   Accounting for Payroll Taxes

Assets		=	Liabilities		+	Owner's Equity			
Debit +	Credit −		Debit −	Credit +		Debit −		Credit +	

| | | | | | | | | | | Social Security Tax Payable | | | | | | | | | | |

Social Security Tax Payable

	312.17

Medicare Tax Payable

	87.51

FUTA Tax Payable

	1.80

SUTA Tax Payable

	16.20

Drawing		Expenses		Revenues	
Debit +	Credit −	Debit +	Credit −	Debit −	Credit +

Payroll Taxes Expense

417.68	

Payroll Taxes Expense

The Social Security, Medicare, FUTA, and SUTA taxes imposed on the employer are expenses of doing business. Each of the employer taxes is debited to Payroll Taxes Expense.

Payroll Taxes Expense

Debit	Credit
Social Security, Medicare, FUTA, and SUTA taxes imposed on the employer	

Social Security and Medicare Taxes Payable

These are the same liability accounts used in Chapter 8 to record the Social Security and Medicare taxes withheld from employees' earnings. The accounts are credited to enter the Social Security and Medicare taxes imposed on the employer. They are debited when the taxes are paid to the IRS. When all of the Social Security and Medicare taxes have been paid, the accounts will have zero balances.

Social Security Tax Payable

Debit	Credit
Payment of Social Security tax	Social Security taxes (1) withheld from employees' earnings and (2) imposed on the employer

Medicare Tax Payable

Debit	Credit
Payment of Medicare tax	Medicare taxes (1) withheld from employees' earnings and (2) imposed on the employer

LEARNING KEY

Employer and employee Social Security and Medicare taxes are credited to the same liability accounts because both of these taxes are due and will be paid to the IRS.

FUTA Tax Payable

A separate liability account entitled FUTA Tax Payable is kept for the employer's FUTA tax. This account is credited for the tax imposed on employers under the Federal Unemployment Tax Act. The account is debited when this tax is paid. When all of the FUTA taxes have been paid, the account will have a zero balance.

FUTA Tax Payable

Debit	Credit
Payment of FUTA tax	FUTA tax imposed on the employer

SUTA Tax Payable

A separate liability account entitled SUTA Tax Payable is kept for the state unemployment tax. This account is credited for the tax imposed on employers under the state unemployment compensation laws. The account is debited when this tax is paid. When all of the state unemployment taxes have been paid, the account will have a zero balance.

SUTA Tax Payable

Debit	Credit
Payment of SUTA tax	SUTA tax imposed on the employer

Total Payroll Cost of an Employee

It is interesting to note what it really costs to employ a person. The employer must, of course, pay the gross wages of an employee. In addition, the employer must pay payroll taxes on employee earnings up to certain dollar limits.

To illustrate, assume that an employee earns $26,000 a year. The total cost of this employee to the employer is calculated as follows:

Gross wages	$26,000
Employer Social Security tax, 6.2% of $26,000	1,612
Employer Medicare tax, 1.45% of $26,000	377
State unemployment tax, 5.4% of $7,000	378
FUTA tax, 0.6% of $7,000	42
	$28,409

Thus, the total payroll cost of employing a person whose stated compensation is $26,000 is $28,409. Employer payroll taxes clearly are a significant cost of doing business. Employer-paid medical insurance and pension plans can further increase total payroll costs.

Checkpoint ✓

Complete Checkpoint-2 on page 340 to test your basic understanding of LO2.

REPORTING AND PAYMENT RESPONSIBILITIES

LO3 Describe employer reporting and payment responsibilities.

Employer payroll reporting and payment responsibilities fall into six areas:

1. Federal income tax withholding and Social Security and Medicare taxes
2. FUTA taxes

3. SUTA taxes

4. Employee Wage and Tax Statement (Form W-2)

5. Summary of employee wages and taxes (Form W-3)

6. Employment eligibility verification (Form I-9)

Federal Income Tax Withholding and Social Security and Medicare Taxes

Three important aspects of employer reporting and payment responsibilities for federal income tax withholding and Social Security and Medicare taxes are:

1. Determining when payments are due

2. Use of electronic funds transfer to make federal tax deposits

3. Use of Form 941, Employer's Quarterly Federal Tax Return

When Payments Are Due

The date by which federal income tax withholding and Social Security and Medicare taxes must be paid depends on the amount of these taxes. Figure 9-5 summarizes the deposit rules stated in *Circular E—Employer's Tax Guide*. In general, the larger the amount that needs to be deposited, the more frequently payments must be made. For simplicity, we will assume that deposits must be made 15 days after the end of each month.

FIGURE 9-5   Summary of Deposit Rules

ACCUMULATED TAX LIABILITY	DEPOSIT DUE
1. Less than $2,500 at the end of the current quarter	1. Pay with Form 941 at end of the month following end of the quarter
2. $2,500 or more at the end of the current quarter and $50,000 or less in total during the lookback period*	2. Deposit 15 days after end of the month
3. $2,500 or more at the end of the current quarter and more than $50,000 in total during the lookback period*	3. Deposit every Wednesday or Friday, depending on day of the week payroll payments are made
4. $100,000 or more on any day during the current quarter	4. Deposit by the end of the next banking day

*Lookback period is the four quarters beginning July 1, two years ago, and ending June 30, one year ago.

Making Federal Tax Deposits

Deposits of employee federal income tax withheld, and Social Security and Medicare taxes must be made using electronic funds transfer. Generally, the Electronic Federal Tax Payment System (EFTPS) is used. The EFTPS is an electronic funds transfer system designed for making federal tax deposits.

On February 15, Westly, Inc., used the EFTPS to deposit $5,850.88 for the following taxes on wages paid in January:

Employees' income tax withheld from wages		$2,526.80
Social Security tax:		
Withheld from employees' wages	$1,346.24	
Imposed on employer	1,346.24	2,692.48
Medicare tax:		
Withheld from employees' wages	$ 315.80	
Imposed on employer	315.80	631.60
Amount of check		$5,850.88

The journal entry for this deposit would be as follows:

5	Feb.	15	Employee Federal Income Tax Payable	2 5 2 6 80		5
6			Social Security Tax Payable	2 6 9 2 48		6
7			Medicare Tax Payable	6 3 1 60		7
8			Cash		5 8 5 0 88	8
9			Deposit of employee federal income tax and			9
10			Social Security and Medicare taxes			10

Form 941

Form 941, Employer's Quarterly Federal Tax Return, must be filed with the IRS at the end of the month following each calendar quarter. This form reports the following taxes for the quarter:

1. Employee federal income tax withheld
2. Employee Social Security and Medicare taxes withheld
3. Employer Social Security and Medicare taxes

If the total amount of taxes due is less than $2,500, payment may be made with Form 941, using Form 941-V.

A completed Form 941 for Westly, Inc., for the first quarter of the calendar year is shown in Figure 9-6. Westly had made its monthly tax deposits using EFTPS. Instructions for completing the form are provided with the form and in *Circular E*.

> If the total tax liability for federal income taxes, Social Security, and Medicare taxes is less than $1,000, Form 944, Employer's Annual Federal Tax Return, may be used. It must be filed by January 31.

FUTA Taxes

Federal unemployment taxes must be calculated on a quarterly basis. If the accumulated liability exceeds $500, the total must be deposited by the end of the month following the close of the quarter. If the liability is $500 or less, no deposit is necessary. The amount is simply added to the amount to be deposited for the next quarter. FUTA taxes are deposited using electronic funds transfer, usually EFTPS.

Assume that an employer's accumulated FUTA tax liability for the first quarter of the calendar year is $508. The employer would deposit this amount on April 30. The journal entry for this transaction would be as follows:

15	Apr.	30	FUTA Tax Payable	5 0 8 00		15
16			Cash		5 0 8 00	16
17			Deposit of federal unemployment tax			17

FIGURE 9-6 Employer's Quarterly Federal Tax Return (Form 941)

Form **941 for 20--:** Employer's **QUARTERLY** Federal Tax Return	950114

(Rev. January 2015)   Department of the Treasury — Internal Revenue Service   OMB No. 1545-0029

Employer identification number (EIN) **4 3 — 0 2 1 1 6 3 0**

Name *(not your trade name)*

Trade name *(if any)* **Westly, Inc.**

Address **5221 Natural Bridge**
     Number   Street   Suite or room number

St. Louis   **MO**   **63115-8230**
City   State   ZIP code

Foreign country name   Foreign province/county   Foreign postal code

Report for this Quarter of 2015
(Check one.)

[X] **1:** January, February, March

[ ] **2:** April, May, June

[ ] **3:** July, August, September

[ ] **4:** October, November, December

Instructions and prior year forms are available at *www.irs.gov/form941.*

Read the separate instructions before you complete Form 941. Type or print within the boxes.

Part 1:   Answer these questions for this quarter.

1   Number of employees who received wages, tips, or other compensation for the pay period including: *Mar. 12* (Quarter 1), *June 12* (Quarter 2), *Sept. 12* (Quarter 3), or *Dec. 12* (Quarter 4)   **1**   **8**

2   Wages, tips, and other compensation   **2**   **65,160.00**

3   Federal income tax withheld from wages, tips, and other compensation   **3**   **7,595.80** ◄— Employee federal income tax withheld

4   If no wages, tips, and other compensation are subject to social security or Medicare tax   [ ] Check and go to line 6.

		Column 1		Column 2	
5a	Taxable social security wages	65,160.00	× .124 =	8,079.84	◄— Employee and employer Social Security taxes
5b	Taxable social security tips	.	× .124 =	.	
5c	Taxable Medicare wages & tips	65,160.00	× .029 =	1,889.64	◄— Employee and employer Medicare taxes
5d	Taxable wages & tips subject to Additional Medicare Tax withholding	.	× .009 =	.	

5e   Add Column 2 from lines 5a, 5b, 5c, and 5d   **5e**   **9,969.48**

5f   Section 3121(q) Notice and Demand—Tax due on unreported tips (see instructions)   **5f**   **.**

6   Total taxes before adjustments. Add lines 3, 5e, and 5f   **6**   **17,565.28**

7   Current quarter's adjustment for fractions of cents   **7**   **.**

8   Current quarter's adjustment for sick pay   **8**   **.**

9   Current quarter's adjustments for tips and group-term life insurance   **9**   **.**

10   Total taxes after adjustments. Combine lines 6 through 9   **10**   **17,565.28**

11   Total deposits for this quarter, including overpayment applied from a prior quarter and overpayments applied from Form 941-X, 941-X (PR), 944-X, 944-X (PR), or 944-X (SP) filed in the current quarter   **11**   **17,565.28**

12   Balance due. If line 10 is more than line 11, enter the difference and see instructions   **12**   **.0**

13   Overpayment. If line 11 is more than line 10, enter the difference   **.**   Check one: [ ] Apply to next return.   [ ] Send a refund.

► You MUST complete both pages of Form 941 and SIGN it.   Next ►

For Privacy Act and Paperwork Reduction Act Notice, see the back of the Payment Voucher.   Cat. No. 17001Z   Form **941** (Rev. 1-20--)

FIGURE 9-6   Employer's Quarterly Federal Tax Return (Form 941) *(concluded)*

```
                                                                                    950214
```

Name *(not your trade name)*	Employer identification number (EIN)

Part 2:   Tell us about your deposit schedule and tax liability for this quarter.

If you are unsure about whether you are a monthly schedule depositor or a semiweekly schedule depositor, see Pub. 15 (Circular E), section 11.

14   Check one: ☐   Line 10 on this return is less than $2,500 or line 10 on the return for the prior quarter was less than $2,500, and you did not incur a $100,000 next-day deposit obligation during the current quarter. If line 10 for the prior quarter was less than $2,500 but line 10 on this return is $100,000 or more, you must provide a record of your federal tax liability. If you are a monthly schedule depositor, complete the deposit schedule below; if you are a semiweekly schedule depositor, attach Schedule B (Form 941). Go to Part 3.

☒   **You were a monthly schedule depositor for the entire quarter.** Enter your tax liability for each month and total liability for the quarter, then go to Part 3.

Tax liability: Month 1   `5,850.88`

Month 2   `5,690.77`

Month 3   `6,023.63`

Total liability for quarter   `17,565.28`   **Total must equal line 10.**

☐   **You were a semiweekly schedule depositor for any part of this quarter.** Complete Schedule B (Form 941), Report of Tax Liability for Semiweekly Schedule Depositors, and attach it to Form 941.

Part 3:   Tell us about your business. If a question does NOT apply to your business, leave it blank.

15   If your business has closed or you stopped paying wages . . . .   ☐ Check here, and

enter the final date you paid wages   `/    /`   .

16   If you are a seasonal employer and you do not have to file a return for every quarter of the year . . .   ☐ Check here.

Part 4:   May we speak with your third-party designee?

Do you want to allow an employee, a paid tax preparer, or another person to discuss this return with the IRS? See the instructions for details.

☐   Yes.   Designee's name and phone number   [   ]   [   ]

Select a 5-digit Personal Identification Number (PIN) to use when talking to the IRS.   ☐ ☐ ☐ ☐ ☐

☒   No.

Part 5:   Sign here. You MUST complete both pages of Form 941 and SIGN it.

Under penalties of perjury, I declare that I have examined this return, including accompanying schedules and statements, and to the best of my knowledge and belief, it is true, correct, and complete. Declaration of preparer (other than taxpayer) is based on all information of which preparer has any knowledge.

✗ **Sign your name here** *William P. Jones*	Print your name here *William P Jones*
	Print your title here *Treasurer*
Date `4 / 30 / --`	Best daytime phone

Paid Preparer Use Only   Check if you are self-employed . . . ☐

Preparer's name		PTIN	
Preparer's signature		Date	`/    /`
Firm's name (or yours if self-employed)		EIN	
Address		Phone	
City		State	ZIP code

Form **941** (Rev. 1-20--)

Form 940

In addition to making quarterly deposits, employers are required to file an annual report of federal unemployment tax using Form 940 (Figure 9-7). If all quarterly deposits have been made, this form must be filed with the IRS by the beginning of the second week of February. Otherwise, it must be filed by January 31. Figure 9-7 shows a completed

FIGURE 9-7 Employer's Annual Federal Unemployment (FUTA) Tax Return (Form 940)

Form **940 for 20--: Employer's Annual Federal Unemployment (FUTA) Tax Return** 850113

Department of the Treasury — Internal Revenue Service OMB No. 1545-0028

Employer identification number (EIN) 4 3 – 0 2 1 1 6 3 0

Name *(not your trade name)*

Trade name *(if any)* Westly, Inc.

Address 5221 Natural Bridge

Number Street Suite or room number

St. Louis MO 63115-8230

City State ZIP code

Foreign country name Foreign province/county Foreign postal code

Type of Return
(Check all that apply.)

☐ **a.** Amended

☐ **b.** Successor employer

☐ **c.** No payments to employees in 2014

☐ **d.** Final: Business closed or stopped paying wages

Instructions and prior-year forms are available at *www.irs.gov/form940.*

Read the separate instructions before you complete this form. Please type or print within the boxes.

Part 1: Tell us about your return. If any line does NOT apply, leave it blank.

1a **If you had to pay state unemployment tax in one state only, enter the state abbreviation** . **1a** M O

1b **If you had to pay state unemployment tax in more than one state, you are a multi-state employer** . . . . . **1b** ☐ Check here. Complete Schedule A (Form 940).

2 **If you paid wages in a state that is subject to CREDIT REDUCTION** . . . . **2** ☐ Check here. Complete Schedule A (Form 940).

Part 2: Determine your FUTA tax before adjustments for 2014. If any line does NOT apply, leave it blank.

3 **Total payments to all employees** **3** 308,917.00

4 **Payments exempt from FUTA tax** **4**

Check all that apply: **4a** ☐ Fringe benefits **4c** ☐ Retirement/Pension **4e** ☐ Other

4b ☐ Group-term life insurance **4d** ☐ Dependent care

5 **Total of payments made to each employee in excess of $7,000** **5** 243,254.00

6 **Subtotal** (line 4 + line 5 = line 6) **6** 243,254.00

7 **Total taxable FUTA wages** (line 3 – line 6 = line 7) (see instructions) . . . . . **7** 65,663.00 ← FUTA taxable wages

8 **FUTA tax before adjustments** (line 7 x .006 = line 8) **8** 393.98

Part 3: Determine your adjustments. If any line does NOT apply, leave it blank.

9 **If ALL of the taxable FUTA wages you paid were excluded from state unemployment tax, multiply line 7 by .054** (line 7 × .054 = line 9). Go to line 12 . . . . . **9** .

10 **If SOME of the taxable FUTA wages you paid were excluded from state unemployment tax, OR you paid ANY state unemployment tax late** (after the due date for filing Form 940), complete the worksheet in the instructions. Enter the amount from line 7 of the worksheet . . **10** .

11 **If credit reduction applies,** enter the total from Schedule A (Form 940) . . . . . **11** .

Part 4: Determine your FUTA tax and balance due or overpayment for 2014. If any line does NOT apply, leave it blank.

12 **Total FUTA tax after adjustments** (lines 8 + 9 + 10 + 11 = line 12) . . . . . **12** 393.98 ← FUTA tax

13 **FUTA tax deposited for the year, including any overpayment applied from a prior year** . **13** . ← FUTA tax paid

14 **Balance due** (If line 12 is more than line 13, enter the excess on line 14.)
- If line 14 is more than $500, you must deposit your tax.
- If line 14 is $500 or less, you may pay with this return. (see instructions) . . . . . **14** 393.98 ← FUTA tax due

15 **Overpayment** (If line 13 is more than line 12, enter the excess on line 15 and check a box below.) . . . . . **15** .

► You **MUST** complete both pages of this form and **SIGN** it. Check one: ☐ Apply to next return. ☐ Send a refund.

Next ►

For Privacy Act and Paperwork Reduction Act Notice, see the back of Form 940-V, Payment Voucher. Cat. No. 11234O Form **940** (20--)

Form 940 for Westly, Inc. Instructions for completing the form are provided with the form and in *Circular E*. If a balance is due, it may be paid using EFTPS, or Form 940-V if the amount due is $500 or less. Figure 9-8 shows a completed Form 940-V for Westly.

SUTA Taxes

Deposit rules and forms for state unemployment taxes vary among the states. Deposits usually are required on a quarterly basis. Assume that Westly's accumulated state

FIGURE 9-7 Employer's Annual Federal Unemployment (FUTA) Tax Return (Form 940) (*concluded*)

850212

Name *(not your trade name)*	Employer identification number (EIN)

Part 5: Report your FUTA tax liability by quarter only if line 12 is more than $500. If not, go to Part 6.

16 Report the amount of your FUTA tax liability for each quarter; do NOT enter the amount you deposited. If you had no liability for a quarter, leave the line blank.

16a 1st quarter (January 1 – March 31)	**16a**	.
16b 2nd quarter (April 1 – June 30)	**16b**	.
16c 3rd quarter (July 1 – September 30)	**16c**	.
16d 4th quarter (October 1 – December 31)	**16d**	.
17 Total tax liability for the year (lines 16a + 16b + 16c + 16d = line 17)	**17**	. **Total must equal line 12.**

Part 6: May we speak with your third-party designee?

Do you want to allow an employee, a paid tax preparer, or another person to discuss this return with the IRS? See the instructions for details.

☐ **Yes.** Designee's name and phone number

Select a 5-digit Personal Identification Number (PIN) to use when talking to IRS

☐ **No.**

Part 7: Sign here. You MUST complete both pages of this form and SIGN it.

Under penalties of perjury, I declare that I have examined this return, including accompanying schedules and statements, and to the best of my knowledge and belief, it is true, correct, and complete, and that no part of any payment made to a state unemployment fund claimed as a credit was, or is to be, deducted from the payments made to employees. Declaration of preparer (other than taxpayer) is based on all information of which preparer has any knowledge.

✗ **Sign your name here** *William P. Jones*

Print your name here: WILLIAM P. JONES

Print your title here: TREASURER

Date: 1/31/--

Best daytime phone

Paid Preparer Use Only — Check if you are self-employed . ☐

Preparer's name		PTIN	
Preparer's signature		Date	/ /
Firm's name (or yours if self-employed)		EIN	
Address		Phone	( ) -
City	State	ZIP code	

Page **2** Form **940** (20--)

FIGURE 9-8 Payment Voucher (Form 940-V)

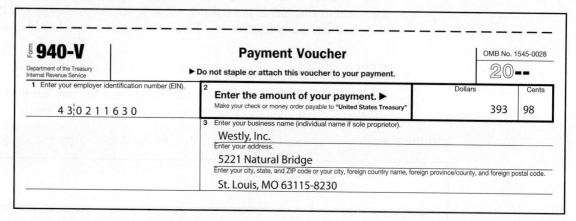

unemployment liability for the first quarter of the calendar year is $2,754. The journal entry for the deposit of this amount with the state on April 30 would be as follows:

19	Apr.	30	SUTA Tax Payable		2 7 5 4 00			19
20			Cash			2 7 5 4 00		20
21			Deposit of state unemployment tax					21

Employee Wage and Tax Statement

By January 31 of each year, employers must furnish each employee with a Wage and Tax Statement, Form W-2 (Figure 9-9). This form shows the total amount of

FIGURE 9-9 Wage and Tax Statement (Form W-2)

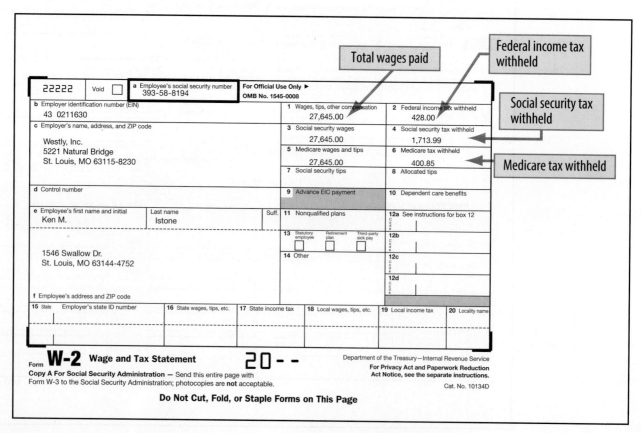

wages paid to the employee and the amounts of taxes withheld during the preceding taxable year. The employee earnings record contains the information needed to complete this form.

Multiple copies of Form W-2 are needed for the following purposes:

- Copy A—Employer sends to Social Security Administration
- Copy B—Employee files with federal income tax return
- Copy C—Employee retains for his or her own records
- Copy D—Employer retains for business records
- Copy 1—Employer sends to state, city, or local tax department
- Copy 2—Employee files with state, city, or local income tax return

The Social Security Administration is encouraging employers to file Form W-3 and Forms W-2 electronically instead of on paper.

Summary of Employee Wages and Taxes

Employers send Form W-3, Transmittal of Wage and Tax Statements (Figure 9-10), with Copy A of Forms W-2 to the Social Security Administration. Form W-3 must be filed by February 28 following the end of each taxable year. This form summarizes

FIGURE 9-10 Transmittal of Wage and Tax Statements (Form W-3)

DO NOT STAPLE

33333	a Control number	**For Official Use Only ▶** **OMB No. 1545-0008**

b Kind of Payer (Check one): 941 ☐ Military ☐ 943 ☐ 944 ☐ CT-1 ☐ Hshld. emp. ☐ Medicare govt. emp. ☐

Kind of Employer (Check one): None apply ☐ 501c non-govt. ☐ State/local non-501c ☐ State/local 501c ☐ Federal govt. ☐

Third-party sick pay (Check if applicable) ☐

c Total number of Forms W-2 / d Establishment number	1 Wages, tips, other compensation 308,917.00	2 Federal income tax withheld 27,370.00
e Employer identification number (EIN)	3 Social security wages 305,217.00	4 Social security tax withheld 18,923.45
f Employer's name	5 Medicare wages and tips 308,917.00	6 Medicare tax withheld 4,479.30
5221 Natural Bridge St.Louis, MO 63115-8230	7 Social security tips	8 Allocated tips
	9	10 Dependent care benefits
g Employer's address and ZIP code	11 Nonqualified plans	12a Deferred compensation
h Other EIN used this year	13 For third-party sick pay use only	12b
15 State MO / Employer's state ID number 21686001	14 Income tax withheld by payer of third-party sick pay	
16 State wages, tips, etc. 276,917.00 / 17 State income tax	18 Local wages, tips, etc.	19 Local income tax
Employer's contact person	Employer's telephone number	For Official Use Only
Employer's fax number	Employer's email address	

Under penalties of perjury, I declare that I have examined this return and accompanying documents and, to the best of my knowledge and belief, they are true, correct, and complete.

Signature ▶ Title ▶ Date ▶

Form **W-3 Transmittal of Wage and Tax Statements** 20-- Department of the Treasury Internal Revenue Service the employee earnings and tax information presented on Forms W-2 for the year. Information needed to complete Form W-3 is contained in the employee earnings records.

Employment Eligibility Verification

Every employee hired after November 6, 1986, must complete Form I-9, Employment Eligibility Verification. The purpose of this form is to document that each employee is authorized to work in the United States. The employee completes Section 1 of the form and provides the employer with evidence of the employee's identity and authorization to work. The employer completes Section 2 of the form indicating what evidence the employer examined.

Form I-9 is not filed with any government agency. Instead, it must be retained by the employer and made available for inspection if requested by the Department of Homeland Security or the Department of Labor.

Summary of Taxes, Reports, and Payments

Keeping track of the many payroll taxes can be a challenge for an employer. Figure 9-11 summarizes the various employee and employer taxes we have discussed in Chapters 8 and 9. Figure 9-12 shows a calendar that highlights the due dates for the various reports and deposits. The calendar assumes the following for an employer:

1. Undeposited FIT (federal income tax) and Social Security and Medicare taxes of $2,500 at the end of each quarter and less than $50,000 during the lookback period.
2. Undeposited FUTA taxes of more than $500 at the end of each quarter.
3. SUTA taxes deposited quarterly.

The combination of payroll taxes, reports, deposit rules, and due dates can make payroll accounting rather complex. In fact, this is a major reason why small businesses often hire an accountant or an outside company to handle payroll.

FIGURE 9-11 Summary of Employee and Employer Taxes

TAX	TAX APPLIES TO	
	EMPLOYEE	EMPLOYER
Federal income tax	X	
State income tax	X	
Social Security	X	X
Medicare	X	X
FUTA		X
SUTA		X*

*Also applies to employees in some states.

Checkpoint ✓

Complete Checkpoint-3 on page 341 to test your basic understanding of LO3.

FIGURE 9-12 Payroll Calendar

File Forms 940, 941, state unemployment tax report, and send W-2 to employees.	File Form 940	File form W-3 with Copy A of W-2s.	File Form 941 and make FUTA and SUTA tax deposits.	Deposit FIT and Social Security and Medicare taxes from previous month.

January

S	M	T	W	T	F	S
			1	2	3	4
5	6	7	8	9	10	11
12	13	14	15	16	17	18
19	20	21	22	23	24	25
26	27	28	29	30	31	

February

S	M	T	W	T	F	S
						1
2	3	4	5	6	7	8
9	10	11	12	13	14	15
16	17	18	19	20	21	22
23	24	25	26	27	28	29

March

S	M	T	W	T	F	S
1	2	3	4	5	6	7
8	9	10	11	12	13	14
15	16	17	18	19	20	21
22	23	24	25	26	27	28
29	30	31				

April

S	M	T	W	T	F	S
			1	2	3	4
5	6	7	8	9	10	11
12	13	14	15	16	17	18
19	20	21	22	23	24	25
26	27	28	29	30		

May

S	M	T	W	T	F	S
					1	2
3	4	5	6	7	8	9
10	11	12	13	14	15	16
17	18	19	20	21	22	23
24	25	26	27	28	29	30
31						

June

S	M	T	W	T	F	S
	1	2	3	4	5	6
7	8	9	10	11	12	13
14	15	16	17	18	19	20
21	22	23	24	25	26	27
28	29	30				

July

S	M	T	W	T	F	S
			1	2	3	4
5	6	7	8	9	10	11
12	13	14	15	16	17	18
19	20	21	22	23	24	25
26	27	28	29	30	31	

August

S	M	T	W	T	F	S
						1
2	3	4	5	6	7	8
9	10	11	12	13	14	15
16	17	18	19	20	21	22
23	24	25	26	27	28	29
30	31					

September

S	M	T	W	T	F	S
		1	2	3	4	5
6	7	8	9	10	11	12
13	14	15	16	17	18	19
20	21	22	23	24	25	26
27	28	29	30			

October

S	M	T	W	T	F	S
				1	2	3
4	5	6	7	8	9	10
11	12	13	14	15	16	17
18	19	20	21	22	23	24
25	26	27	28	29	30	31

November

S	M	T	W	T	F	S
1	2	3	4	5	6	7
8	9	10	11	12	13	14
15	16	17	18	19	20	21
22	23	24	25	26	27	28
29	30					

December

S	M	T	W	T	F	S
		1	2	3	4	5
6	7	8	9	10	11	12
13	14	15	16	17	18	19
20	21	22	23	24	25	26
27	28	29	30	31		

WORKERS' COMPENSATION INSURANCE

LO4 Describe and account for workers' compensation insurance.

Most states require employers to carry workers' compensation insurance. Workers' compensation insurance provides insurance for employees who suffer a work-related illness or injury.

The employer usually pays the entire cost of workers' compensation insurance. The cost of the insurance depends on the number of employees, riskiness of the job, and the company's accident history. For example, the insurance premium for workers in a chemical plant could be higher than for office workers. Employers generally obtain the insurance either from the state in which they operate or from a private insurance company.

The employer usually pays the premium at the beginning of the year, based on the estimated payroll for the year. At the end of the year, after the actual amount of payroll is known, an adjustment is made. If the employer has overpaid, a credit is received from the state or insurance company. If the employer has underpaid, an additional premium is paid.

A Broader View

Dealing with Payroll Complexity—Let Someone Else Do It

A common way for both small and large businesses to deal with the complexity of payroll reports, deposit rules, and due dates is to hire an outside company to handle the payroll. Payroll processing companies have combined payroll expertise with the power of computers to create a major business enterprise based on the efficient and effective provision of payroll services.

The extent to which businesses use outside companies to handle payroll can be seen in the two largest payroll processing companies: Automatic Data Processing, Inc. (ADP) and Paychex, Inc. ADP has operations in the United States, Canada, Europe, South America, Africa, the Mid-East, Australia, and Asia; provides payroll services to 610,000 clients; and has revenues of over $12 billion. Paychex has more than 100 locations nationwide, provides services to 580,000 clients, and has revenues of $2.5 billion. These companies prepare employee paychecks, journals, and summary reports; collect and remit funds for federal, and local payroll taxes; and file all required forms with government taxing authorities.

To illustrate the accounting for workers' compensation insurance, assume that Lockwood Co. expects its payroll for the year to be $210,000. If Lockwood's insurance premium rate is 0.2%, its payment for workers' compensation insurance at the beginning of the year would be $420.

Estimated Payroll	×	Rate	=	Estimated Insurance Premium
$210,000		0.002		$420.00

The journal entry for the payment of this $420 premium would be as follows:

7	Jan.	2	Workers' Compensation Insurance Expense		4 2 0 00			7
8			Cash			4 2 0 00		8
9			Paid insurance premium					9

If Lockwood's actual payroll for the year is $220,000, Lockwood would owe an additional premium of $20 at year-end.

Actual Payroll	×	Rate	=	Insurance Premium
$220,000		0.002		$440.00
Less premium paid				420.00
Additional premium due				$ 20.00

The adjusting entry at year-end for this additional expense would be as follows:

11	Dec.	31	Workers' Compensation Insurance Expense			2 0 00			11
12			Workers' Compensation Insurance Payable				2 0 00		12
13			Adjustment for insurance premium						13

In T account form, the total Workers' Compensation Insurance Expense of $440.00 would look like this:

Workers' Compensation Insurance Expense

Debit	Credit
420.00	
20.00	
440.00	

If Lockwood's actual payroll for the year is only $205,000, Lockwood would be due a refund of $10:

Payroll	×	Rate	=	Insurance Premium
$205,000		0.002		$410.00
Less premium paid				420.00
Refund due				$ (10.00)

The adjusting entry at year-end for this refund due would be as follows:

16	Dec.	31	Insurance Refund Receivable			1 0 00			16
17			Workers' Compensation Insurance Expense				1 0 00		17
18			Adjustment for insurance premium						18

In T account form, the total Workers' Compensation Insurance Expense of $410 would look like this.

Workers' Compensation Insurance Expense

Debit	Credit
420.00	10.00
410.00	

Checkpoint ✓

Complete Checkpoint-4 on page 341 to test your basic understanding of LO4.

Self-Study

LO1 Describe and calculate employer payroll taxes.

LO2 Account for employer payroll taxes expense.

Employer payroll taxes include FICA, FUTA, and SUTA taxes. These taxes represent additional payroll expenses of the employer. The journal entry for payroll taxes is as follows:

8		Payroll Taxes Expense			x	x	x	xx					8
9		Social Security Tax Payable							x	x	x	xx	9
10		Medicare Tax Payable							x	x	x	xx	10
11		FUTA Tax Payable							x	x	x	xx	11
12		SUTA Tax Payable							x	x	x	xx	12

The steps to be followed in preparing this journal entry are as follows:

1. Obtain the total earnings and taxable earnings amounts from the Earnings—Total and Taxable Earnings columns of the payroll register.
2. Compute the amount of employer Social Security tax by multiplying the Social Security taxable earnings by 6.2%.
3. Compute the amount of employer Medicare tax by multiplying total earnings by 1.45%.
4. Compute the amount of FUTA tax by multiplying the Unemployment Taxable earnings by 0.6%.
5. Compute the amount of SUTA tax by multiplying the Unemployment Taxable earnings by 5.4%.
6. Prepare the appropriate journal entry using the amounts computed in steps 2–5.

LO3 Describe employer reporting and payment responsibilities.

Employer payroll reporting and payment responsibilities fall into six areas.

1. Federal income tax withholding and Social Security and Medicare taxes
2. FUTA taxes
3. SUTA taxes
4. Employee Wage and Tax Statement (Form W-2)
5. Summary of employee wages and taxes (Form W-3)
6. Employment eligibility verification (Form I-9)

Most federal tax deposits are made using the EFTPS. In addition, two forms are needed in reporting and paying employer payroll taxes:

1. Form 941, Employer's Quarterly Federal Tax Return
2. Form 940, Employer's Annual Federal Unemployment Tax Return

By January 31 of each year, employers must provide each employee with a Wage and Tax Statement, Form W-2.

By February 28 of each year, employers must file Form W-3 and Copy A of Forms W-2 with the Social Security Administration.

LEARNING OBJECTIVES	Key Points to Remember
LO4 Describe and account for workers' compensation insurance.	Workers' compensation insurance provides insurance for employees who suffer a work-related illness or injury. Employers generally are required to carry and pay the entire cost of this insurance.

DEMONSTRATION PROBLEM

The Totals line from Hart Company's payroll register for the week ended December 31, 20--, is as follows:

(left side)									PAYROLL REGISTER	
	NAME	EMPLOYEE NUMBER	ALLOWANCES	MARITAL STATUS	EARNINGS				TAXABLE EARNINGS	
					REGULAR	OVERTIME	TOTAL	CUMULATIVE TOTAL	UNEMPLOYMENT COMPENSATION	SOCIAL SECURITY
21	Totals				3 5 0 0 00	3 0 0 00	3 8 0 0 00	197 6 0 0 00	4 0 0 00	3 8 0 0 00

								(right side)	
—PERIOD ENDED December 31, 20--									
			DEDUCTIONS					NET PAY	CHECK NO.
FEDERAL INCOME TAX	SOCIAL SECURITY TAX	MEDICARE TAX	HEALTH INSURANCE	UNITED WAY	OTHER		TOTAL		
3 8 0 00	2 3 5 60	5 5 10	5 0 00	1 0 0 00			8 2 0 70	2 9 7 9 30	21

Payroll taxes are imposed as follows: Social Security, 6.2%; Medicare, 1.45%; FUTA, 0.6%; and SUTA, 5.4%.

REQUIRED

1. a.   Prepare the journal entry for payment of this payroll on December 31, 20--.

   b.   Prepare the journal entry for the employer's payroll taxes for the period ended December 31, 20--.

2. Hart Company had the following balances in its general ledger *after* the entries for requirement (1) were made:

Employee Federal Income Tax Payable	$1,620.00
Social Security Tax Payable	1,847.00
Medicare Tax Payable	433.00
FUTA Tax Payable	27.20
SUTA Tax Payable	183.60

   a.   Prepare the journal entry for payment of the liabilities for employee federal income taxes and Social Security and Medicare taxes on January 15, 20--.

   b.   Prepare the journal entry for payment of the liability for FUTA tax on January 31, 20--.

   c.   Prepare the journal entry for payment of the liability for SUTA tax on January 31, 20--.

3. Hart Company paid a premium of $280 for workers' compensation insurance based on estimated payroll as of the beginning of the year. Based on actual payroll as of the end of the year, the premium is $298. Prepare the adjusting entry on December 31 for the additional workers' compensation insurance premium.

Solution 1.

	DATE		DESCRIPTION	POST. REF.	DEBIT	CREDIT	
	20--		GENERAL JOURNAL			PAGE 1	
1	Dec.	31	Wages and Salaries Expense		3 8 0 0 00		1
2			Employee Federal Income Tax Payable			3 8 0 00	2
3			Social Security Tax Payable			2 3 5 60	3
4			Medicare Tax Payable			5 5 10	4
5			Health Insurance Premiums Payable			5 0 00	5
6			United Way Contributions Payable			1 0 0 00	6
7			Cash			2 9 7 9 30	7
8			To record Dec. 31 payroll				8
9							9
10		31	Payroll Taxes Expense		3 1 4 70		10
11			Social Security Tax Payable			2 3 5 60	11
12			Medicare Tax Payable			5 5 10	12
13			FUTA Tax Payable			2 40	13
14			SUTA Tax Payable			2 1 60	14
15			Employer payroll taxes for week ended Dec. 31				15

2. and 3.

	DATE		DESCRIPTION	POST. REF.	DEBIT	CREDIT	
18	Jan.	15	Employee Federal Income Tax Payable		1 6 2 0 00		18
19			Social Security Tax Payable		1 8 4 7 00		19
20			Medicare Tax Payable		4 3 3 00		20
21			Cash			3 9 0 0 00	21
22			Deposit of employee federal income tax and				22
23			Social Security and Medicare taxes				23
24							24
25		31	FUTA Tax Payable		2 7 20		25
26			Cash			2 7 20	26
27			Paid FUTA tax				27
28							28
29		31	SUTA Tax Payable		1 8 3 60		29
30			Cash			1 8 3 60	30
31			Paid SUTA tax				31
32							32
33	Dec.	31	Workers' Compensation Insurance Expense		1 8 00		33
34			Workers' Compensation Insurance Payable			1 8 00	34
35			Adjustment for insurance premium				35

KEY TERMS

Electronic Federal Tax Payment System (EFTPS) (324)   An electronic funds transfer system for making federal tax deposits.

employer FICA taxes (318)   Taxes levied on employers at the same rates and on the same earnings bases as the employee FICA taxes.

experience-rating system (320)   A system to encourage employers to provide regular employment to workers.

FUTA (Federal Unemployment Tax Act) tax (319)   A tax levied on employers to raise funds to administer the federal/state unemployment compensation program.

Self-Employment Contributions Act (SECA) (319)   A government Act that requires self-employed individuals to pay tax on net self-employment income.

self-employment income (319)   The net income of a trade or business run by an individual.

self-employment tax (319)   A tax on the earnings of a self-employed person at double the Social Security and Medicare rates.

SUTA (state unemployment tax) tax (320)   A tax levied on employers to raise funds to pay unemployment benefits.

workers' compensation insurance (333)   Insurance carried by employers for employees who suffer a work-related illness or injury.

SELF-STUDY TEST QUESTIONS

True/False

1. **LO1**   Employer payroll taxes are deducted from the employee's pay.

2. **LO1**   The payroll register is a key source of information for computing employer payroll taxes.

3. **LO1**   Self-employment income is the net income of a trade or business owned and run by an individual.

4. **LO1**   The FUTA tax is levied only on the employees.

5. **LO3**   The W-4, which shows total annual earnings and deductions for federal and state income taxes, must be completed by the employer and given to the employee by January 31.

Multiple Choice

1. **LO2**   The general ledger accounts commonly used to record the employer's Social Security, Medicare, FUTA, and SUTA taxes are classified as

   (a) assets.
   (b) liabilities.
   (c) expenses.
   (d) owner's equity.

2. **LO2**   Joyce Lee earns $30,000 a year. Her employer pays a matching Social Security tax of 6.2% on the first $118,500 in earnings, a Medicare tax of 1.45% on gross earnings, and a FUTA tax of 0.6% and a SUTA tax of 5.4%, both on the first $7,000 in earnings. What is the total cost of Joyce Lee to her employer?

(a) $32,295   (c) $30,420
(b) $30,000   (d) $32,715

3. **LO3**   The Form 941 tax deposit includes which of the following types of taxes withheld from the employee and paid by the employer?

(a) Federal income tax and FUTA tax
(b) Federal income tax and Social Security and Medicare taxes
(c) Social Security and Medicare taxes and SUTA tax
(d) FUTA tax and SUTA tax

4. **LO4**   Workers' compensation provides insurance for employees who

(a) are unemployed due to a layoff.
(b) are unemployed due to a plant closing.
(c) are underemployed and need additional compensation.
(d) suffer a work-related illness or injury.

5. **LO4**   The journal entry at the end of the year that recognizes an additional premium owed under workers' compensation insurance will include a

(a) debit to Workers' Compensation Insurance Expense.
(b) debit to Cash.
(c) debit to Workers' Compensation Insurance Payable.
(d) credit to Workers' Compensation Insurance Expense.

Checkpoint Exercises

1. **LO1**   Total earnings for the employees of Gary's Grill for the week ended January 14, 20--, were $6,400. The following payroll taxes were levied on these earnings:

Social Security	6.2%
Medicare	1.45%
FUTA	0.6%
SUTA	5.4%

Calculate Gary's payroll taxes expense for the week ended January 14, 20--.

2. **LO2**   Liu's Lounge had the following payroll taxes expense for the week ended February 10, 20--:

Social Security	$595.20
Medicare	139.20
FUTA	76.80
SUTA	518.40

Prepare the journal entry for these payroll taxes.

3. **LO3**   ARC Co. owes the following amounts for payroll taxes and employees' withholding of Social Security, Medicare, and federal income tax as of April 15:

Social Security Tax Payable	$6,750.00
Medicare Tax Payable	1,575.00
FUTA Tax Payable	360.00
SUTA Tax Payable	2,646.00
Employee Federal Income Tax Payable	4,095.00

Prepare the journal entries for:
(a)   Deposit of the employees' federal income taxes and the Social Security and Medicare taxes on April 15.
(b)   Deposits of the FUTA and SUTA taxes on April 30.

4. **LO4**   LC Co. estimates that its total payroll for the year will be $260,000. LC's workers' compensation insurance premium rate is 0.22%. Calculate LC's estimated workers' compensation insurance premium and prepare the journal entry for the payment of this amount.

The answers to the Self-Study Test Questions are at the end of the chapter (pages 351–352).

Applying Your Knowledge

REVIEW QUESTIONS

LO1   1.   Why do employer payroll taxes represent an additional expense to the employer, whereas the various employee payroll taxes do not?

LO1   2.   At what rate and on what earnings base is the employer's Social Security tax levied?

LO1   3.   What is the purpose of the FUTA tax, and who must pay it?

LO1   4.   What is the purpose of the state unemployment tax, and who must pay it?

LO2   5.   What accounts are affected when employer payroll tax expenses are properly recorded?

LO2   6.   Identify all items that are debited or credited to Social Security Tax Payable and to Medicare Tax Payable.

LO2   7.   Explain why an employee whose gross salary is $20,000 costs an employer more than $20,000 to employ.

LO3   8.   What is the purpose of the EFTPS?

LO3   9.   What is the purpose of Form 941, Employer's Quarterly Federal Tax Return?

LO3 10. What is the purpose of Form 940, Employer's Annual Federal Unemployment Tax Return?

LO3 11. What information appears on Form W-2, the employee's Wage and Tax Statement?

LO3 12. What is the purpose of Form I-9, Employment Eligibility Verification?

LO4 13. What is the purpose of workers' compensation insurance, and who must pay for it?

SERIES A EXERCISES

E 9-1A   (LO1/2)
✓ SUTA tax: $567

CALCULATION AND JOURNAL ENTRY FOR EMPLOYER PAYROLL TAXES
Portions of the payroll register for Barney's Bagels for the week ended July 15 are shown below. The SUTA tax rate is 5.4%, and the FUTA tax rate is 0.6%, both of which are levied on the first $7,000 of earnings. The Social Security tax rate is 6.2% on the first $118,500 of earnings. The Medicare rate is 1.45% on gross earnings.

Barney's Bagels
Payroll Register

	Total Taxable Earnings of All Employees	
Total Earnings	Unemployment Compensation	Social Security
$12,200	$10,500	$12,200

Calculate the employer's payroll taxes expense and prepare the journal entry to record the employer's payroll taxes expense for the week ended July 15 of the current year.

E 9-2A   (LO1/2)
✓ Medicare tax: $58

CALCULATION AND JOURNAL ENTRY FOR EMPLOYER PAYROLL TAXES
Earnings for several employees for the week ended March 12, 20--, are as follows:

		Taxable Earnings	
Employee Name	Current Earnings	Unemployment Compensation	Social Security
Aus, Glenn E.	$ 700	$200	$ 700
Diaz, Charles K.	350	350	350
Knapp, Carol S.	1,200	—	1,200
Mueller, Deborah F.	830	125	830
Yeager, Jackie R.	920	35	920

Calculate the employer's payroll taxes expense and prepare the journal entry as of March 12, 20--, assuming that FUTA tax is 0.6%, SUTA tax is 5.4%, Social Security tax is 6.2%, and Medicare tax is 1.45%.

E 9-3A   (LO1/2)

✓ Soc. Sec. tax: $672.70

CALCULATION OF TAXABLE EARNINGS AND EMPLOYER PAYROLL TAXES AND PREPARATION OF JOURNAL ENTRY Selected information from the payroll register of Joanie's Boutique for the week ended September 14, 20--, is as follows. Social Security tax is 6.2% on the first $118,500 of earnings for each employee. Medicare tax is 1.45% of gross earnings. FUTA tax is 0.6% and SUTA tax is 5.4% on the first $7,000 of earnings.

| | | | Taxable Earnings | |
| | Cumulative Pay Before Current | Current | Unemployment | Social |
Employee Name	Earnings	Gross Pay	Compensation	Security
Jordahl, Stephanie	$ 6,600	$1,190		
Keesling, Emily	6,150	1,070		
Palmer, Stefan	55,200	2,410		
Soltis, Robin	54,300	2,280		
Stout, Hannah	29,050	2,030		
Xia, Xu	116,630	2,850		

Calculate the amount of taxable earnings for unemployment, Social Security, and Medicare taxes, and prepare the journal entry to record the employer's payroll taxes as of September 14, 20--.

E 9-4A   (LO1/2)

✓ Soc. Sec. Tax: $2,170

TOTAL COST OF EMPLOYEE Mandy Feng employs Jay Johnson at a salary of $35,000 a year. Feng is subject to employer Social Security taxes at a rate of 6.2% and Medicare taxes at a rate of 1.45% on Johnson's salary. In addition, Feng must pay SUTA tax at a rate of 5.4% and FUTA tax at a rate of 0.6% on the first $7,000 of Johnson's salary.

Compute the total cost to Feng of employing Johnson for the year.

E 9-5A   (LO3)

✓ 941 deposit: $20,700

SHOW
ME HOW

JOURNAL ENTRIES FOR PAYMENT OF EMPLOYER PAYROLL TAXES Angel Ruiz owns a business called Ruiz Construction Co. He does his banking at Citizens National Bank in Portland, Oregon. The amounts in his general ledger for payroll taxes and the employees' withholding of Social Security, Medicare, and federal income tax payable as of April 15 of the current year are as follows:

Social Security tax payable (includes both employer and employee)	$11,250
Medicare tax payable (includes both employer and employee)	2,625
FUTA tax payable	600
SUTA tax payable	4,050
Employee income tax payable	6,825

Journalize the quarterly payment of the employee federal income taxes and Social Security and Medicare taxes on April 15, 20--, and the payments of the FUTA and SUTA taxes on April 30, 20--.

E 9-6A   (LO4)

✓ 2. Additional premium due: $12

SHOW
ME HOW

WORKERS' COMPENSATION INSURANCE AND ADJUSTMENT Specialty Manufacturing estimated that its total payroll for the coming year would be $450,000. The workers' compensation insurance premium rate is 0.2%.

REQUIRED

1. Calculate the estimated workers' compensation insurance premium and prepare the journal entry for the payment as of January 2, 20--.

2. Assume that Specialty Manufacturing's actual payroll for the year is $456,000. Calculate the total insurance premium owed and prepare a journal entry as of December 31, 20--, to record the adjustment for the underpayment. The actual payment of the additional premium will take place in January of the next year.

SERIES A PROBLEMS

P 9-7A   (LO1/2)

✓ Soc. Sec. tax: $455.08

SHOW
ME HOW

CALCULATING PAYROLL TAXES EXPENSE AND PREPARING JOURNAL ENTRY Selected information from the payroll register of Ebeling's Dairy for the week ended July 7, 20--, is shown below. The SUTA tax rate is 5.4%, and the FUTA tax rate is 0.6%, both on the first $7,000 of earnings. Social Security tax on the employer is 6.2% on the first $118,500 of earnings, and Medicare tax is 1.45% on gross earnings.

Employee Name	Cumulative Pay Before Current Earnings	Current Weekly Earnings	Taxable Earnings	
			Unemployment Compensation	Social Security
Click, Katelyn	$ 6,650	$ 800		
Coombs, Michelle	6,370	720		
Fauss, Erin	23,460	1,200		
Lenihan, Marcus	6,930	900		
McMahon, Drew	117,150	3,440		
Newell, Marg	25,470	1,110		
Stevens, Matt	28,675	1,260		

REQUIRED

1. Calculate the total employer payroll taxes for these employees.

2. Prepare the journal entry to record the employer payroll taxes as of July 7, 20--.

P 9-8A   (LO2/3)

✓ Payroll taxes expense: $3,864

CLGL

JOURNALIZING AND POSTING PAYROLL ENTRIES Cascade Company has four employees. All are paid on a monthly basis. The fiscal year of the business is June 1 to May 31.

The accounts kept by Cascade include the following:

Account Number	Title	Balance on June 1
101	Cash	$70,200
211	Employee Federal Income Tax Payable	3,553
212	Social Security Tax Payable	5,103
213	Medicare Tax Payable	1,197
218	Savings Bond Deductions Payable	1,225
221	FUTA Tax Payable	574
222	SUTA Tax Payable	2,835
511	Wages and Salaries Expense	0
530	Payroll Taxes Expense	0

The following transactions relating to payrolls and payroll taxes occurred during June and July:

June 15 Paid $9,853 covering the following May taxes:

Social Security tax	$5,103
Medicare tax	1,197
Employee federal income tax withheld	3,553
Total	$9,853

30 June payroll:

Total wages and salaries expense		$42,000
Less amounts withheld:		
Social Security tax	$2,604	
Medicare tax	609	
Employee federal income tax	3,570	
Savings bond deductions	1,225	8,008
Net amount paid		$33,992

30 Purchased savings bonds for employees, $2,450

30 Employer payroll taxes expenses for June were:

Social Security	$2,604
Medicare	609
FUTA	84
SUTA	567
Total	$3,864

July 15 Paid $9,996 covering the following June taxes:

Social Security tax	$5,208
Medicare tax	1,218
Employee federal income tax withheld	3,570
Total	$9,996

31 Paid SUTA tax for the quarter, $3,402

31 Paid FUTA tax, $658

REQUIRED

1. Journalize the preceding transactions using a general journal.

2. Open T accounts for the payroll expenses and liabilities. Enter the beginning balances and post the transactions recorded in the journal.

P 9-9A   (LO4)

✓ 3. Refund due: $48

WORKERS' COMPENSATION INSURANCE AND ADJUSTMENT Willamette Manufacturing estimated that its total payroll for the coming year would be $650,000. The workers' compensation insurance premium rate is 0.3%.

REQUIRED

1. Calculate the estimated workers' compensation insurance premium and prepare the journal entry for the payment as of January 2, 20--.

2. Assume that Willamette Manufacturing's actual payroll for the year was $672,000. Calculate the total insurance premium owed and prepare a journal entry as of December 31, 20--, to record the adjustment for the underpayment. The actual payment of the additional premium will take place in January of the next year.

3. Assume instead that Willamette Manufacturing's actual payroll for the year was $634,000. Prepare a journal entry as of December 31, 20--, for the total amount that should be refunded. The refund will not be received until the next year.

SERIES B EXERCISES

E 9-1B   (LO1/2)
✓ SUTA tax: $664.74

CALCULATION AND JOURNAL ENTRY FOR EMPLOYER PAYROLL TAXES
Portions of the payroll register for Kathy's Cupcakes for the week ended June 21 are shown below. The SUTA tax rate is 5.4%, and the FUTA tax rate is 0.6%, both on the first $7,000 of earnings. The Social Security tax rate is 6.2% on the first $118,500 of earnings. The Medicare rate is 1.45% on gross earnings.

Kathy's Cupcakes
Payroll Register

	Total Taxable Earnings of All Employees	
Total Earnings	Unemployment Compensation	Social Security
$15,680	$12,310	$15,680

Calculate the employer's payroll taxes expense and prepare the journal entry to record the employer's payroll taxes expense for the week ended June 21 of the current year.

E 9-2B   (LO1/2)
✓ Medicare tax: $79.24

CALCULATION AND JOURNAL ENTRY FOR EMPLOYER PAYROLL TAXES
Earnings for several employees for the week ended April 7, 20--, are as follows:

		Taxable Earnings	
Employee Name	Current Earnings	Unemployment Compensation	Social Security
Boyd, Glenda L.	$ 850	$300	$ 850
Evans, Sheryl N.	970	225	970
Fox, Howard J.	830	830	830
Jacobs, Phyllis J.	1,825	—	1,825
Roh, William R.	990	25	990

Calculate the employer's payroll taxes expense and prepare the journal entry as of April 7, 20--, assuming that FUTA tax is 0.6%, SUTA tax is 5.4%, Social Security tax is 6.2%, and Medicare tax is 1.45%.

E 9-3B   (LO1/2)
✓ Soc. Sec. tax: $569.16

CALCULATION OF TAXABLE EARNINGS AND EMPLOYER PAYROLL TAXES, AND PREPARATION OF JOURNAL ENTRY Selected information from the payroll register of Howard's Cutlery for the week ended October 7, 20--, is presented below. Social Security tax is 6.2% on the first $118,500 of earnings for each employee. Medicare tax is 1.45% on gross earnings. FUTA tax is 0.6% and SUTA tax is 5.4% on the first $7,000 of earnings.

			Taxable Earnings	
Employee Name	Cumulative Pay Before Current Earnings	Current Gross Pay	Unemployment Compensation	Social Security
Carlson, David J.	$ 6,635	$ 950		
Delgado, Luisa	6,150	1,215		
Lewis, Arlene S.	54,375	2,415		
Nixon, Robert R.	53,870	1,750		
Shippe, Lance W.	24,830	1,450		
Watts, Brandon Q.	117,100	2,120		

Calculate the amount of taxable earnings for unemployment, Social Security, and Medicare taxes, and prepare the journal entry to record the employer's payroll taxes as of October 7, 20--.

E 9-4B   (LO1/2)

✓ Soc. Sec. tax: $2,852

TOTAL COST OF EMPLOYEE B. F. Goodson employs Eduardo Gonzales at a salary of $46,000 a year. Goodson is subject to employer Social Security taxes at a rate of 6.2% and Medicare taxes at a rate of 1.45% on Gonzales's salary. In addition, Goodson must pay SUTA tax at a rate of 5.4% and FUTA tax at a rate of 0.6% on the first $7,000 of Gonzales's salary.

Compute the total cost to Goodson of employing Gonzales for the year.

E 9-5B   (LO3)

✓ 941 deposit: $19,058

SHOW
ME HOW

JOURNAL ENTRIES FOR PAYMENT OF EMPLOYER PAYROLL TAXES Francis Baker owns a business called Baker Construction Co. She does her banking at the American National Bank in Seattle, Washington. The amounts in her general ledger for payroll taxes and employees' withholding of Social Security, Medicare, and federal income tax payable as of July 15 of the current year are as follows:

Social Security tax payable (includes both employer and employee)	$9,563
Medicare tax payable (includes both employer and employee)	2,250
FUTA tax payable	504
SUTA tax payable	3,402
Employee federal income tax payable	7,245

Journalize the quarterly payment of the employee federal income taxes and Social Security and Medicare taxes on July 15, 20--, and the payments of the FUTA and state unemployment taxes on July 31, 20--.

E 9-6B   (LO4)

✓ 2. Additional premium due: $22

SHOW
ME HOW

WORKERS' COMPENSATION INSURANCE AND ADJUSTMENT Columbia Industries estimated that its total payroll for the coming year would be $385,000. The workers' compensation insurance premium rate is 0.2%.

REQUIRED

1. Calculate the estimated workers' compensation insurance premium and prepare the journal entry for the payment as of January 2, 20--.

2. Assume that Columbia Industries' actual payroll for the year is $396,000. Calculate the total insurance premium owed and prepare a journal entry as of December 31, 20--, to record the adjustment for the underpayment. The actual payment of the additional premium will take place in January of the next year.

SERIES B PROBLEMS

P 9-7B   (LO1/2)

✓ Soc. Sec. tax: $543.74

SHOW
ME HOW

CALCULATING PAYROLL TAXES EXPENSE AND PREPARING JOURNAL ENTRY Selected information from the payroll register of Wray's Drug Store for the week ended July 14, 20--, is shown below. The SUTA tax rate is 5.4%, and the FUTA tax

(continued)

rate is 0.6%, both on the first $7,000 of earnings. Social Security tax on the employer is 6.2% on the first $118,500 of earnings, and Medicare tax is 1.45% on gross earnings.

Employee Name	Cumulative Pay Before Current Earnings	Current Weekly Earnings	Taxable Earnings	
			Unemployment Compensation	Social Security
Ackers, Alice	$ 6,460	$ 645		
Conley, Dorothy	27,560	1,025		
Davis, James	6,850	565		
Lawrence, Kevin	52,850	2,875		
Rawlings, Judy	16,350	985		
Tanaka, Sumio	22,320	835		
Vadillo, Raynette	116,660	3,540		

REQUIRED

1. Calculate the total employer payroll taxes for these employees.

2. Prepare the journal entry to record the employer payroll taxes as of July 14, 20--.

P 9-8B   (LO2/3)

✓ Payroll taxes expense: $2,105.33

JOURNALIZING AND POSTING PAYROLL ENTRIES Oxford Company has five employees. All are paid on a monthly basis. The fiscal year of the business is June 1 to May 31.

The accounts kept by Oxford Company include the following:

Account Number	Title	Balance on June 1
101	Cash	$69,500.00
211	Employee Federal Income Tax Payable	2,018.00
212	Social Security Tax Payable	2,735.00
213	Medicare Tax Payable	641.00
218	Savings Bond Deductions Payable	787.50
221	FUTA Tax Payable	540.00
222	SUTA Tax Payable	1,380.00
511	Wages and Salaries Expense	0.00
530	Payroll Taxes Expense	0.00

The following transactions relating to payrolls and payroll taxes occurred during June and July:

June 15   Paid $5,394.00 covering the following May taxes:

Social Security tax	$2,735.00
Medicare tax	641.00
Employee federal income tax withheld	2,018.00
Total	$5,394.00

30   June payroll:

Total wages and salaries expense		$22,050.00
Less amounts withheld:		
Social Security tax	$1,367.10	
Medicare tax	319.73	
Employee federal income tax	1,920.00	
Savings bond deductions	787.50	4,394.33
Net amount paid		$17,655.67

30	Purchased savings bonds for employees, $1,575.00	
30	Employer payroll taxes expenses for June were:	
	Social Security	$1,367.10
	Medicare	319.73
	FUTA	54.00
	SUTA	364.50
	Total	$2,105.33

July 15	Paid $5,293.66 covering the following June taxes:	
	Social Security tax	$2,734.20
	Medicare tax	639.46
	Employee federal income tax withheld	1,920.00
	Total	$5,293.66
31	Paid SUTA tax for the quarter, $1,744.50	
31	Paid FUTA tax, $594.00	

REQUIRED

1. Journalize the preceding transactions using a general journal.

2. Open T accounts for the payroll expenses and liabilities. Enter the beginning balances and post the transactions recorded in the journal.

P 9-9B   (LO4)

✓ **3. Refund due: $16**

WORKERS' COMPENSATION INSURANCE AND ADJUSTMENT Multnomah Manufacturing estimated that its total payroll for the coming year would be $540,000. The workers' compensation insurance premium rate is 0.2%.

REQUIRED

1. Calculate the estimated workers' compensation insurance premium and prepare the journal entry for the payment as of January 2, 20--.

2. Assume that Multnomah Manufacturing's actual payroll for the year was $562,000. Calculate the total insurance premium owed and prepare a journal entry as of December 31, 20--, to record the adjustment for the underpayment. The actual payment of the additional premium will take place in January of the next year.

3. Assume instead that Multnomah Manufacturing's actual payroll for the year was $532,000. Prepare a journal entry as of December 31, 20--, for the total amount that should be refunded. The refund will not be received until the next year.

MANAGING YOUR WRITING

Check List
☑ Check List
☐ Managing
☐ Planning
☐ Drafting
☐ Break
☐ Revising
☐ Managing

The director of the art department at an advertising company, Wilson Watson, wants to hire new office staff. His boss tells him that to do so he must find in his budget not only the base salary for this position but an additional 30% for "fringe benefits." Wilson explodes: "How in the world can there be 30% in fringe benefits?" Write a memo to Wilson Watson explaining the costs that probably make up these fringe benefits.

ETHICS CASE

Bob Estes works at Cliffrock Company in the central receiving department. He unpacks incoming shipments and verifies quantities of goods received. Over the weekend, Bob pulled a muscle in his back while playing basketball. When he came to work on Monday and started unpacking shipments, his back started to hurt again. Bob called the human resources department and told them he hurt his back lifting a package at work. He was told to fill out an accident report and sent to an orthopedic clinic with a workers' compensation form. The doctor at the clinic told Bob not to lift anything heavy for two weeks and to stay home from work for at least one week.

1. Is Bob entitled to workers' compensation? Why or why not?

2. What effect will Bob's claim have on Cliffrock Company's workers' compensation insurance premium?

3. Write a short memo from the human resources department to Cliffrock Company's employees explaining the purpose of workers' compensation.

4. In small groups, discuss the job-related illness or injury risks of a computer input operator and measures an employer might take to minimize these risks.

MASTERY PROBLEM

✓ Payroll taxes expense: $720.75

The totals line from Nix Company's payroll register for the week ended March 31, 20--, is as follows:

(left side)

PAYROLL REGISTER

| | NAME | EMPLOYEE NUMBER | ALLOWANCES | MARITAL STATUS | EARNINGS | | | | TAXABLE EARNINGS | |
					REGULAR	OVERTIME	TOTAL	CUMULATIVE TOTAL	UNEMPLOYMENT COMPENSATION	SOCIAL SECURITY
21	Totals				5 4 0 0 00	1 0 0 00	5 5 0 0 00	71 5 0 0 00	5 0 0 0 00	5 5 0 0 00

—PERIOD ENDED March 31, 20--   (right side)

| DEDUCTIONS | | | | | | | NET PAY | CHECK NO. |
FEDERAL INCOME TAX	SOCIAL SECURITY TAX	MEDICARE TAX	HEALTH INSURANCE	LIFE INSURANCE	OTHER	TOTAL		
5 0 0 00	3 4 1 00	7 9 75	1 6 5 00	2 0 0 00		1 2 8 5 75	4 2 1 4 25	21

Payroll taxes are imposed as follows: Social Security tax, 6.2%; Medicare tax, 1.45%; FUTA tax, 0.6%; and SUTA tax, 5.4%.

REQUIRED

1. a. Prepare the journal entry for payment of this payroll on March 31, 20--.

   b. Prepare the journal entry for the employer's payroll taxes for the period ended March 31, 20--.

2. Nix Company had the following balances in its general ledger before the entries for requirement (1) were made:

Employee federal income tax payable	$2,500
Social Security tax payable	2,008
Medicare tax payable	470
FUTA tax payable	520
SUTA tax payable	4,510

a. Prepare the journal entry for payment of the liabilities for federal income taxes and Social Security and Medicare taxes on April 15, 20--.

b. Prepare the journal entry for payment of the liability for FUTA tax on April 30, 20--.

c. Prepare the journal entry for payment of the liability for SUTA tax on April 30, 20--.

3. Nix Company paid a premium of $420 for workers' compensation insurance based on the estimated payroll as of the beginning of the year. Based on actual payroll as of the end of the year, the premium is only $400. Prepare the adjusting entry to reflect the overpayment of the insurance premium at the end of the year (December 31, 20--).

CHALLENGE PROBLEM

This problem challenges you to apply your cumulative accounting knowledge to move a step beyond the material in the chapter.

✓ Payroll taxes expense: $1,281.25

Payrex Co. has six employees. All are paid on a weekly basis. For the payroll period ending January 7, total employee earnings were $12,500, all of which were subject to SUTA, FUTA, Social Security, and Medicare taxes. The SUTA tax rate in Payrex's state is 5.4%, but Payrex qualifies for a rate of 2.0% because of its good record of providing regular employment to its employees. Other employer payroll taxes are at the rates described in the chapter.

REQUIRED

1. Calculate Payrex's FUTA, SUTA, Social Security, and Medicare taxes for the week ended January 7.

2. Prepare the journal entry for Payrex's payroll taxes for the week ended January 7.

3. What amount of payroll taxes did Payrex save because of its good employment record?

Answers to Self-Study Test Questions

True/False

1. F (these taxes are paid by the employer)
2. T
3. T
4. F (FUTA tax is levied on employers)
5. F (this Form is W-2)

Multiple Choice

1. b   2. d   3. b   4. d   5. a

Checkpoint Exercises

1. Social Security	$396.80
Medicare	92.80
FUTA	38.40
SUTA	345.60
Total	$873.60

2. Payroll Taxes Expense 1,329.60
    Social Security Tax Payable   595.20
    Medicare Tax Payable   139.20
    FUTA Tax Payable   76.80
    SUTA Tax Payable   518.40
    Employer payroll taxes for week ended Feb. 10

3. (a) Social Security Tax Payable 6,750.00
    Medicare Tax Payable 1,575.00
    Employee Federal Income Tax Payable 4,095.00
    Cash   12,420.00
    Deposit of employee federal income tax
    and Social Security and Medicare taxes

  (b) FUTA Tax Payable
    Cash 360.00
    Paid FUTA tax   360.00

    SUTA Tax Payable
    Cash 2,646.00
    Paid SUTA tax   2,646.00

4. Workers' Compensation Insurance Expense
    Cash 572.00
    Paid insurance premium   572.00

Index

*Page references in bold indicate defined terms.

THE ACCOUNTING EQUATION

$$\text{Assets} = \text{Liabilities} + \text{Owner's Equity}$$

FINANCIAL STATEMENTS

Income Statement   Revenues − Expenses = Net Income or Loss

Statement of Owner's Equity   Beginning Capital + Investments + Net Income − Withdrawals = Ending Capital

Balance Sheet   Assets = Liabilities + Owner's Equity

T ACCOUNT

Title

Debit = Left	Credit = Right

EXPANDED ACCOUNTING EQUATION SHOWING RULES OF DEBIT AND CREDIT

Assets

Dr.	Cr.
+	−

=

Liabilities

Dr.	Cr.
−	+

+

Owner's Equity

Dr.	Cr.
−	+

Drawing

Dr.	Cr.
+	−

Expenses

Dr.	Cr.
+	−

Revenue

Dr.	Cr.
−	+

STEPS IN MAJOR ACCOUNTING PROCESSES

Steps in Journalizing a Transaction

1. Enter the date.
2. Enter the account title and debit amount.
3. Enter the account title and credit amount.
4. Enter the explanation.

Steps in Posting from the Journal to the Ledger

In the ledger:

1. Enter the date in the Date column.
2. Enter the amount of each transaction in the Debit or Credit column.
3. Enter the new balance in the Balance column under Debit or Credit.
4. Enter the page number of the journal from which each transaction is posted in the Posting Reference column.

In the journal:

5. Enter the ledger account number in the Posting Reference column in the journal.

Steps in Preparing the Work Sheet

1. Prepare the trial balance.
2. Prepare the adjustments.
3. Prepare the adjusted trial balance.
4. Extend adjusted balances to the Income Statement and Balance Sheet columns.
5. Complete the work sheet.

Steps in the Closing Process

1. Close the revenue accounts to Income Summary.
2. Close the expense accounts to Income Summary.
3. Close Income Summary to the owner's capital account.
4. Close the drawing account to the owner's capital account.

STEPS IN THE ACCOUNTING CYCLE

Source Documents

Rohan's Campus Delivery
Income Statement
For Month Ended June 30, 20 --

Revenues:	
Delivery fees	$2,150
Expenses:	
Wages expense	$650
Rent expense	200
Phone expense	50
Total expenses	900
Net income	$1,250

Rohan's Campus Delivery
Statement of Owner's Equity
For Month Ended June 30, 20 --

Rohan Macsen, capital, June 1, 20--	$ —
Investments during June	2,000
Total investment	$2,000
Net income for June	$1,250
Less: withdrawals for June	150
Increase in capital	1,100
Rohan Macsen, capital, June 30, 20--	$3,100

Rohan's Campus Delivery
Balance Sheet
June 30, 20 --

Assets		Liabilities	
Cash	$ 370	Accounts payable	$1,800
Accounts receivable	650		
Supplies	80	Owner's Equity	
Prepaid insurance	200	Rohan Macsen, capital	3,100
Delivery equipment	3,600		
		Total liabilities and	
Total assets	$4,900	owner's equity	$4,900

Steps in the Accounting Cycle

During Accounting Period:
1. Analyze source documents.
2. Journalize the transactions.
3. Post to the ledger accounts.

End of Accounting Period:
4. Prepare a trial balance.
5. Determine and prepare the needed adjustments on the work sheet.
6. Complete an end-of-period work sheet.
7. Journalize and post the adjusting entries.
8. Prepare an income statement, statement of owner's equity, and balance sheet.
9. Journalize and post the closing entries.
10. Prepare a post-closing trial balance.

Note: While for a specific company each account number used would have only one title, titles vary from company to company as needed. Particularly for the Owner's Equity accounts, the accounts used depend on the company ownership structure (proprietorship, partnership, or corporation).

Assets (100–199)

100s—Cash Related Accounts
101 Cash
105 Petty Cash

120s—Receivables
121 Notes Receivable
122 Accounts Receivable
122.1 Allowance for Bad Debts
123 Interest Receivable (Also Accrued Interest Receivable)

130s—Inventories
131 Merchandise Inventory
132 Raw Materials
133 Work in Process
134 Finished Goods

140s—Prepaid Items
141 Supplies (Specialty items like Medical, Bicycle, Tailoring, etc.)
142 Office Supplies
144 Food Supplies
145 Prepaid Insurance

150s—Long-Term Investments
153 Bond Sinking Fund

160s—Land
161 Land
162 Natural Resources
162.1 Accumulated Depletion

170s—Buildings
171 Buildings
171.1 Accumulated Depreciation—Buildings

180s—Equipment
181 Office Equipment (Also Store Equipment)
181.1 Accumulated Depreciation—Office Equipment (Also Store Equipment)
182 Office Furniture
182.1 Accumulated Depreciation—Office Furniture
183 Athletic Equipment (Also Tailoring, Lawn, Cleaning)
183.1 Accumulated Depreciation—Athletic Equipment (Also Tailoring, Lawn, Cleaning)
184 Tennis Facilities (Also Basketball Facilities)
184.1 Accumulated Depreciation—Tennis Facilities (Also Basketball Facilities)
185 Delivery Equipment (Also Medical, Van)
185.1 Accumulated Depreciation—Delivery Equipment (Also Medical, Van)
186 Exercise Equipment
186.1 Accumulated Depreciation—Exercise Equipment
187 Computer Equipment
187.1 Accumulated Depreciation—Computer Equipment

190s—Intangibles
191 Patents
192 Copyrights

Liabilities (200–299)

200s—Short-Term Payables
201 Notes Payable
201.1 Discount on Notes Payable
202 Accounts Payable (Also Vouchers Payable)
203 United Way Contribution Payable
204 Income Tax Payable
205 Common Dividends Payable
206 Preferred Dividends Payable
207 Interest Payable (Also Bond Interest Payable)

210s—Employee Payroll Related Payables
211 Employee Income Tax Payable
212 Social Security Tax Payable
213 Medicare Tax Payable
215 City Earnings Tax Payable
216 Health Insurance Premiums Payable
217 Credit Union Payable
218 Savings Bond Deductions Payable
219 Wages Payable

220s—Employer Payroll Related Payables
221 FUTA Tax Payable
222 SUTA Tax Payable
223 Workers' Compensation Insurance Payable

230s—Sales Tax
231 Sales Tax Payable

240s—Deferred Revenues and Current Portion of Long-Term Debt
241 Unearned Subscription Revenue (Also Unearned Ticket Revenue, Unearned Repair Fees)
242 Current Portion of Mortgage Payable

250s—Long-Term Liabilities
251 Mortgage Payable
252 Bonds Payable
252.1 Discount on Bonds Payable
253 Premium on Bonds Payable

Owner's Equity (300–399)

311 Rohan Macsen, Capital
312 Rohan Macsen, Drawing
313 Income Summary
321 Common Stock
321.1 Common Treasury Stock
322 Paid in Capital in Excess of Par/Stated Value—Common Stock
323 Preferred Stock
323.1 Preferred Treasury Stock
324 Paid in Capital in Excess of Par/Stated Value—Preferred Stock
327 Common Stock Subscribed
327.1 Common Stock Subscriptions Receivable
328 Preferred Stock Subscribed
328.1 Preferred Stock Subscriptions Receivable
329 Paid in Capital from Sale of Treasury Stock
331 Retained Earnings
332 Retained Earnings Appropriated for…
333 Cash Dividends
334 Stock Dividends

Revenues (400–499)

400s—Operating Revenues

401 Delivery Fees
401 Appraisal Fees
401 Medical Fees
401 Service Fees
401 Repair Fees
401 Sales
401.1 Sales Returns and Allowances
401.2 Sales Discounts
402 Boarding and Grooming Revenue
403 Subscriptions Revenue (if main line of business)

410s—Other Revenues

411 Interest Revenue
412 Rent Revenue
413 Subscriptions Revenue (if not main line of business)
414 Sinking Fund Earnings
415 Uncollectible Accounts Recovered
416 Gain on Sale/Exchange of Equipment
417 Gain on Bonds Redeemed

Operating Expenses (500–599)

500s—Cost of Goods Sold

501 Purchases
501.1 Purchases Returns and Allowances
501.2 Purchases Discounts
502 Freight-In
504 Overhead
505 Cost of Goods Sold

510s—Selling Expenses

511 Wages Expense (Also Wages and Salaries Expense)
512 Advertising Expense
513 Bank Credit Card Expense
514 Store Supplies Expense
515 Travel and Entertainment Expense
516 Cash Short and Over
519 Depreciation Expense—Store Equipment and Fixtures

520s–40s—General and Administrative Expenses

521 Rent Expense
522 Office Salaries Expense
523 Office Supplies Expense (Also Medical)
524 Other Supplies: Food Supplies Expense (Also Medical)
525 Phone Expense
526 Transportation/Automobile Expense (Also Laboratory, Travel)
527 Collection Expense
528 Inventory Short and Over
529 Loss on Write Down of Inventory
530 Payroll Taxes Expense
531 Workers' Compensation Insurance Expense
532 Bad Debt Expense
533 Electricity Expense, Utilities Expense
534 Charitable Contributions Expense
535 Insurance Expense
536 Postage Expense
537 Repair Expense
538 Oil and Gas Expense (Also Automobile Expense)
540 Depreciation Expense—Building
541 Depreciation Expense—Equipment (Also Tennis Facilities, Delivery Equipment, Office Equipment, Furniture)
542 Depreciation Expense—Other Equipment (Medical Equipment, Exercise Equipment, Computer Equipment)
543 Depletion Expense
544 Patent Amortization
545 Organization Expense
549 Miscellaneous Expense

550s—Other Expenses

551 Interest Expense (Also Bond Interest Expense)
552 Loss on Discarded Equipment
553 Loss on Sale/Exchange of Equipment
554 Loss on Bonds Redeemed
555 Income Tax Expense